RELIGION AND CULTURE IN THE MIDDLE AGES

Cognitive Sciences and Medieval Studies

RELIGION AND CULTURE IN THE MIDDLE AGES

Cognitive Sciences and Medieval Studies

An Introduction

edited by

JULIANA DRESVINA AND VICTORIA BLUD

UNIVERSITY OF WALES PRESS
2020

www.uwp.co.uk

British Library Cataloguing-in-Publication Data
A catalogue record for this book is available from the British Library.

ISBN 978-1-78683-674-8
e-ISBN 978-1-78683-675-5

Typeset by Eira Fenn Gaunt, Pentyrch, Cardiff
Printed by CPI Antony Rowe, Melksham, Wiltshire

Contents

Series Editors' Preface

Religion and Culture in the Middle Ages aims to explore the interface between medieval religion and culture, with as broad an understanding of those terms as possible. It puts to the forefront studies which engage with works that significantly contributed to the shaping of medieval culture. However, it also gives attention to studies dealing with works that reflect and highlight aspects of medieval culture that have been neglected in the past by scholars of the medieval disciplines. For example, devotional works and the practice they infer illuminate our understanding of the medieval subject and its culture in remarkable ways, while studies of the material space designed and inhabited by medieval subjects yield new evidence on the period and the people who shaped it and lived in it. In the larger field of religion and culture, we also want to explore further the roles played by women as authors, readers and owners of books, thereby defining them more precisely as actors in the cultural field. The series as a whole investigates the European Middle Ages, from *c*.500 to *c*.1500. Our aim is to explore medieval religion and culture with the tools belonging to such disciplines as, among others, art history, philosophy, theology, history, musicology, the history of medicine, and literature. In particular, we would like to promote interdisciplinary studies, as we believe strongly that our modern understanding of the term applies fascinatingly well to a cultural period marked by a less tight confinement and categorization of its disciplines than the modern period. However, our only criterion is academic excellence, with the belief that the use of a large diversity of critical tools and theoretical approaches enables a deeper understanding of medieval culture. We want the series to reflect this diversity, as we believe that, as a collection of outstanding contributions, it offers a more subtle representation of a period that is marked by paradoxes and contradictions and which necessarily reflects diversity and difference, however difficult it may sometimes have proved for medieval culture to accept these notions.

Acknowledgements

During the writing and editing of this volume we have been the grateful recipients of advice, feedback and responses from scholars both within and outside the 'cognitive medievalism' enclave. This volume is much the richer for the expertise and academic kindnesses of numerous colleagues and friends, and in particular we would like to thank: Alex Anokhina, Alan Costall, Rick Cooper, Laura Crombie, Greg Currie, Line Engh, Daniel Gerrard, Michael Moore, Sarah Salih, Debs Thorpe, Stephanie Trigg and Kathleen Walker-Meikle. We would also like to acknowledge the support of our respective institutions, the University of Oxford and the University of York, and particularly The Oxford Research Centre in the Humanities (TORCH) for their help in securing images. Several chapters in this volume were also supported by individual grants, which are acknowledged separately. The two anonymous readers for University of Wales Press gave us some tremendously helpful insight and incisive suggestions, and we thank them for helping us make this a better volume. Finally, our heartfelt thanks go to Sian Chapman, Dafydd Jones, Bethan Phillips and all the team at University of Wales Press, to Heather Palomino for her careful copyediting, and especially to Sarah Lewis, our endlessly patient and supportive editor.

ILLUSTRATIONS

Notes on Contributors

Victoria Blud is a research associate in English at the University of York. She is the author of *The Unspeakable, Gender, and Sexuality in Medieval Literature* (Boydell & Brewer, 2017) and her research focuses on studies of gender, transgressive speech, non/human bodies, materiality, emotion and cognition in the Middle Ages. Her most recent project (funded by the British Academy/Leverhulme Trust) examined the afterlives of medieval mysticism in early modern convents in exile, looking particularly at learning communities and cognitive scaffolding.

Juliana Dresvina is a member of the History Faculty, University of Oxford, where she works on late-medieval devotion and on how people of the past strived to make sense of their lives in general and their unusual experiences in particular, using a variety of modern methods, such as attachment theory and fanfiction studies. She is the author of *A Maid with a Dragon: The Cult of St Margaret of Antioch in Medieval England* (Oxford University Press, 2016) and a forthcoming study of attachment and pre-modern history (Brill, 2021).

Antonina Harbus is Professor of English at Macquarie University, Sydney, Australia. Her current research on medieval and more recent English texts combines literary analysis with ideas and methods from cognitive science to investigate how the mind makes meaning from a text. Her most recent book is *Cognitive Approaches to Old English Poetry* (2012). Her wide-ranging research programme, supported by Australian Research Council Discovery Project funding, includes investigations into literature and emotion, ideas about the self and autobiographical memory in literature, metaphor and concepts of the mind, and narrative poetry.

Ralph W. Hood Jr is a professor of psychology, LeRoy A. Martin Distinguished Professor of Religious Studies at the University of Tennessee at Chattanooga, and UT Alumni Association Distinguished Professor. He currently is co-editor of *Research in the Social Scientific Study of Religion* and Editor-in-Chief of *Psychology and Religion*. He is a past president of division 36 of the American Psychological Association and a recipient of its William James award for research in the psychology of religion.

John Onians is Professor Emeritus of World Art at the University of East Anglia, Norwich. His interests range from the close analysis of Italian Renaissance Architecture and Greek and Roman Art to experimentation with broad approaches to art as a worldwide phenomenon, such as art geography. Most recently he has explored the use of neuroscience for the study of art-related behaviours, pioneering neuroarthistory, neuroarchaeology, neuroanthropology and neuromuseology. His most recent book is *European Art: A Neuroarthistory* (Yale, 2016).

Nadia Pawelchak received her doctorate in art history from Florida State University in 2014, with emphases in medieval and modern art. Her research primarily focuses on cognitive neuroscience and medieval reception. She is especially interested in how medieval viewers may have responded to manuscripts and luxury secular objects. She currently teaches at Rocky Mountain College of Art and Design as well as Tallahassee Community College.

Godelinde Gertrude Perk is a Marie Skłodowska-Curie Fellow at the Faculty of Medieval and Modern Languages (University of Oxford) and Fulford Junior Research Fellow (Somerville College). Her project, 'Women Making Memories', juxtaposes medieval women's writings in four north-western European vernaculars and considers the intersection of holy women's texts, medieval literary theory, materiality, and folklore. Other research interests include cognitive literary approaches, research-by-performance explorations, and excursions to modern artists such as *fin-de-siècle* designer Karin Larsson.

Matthew Rampley is a research fellow of the Institute of Art History of the Czech Academy of Sciences. His current research is concerned with the cultural politics of interwar art and architecture in central Europe, focusing in particular on the memory and legacy of the Habsburg Empire. His recent publications include: *The Seductions of Darwin* (2017) and *Liberalism, Nationalism and Design Reform in Austria-Hungary* (2020), with Markian Prokopovych and Nóra Veszprémi.

Jeff Rider is a professor of the literature and history of north-western medieval Europe. He is the author, editor or translator of eleven books and has published over forty articles, essays or chapters in collective works. Rider has received grants from the National Endowment for the Humanities, the Fulbright Commission, the American Philosophical Society, the Fondation des Treilles, the Herzog August Bibliothek, the Fondation Nationale de Recherche Scientifique, and the Royal Flemish Academy of Belgium for Science and the Arts. He is working on editions of the earliest works of the medieval Flemish historical tradition, translations of Walter of Thérouanne's hagiographical works, and a book on the usefulness of the Middle Ages.

José Filipe Silva is a professor of medieval philosophy at the University of Helsinki, where he directs the ERC research project Rationality in Perception: Transformations of Mind and Cognition 1250–1550. He is the author of *Robert Kilwardby on the Human Soul: Plurality of Forms and Censorship in the Thirteenth Century* (Brill, 2012) and editor of *Active Perception in the History of Philosophy* (Springer 2014, with M. Yriönsuuri) and *The Senses and the History of Philosophy* (Routledge, 2019, with B. Glenney).

Daniel Lord Smail is Frank B. Baird Jr Professor of History at Harvard University, where he works on deep human history and the history and anthropology of Mediterranean societies between 1100 and 1600. His current research approaches transformations in the material culture of later medieval Mediterranean Europe using household inventories and inventories of debt collection from Lucca and Marseille, and he is also embarking on a study of slavery in later medieval Provence. His books include *Legal Plunder: Households and Debt Collection in Late Medieval Europe* (2016); *On Deep History and the Brain* (2008); and *The Consumption of Justice: Emotions, Publicity, and Legal Culture in Marseille, 1264–1423* (2003).

Wendy Turner is a professor of history at Augusta University. She is a medieval historian, researching the intersection between law and medicine in medieval England, with special attention given to disabilities. She is also a professor with the Center for Bioethics and Health Policy. Other research includes medieval law more generally, medicine, alchemy, and power. Her publications include *Madness in Medieval Law and Custom* (Brill, 2010) and *Care and Custody of the Mentally Ill, Incompetent, and Disabled in Medieval England* (Brepols, 2013).

Introduction: Cognitive Sciences and Medieval Studies

VICTORIA BLUD AND JULIANA DRESVINA

The Cognitive Turn

Why look at medieval studies alongside cognitive science? The cognitive sciences are some of the most rapidly developing fields of human knowledge, and their findings frequently generate talking points among researchers and the reading public alike, as witnessed by the soaring sales of researchers like David Eagleman, Douglas Hofstadter, or most recently Gina Rippon, and the allure of titles such as *Proust Was a Neuroscientist* or *Jane on the Brain*.[1] As the interdisciplinary conversations between neuroscience, computer science, psychology, philosophy, linguistics and anthropology address fundamental questions about what the mind is and how we perceive it, these methods become increasingly important in the humanities as well. On the face of it, medieval studies and cognitive science might not seem the most intuitive pairing. Of the six parent disciplines in cognitive science, four have developed (even taking a rather long view of things) largely over the past two centuries, and cognitive science itself is generally agreed to have been established in the 1950s – or 11 September 1956, as George Miller declared[2] – comfortably out of range of the Middle Ages. Yet the debates that drive exploration in the cognitive sciences are questions with long philosophical pedigrees: the difference between human and nonhuman minds, the mind–body question, the nature–nurture debate, the character of language, the existence of free will, the question of consciousness, to name a few.[3] As cognitive, neuro- and bioscientists investigate cognition, emotional experience, neurological disorders and other mental states and phenomena, cognitive science and the humanities come closer together in the effort to situate these phenomena within longer histories. *Cognitive Sciences and Medieval Studies* is aimed at scholars of medieval studies who are engaged in this endeavour, applying and evaluating the methodologies of cognitive studies in order to explore psychic and mental processes, phenomenological experience and emotional states of individuals from the past, as related through the documents, narratives, visions, locutions and art of their cultural idiom.

The study of the Middle Ages, like other modern humanities specialisms, is always already interdisciplinary: in the past, an accomplished medievalist was obliged to be a historian, linguist, theologian, palaeographer, and later a theorist as well, but the list of desiderata is now expanding to the social and bio-sciences. Projects that embrace cognitive approaches often require their participants to keep abreast of two (or frequently more) sizeable and very different fields of knowledge, as witnessed in collaborative research projects.[4] The potential obstacles that arise alongside these opportunities are brilliantly anatomised in Marilyn Strathern's 2005 address to the British Academy. The appeal and power of interdisciplinarity is its capacity to bring fields and scholars together. As Strathern remarks, however, 'that relational faculty frequently becomes overdetermined by the notion of communication'; interdisciplinary endeavours are often beset by the concern that accessibility and legibility are obtained at the expense of detail and nuance.[5] Yet the effort to relate one field to another and to raise the stakes for communicating well is also generative, expansive and connective. At a time when education policies pit STEM and humanities subjects against one another in the name of employability and social value, the advantages of bringing the two together increase exponentially.

Philosophy and neuroscience have a long history together: the study of the brain has sometimes clashed with the study of the mind, particularly as regards the respective claims of neuroscientists and philosophers to describe and analyse neural activity on the one hand, and conceptual questions of mind on the other.[6] The impact of modern advances in various branches of biology and the influence of biocentrism in art and architecture have resulted not only in the 'BioArt' movement, which incorporates processes from biotechnology in order to create works of art using living organisms, but a new branch of academic discussion that brings together art and science.[7] Literary scholars have explored the relationship between science fiction and scientific reality, and whether the one may affect the other. As John Canaday observes, 'Before they became physical facts, atomic weapons existed as literary fictions', and scientists could read fiction just like everyone else.[8] Conversely, the literature and wider cultural discourse of the past has been analysed via influential scientific notions, and new schools of scientific thought (including cognitive science) used to open up new hermeneutics for studies of the past.[9] The sciences and humanities are also mutually informative and valuable at the level of theory in the work of scholars like Donna Haraway and Karen Barad. Haraway's research defies species barriers and interrogates 'human' nature, from her seminal 'Cyborg Manifesto' to recent work on ecofeminism and posthumanist theory.[10] Barad, meanwhile, combines theoretical physics and feminist and queer theory, for instance taking inspiration from 1950s horror movie *The Blob*, colonies of amoebas, and 'the queerness of one of the most pervasive of all critters – atoms' to challenge assumptions about nature, agency, morality and queerness itself.[11]

In the case of the cognitive turn, scholars of literature and the arts can give abstract principles a human face, while cognitive scientists reveal how an experience that seems otherwise intangible can be observed, measured, recorded, giving rise to an emerging and expanding field of publications.[12] An early adopter in literary studies was Mark Turner in *Reading Minds* (1991) and *The Literary Mind* (1996), which respectively theorised the role of the arts in the cognitive revolution and how narrative and parable provide models for cognitive processes that underpin everyday problem-solving and social interactions.[13] Since then, Lisa Zunshine has explored Theory of Mind as a framework for a theory of the novel, and analysed the utility of cognitive approaches for understanding fictional moments that depend on us acknowledging that we all 'live in other people's heads'.[14] The engagement with neuroscience and neuropsychology in the humanities was spearheaded by Suzanne Nalbantian and Paul Mathews (on studies of memory), Ann Taves, and Patrick McNamara (on theology and religious experience).[15] In a related vein, Patrick Colm Hogan has argued for the value of dialogue between cognitive sciences and comparative literature, drawing reciprocal insights from a temporally and geographically diverse range of literary works and cognitive psychology and philosophy, particularly the study of emotion and identity.[16] Evelyn Tribble, meanwhile, has written extensively on how contemporary cognitive philosophy furnishes the Renaissance scholar with powerful tools for understanding how the feats of memory were achieved on which early modern theatre depended.[17]

In the field of medieval studies, this approach was pioneered in a special issue of *postmedieval: a journal of medieval cultural studies* dedicated to 'neuromedievalism'.[18] Another established area of neuro-adjacent study, the history of emotions, has also been a subject of fascination for medievalists.[19] Jill Stevenson and Clare Wright, following Tribble's lead, have written persuasively on the transformative potential of applying cognitive theory to the study of drama in the Middle Ages contributing to a longer history of neurology and psychology, especially the history of emotions and medieval understanding of neurological disease and impairment.[20] Julia Bourke explores the 'neurohistory' of anchoritic writing by applying the insights of modern research into emotions such as compassion.[21] Deborah Thorpe demonstrates the utility of cognitive approaches and the findings of clinical neuroscience in her work on modern and medieval neurology.[22] Antonina Harbus's *Cognitive Approaches to Old English Poetry* has made cognitive literary studies accessible to scholars of early medieval English and opened up the widest scope of English literature to cognitive studies.[23] Line Engh, meanwhile, discusses how scholars in the cognitive sciences benefit from the questions raised by assembling detailed contextual information with which to make representations useful – a skill in which humanities researchers are already highly trained.[24] In this point, she echoes Anne L. Clark's observation that 'Cognitive theory offers a concrete reminder of powerful aspects of human existence that historians cannot directly see', but, on the other hand, 'cognitive theorists strive for simplicity, formulating what they consider the most basic blueprints of mental processing': the exchanges between cognitive sciences and the humanities are remarkable and attractive not for their novelty but for their genuine reciprocity.[25]

What is Cognitive Science?

The following chapters ask a series of questions about how this reciprocal benefit can be explored and assessed, so in the interests of practicality we turn first to the question of how *cognitive science* is to be understood. Cognitive science is an interdisciplinary field for the study and understanding of the mind: its practitioners are drawn from a range of scientific backgrounds, united by such principal and fundamental questions as *What is the mind?* and *How does it work?* While the disciplinary members that make up *the cognitive sciences*[26] are not always fixed, the six branches of the 'cognitive hexagon' drawn up in the Sloan Foundation's 1978 'State of the Art' Report are often still taken as paradigmatic, and comprise of philosophy, linguistics, anthropology, neuroscience, computer science and psychology.[27] *Computer science* has since been updated and refined to more precise branches such as *computational psychology*, *computational intelligence*, or *artificial intelligence.* The place of anthropology in particular has been subject to alteration, broadened under variants such as *cognition and culture*, or sometimes omitted altogether.[28] Regardless of number, however, the principle of cognitive science is at heart interdisciplinary, and as such, any attempt to sketch the development and interconnection of cognitive science's component disciplines can only be precisely that.[29]

The *cognitive revolution* was the name eventually given to a trend that began in the 1950s as a movement combining psychology, linguistics and the developing computer sciences with the goal of applying scientific method to the study of the human brain. Cognitive science emerged with development of computing as a discipline, as part of the pushback against behaviourism in psychology and as a wider paradigm;[30] subsequent interventions by scholars like Noam Chomsky, George Miller, Hilary Putnam, and Jerry Fodor are cited as watershed moments.[31] Though the exponents of cognitive science came from different disciplines and espoused a variety of philosophical positions, they shared a scepticism of behaviourism and were inspired by the potential of the analogy of the human mind with the computer, or Turing machine. The idea of nonhuman or mechanical intelligence had been around since the Enlightenment and could be traced back to antiquity; however, the modern concept of *artificial intelligence* was first articulated by Alan Turing in the 1950s. The cognitive sciences encompass research into AI, since the latter's goal is to delineate the process of human cognition so precisely that it may be reproduced in nonhuman form; modern cognitive studies also frequently incorporate computational modelling, in part in order to test and augment theories arising from the other branches of cognitive science.[31] The other significant legacy of computational theory in cognitive science is the tendency among its practitioners to approach questions as input-processing-output models; this tendency is being revised in more recent work, however, in particular with the rise of embodied cognition (which is explored in several chapters of this volume).

Cognitive psychology explores the scientific study of mental functions such as memory, learning, attention, reasoning, language, decision-making. It emerged partly as a reaction to behavioural psychology and behaviourism in general, which held sway in the United States from the 1920s to the 1950s, but in Europe represented rather a continuation of the pioneering work of Jean Piaget on the cognitive development of children. (The term itself was coined in the 1960s and popularised by Ulric Neisser in his book of the same name.)[33] Cognitive psychology looks at the question of how learning occurs specifically in the mind, as distinct from the behaviourist approach, which privileged observable behaviour over mental processes. As well as Piaget, other early instigators included Donald Broadbent and James Gibson, both of whom drew on William James's functionalism and radical empiricism. James's work proved enduringly influential in the psychology of religion, on attention (in Broadbent's work), and on emotion, this being taken up in earnest with the advent of embodied cognition. (For further discussion of James's work on the psychology of religion, see Ralph Hood's chapter in this volume.) Cognitive psychology also encompasses the contribution of language, as in Eleanor Rosch's work on semantic categorisation and cognitive representation. Rosch is also one of the foremothers of embodied cognition (discussed in more detail below).[34]

Closely allied with cognitive psychology, *cognitive linguistics* arose out of the impulses of the original cognitive revolution but the modern practice emerged in the 1980s, particularly with George Lakoff's work on conceptual metaphor theory.[35] Cognitive linguistics is concerned with language as an instrument for processing and conveying information, and asks, what does language tell us about cognition? It reacts against the generative paradigm of Chomsky in that cognitive linguists hold that capacity for language, though it may be innate as Chomsky argued, is not separate from the rest of cognition. Rather, language knowledge is acquired through, and its structure shaped by, language use. Thus in cognitive grammar, communication or interpretation of an event or concept is influenced by grammatical structure influences; grammatical construction can reveal something about cognitive processes.[36]

As academic legend has it, *cognitive neuroscience* as a term was born in the late 1970s in a New York cab transporting George Miller and Michael Gazzaniga, but its roots reach all the way back to Aristotelian and Galenic hypotheses concerning the connection of brain and mind. It emerged in the twentieth century from neuropsychology, building on the work of predecessors like physiologist Korbinian Brodmann on brain architecture, Pierre Broca and Carl Wernicke on language centres and locations in the brain, and neuroscientists Santiago Ramón y Cajal and Camillo Golgi on the structure and connection of neurons. *Cognitive neuroscience* is concerned with the biological processes underlying cognition – the activity in the brain at a cellular and molecular level, the activity of neurons and neural networks in tasks like memory, perception, attention, language.[37] Recent significant discussions have coalesced around the discovery of mirror neurons in the 1990s,[38] the neuroscience of emotion,[39] and the connection between emotion and reason.[40]

Where cognitive psychology analyses the cognitive processes of individuals, the cognitive aspects of larger social and cultural processes are the subject of *cognitive anthropology*. Developing from earlier work by Claude Lévi-Strauss and Marcel Mauss, among others, cognitive anthropology was developed in the 1950s and 60s as the study of shared cultural knowledge, knowledge that appears implicit, and the transmission of ideas – 'the way knowledge is conventionalised into *culture*', as Roy D'Andrade put it.[41] Its methods draw on ethnology, linguistics and psychology to investigate how knowledge is embedded in language, artefacts, and cultural practices. A wariness of computational methods, a break with psychology in the 1970s (represented by the work of Clifford Geertz, among others), and the relatively small numbers of cognitive anthropologists to begin with, all contributed to a decline in the discipline.[42] This was partly symptomatic of a general erosion of the remit of anthropology and a suspicion that anthropology was not sufficiently scientific in its methods, leaving some scholars feeling they were simply not being taken seriously.[43] With the rise of poststructuralist and postcolonial theory, earlier anthropology was also open to criticism. While cognitive anthropology has sometimes been less populated and undervalued in comparison with its sister disciplines, it has been given a boost by the enduring popularity of the cognitive sciences and by its intersection with evolutionary biology;[44] the work of Edwin Hutchins has also brought the field more attention in recent years as the concept of distributed cognition has gained momentum in the cognitive sciences.

Hutchins's work has been adopted by advocates of *embodied cognition*, which challenges the input–output models of classical cognitivism and enlarges the focus of study to the body and environment – a move that shifts towards the discipline that arguably overlooks all the other aspects of cognitive science, as well as preceding them chronologically. The *philosophy of cognitive science* can relate to the ethical and epistemological implications of the theories and methods of the other branches, but it also encompasses philosophy of mind. Descending from ancient questions about the nature of the mind and the relationship of mind to body, the philosophy of cognitive science also considers myriad other debates, including – as neurobiology intervenes and AI presents new challenges – the nature and cognitive role of consciousness, emotion, differences in computation in the brain, social aspects of cognition, ethical issues in artificial intelligence, theory of mind or 'mindreading'.[45]

As the research landscape of cognitive science continues to develop and change, so does the degree of consilience (to invoke another voguish term) with the humanities.[46] More recently, while the interdisciplinary and philosophical dimension of cognitive science has remained a constant, the de-prioritising of lived experience has been countered by the rise of embodied cognition, that is, the reintroduction of the body and the world into previously computational–representational models. For the purposes of an investigation into the cross-disciplinary possibilities of cognitive science and medieval studies, there are more opportunities to engage with some disciplines than with others: there are no live subjects to observe or wire up; the methodological character of computational studies does not always mesh with the contemplation of an age before computers. However, with regard to the re-embodiment of cognition and its attendant philosophical, anthropological, linguistic, and psychological implications, the place of the humanities in this broader picture comes into focus.

Aims of this Collection

The aims and objectives of this collection therefore are to gather researchers from a variety of backgrounds to suggest, using both theoretical approaches and concrete examples, how their methods and findings can be utilised by other scholars in adjacent fields. We seek to inspire scholars within the humanities to engage with the tools and investigative methodologies deriving from cognitive sciences, while at the same time striving to address the estrangement that still persists between the sciences and the humanities, particularly in a climate in which the utility, communicability and impact of knowledge are so pressing. The contributors to this volume engage with novel hermeneutics for interpreting texts and images/artefacts (perhaps especially the hermeneutics of embodiment), and identify some practical principles. The resulting chapters examine what is helpful, how certain methods can generate new ways of looking at medieval texts, art and experience, and where this methodology exposes biases in our existing assumptions about the past and the way in which we study it. At the same time, we also aim to show where the study of the past overlaps with the study of modern psychology, neurobiology and other fields, and where the longer histories for some of these concepts might be (Wendy Turner's chapter in particular provides valuable precedents). The humanities play an important role in formulating and refining the complex models of the human mind and the way it is experienced, extended, and enacted in time and space. We want to offer a book in which readers can find a variety of methods and problems, and which we hope will encourage broader interest in the field and act as a resource both for humanities scholars who are researching and teaching courses that engage with the cognitive sciences, and students gaining a foothold and pursuing interests in these areas.

Several of the methods mentioned in this volume, especially older versions of psychohistory and classic psychoanalysis, have been in use within the humanities for a while, though the extent to which medievalists could embrace newer scientific approaches – especially those involving a degree of interaction with individuals being analysed, the tools they use and the environments in which they live and learn – has been limited. This is partly because surviving evidence of this type from the Middle Ages is often fragmentary and often unique (or at least anchored to a very specific context), as well as, of course, being significantly distant from twenty-first century methods and norms, both temporally and culturally. Yet just as methods in the biosciences undergo revision in the light of new research (as in the case of group and multilevel selection in biology and anthropology),[47] the humanities' attitude towards more bioscience-informed theories is undergoing revision, particularly outside the areas of anthropology, prehistory and modern/contemporary history and culture. The work of scholars like John Onians, David Freedberg and Iain McGilchrist demonstrate how successfully cultural material from a distant past can be studied and interpreted through new scientific lenses.[48]

Encounters between the cognitive sciences and the humanities have not been without controversy. The effects of mirror neurons, for example, have proven a fertile area of cross-disciplinary investigation for scholars of literature and art history in particular: this is a class of neurons first identified in macaques, which it was discovered would discharge in the same way in a subject performing an action and in another subject observing the same action (the Mirror Mechanism).[49] The same mechanism, and the existence of the same neurons, has been hypothesised for human subjects: the implications of this phenomenon have since become a source of fascination in the humanities and have been effectively mined by scholars asking how and why we respond to, learn from and personally invest in works of art and literature.[50] Freedberg and Onians, for example, have embraced the possibilities this hypothesis offers in art history.[51] Ben Morgan has also noted that the principles of 'Simulation Theory' are potentially illuminating in the study of mysticism and identity.[52] Among both neuroscientists and humanities scholars, however, there has also been a measure of pushback and scepticism with regard to what Raymond Tallis has called 'neuromania'.[53] Matthew Rampley, who contributes to this volume (and discusses mirror neurons at length), identifies somewhat more constructively that a key methodological difficulty in realising the potential of the neuroaesthetic turn is 'articulating the relation between, on the one hand, the generalized categories of the brain and its functions and, on the other, the individuated historical artistic and cultural practices it purports to explain'.[54] Anthropologists, too, have warned of the potential insensitivity of neuroscience to various cultural issues; the new discipline of cultural neuroscience consequently emerged in the late 2000s, striving to present a more nuanced picture as opposed to the universalising trends of mainstream bioscience.[55]

As was the case in previous decades in critiques of psychohistory, the lack of material for an experimental clinical study is a substantial issue. Pre-modern brains have not been preserved in sufficient condition or quantity for modern science to test their structural resemblance to contemporary brains, and the implications of neuroplasticity – the brain's capacity to change and 'rewire' itself over the course of an individual's life – makes it plausible that, even if they were morphologically identical, pre-modern brains may have been 'wired' rather differently from present-day brains. It is also possible to argue, however, that we can find recognisable traits, both behavioural and cultural, in sources from the past. While it is wise to be cautious and avoid reducing the study of aesthetics, history or literature to the methods of biological or 'brain' science, it is arguably reductive as well to elide the fact that all of the above are the products of an embodied mind, whose complexity demands an approach that pays due attention to physical, intellectual and cultural environment and to the experience of individual lived bodies.

Questions and Approaches

Without giving too much credence to the oft-cited suspicion that the humanities' concern with 'theory' has become too abstract and too ubiquitous, the cognitive turn in the humanities tends to coincide with the shift in the cognitive sciences themselves, prompted by the rise of 'embodied' cognition, which questioned previously held convictions of classical cognitivism just as cognitivism had challenged behaviourism. *Embodied cognition* has its philosophical roots in the anti-Cartesianism of James and Dewey and the concern for body and world in Heidegger's *Dasein* and Merleau-Ponty's embodied phenomenology. Incorporating into the work of cognition the state of the body, its feedback, and the information and conditions of the environment, this model thus moves beyond the computational model and locates cognition back in the world (see the contributions by Godelinde Gertrude Perk and Victoria Blud in this volume). Modern readers have the sense of a shared point of departure in the exploration of modern cognitive science and medieval thought on cognition: we have brains, minds, bodies, a stake in the world around us. There is an appeal to the idea of shared human experience, too, in the thought that although culture has changed, we can still recognise what we imagine to be basic physiological and sensory givens in, for instance, accounts of the five senses that read much the same today as in the Middle Ages.[56]

However, we must also be aware of and acknowledge the dangers of assuming continuity not only between one mind/body and another, but also between minds/bodies of one period and another. Studies in the field of anthropology add nuance and advise caution here. Kathryn Geurts makes the point that cognitive approaches should not overlook their own Western assumptions regarding, for instance, the concept of the senses: 'Despite the belief of many Euro-Americans, the five-senses model is not a scientific fact . . . From Aristotle to Aquinas and Descartes, however, cultural traditions have sustained a five-senses model that privileges mental representations and external modes of knowing. This construct, I argue, is essentially a folk ideology'.[57] Scholars of race, culture, disability, gender and sexuality have also offered incisive comments on the necessity of interrogating the assumptions that inform cognitive theory; they also show the potential of extending and applying these ideas to scenarios that engage with groups who were not necessarily envisaged in the sometimes homogenised landscape of cognitive theory. On the embodied- and embedded-ness of recent cognitive investigations, Ralph James Saverese notes that, 'By this logic, then, the sensing and acting associated with congenital deafness or autism or even impaired mobility would spawn a different kind of cognition'.[58] Zoe Drayson and Andy Clark have also written very recently on the implications of embodied models such as Clark's extended mind for subjects with cognitive disabilities.[59] J. Keith Vincent, meanwhile, writes on theory of mind and its place in the development of queer theory, especially the continuity with 'the preoccupation with *what other people are thinking*, and whether or not it is possible to find out', which might be far from innocuous wondering.[60]

To these considerations of divergence from an assumed norm we could add occupation, class, religion, and more. The study of religion, in particular, is one area where the geographical and cultural extent of the intersection of medieval studies and cognitive humanities becomes broader (see below). The contributions in this volume are mostly concerned with the culture of Western Europe in the Middle Ages, and adapt their methodologies from European and American schools of thought. While the essays here have this in common with much of the existing work on the cognitive turn in medieval studies, recent developments in both fields have seen its researchers attempting to come to terms with the Eurocentric influences that shaped and informed their fields. The need to recognise and re-evaluate implicit biases in the foundations of, and approaches to, scholarship is now changing and revising perspectives and methodologies, and has the potential to enrich both avenues of study.

With regard to cognitive studies of the Middle Ages, this is especially true. Islamic medicine in particular was hugely influential in Western Europe, where works like al-Rāzī's ninth-century *al-Kitab al-Hāwi* (translated as *Liber continens* in 1279) and Ibn Sīna's *al-Qānūn fī aṭ-Ṭibb* (*Canon of medicine*, completed 1025) were widely translated and transmitted; both became foundational texts in the Western study of medicine, the *Canon* remaining on the university syllabus at Padua until the eighteenth century. Arabic sources also present some of the most significant medieval contributions to cognitive science, including the development of ocular theory and ophthalmology (which later inspired Roger Bacon), the neuropsychology of memory, post-Galenic enquiry into the faculties and ventricles of the brain, theories of self-awareness, the treatment of brain injuries, certain terminology (Latin *dura mater* and *pia mater* for the meninges are translated from Arabic terms, for example), and clinical descriptions of neurosurgery to treat hydrocephalus in al-Rāzī and in al-Zahrāwī's *Kitab al-Taṣrīf* (*c.*1000).[61] Peter Pormann and Emilie Savage-Smith point to Chaucer's introduction to the Physician in the General Prologue to the *Canterbury Tales*, where he lists as medical authorities not only Hippocrates and Galen but also Rhazes (al-Rāzī), Avicenna (Ibn Sīna), Serapion (Ibn Sarābiyūn) and Haly ('Alī ibn Riḍwān): 'That Chaucer would so casually refer to medieval Islamic medical writers in a narrative poem that met with immediate popularity clearly illustrates the profound influence that the Islamic medical tradition had in Europe'.[62]

With regard to the medieval or pre-modern heritage of cognitive studies beyond Europe, scholarship in English is often still rooted in classical philosophy and dominated by Western thinkers, with key exceptions such as Avicenna and Averroes. However, Alexander Key has recently written on cognitive theories of reading expounded by eleventh-century Arabic thinkers, which anticipate in some respects the theories of later Western scholars.[63] Islamic and Jewish mysticism has been a particular flashpoint for engagement with the cognitive sciences, just as it has in European contexts.[64] Elham Sayyedan has recently written on the possibilities of interpreting the paradoxes of Sufi writings through cognitive linguistic approaches.[65] Among scholars of medieval Kabbalah, Brian L. Lancaster has explored the cognitive neuroscience of mystic experience in a series of publications;[66] Gabriel Levy looks at affordances alongside Andy Clark's reconsideration of language as a material artefact.[67] Reuven Tsur, the prolific scholar of cognitive poetics, has presented cognitive linguistics-based analyses of medieval Hebrew poetry, examining the impact of rhyme, metaphor and (drawing on D'Andrade's principles in cognitive anthropology) cognitive devices in poetry.[68] Neuroscientist Shahar Arzy and Kabbalah scholar Moshe Idel have also looked to cognitive neuroscience as a means of expanding the available 'toolkit' for engaging with mystic experience.[69] The number of researchers who specialise in both global medievalism and cognitive humanities is relatively small as yet, but the scope for cross-pollination and mutual enrichment is great, and continuing developments in this area are eagerly anticipated.

Overview

The present volume also begins by considering how the landscape of relations between the sciences has evolved, getting to grips with some difficult preliminary considerations: how similar the medieval understanding of the mind may be to the mind as conceived in modern neuroscience and cognitive psychology; the feasibility and usefulness of consilience as a methodology and objective; and the challenges of embarking on this venture in the first place. Parts II–IV, meanwhile, offer worked examples of how the disciplines of medieval studies can engage with methodologies drawn from cognitive studies, to what end, and with what effects. Broadly speaking, the organisation of the volume also moves from longer-established areas of study (philosophy of mind, psychology of religion and history of medicine) to the implications of more recent schools of thought, chiefly embodied cognition. The latter three sections are also thematically organised to coalesce around the study of stress, the psychology and cognitive experience of mysticism, and the historical and contemporary encounter with medieval visual and material culture.

The contributors in Part I, Questions of Method, define the scope of this interdisciplinary enquiry and identify some of the key areas of continuity and conflict. José Filipe Silva first draws parallels between medieval theories of mind and cognition – in which the faculties were seen as hierarchical and largely independent from one another – and the modular model of the mind found in contemporary debates, asking: Does the contemporary idea of modularity represent any continuity with the historical idea? Silva argues that this is a useful exegetical exercise for both cognitive psychology and medieval studies, pointing out that these medieval theories share with modularity (as theorised by Fodor) a principled distinction between modular perceptual processes and non-modular higher order cognitive processes, which in the medieval case apply only to rational processes.

Ralph W. Hood Jr engages with the psychology of religion: this chapter brings cognitive psychology and the history of the discipline to a wide-ranging engagement with medieval theology and mysticism. Re-contextualising William James's views on mystic thought, particularly his foundational contribution to cognitive psychology and the intersections of his work with the study of medieval mysticism, Hood examines how later receptions of *Varieties of Religious Experience* – rooted in psychology but more widely read now in religious studies – led James to be 'both silenced and a participant in this unrealised conversation' between religion and psychology (p. 41). Like Silva, he advocates the importance of developing loci for genuine conversations that may be realised between cognitive and medieval studies.

The final chapter in this section is a note of caution from Matthew Rampley, speaking predominantly from the perspective of art history and warning about the dangers of overenthusiastic and insufficiently informed forays into 'neurohumanities'. What does all this new data actually offer us, and how can we use it? In particular, he pays detailed attention to the functionality of modern technology and apparatus such as the fMRI scan, and the nuances of interpreting the data such innovations provide. He also considers the problems of transferring the insights of research into mirror neurons. Rampley's contribution highlights the difficulties and limitations of this emerging, often amorphous interdisciplinary approach, a voice of caution to those of us rushing to apply new scientific methods, findings and technologies to our medieval material.

The chapters in Part II draw on historical engagement with cognitive studies and together present a discussion of the historian's intervention in accounts of psychological stress. Daniel Lord Smail explores the potential of marrying neuroscience and history, arguing that 'neurohistory' offers 'a model where the nervous system itself is involved in a complex, never-ending dialectic with the cultural formations of the human past' (p. 84). In his chapter, Smail looks at the neurobiology of stress as a historical subject, drawing on ways in which we can use neuroscience for the study of environmental history, broadly conceived, and observing the reciprocal influence of humans, their natural environment, and their own nervous systems. Specifically, he discusses stress and patterns of violence in the late-medieval Western Europe, suggesting that a complex historical view on stress has the potential to be as useful as other political and social factors when evaluating historical violence and uprisings.

Wendy Turner also looks at stress disorders in the medieval period, from the perspective of history of medicine. She advances a 'parallel diagnosis' in order to compare symptoms using neutral terminology in the light of the limitations of historical distance. Rather than looking at accounts of conditions linked with highly stressful events as analogous to PTSD or psychosis, Turner analyses how the conditions arose, the extent to which sufferers of mental health problems were held accountable for their actions, the legal measures designed to help sufferers, and their success. In her examination of legal and medical terminology applied to mental health issues in medieval England, Turner reveals a nuanced and often compassionate picture of contemporary medieval understanding and definition of those underlying conditions, which led people to become a potential danger to themselves and society.

The final chapter in this section, by Juliana Dresvina, picks up the topics raised by Smail and Turner, narrowing this broad discussion down to one approach: the application of attachment theory to the study of the heightened religiosity of the past. Dresvina connects attachment theory with more recent developments in the field of cognitive neuroscience, analysing stress responses and adult psychology. In the light of the instability of interpersonal circumstances in the Middle Ages, Dresvina suggests that God emerges as a significant attachment figure: she offers Margery Kempe as a potential example of attachment anxiety being resolved through reorientation towards the deity, special saints and religious authorities.

Part III develops some of these threads with regard to the study of medieval literature: moving into the realm of embodied cognition, these chapters focus first on the incredibly rich accounts of individual intellectual and cognitive experience in medieval mysticism, before broadening the discussion to the reader experience of affect in literature. Like Hood, Godelinde Gertrude Perk contemplates medieval mysticism in particular and what it may offer contemporary studies of cognition, but here adopts a rather different methodology. She looks to the text of Julian of Norwich's visions as inspiration for applying the insights of situated and embodied cognitive theory: here, the text is paired with a process it particularly evokes – knitting. Focusing especially on Julian's use of the word 'knot' (here interpreted as an 'echo object' that participates in the same mental process that it signifies), Perk traces the ravelling and unravelling associations and semantics threaded through Julian's text through the repetitions of this image, asking 'How can Julian's knitting of words transform ours?' (p. 146).

Like Perk and Dresvina, Victoria Blud looks to Julian of Norwich's text of her showings and the conditions under which it was written and expanded, investigating the growing influence of the so-called '4 Es' of new cognitive philosophy. Reacting against traditional cognitivism, this set of theories posits that the mind is embodied, embedded, enacted and extended. This last has often been the most disputed, since it suggests that not only extra-cranial but extra-bodily and non-organic components may be considered part of cognitive processes. Blud investigates the potential mutual benefits for medievalists and cognitive studies of an intersection of 4E cognition and medieval texts and culture, which are likewise the products of a culture that does not see intellectual activity as being confined to the head.

Extending the discussion back further, Antonina Harbus brings a diachronic perspective to the study of emotion and asks how contemporary readers can affectively engage with past cultures, focusing on the role of art in the experience and stimulation of emotion, rather than simply its representation. Like Perk and Blud, Harbus explores embodied cognition, bringing 'mirroring' theory to bear on an analysis of how two poems from the Exeter Book 'enact the process of emotional remembering' in order to stimulate the reader's engagement. Significantly, her reading makes a highly practical virtue of the modern reader's linguistic, cultural and temporal distance from such texts, since this quality of difference demonstrates how between early medieval and modern experience there is 'a core degree of intelligibility' grounded in 'the human experience of an embodied mind and . . . a hard-wired predisposition for narrative' (pp. 186–7).

Finally, Part IV shifts to engagement with medieval artwork or artefacts, while staying broadly in the realm of embodied cognition and continuing to develop this perspective. The embodiment of the mind and its potential implications for art historians is the subject of Nadia Pawelchak's chapter, which explores the cognitive neuroscience and biological processes underlying artistic reception. In her analysis of a fourteenth-century ivory mirror case, Pawelchak draws on the anthropological concept of 'cognitive maps' and, like Harbus, examines the embodied responses elicited by the depicted postures and symbolism of the artwork in the light of the fascinating possibilities presented by mirror neurons. Perhaps most importantly, in engaging questions such as the extent to which brain activity and mental processes coincide (or not) with selfhood, personality, taste, or the limitations on reconstructing a cognitive map from a distant past, Pawelchak considers the caveats of applying neuroscientific study to art history, and suggests how art historians working in the neurohumanities can most fruitfully refine their methodology.

Jeff Rider turns to archaeology and the cognitive psychology of perception, demonstrating how examining and sensorily engaging with medieval artefacts – in the present, as much as in the Middle Ages – can not only stimulate but enhance our cognitive processes. Rider takes as his examples both physical artefacts – a spoon and a whorl – and the records of organised physical activity, specifically descriptions of dances and choreography. In his exploration of the role of such artefacts in cognitive processes, Rider builds on a particular strand of the embodied theories of cognition by offering a thorough introduction to the study of affordances (the properties that reveal a subject's possible interactions with a particular object) in medieval culture. He also argues for the vital role of artefacts in preserving, and in some scenarios constituting, the repertoire of human experience and neurocognitive abilities.

The volume ends with an Afterword from John Onians, reflecting on the foregoing chapters, responding to Rampley's reservations, and offering a broader perspective on one of the fundamental stakes of this endeavour – what the value of the cognitive humanities will turn out to be. While we aim to demonstrate that value by bringing together historians, art historians, literary scholars, philosophers and psychologists, as well as a 'neurosceptic', both the list of the disciplines involved and the variety of topics covered will always be incomplete. We hope, however, that this volume will contribute to the ongoing conversation about the ways in which cognitive sciences can be successfully applied to the study of the distant past.

Notes

1 David Eagleman, *Incognito: The Secret Lives of the Brain* (Edinburgh: Canongate, 2011), idem, *The Brain* (Edinburgh: Canongate, 2015); Douglas Hofstadter, *I Am a Strange Loop* (New York: Basic Books, 2007); Gina Rippon, *The Gendered Brain: The New Neuroscience that Shatters the Myth of the Female Brain* (London: Vintage, 2019); Jonah Lehrer, *Proust Was a Neuroscientist* (Edinburgh: Canongate, 2012); Wendy S. Jones, *Jane on the Brain: Exploring the Science of Social Intelligence with Jane Austen* (New York: Pegasus Books, 2017).

2 The date of a landmark research presentation at MIT. See Howard Gardner, *The Mind's New Science* (New York: Basic Books, 1987), p. 28.

3 On the major areas of study and debates in the field, see, for instance, William Bechtel and George Graham (eds), *A Companion to Cognitive Science* (Oxford: Blackwell, 1998), pp. 107–337.

4 See, for example, the Wellcome-funded Hearing the Voice project on hallucination at Durham University (*http://hearingthevoice.org*); a study of how people relate to and interpret unusual experiences conducted by the UNIQUE research group (Institute of Psychiatry, King's College London: *https://www.kcl.ac.uk/ioppn/depts/psychology/research/researchgroupings/the-unique-research-group*); the Religion, Experience, and Mind (REM) Lab Group (University of California: *https://remlab.religion.ucsb.edu*); The Eye's Mind project at the University of Exeter (*http://sites.exeter.ac.uk/eyesmind/*); and the AHRC History of Distributed Cognition Project (*http://www.hdc.ed.ac.uk*), to name a few.

5 Marilyn Strathern, 'Useful Knowledge', *Proceedings of the British Academy*, 139 (2006), 73–109 (p. 78).

6 For a detailed account of these debates, see Maxwell Bennett, Daniel Dennett, Peter Hacker, John Searle and Daniel Robinson, *Neuroscience and Philosophy: Brain, Mind, and Language* (New York: Columbia University Press, 2007). John Bickle argues that philosophers need to branch out even further from the relatively familiar theoretical level of cognitive neuroscience and look to the more challenging neuroscientific research in molecular biology and cellular physics. See *Philosophy and Neuroscience: A Ruthlessly Reductive Account* (Norwell, MA: Springer, 2003).

7 For a broad survey and overview of these developments, see Charissa N. Terranova and Meredith Tromble (eds), *The Routledge Companion to Biology in Art and Architecture* (New York: Routledge, 2017).

8 John Canaday, *The Nuclear Muse: Literature, Physics, and the First Atomic Bombs* (Madison, WI: University of Wisconsin Press, 2000), p. 3.

9 In addition to the works by medievalists below, recent examples in literary studies include Barri J. Gold, *Thermopoetics: Energy in Victorian Literature and Science* (Cambridge, MA: MIT Press, 2010); Sarah C. Alexander, *Victorian Literature and the Physics of the Imponderable* (London: Taylor & Francis, 2015); Courtney Weiss Smith, *Empiricist Devotions: Science, Religion, and Poetry in Early Eighteenth-Century England* (Charlottesville, VA: University of Virginia Press, 2016); Michael Tondre, *The Physics of Possibility: Victorian Fiction, Science, and Gender* (Charlottesville, VA: University of Virginia Press, 2018); Karin Kukkonen, *4E Cognition and Eighteenth-Century Fiction: How the Novel Found its Feet* (Oxford: Oxford University Press, 2019).

10 See Donna J. Haraway, 'Manifesto for Cyborgs: Science, Technology, and Socialist Feminism in the 1980s', *Socialist Review*, 80 (1985), 65–108; *When Species Meet* (Minneapolis: University of Minnesota Press, 2007); *Staying with the Trouble: Making Kin in the Chthulucene* (Durham, NC: Duke University Press, 2016).

11 Karen Barad, 'Nature's queer performativity', *Kvinder, Køn & Forskning*, 1–2 (2012), 25–53 (p. 29). See also Barad, 'Queer causation and the ethics of mattering', in Noreen Giffney and Myra J. Hird (eds), *Queering the Non/Human* (Aldershot: Ashgate, 2008), pp. 311–38.

12 See, for example, Suparna Choudhury and Jan Slaby (eds), *Critical Neuroscience: A Handbook of the Social and Cultural Contexts of Neuroscience* (Chichester: Wiley-Blackwell, 2012); Cristian Tileagă and Jovan Byford (eds), *Psychology and History: Interdisciplinary Explorations* (Cambridge: Cambridge University Press, 2014).

13 Mark Turner, *Reading Minds: The Study of English in the Age of Cognitive Science* (Princeton, NJ: Princeton University Press, 1991); *The Literary Mind: The Origins of Thought and Language* (Oxford: Oxford University Press, 1996).

14 Lisa Zunshine, *Why We Read Fiction: Theory of Mind and the Novel* (Columbus, OH: Ohio State University Press, 2006); *Getting Inside Your Head: What Popular Science Can Tell Us about Popular Culture* (Baltimore: Johns Hopkins University Press, 2012), p. xi. Zunshine has also edited the *Introduction to Cognitive Cultural Studies* (Baltimore: Johns Hopkins University Press, 2010) and the *Oxford Handbook of Cognitive Literary Studies* (Oxford: Oxford University Press, 2015).

15 Suzanne Nalbantian, Paul M. Matthews; James L. McClelland, *The Memory Process: Neuroscientific and Humanistic Perspectives* (Cambridge, MA: MIT Press, 2010); Suzanne Nalbantian, *Memory in Literature: From Rousseau to Neuroscience* (Basingstoke: Palgrave Macmillan, 2003); Paul M. Matthews and Jeff McQuain, *The Bard on the Brain: Understanding the Mind Through the Art of Shakespeare and the Science of Brain Imaging* (New York: Dana, 2003); Ann Taves, *Religious Experience Reconsidered: A Building-Block Approach to the Study of Religion and Other Special Things* (Princeton, NJ: Princeton University Press, 2009); Patrick McNamara (ed.), *Where God and Science Meet: How Brain and Evolutionary Studies Alter Our Understanding of Religion*, 3 vols (Westport, CT: Praeger, 2006).

16 See *Cognitive Science, Literature, and the Arts: A Guide for Humanists* (New York: Routledge, 2003); *Understanding Nationalism: On Narrative, Cognitive Science, and Identity* (Columbus, OH: Ohio State University Press, 2009); *What Literature Teaches Us About Emotion* (Cambridge: Cambridge University Press, 2011).

17 See especially 'Distributing Cognition in the Globe', *Shakespeare Quarterly*, 56/2 (2005), 135–55; *Cognition in the Globe: Attention and Memory in Shakespeare's Theatre* (New York and Basingstoke: Palgrave Macmillan, 2011); *Early Modern Actors and Shakespeare's Theatre: Thinking with the Body* (London: Bloomsbury, 2017). In a similar vein, Mary Thomas Crane explored Shakespeare's plays through the lens of embodied cognition and cognitive linguistics in *Shakespeare's Brain: Reading with Cognitive Theory* (Princeton, NJ: Princeton University Press, 2001).

18 Jane Chance and Anthony Passaro (eds), *postmedieval: a journal of medieval cultural studies* 3/3 (2012). See especially Jane Chance's introduction, 'Cognitive alterities: From cultural studies to neuroscience and back again', 247–61.

19 On cognition and emotions, see Sino Knuuttila, *Emotions in Ancient and Medieval Philosophy* (Oxford: Clarendon, 2004); Martin Pickavé and Lisa Shapiro (eds), *Emotion and Cognitive Life in Medieval and Early Modern Philosophy* (Oxford: Clarendon, 2012); Frank Brandsma, Carolyne

Larrington and Corinne Saunders (eds), *Emotions in Medieval Arthurian Literature: Body, Mind, Voice* (Cambridge: D. S. Brewer, 2015); Victoria Blud, 'Emotional Bodies: Cognitive Neuroscience and Mediaeval Studies', *Literature Compass*, 13/6 (2016), 457–66.

20 Jill Stevenson, *Performance, Cognitive Theory, and Devotional Culture: Sensual Piety in Late Medieval York* (Basingstoke: Palgrave Macmillan 2010); Clare Wright, 'Enculturated, Embodied, Social: Medieval Drama and Cognitive Integration', in Miranda Anderson and Michael Wheeler (eds), *Distributed Cognition in Medieval and Renaissance Culture* (Edinburgh: Edinburgh University Press, 2019).

21 See also Julia Bourke, 'An Experiment in "Neurohistory": Reading Emotions in Aelred's *De Institutione Inclusarum (Rule for a Recluse)*', *Journal of Medieval Religious Cultures*, 42/1 (2016), 124–42, Special Issue: Anchoritic Studies and Liminality.

22 See Deborah Thorpe (ed.), *The Medieval Brain*, Special Collection: Open Library of Humanities, 5(1), 2018: *https://olh.openlibhums.org/collections/special/the-medieval-brain/* (accessed 3 September 2019). On the neurology of scribes see, for example, Thorpe, 'Tracing Neurological Disorders in the Handwriting of Medieval Scribes: Using the Past to Inform the Future', *The Journal of the Early Book Society for the Study of Manuscripts and Printing History*, 18 (2015), 241–8.

23 Antonina Harbus, *Cognitive Approaches to Old English Poetry* (Woodbridge: Boydell & Brewer, 2012).

24 Line Engh (ed.), *The Symbolism of Marriage in Early Christianity and the Latin Middle Ages* (Amsterdam: Amsterdam University Press, 2019): the volume focuses on cognitive linguistics and Conceptual Metaphor Theory (CMT) as a broader framework for encountering cultural and anthropological questions.

25 'Why All the Fuss About the Mind? A Medievalists Perspective on Cognitive Theory', in Rachel Fulton and Bruce W. Holsinger (eds), *History in the Comic Mode: Medieval Communities and the Matter of Person* (New York: Columbia University Press, 2007), pp. 170–81.

26 The terms *cognitive science* and *cognitive sciences* are both used in the literature.

27 Sloan Foundation, *Cognitive Science, 1978*: Report of the State of the Art Committee to the Advisors of the Alfred P. Sloan Foundation. Archived at *http://csjarchive.cogsci.rpi.edu/misc/CognitiveScience1978_OCR.pdf.*

28 *The Dictionary of Cognitive Science* (translated from French) lists five core disciplines: cognitive neuroscience, cognitive psychology, AI, cognitive linguistics and the philosophy of mind. See 'Introduction: A New Puzzle of the Mind', in Oliver Houdé, Daniel Kayser, Oliver Koenig, Joëlle Proust, François Rastier (eds), *Dictionary of Cognitive Science* (London: Routledge, 2004), pp. xxi–xxxviii (p. xxi). The recent *Oxford Handbook of Cognitive Science* focuses on psychology, linguistics and computational psychology, with less space devoted to philosophy of mind, cognitive anthropology – whose study has a 'sad history' – and even to AI and neuroscience. See Susan E. F. Chipman, 'An Introduction to Cognitive Science', in *The Oxford Handbook of Cognitive Science* (Oxford: Oxford University Press, 2017), pp. 1–12 (p. 7).

29 For a recent history and detailed evaluation not only of how the cognitive sciences developed but of the debates and controversies that informed and continue to shape the discipline, see Margaret A. Boden's magisterial *Mind as Machine: A History of Cognitive Science*, 2 vols (Oxford: Clarendon Press, 2006). Michael I. Posner first surveyed the development of the combined discipline, its methods and background, in the late 1980s; see *Foundations of Cognitive Science* (Cambridge, MA: MIT Press, 1989).

30 In particular, see Chomsky, 'A Review of B.F. Skinner's *Verbal Behavior*', *Language*, 35 (1959), 26–58.

31 See, for example, Miller, 'The magical number seven, plus or minus two: Some limits on our capacity for processing information', *Psychological Review*, 63/2 (1956), 81–97; Chomsky, *Aspects of the Theory of Syntax* (Cambridge, MA: MIT Press, 1965); Putnam, *Mind, Language, and Reality*, 2 vols (Cambridge: Cambridge University Press, 1975); Fodor, *The Language of Thought* (New York: Crowell, 1975); Miller and Philip Johnson-Laird, *Language and Perception* (Cambridge, MA: Harvard University Press, 1976). For a detailed history, see chapters 5–6 in Boden, *Mind as Machine*, vol. I.

32 The classic foundational studies include Alan Turing, 'Computing Machinery and Intelligence', *Mind*, 59 (1950), 433–60; Alan Newell and Herbert A. Simon, *Human Problem Solving* (Englewood Cliffs, NJ: Prentice-Hall, 1972).

33 Neisser, *Cognitive Psychology* (Englewood Cliffs, NJ: Prentice-Hall, 1967).

34 See Francisco J. Varela, Eleanor Rosch and Evan Thompson, *The Embodied Mind: Cognitive Science and Human Experience* (Cambridge, MA: MIT Press, 1992; rev. edn 2017).

35 See George Lakoff and Mark Johnson, *Metaphors We Live By* (Chicago: University of Chicago Press, 1980); George Lakoff, *Women, Fire, and Dangerous Things: What Categories Reveal About the Mind* (Chicago: University of Chicago Press, 1987).

36 See Ronald W. Langacker, *Foundations of Cognitive Grammar* (Stanford, CA: Stanford University Press, 1987); Gilles Fauconnier, *Mental Spaces: Aspects of Meaning Construction in Natural Language* (Cambridge: Cambridge University Press, 1994); Adele Goldberg, *Constructions: A Construction Grammar Approach to Argument Structure* (Chicago: University of Chicago Press, 1995); John R. Taylor, *Cognitive Grammar* (Oxford: Oxford University Press, 2002).

37 See Michael S. Gazzaniga (ed.), *Handbook of Cognitive Neuroscience* (New York: Plenum, 1984); Michael S. Gazzaniga, R. B. Ivry and G. R. Mangun (eds), *Cognitive Neuroscience: The Biology of the Mind*, 2nd edn (New York: W. W. Norton, 2002); C. R. Gallistel and Adam Philip King, *Memory and the Computational Brain: Why Cognitive Science Will Transform Neuroscience* (New York: Wiley-Blackwell, 2009).

38 The landmark paper on mirror neurons is Vittorio Gallese, Luciano Fadiga, Leonardo Fogassi and Giacomo Rizzolatti, 'Action Recognition in the Premotor Cortex', *Brain*, 119 (1996): 593–609. For studies on mirror neurons, embodied simulation and their applications, see Vittorio Gallese and Alvin Goldman, 'Mirror Neurons and the Simulation Theory of Mind-Reading', *Trends in Cognitive Sciences*, 2/12 (1998), 493–501; Marco Iacoboni, *Mirroring People: The New Science of How We Connect With Others* (New York: Farrar, Strauss & Giroux, 2009).

39 See, for example, Joseph LeDoux, *The Emotional Brain: The Mysterious Underpinnings of Emotional Life* (New York: Simon & Schuster, 1996); Jaak Panksepp, *Affective Neuroscience: The Foundations of Human and Animal Emotion* (Oxford: Oxford University Press, 1998); Jesse Prinz, *Gut Reactions: A Perceptual Theory of Emotion* (Oxford: Oxford University Press, 2004). William James was also a founding father in this area: see James, 'What is an Emotion?' *Mind*, 9/34 (1884), 188–205.

40 Particularly in the work of Antonio Damasio, *Descartes' Error: Emotion, Reason, and the Human Brain* (New York: Putnam, 1994); *Looking for Spinoza: Joy, Sorrow, and the Feeling Brain* (London: William Heinemann, 2003).

41 Roy D'Andrade, *The Development of Cognitive Anthropology* (Cambridge: Cambridge University Press, 1995), p. xiv (original emphasis).

42 For the history and defence of cognitive anthropology's place in the discipline, see Boden, 'The Mystery of the Missing Discipline', in *Mind as Machine*, vol. I, pp. 515–90.

43 'That this feeling is at least partly justified can be seen from *The German Dictionary of Cognitive Sciences* (Strube et al., 1996). Its cover is illustrated with a pentagon instead of the hexagon depicting the classic cognitive sciences – and guess which discipline is missing?' Sieghard Beller, Andrea Bender and Douglas L. Medin, 'Should Cognitive Anthropology Be Part of Cognitive Science?' *Topics in Cognitive Science*, 4 (2012), 342–53 (p. 344).

44 See Roy D'Andrade, 'The Sad Story of Anthropology 1950–1999', *Cross-Cultural Research*, 3/3 (2000), 219–32.

45 See William G. Lycan and Jesse Prinz (eds), *Mind and Cognition: A Reader* (Oxford: Blackwell, 1990); David Braddon-Mitchel and Frank Jackson, *Philosophy of Mind and Cognition* (Oxford: Blackwell, 1996); Jaegwon Kim, *Philosophy of Mind* (Boulder, CO: Westview, 1996); George Lakoff and Mark Johnson, *Philosophy in the Flesh* (New York: Basic Books, 1999).

46 Coined by William Whewell and revived by E. O. Wilson in his book of the same name, *consilience* has not been without its controversies – Louis Menard declaring it 'a bargain with the devil' – but has found adopters and commentators in both the sciences and the humanities as the trend towards cross-disciplinary research joining the humanities and the sciences continues apace. See E. O.

Wilson, *Consilience: The Unity of Knowledge* (New York: Knopf, 1998); Edward Slingerland, *What Science Offers the Humanities: Integrating Body and Culture* (Cambridge: Cambridge University Press, 2008); Edward Slingerhand and Mark Collard, *Creating Consilience: Integrating the Sciences and the Humanities* (Oxford: Oxford University Press, 2012).

47 David Sloan Wilson, *Darwin's Cathedral: Evolution, Religion, and the Nature of Society* (Chicago: University of Chicago Press, 2002), or Jonathan Haidt, *The Righteous Mind: Why Good People Are Divided by Politics and Religion* (London: Penguin, 2012).

48 John Onians, *European Art: A Neuroarthistory* (New Haven, CT: Yale University Press, 2016); David Freedberg and Vittorio Gallese, 'Motion, Emotion and Empathy in Esthetic Experience', *Trends in Cognitive Science*, 11/5 (2007), 197–203 and David Freedberg, 'From Absorption to Judgment: Empathy in Aesthetic Response', in Vanessa Lux (ed.), *Empathy: Epistemic Problems and Cultural-Historical Perspectives of a Cross-Disciplinary Concept* (London: Palgrave MacMillan, 2017), pp. 139–80; Iain McGilchrist, *The Master and His Emissary: The Divided Brain and the Making of the Western World* (New Haven, CT: Yale University Press, 2009).

49 James M. Kilner and Roger N. Lemon survey the hype surrounding the discovery in 'What We Currently Know About Mirror Neurons', *Current Biology*, 23 (2013), 1057–62.

50 For early literary engagements, see Gerhard Lauer, 'Going Empirical: Why We Need Cognitive Literary Studies', *Journal of Literary Theory*, 3/1 (2009), 145–54; Blakey Vermeule, *Why Do We Care about Literary Characters?* (Baltimore: Johns Hopkins University Press, 2010); Paula Leverage, Howard Mancing, Richard Schweikert and Jennifer Marston William (eds), *Theory of Mind and Literature* (West Lafayette, IN: Purdue University Press, 2011), esp. Breithaupt and Zunshine.

51 See, for example, Freedberg and Gallese, 'Motion, Emotion and Empathy in Esthetic Experience'; Gallese and Freedberg, 'Mirror and Canonical Neurons are Crucial Elements in Esthetic Experience', *Trends in Cognitive Science*, 11/10 (2007), 411; Onians, *Neuroarthistory: From Aristotle and Pliny to Baxendall and Zeki* (New Haven, CT: Yale University Press, 2007); Onians, *European Art: A Neuroarthistory*.

52 Ben Morgan, *On Becoming God: Late Medieval Mysticism and the Modern Western Self* (New York: Fordham University Press, 2013), pp. 40–4.

53 Vigorously opposed to biologism and the tendency to view the mind as identical with the individual's brain activity, Tallis argues that neuroscience has little to contribute to the humanities and almost nothing to studies of the past. Private correspondence; see also Tallis, *Aping Mankind: Neuromania, Darwinitis and the Misrepresentation of Humanity*, 2nd edn (London: Routledge, 2016).

54 Matthew Rampley, 'Fish, volcanoes and the art of brains: Review of John Onians, *European Art: A Neuroarthistory*', *Journal of Art Historiography*, 15 (December 2016): (accessed 15 September 2019). *https://arthistoriography.files.wordpress.com/2016/10/rampley-review-2.pdf* (accessed 15 September 2019). See also Rampley, *The Seductions of Darwin: Art, Evolution, Neuroscience* (University Park, PA: The Pennsylvania State University Press, 2017), and the chapter in this volume.

55 A good introduction to the debate can be found in Rebecca Seligman and Ryan A. Brown, 'Theory and method at the intersection of anthropology and cultural neuroscience', *Social Cognitive and Affective Neuroscience*, 5/2–3 (2010), 130–7.

56 For accounts of the five senses' descent from antiquity but also the way in which the senses were conceptualised differently in the Middle Ages, see C. M. Woolgar, *The Senses in Late Medieval England* (New Haven, CT: Yale University Press, 2006) and more recently Richard G. Newhauser (ed.), *A Cultural History of the Senses in the Middle Ages* (London: Bloomsbury, 2016).

57 Kathryn Linn Geurts, *Culture and the Senses: Bodily Ways of Knowing in an African Community* (Berkeley, CA: University of California Press, 2002), p. 7. See also David Howes, *The Varieties of Sensory Experience: A Sourcebook in the Anthropology of the Senses* (Toronto: University of Toronto Press, 1991); Kathryn Linn Geurts, 'Consciousness as "Feeling in the Body": A West African Theory of Embodiment, Emotion and the Making of Mind', in David Howes (ed.), *Empire of the Senses: The Sensual Culture Reader* (Oxford: Berg, 2005), pp. 164–78.

58 Ralph James Saverese, 'Cognition', in Rachel Adams, Benjamin Reiss and David Serlin (eds), *Keywords for Disability Studies* (New York: New York University Press, 2015), pp. 40–2 (p. 40).

For an excellent discussion of the potential benefits and necessary cautions that disability studies have for cognitive approaches to the humanities – particularly with regard to mindblindness, subalternity, and myths about autism and theory of mind – see as well Ralph James Savarese and Lisa Zunshine, 'The Critic as Neurocosmopolite; Or, What Cognitive Approaches to Literature Can Learn from Disability Studies: Lisa Zunshine in Conversation with Ralph James Savarese', *Narrative*, 22/1 (2014), 17–44.

59 Zoe Drayson and Andy Clark, 'Cognitive Disability and Embodied, Extended Minds', in Adam Cureton and David T. Wasserman (eds), *The Oxford Handbook of Philosophy and Disability* (Oxford: Oxford University Press, forthcoming; published online March 2019). Retrieved 3 September 2019, from *https://www.oxfordhandbooks.com/view/10.1093oxforhb/9780190622879.001.0001/oxfordhb-9780190622879*. See also Pia C. Kontos, '"The Painterly Hand": Embodied Consciousness and Alzheimer's Disease', *Journal of Aging Studies*, 17 (2003), 151–70. D. Corina and J. Singleton, 'Developmental Social Cognitive Neuroscience: Insights from Deafness', *Child Development*, 80 (2009), 952–67. Caroline King, 'Learning Disability and the Extended Mind', *Essays in Philosophy*, 17/2 (2016), 38–68. Surveying the role of cognitive sciences in the last fifty years of advances in neuropsychological research, see Jack M. Fletcher and Elena L. Grigorenko, 'Neuropsychology of Learning Disabilities: The Past and the Future', *Journal of the International Neuropsychological Society*, 23/9–10 (2017), 930–40.

60 J. Keith Vincent, 'Sex on the Mind: Queer Theory Meets Cognitive Theory', in Lisa Zunshine (ed.), *The Oxford Handbook of Cognitive Literary Studies* (Oxford: Oxford University Press, 2015), pp. 199–224 (p. 202, emphasis original).

61 For a selection of works surveying the history and impact of Islamic medicine on Europe, see F. Rahman (trans.), *Avicenna's Psychology* (Oxford: Oxford University Press, 1952); A. Z. Iskandar, *A Catalogue of Arabic Manuscripts on Medicine and Science in the Wellcome Historical Medical Library* (London: Wellcome Institute, 1967), esp. Introduction, pp. 1–73; Manfred Ullmann, *Islamic Medicine* (Edinburgh: Edinburgh University Press, 1997) and *Medizin im Islam* (Leiden: Brill, 1970); Dimitri Gutas, *Avicenna and the Aristotelian Tradition: Introduction to Reading Avicenna's Philosophical Works* (Leiden: Brill, 1988); Danielle Jacquart, 'The Influence of Arabic Medicine in the Medieval West', in Roshdi Rashid (ed.), *Encyclopaedia of the History of Arabic Science*, 3 vols (London: Routledge, 1996), vol. III, pp. 963–84; Danielle Jacquart and Françoise Micheau, *La médecine arabe et l'Occident médiéval* (Paris: Maisonneuve et Larose, 1996); Dag N. Hasse and Amos Bertolacci (eds), *The Arabic, Hebrew and Latin Reception of Avicenna's Metaphysics* (Berlin: De Gruyter, 2012).

62 Peter E. Pormann and Emilie Savage-Smith, *Medieval Islamic Medicine* (Edinburgh: Edinburgh University Press, 2007), p. 162.

63 Alexander Key, *Language between God and the Poets: Maʿnā in the Eleventh Century* (California: University of California Press, 2018).

64 See Jerome Kroll and Bernard Bachrach, *The Mystic Mind: The Psychology of Medieval Mystics and Ascetics* (New York and London: Routledge, 2005), and on meditation, Michelle Karnes, *Imagination, Meditation and Cognition in the Middle Ages* (Chicago: University of Chicago Press, Chicago, 2011).

65 Elham Sayyedan, 'A Cognitive Approach to Motion Verbs in Ruzbihan Baqli's Sharhe-Shathiyat', *Textual Criticism of Persian Literature*, 11/1 (2019), 109–25.

66 See B. L. Lancaster, 'On the Relationship Between Cognitive Models and Spiritual Maps. Evidence from Hebrew Language Mysticism', *Journal of Consciousness Studies*, 7/11–12 (2000), 231 50; Brian L. Lancaster, *Approaches to Consciousness: The Marriage of Science and Mysticism* (London: Routledge, 2004), pp. 148–92; B. L. Lancaster, 'The Hard Problem Revisited: From Cognitive Neuroscience to Kabbalah and Back Again', in Harald Walach, Stefan Schmidt and Wayne B. Jonas (eds), *Neuroscience, Consciousness and Spirituality. Studies in Neuroscience, Consciousness and Spirituality* (Springer: Dordrecht, 2011), pp. 229–52.

67 Gabriel Levy, '"I was El Shaddai, but now I'm Yah'weh": God Names and the Informational Dynamics of Biblical Texts', in István Czachesz and Risto Uro (eds), *Mind, Morality and Magic:*

Cognitive Science Approaches in Biblical Studies (London: Routledge, 2014), pp. 98–119 (p. 100).

68 See Reuven Tsur, 'What Can we Know about the Mediaeval Reader's Response to Rhyme?' in Jean Perrot (ed.), *Polyphonie pour Ivan Fonagy* (Paris: Harmattan, 1997), pp. 467–78; 'Light, Fire, Prison: A Cognitive Analysis of Religious Imagery in Poetry', *PSYART: A Hyperlink Journal for the Psychological Study of the Arts* (1998): *http://psyartjournal.com/article/show/tsur-light_fire_prison_a_cognitive_analysis_o* (accessed 3 September 2019); 'Poetic Conventions as Fossilized Cognitive Devices; The Case of Mediaeval and Renaissance Poetics', *PSYART: A Hyperlink Journal for the Psychological Study of the Arts (2008): http://psyartjournal.com/article/show/tsur-poetic_conventions_as_fossilized_cogniti* (accessed 3 September 2019).

69 Shahar Arzy and Moshe Idel, *Kabbalah: A Neurocognitive Approach to Mystic Experiences* (New Haven, CT: Yale University Press, 2015).

Select Bibliography

Boden, Margaret A., *Mind as Machine: A History of Cognitive Science*, 2 vols (Oxford: Clarendon Press, 2006).

Chance, Jane, 'Cognitive alterities: From cultural studies to neuroscience and back again', *postmedieval*, 3/3 (2012), 247–61.

Clark, Anne L., 'Why All the Fuss About the Mind? A Medievalist's Perspective on Cognitive Theory', in Rachel Fulton and Bruce W. Holsinger (eds), *History in the Comic Mode: Medieval Communities and the Matter of Person* (New York: Columbia University Press, 2007), pp. 170–81.

Freedberg, David and Vittorio Gallese, 'Motion, Emotion and Empathy in Esthetic Experience', *Trends in Cognitive Science*, 11/5 (2007), 197–203.

Gardner, Howard, *The Mind's New Science* (New York: Basic Books, 1987).

Gazzaniga, Michael S., R. B. Ivry and G. R. Mangun (eds), *Cognitive Neuroscience: The Biology of the Mind*, 2nd edn (New York: W. W. Norton, 2002).

Hogan, Patrick Colm, *What Literature Teaches Us About Emotion* (Cambridge: Cambridge University Press, 2011).

Lakoff, George and Mark Johnson, *Metaphors We Live By* (Chicago: University of Chicago Press, 1980).

McGilchrist, Iain, *The Master and His Emissary: The Divided Brain and the Making of the Western World* (New Haven, CT: Yale University Press, 2009).

McNamara, Patrick (ed.), *Where God and Science Meet: How Brain and Evolutionary Studies Alter Our Understanding of Religion*, 3 vols (Westport, CT: Praeger, 2006).

Nalbantian, Suzanne, *Memory in Literature: From Rousseau to Neuroscience* (Basingstoke: Palgrave Macmillan, 2003).

Nalbantian, Suzanne, Paul M. Matthews and James L. McClelland, *The Memory Process: Neuroscientific and Humanistic Perspectives* (Cambridge, MA: MIT Press, 2010).

Onians, John, *European Art: A Neuroarthistory* (New Haven, CT: Yale University Press, 2016).

Panksepp, Jaak, *Affective Neuroscience: The Foundations of Human and Animal Emotion* (Oxford: Oxford University Press, 1998).

Pickavé, Martin and Lisa Shapiro (eds), *Emotion and Cognitive Life in Medieval and Early Modern Philosophy* (Oxford: Clarendon, 2012).

Rampley, Matthew, *The Seductions of Darwin: Art, Evolution, Neuroscience* (University Park, PA: The Pennsylvania State University Press, 2017).

Slingerland, Edward, *What Science Offers the Humanities: Integrating Body and Culture* (Cambridge: Cambridge University Press, 2008).

Tribble, Evelyn, *Cognition in the Globe: Attention and Memory in Shakespeare's Theatre* (New York and Basingstoke: Palgrave Macmillan, 2011).

Turner, Mark, *The Literary Mind: The Origins of Thought and Language* (Oxford: Oxford University Press, 1996).

Varela, Francisco J., Eleanor Rosch and Evan Thompson, *The Embodied Mind: Cognitive Science and Human Experience* (Cambridge, MA: MIT Press, 1992; rev. edn 2017).

Wilson, E. O., *Consilience: The Unity of Knowledge* (New York: Knopf, 1998).

Zunshine, Lisa, *Why We Read Fiction: Theory of Mind and the Novel* (Columbus, OH: Ohio State University Press, 2006).

Zunshine, Lisa (ed.), *The Oxford Handbook of Cognitive Literary Studies* (Oxford: Oxford University Press, 2015).

I

Questions of Method

1

How Modular are Medieval Cognitive Theories?

JOSÉ FILIPE SILVA

Traditional overviews of medieval theories of mind and cognition offer a picture in which the human soul is constituted by distinct cognitive faculties that process different kinds of information – or the same kind in different ways. These faculties are disposed in a hierarchical structure and are largely independent from one another, very much like the modular model of the mind in contemporary debates. However, the similarities do not stop here. In this chapter, I argue that medieval theories of mind share with Fodor's style modularity a distinction between modular perceptual processes and non-modular higher order cognitive processes, which in the medieval case apply only to rational processes. The aim of this chapter is therefore to connect historical sources, especially late medieval Latin commentaries on Aristotle's *De anima*, with contemporary debates on the philosophy of mind, in particular the question of mental architecture.

There are many ways to approach and interpret medieval cognitive theories, but often this is attempted on the basis of very broad theoretical frameworks and philosophical traditions: Aristotelianism versus Augustinianism, realism versus nominalism, and so on. Another way, which will be essayed here, is to look at those late medieval theories from the perspective of a basic contemporary notion, in this case that of modularity. Modularity is a philosophical assumption about the structure of the mind, more specifically a view of the mind as carved up, at least partially, into distinct operating mechanisms, like that responsible for vision. The aim is not to be anachronistic – that is, to claim that late medieval thinkers made use of notions that they would not be amenable to – but rather to test the hypothesis that using conceptual apparatus of contemporary debates on epistemology and philosophy of mind may be of exegetical value in understanding medieval models. Here, I focus on whether the modularity of mind thesis is appropriate *and* useful for interpreting medieval faculty psychology. Faculty psychology is the study of the soul and its powers or capacities or faculties, by means of which a living thing is capable of performing the operations proper to its kind of life, according to a division proposed by Aristotle and adopted by the majority of late medieval thinkers. These are growth and reproduction in the case of plants; growth, reproduction, motion and perception in the case of animals; growth, reproduction, motion, sensation and understanding in the case of human beings. To test this, we may ask whether, for medieval authors, perceptual faculties like sight or common sense are encapsulated – that is, closed to the flow of information from other faculties – or subject to horizontal and/or vertical influences from other processes (or modules).[1] In other words, the focus is on the nature of 'mental' processes and whether higher cognitive faculties play any role in lower mental functions: are low level cognitive processes, like perception, sensitive to reason or reason-like abilities, and to what extent are psychological faculties really independent, domain specific, etc.? I will not consider the difference between rational and non-rational perceivers, but instead focus on human beings, who are endowed with rational abilities, because only this way can the question of whether these rational abilities play a role in perceptual cognitive processes be properly assessed. (It would make little sense to ask whether rational abilities or capacities play a role in perceptual processes in beings lacking rational abilities or capacities; medieval thinkers thought that animals, by and large, lacked such abilities or capacities. It is altogether a different issue whether they thought animals could perform actions that *appeared* rational, but this is not my concern here.) At the same time, a secondary aim is to understand whether the contemporary concept of modularity is the result of historical influences, namely of medieval faculty psychology. In that sense, I take Jerry Fodor's contemporary version of modularity as paradigmatic because of his explicit engagement with historical sources.

I. Setting the Stage

A good starting point is to be clear about terminology: there is a wide range of interpretations of what a 'module' is. I suggest following the definition advocated by a major figure in the development of the modularity thesis, Jerry Fodor. According to Fodor, the basic properties of modules are:

> (i) domain specificity, meaning that each module operates with a specific type of input; (ii) encapsulation, meaning that each module functions largely on its own, without appealing to other psychological systems to perform its specific functions; (iii) fast, as modules operate a set of functions with very specific input, and mandatory once the appropriate input is present: input of a certain kind turns the system on; (iv) shallow output, meaning that it is non-conceptual; (v) localized, meaning that each module is located in a specific brain region/area.[2]

With these characteristics in mind, we can define a module as a sub-system capable of processing a certain kind of information that it takes as input and processes according to a set of rules specific to that module.[3] An example Fodor gives is the use of the rules of grammar of a certain language by a parsing mechanism. This means that it operates on the basis of these rules, without taking extra input from other modules, up- or downstream – that is, from those modules that feed information to the module in question or those modules further down the line in the processing sequence that receive the information from the module in question. If the module were to take such input other than the specific input that characterises it, it would not be functionally independent and thus would not be encapsulated. By rules here, I mean nothing other than the general operating principles of a given module, something akin to: 'when you receive information of type x, perform the operation y'.

That means that one of the questions about the modules is the origin of their set of rules (or principles) of operation – whether this is at the outset of their constitution or whether their database of rules is constituted and continually updated by external factors (external either to the module or to the whole cognitive system of which it is part). Now, the answer to the question of whether modules can retrieve or access stored information depends on how modules are conceived, which leads us to a central question of the present comparison between medieval and contemporary modules: How (broadly or narrowly) do modules characterise our mental architecture? That is, is the mind a completely modular system, and is this a model of mental facts and processes that it makes sense to apply to medieval faculty psychology? In what follows, I will try to show that this is the case and further qualify this claim, adjusting it to the structures of mental life, medieval style.

I take Fodor as the paradigmatic contemporary model of modularity for two main reasons. First, his is the standard against which other versions of modularity have developed (on alternative models, see Section V below). For the purposes of this chapter, a standard notion is better than any of the qualified versions that follow (massive modularity, etc.) because I wish to exploit the exegetical value of the concept in a historical setting, rather than debate the merits (and difficulties) of a particular version of a theory of modularity. Secondly, Fodor explicitly recognises himself as an heir to the tradition of faculty psychology, even if his historical references are limited to Plato, Descartes and Locke. He thus warrants our investigation into the historical predecessors of his concept of modules, conceived as cognitive mechanisms that are functionally differentiated and that together account for the different processes the cognitive system is capable of performing. The focus on the medieval period is justified by the fact that in this period an explanation of the different kinds of operations (cognitive, volitional) a being is capable of performing is given by appealing to different psychological units, called faculties or powers (*virtutes*, *potentiae*). The question worth asking is whether these powers or faculties can be con ceived of as 'modules' in Fodor's sense. I argue that they can, and that to understand mental faculties in terms of modules provides new insight into medieval faculty psychology, at least at a very general level, because Fodor's modules and medieval faculties share a number of significant characteristics, like domain specificity and encapsulation. But I also argue, on a more specific level, that medieval theories of mind share with Fodor's style of modularity the distinction between modular perceptual processes and non-modular higher order cognitive processes, which in the medieval case apply only to rational processes.

In order to investigate these claims, I first consider the basic Aristotelian scheme of the cognitive faculties. But the medieval model of faculty psychology was not directly and purely taken from Aristotle (384–322 BC); rather, it was based on a re-elaboration originating with Ibn Sina (Avicenna, 980–1037). For that reason, I compare this Avicennian scheme to the Aristotelian basic model. Next, I illustrate briefly two different modes of reception of this Aristotelian–Avicennian model in the Latin West, those of Albert the Great (1200–1280) and Nicholas Oresme (1320–1382). I conclude by bringing the issue back to the way the contemporary concept of modularity is helpful in understanding the medieval developments in faculty psychology.[4]

II. Aristotle

One of the basic theses in Aristotle's philosophy of mind and epistemology is that psychological faculties as powers are determined and defined by what they do, and in turn these activities are determined by what they are about.[5] What they are about (say, vision is about colour) is precisely what triggers them into action, moving them from a state of potentiality to actuality (actually seeing). Perception is thus largely explained in causal terms: actual-x brings y, which is 'y-potentially-cognising x' into 'y-cognising x in actuality'. That is the very general picture that needs to be fleshed out.

As far as sensation is concerned, Aristotle distinguishes between the external and internal senses, in terms of powers, and between sensibles *per se* (proper and common) and sensibles *per accidens*, in terms of objects. Whereas proper sensibles are the objects of one sense modality only (like colour to sight), common sensibles (like motion, shape, number) are the objects of at least two sense modalities. There have been lengthy discussions in the literature about the nature of the central perceptual faculty in Aristotle – the common sense – namely, whether it is a faculty above and beyond the five sense modalities, or rather just the five external senses jointly operating.[6] The incidental sensible on the other hand is that which is perceived by accident, that is to say, together with but not *as* a primary perceptible object (like colour). A good example is the perception of my cat, when I perceive its colour, black. Black is the proper object of sight, whereas the cat's shape and size, as well as its being a/my cat, are respectively common and incidental sensibles. But if objects in the world have properties to be perceived, cognitive subjects must have powers capable of perceiving them. These are psychological faculties, which receive, process, retain, combine and judge sensory information.[7] The internal senses are those powers of the soul that process sensory information without being in direct contact with the external things they (help) cognising. Some of these faculties only operate online, i.e. while the external object is present, whereas others operate only offline, i.e. when the object is not present, and still others are neutral to the presence of the object. Aristotle's faculty psychology is limited to the powers of common sense, imagination or *phantasia* and memory.[8]

Historically, Aristotle is essential as the backdrop against which different authors developed their ideas about how we can know the world and the psychological structures (and mechanisms) that make this possible. However, the truth of the matter is that his faculty psychology model fell short in some respects: for instance, in what concerns the explanation of perceptual illusions and the perception of extra-sensible features of things, like the way these things relate to us. It is precisely this last aspect that Aristotle's Arabic commentator, Avicenna, addresses with his theory of intentions (see below). It is important to stress that the two sets of works – those of the Greek philosopher and of his Arabic commentator – arrived in the Latin West at roughly the same time (from the mid-twelfth century), so that in a way the reception of Aristotle *is* the reception of Avicenna. In no other area of enquiry has this been more significant than in natural philosophy, and in particular in what concerns the soul and its cognitive processes. I will therefore spend the rest of this chapter examining this reception, rather than Aristotle's faculty psychology proper, even though the former largely depends on the latter.

III. Avicenna

Among the reasons that seem to explain the development of a more complex psychological model in the late medieval period is something akin to what we would call nowadays the 'poverty of stimulus' argument. In contemporary philosophy this argument is intended to show that the information we receive from the world is simply too poor to account for our successful behaviour in negotiating the environment. It is particularly used by supporters of the cognitive penetration of perception, the view that perception is determined (guided) by the influence higher cognitive powers exert on lower perceptual processes/powers. To put it simply: if perpetual success cannot be explained solely by the incoming stimulus, then our cognitive system must fill in the gaps, most likely by appealing to stored background information *on how we know and thus expect the world to be*. How the details of this filling-in can be explored is open to interpretation. The original Aristotelian model seems to fail to explain two important aspects of our perceptual experience. The first is how we perceive sensible features of things that are not immediately available to us; hence, our perception of them cannot be the result of *their causal action* on our sense organs. The second is the categorisation of sensory information that human beings carry out as soon as they get in direct contact with external things: the way we recognise 'this' coloured thing as a *dog* or a *chair* and, at a simpler level, how we are able to identify *that thing which is white* to be also *at a certain distance* and *to have a certain shape*. It is thus amazing that, on the basis of what seems very basic sensory information, we do achieve quite an impressive degree of accuracy. But if what we get from the world is not enough on its own to explain it, what would explain it, if not the nature of our own cognitive capacities and the nature of their cooperation? Scholars have of course debated whether Aristotle has solutions for these issues, but even if that is the case, these are at least not immediately evident.

Avicenna intended to tackle some of those concerns by elaborating on the sparse faculty psychology model of Aristotle. Avicenna considers four basic (functional) distinctions between powers:[9] (1) on the basis of their objects, there is a distinction between the common sense, which deals with sensible forms, and the estimative power, which deals with connotational attributes; (2) there is a difference between those faculties that are receptive (like common sense and estimation), which receive information directly from the external senses, and those faculties that retain this information (the retentive imagination and the memory); (3) there is a distinction between the retentive faculties on the basis of the kind of information they retain: retentive imagination retains sensory information, memory retains the connotational attributes; and (4) there is a distinction between the nature of the faculties, between those that are passive, namely the common sense and estimative power, and the active power of compositional imagination, which combines previously received sense information in ways that do not have to conform to the way things are in the external world. In addition to distinctions based on function, Avicenna also attributes differences between powers to their bodily location, but this latter kind of distinction seems to be parasitical on the former (functional) kind.

The key innovation in Avicenna's model is the estimative power, which has the functions of apprehending the intentions (also called 'connotational attributes') together with the sensible forms, in order to explain behaviour in a way that is species-specific and not based on previously acquired knowledge. His famous example is of a sheep that runs from a wolf without ever having encountered one before, because it apprehends the wolf's intention of 'harmfulness' or 'enmity' together with its shape and colour. The estimative power thus conceived shares two central features of a module in Fodor's account: it is encapsulated and it is domain specific. There is an immediate (i.e. direct) connection between the intention received by the estimative power and the behaviour of the animal that receives such an intention: if it is harmfulness, the animal runs away; if friendship, the animal looks for its friend. But this raises the following worry: What happens in the case of rational animals that receive also the intention of harmfulness or friendliness? Here the explanation must be slightly more complex, because human behaviour is not simply conditioned, at least not in the same degree as that of animals. In face of a dangerous animal, I can decide to fight or pick up a gun or start a fire, if I have the background information that tells me that this is the kind of animal that is afraid of fire. And of course, if I have a door between myself and the dangerous beast – and I know the door is strong enough to keep the animal at bay – I can close it. When I was recently at the zoo with my son, in a glass tunnel surrounded by the lions' pit – with the lions actually on top of the 'ceiling' of the tunnel – I may well have been receiving such intentions of harmfulness from those lions, but I certainly was not afraid because my background information overrode those intentions. Hard glass structures in zoos trump lions every day of the week, as far as I am concerned! Similar worries led later medieval thinkers, for instance Thomas Aquinas (1224–1274), to propose an essential distinction between the human estimative power – which he renamed cogitative power and nicknamed 'particular reason' – and the estimative power of non-rational animals, precisely to account for that kind of difference in behaviour and cognitive reach.[10]

At a very basic level, the story Avicenna wants to tell is that there is a basic distinction between the kind of responses sensory stimuli elicit in the different kinds of beings and within each subject between different types of psychological faculties: on the one hand, in the case of those faculties that are cognitive, the reception of the stimulus of a certain kind is simply the actualisation (i.e. realisation) of its proper function: the reception of colour simply is the act of seeing a coloured object. But the reception of the 'intentional' stimulus is the triggering of a behavioural reaction of the kind of 'running away' or 'befriending'. Neither of these stimuli lead to any other kind of reaction because they are not the proper objects of those powers. Each power has proper objects and specific functions, allowing Avicenna to offer a model of completely encapsulated and domain-specific psychological faculties that is akin to Fodor's modular account of the mind. These powers, like the common sense and estimation, behave like modules in the sense that their outcome is flat, i.e. the information they generate is not complex: it is either this or that, harmful or beneficial. Comparing the two models, however, there is an immediate important difference: Fodor argues for a version of horizontal faculties in which what matters for its distinction from other modules is the function the module produces, rather than the content it deals with. So there is a memory module the function of which is to retain information for future use, no matter what kind of information – be that about blue cars or dangerous bears. But for Avicenna and people adopting his model, there are different retentive powers, which are distinguished on the basis of the *kinds* of information they retain: whereas sensible forms are kept by imagination, intentions are kept by memory.

A different (and complex) question is whether perception for medieval thinkers is 'smart', in the sense of entailing inferential processes built into the system, thus being similar to cognition. In other words, the question is whether for medieval thinkers basic perceptual episodes require the use of inferential capacities, namely whether seeing a white object entails the identification of that object as this or that kind of object (say, a table or a horse). To answer this would take us too far from the main focus of this article. Let me just say here that, in a sense, the question is misguided, at least in what concerns basic perceptual functions. For medieval thinkers, like Avicenna, seeing colours or avoiding dangerous things does not require inferential processes because the appropriated reaction to a stimulus of a given kind is determined by the metaphysical level of explanation, rather than the content it brings to bear on the epistemic subject. The wolf is perceived as dangerous by the sheep because the sheep receives the sensible properties of the wolf's colour, shape and so on *together* with the intention of hostility or harmfulness. It is the reception of these sensible forms plus intentions that explains the reaction, rather than the reception of these sensible features giving rise to higher processes of categorisation – '*this* is a *wolf*' – and inference – 'this is a wolf, wolves are dangerous, I must run away'. There is no processing that is not transmission and proper functioning of encapsulated and domain specific psychological faculties or modules. What information any given module processes – its input – is restricted to a specific kind of property it receives from the extra-mental object and its operation is restricted to that property-kind. Those received features are metaphysically constitutive of what the object perceived is and there is no contribution of the perceptual powers *to constitute the object as being in a certain way*, i.e. to represent it in a way that is not both grounded *and* restricted to what is made available from the senses.

One does not, however, simply perceive colour but an object with a certain shape and size, standing at a certain distance, and probably with a certain smell and texture. The perception of those proper and common sensibles, as they are called in this model, results in the perception of a (roughly) unified entity. How unified is a matter of dispute and gives rise to the question of whether higher order cognitive processes, like identification and recognition, have any role to play in perception. In other words, does the content of perceptual experiences include the identification of the *kind* to which *that thing* one perceives as having such and such properties belongs? Medieval thinkers thought there were two ways to deal with this question: the dominant view denies that such identification can occur at the sensory level, claiming instead that it would have to occur upstream, at the level of the intellect; some authors seem to allow for some instances of sensory identification or recognition of 'low level universals' or at least of vague universals by some cognitive beings,[11] namely of the rational kind (and in this case as the result of the influence of reason). The reason why this question is significant for our purposes is that similar questions arise in the case of modularity of mind Fodor's style, namely whether higher order cognitive processes escape the modularity structure and how exactly to carve the distinction between the modules that cover the basic perceptual categories. I return to this issue in Section V. In brief, Avicennian psychological faculties are very much like Fodor's modules: faculties, like modules, are exclusively dedicated to certain kinds of information; their operations cannot be interfered with by other modules, and every module/faculty has a specific location.

IV. The Medieval Latin West

The reception of Aristotle and Avicenna's natural philosophy in the Latin West was characterised by the adoption of their models of mind and cognition. There is a wide range of scholarship on this topic, beyond the scope of this chapter.[12] I will present briefly two examples: first, the Dominican Albert the Great, an author of the second generation to comment on these works and who remains (with important qualifications) within the Avicennian framework; secondly, a fourteenth-century philosopher who proposes a more heterodox model of the mind, Nicole Oresme. The aim of this section is to show how the hypothesis of conceiving the human soul in modular terms was both confirmed (by Albert) and refuted (by Oresme).

Following Avicenna in his classification of internal senses, Albert argues that the sensitive part of the human soul is divided into the powers of common sense, the power of imagination, estimative power, fantasy (*phantasia*) and memory. Common sense is conceived as the root or fountain of the five external senses.[13] The sensory information feeds also into the other faculties: sensible forms are fed into the imagination to be retained, intentions into the memory for keeping. The common sense performs two main functions: first, it is responsible for our awareness of experiencing something, so for instance our awareness that we are seeing (literally, 'when we see, we apprehend ourselves seeing': 'nos apprehendimus nos videre, quando videmus', *De anima* II.4.7, 157); secondly, it is responsible for comparing and judging the information received from the different sense modalities, so that we can adjudicate that 'this citrus is sweet' ('citrinum esse dulce', *De anima* II.4.7, 157). Another central psychological faculty is (the) phantasy, which explains why and how we are able to bring together sensible forms and/or intentions of things previously sensed, that do not necessarily correspond to the way those sensed things are on their own. I am able to imagine a human being with two heads or a golden mountain. For reasons of space, I cannot dwell on Albert's faculty psychology, but proceed to present an author with a different approach to the question of the 'internal senses', Nicole Oresme.

Oresme lists the internal processing faculties of common sense, fantasy, cogitative and memory. These are called 'internal', he remarks, because they receive their information from the external senses and do not have any direct contact with the external objects. In other words, these are not located in the external senses' organs, which would allow them to be in contact with the objects. Oresme notes that one of the motivation to postulate such internal processing mechanisms is the fact that we are able to bring to view sensible things in their absence as well as to organise the sensory information in a more complex way than the way that information is made available to us: I can not only bring together and adjudicate disparate information acquired via different sense modalities – sweet from taste and white from sight – as I can combine sense data in a way that does not correspond to the way things are (e.g. a golden mountain) and am even able to perceive privation for instance of light (the assumption is that privation of light means the awareness of something as being a state other than what was expected).[14] But the fact that 'internal' mechanisms are necessary does not make it necessary that there is a plurality of such powers. That plurality needs to be argued for, so the basic question is how to distinguish between them.

One way to do so is in terms of functions, that is to say, what operations each power performs. Another way is to consider their location within the human body. Two immediate objections appear: the first is that there seems to be just one such organ, the brain, which is the subject for all these operations. Thus bodily or organic location cannot be the principle of distinction. Even those who wish to argue for the localisation criterion by noting the existence of ventricles or cavities in the brain must admit that there are only three such structures, suggesting at most three psychological faculties.[15] Secondly, each of these faculties seems to be responsible for a number of functions, which means that the 'number of functions' cannot on its own be the principle of distinction among powers.

The argument that slowly emerges is that one and the same faculty would be able to perform all the functions, as Oresme explicitly states:

> It is clear that one internal sense, namely the common sense, suffices in what concerns all the sensible [things], just like a single intellect in man suffices for everything that he understands.[16]

The question, then, is why postulate many internal senses if one is enough for the job? The common sense is well able to both judge the incoming sensory information and to compose and divide that sensory information at will. In addition, the common sense is also able to cognise or perceive what is not directly available to the external senses, the non-sensed intentions attributed by Avicenna to the estimative/cogitative faculty. Now, by operating under this simplification assumption, Oresme is able to offer an interesting model that can be interpreted in two ways: (1) as an anti-modular system; and (2) as the sensitive *mechanisms* together constituting a vast and unique processing *module*. But there is a clear difficulty with this model, which is the fact that different faculties seem to have contrary requirements for their operation. Some are intended to process information, others to simply retain that information. Moreover, these are found in different parts of the brain. Oresme's solution is to follow the suggestion of some authors that there exist *two* major internal senses: one that combines the functions of the common sense, imagination and cogitative powers and is properly called a 'cognitive' faculty (*cognoscitiva*), and the other which is a retentive faculty (*reservativa*), keeping both the sensible forms and the intentions and organising them according to time: the short-term memory is the function of the imagination, whereas the long-term memory is the function of memory proper. The implication, never stated, is that this second power is not cognitive as such but serves the purposes of assisting the cognitive power in its functions. The evidence for this split division – rather than the unified version – is that damage to one side of the brain (the back part) causes the loss of functions related to memory, and damage to the frontal part of the brain causes the loss of cognitive functions (*Expositio* II.21, 303). Lesions in the brain cause impairments in specific cognitive functions.

With his defence of a reductive version of the doctrine of the internal senses, Oresme positions himself in a certain philosophical tradition, according to which we can reduce the number of internal senses to just two (Manuel de Góis) or even one (Peter John Olivi, John Buridan, Francisco Suárez). Olivi, Buridan and Suárez conceived the different mental functions as modes of operation of one single entity, instead of ontologically carving these functions out of the human soul as distinct psychological faculties.[17] The only way to apply the modularity thesis to these authors is to take the sensory functions together as constituting one module – what we could call the 'massive module hypothesis', to contrast it with the other extreme view, the 'massive modularity hypothesis'. Otherwise, the contemporary modularity thesis fails to apply to this tradition of medieval faculty psychology.[18]

V. How Modular is the Mind?

In the previous sections, I have attempted to show how psychological faculties are conceived by some medieval thinkers as encapsulated, domain specific – i.e. operate with information of a specific kind, located in specific areas, operating fast and providing shallow outputs, just like the 'modules' theorised by Fodor. This seems to confirm the initial suggestion that there are some significant similarities between the medieval faculty psychology and the contemporary modularity of mind hypothesis. But there is another element of comparison that I wish to explore, namely the difference between the operation of lower sensory modules/faculties and higher rational cognitive processes. In order to do so, I must describe the issue in contemporary terms and only then consider its application to the medieval sources, in particular to Oresme.

Fodor thought that modularity explains the structure and functioning of lower perceptual powers (or, 'input systems'), but it does not concern higher cognitive functions, which he referred to as 'central systems'. In contrast, later authors have proposed to extend the modularity thesis to the whole mind, claiming that all mental mechanisms are modular in nature. This is the 'massive modularity hypothesis'.[19] For Fodor, however, lower functions are encapsulated inferential capacities restricted to input, whereas higher functions do not display similar restrictions and are instead holistic and wider reaching, thus are not subjected to the paradigm of modularity. Likewise, for most medieval thinkers there is a clear contrast between the perceptual faculties (examined above), which have the properties of Fodor's modules, and the rational powers that operate outside the scope of modularity. The reason for this contrast is that, whereas perceptual faculties are restricted in their operations to the bodily organs and to the received sensory information, the intellect does not require bodily organs to perform its operations and can access the information available to/in other (perceptual) faculties – thus, it is not encapsulated. There are two issues to consider here: first, what does it mean to say that the intellect does not need to operate via bodily organs, but is a part of the soul distributed throughout the body? Secondly, what does this mean, if anything, for those operations (like perception) performed by rational beings but also found in non-rational animals? The first question allows us to consider the extension of the modularity thesis, namely whether medieval thinkers would side with Fodor's modularity thesis limited to perceptual processes or with the massive modularity thesis, which takes the whole mind to be subject to modularity constraints. The second question allows us to test the encapsulation of lower sensory modules, i.e. whether they are really impermeable to the influence of higher cognitive powers.

Already Aristotle defends a basic separation between the realm of operations of the intellect and the rest of the psychological functions of a human being, namely those that are cognitive in nature, like perception, and those that are about basic life functions, like digestion. Understanding does not require any bodily organ, even though it requires, for its operation, information acquired via sensation and thus the sense organs, but it can only really operate if it is isolated from the constraint of material operation. The argument presented in Aristotle and developed by medieval authors to become a cornerstone of medieval epistemology is that the intellect's capacity to know all things depends on it being no one thing – i.e. having no material determination – on its own prior to the encounter with the object to be known. The key in this argument is the assumption that whatever is of a certain material constitution is disposed only to what falls within a certain spectrum of opposing properties, so that everything that falls outside that range is not considered from the epistemic point of view. For example, the eye must be transparent in order to allow for the perception of colour; if the eye were coloured itself, it would not be able to make us aware of the full range of colours, but our seeing would be 'contaminated' or 'filtered' by the colour the eye would be made of. At the same time, in order to be transparent, the eye must be constituted of a certain kind of matter – watery, to simplify – which makes it unfit to be the organ for the sense of say smell (which must be 'airy'). An interesting and often overlooked aspect in this argument is that the intellect is being considered primarily in comparison not with the internal senses, i.e. the processing faculties, as one would suppose, but with the external senses. (I think there is something to be said about why this is so, both from the point of view of what concerns the intellect as from the point of view of what concerns the internal senses, but that is a subject for another article.)

What does Oresme have to say about the issue of the un-instantiated bodily nature of the intellect? Oresme notes that being 'not organic' does not mean to lack location, as the soul is the soul to/of this body. The soul is 'whole in every single part of the body' (*in qualibet parte corporis tota*), meaning that it is not extended according to the extension of the body, which explains why there is no lag between an affection of the body – like a piercing of my skin – and the awareness of it by the soul. It also means, in something that is dear to the medieval heart, that there is no privileged place in the body for any given psychological cognitive function, so that one could attribute ownership of it to that bodily part. Instead, all those are functions of the human soul or the human composite, depending on whether they are performed by means of bodily organs or not. It is me who feels the heel pain rather than my heel. But it is also true that I think as much in my foot as in any other part of my body.[20] This notion introduces a conflict – or at least a tension – with the clearly spelled out argument for the location of certain psychological functions in bodily parts, like sight in the eyes and memory in the brain ventricles or cavities. How is one to equate one claim with the other, and more importantly, how is this related to the modularity thesis? I claim that this is evidence that medieval philosophers were as uncertain as contemporary ones about how far to go in explaining the phenomena that gave rise to the modularity thesis, i.e. whether the whole cognitive system is modular or only partially modular (modular in the lower cognitive functions as opposed to 'central' systems).

The presence of the intellect has implications for the animal–human divide. Oresme claims that the human soul is far superior to the soul of non-rational animals in its sheer epistemic power. That is not to say that other animals lack cognitive power to perform even pretty complex operations, and in this Oresme is willing to go well beyond what many of his contemporaries were ready to admit were non-rational animals' cognitive capacities, namely by attributing to some of them, like apes, reasoning-like abilities.[21] Although this is not the focus of this chapter, it is worth pointing out that Oresme accepts the existence of degrees of perfection in animal cognition and that he explicitly connects this with the nobility of disposition of their organs of sense. What the previous discussion shows is the encapsulated nature of perceptual modules, so that including more extended or more restrictive cognitive reach results even then in operations contained in each of those modules: judging the external senses is a function of sense. But the main issue is whether or not certain operations that require reason-like abilities do entail the use of reason. In some cases, perception of sensibles cannot be achieved merely by the internal sense faculties but require the concurrence of higher cognitive powers, for instance of reason. That is the real challenge to the modularity thesis that we find to be so strongly observed in medieval philosophy. If they do, then the modularity thesis is put in question because the key encapsulated nature of the module is challenged. A good example of this possible challenge is Oresme's examination of the different levels of perceptual judgment.

According to Oresme, all cognitive powers judge, so the sense once in direct contact with a coloured object, judges that this object is coloured. At this stage, the sensible object is colour and only in a second stage/moment does the sense judge this colour to be white or black or red. Finally, in a third moment, the sense judges the colour white or black or red to be of a given shade or hue (*in quo gradu*) of white/black/red. Oresme calls the first a general judgment (*iudicium universale*), the second a special judgment (*iudicium speciale*), and finally the third an articulated judgment (*iudicium dearticulatum*).[22] What characterises the last type of judgment, which he also calls more particular (*iudicium magis particulare*) is that it requires a certain degree of reasoning, i.e. collation and comparison between different colours (and other hues of the same colour) in order to judge *this* as *x-white* ('x' standing for whatever hue of white, like pearl, bone, or snow-white), say, and the perception of a common sensible: for Oresme, the perception of hue is the perception of the quantity of e.g. white (*Expositio* II.10, 294). But Oresme also notes that, 'It seems thus that sense can judge; and this is universally in all animals that have sense'.[23]

Oresme denies that such operations are exclusive to rational animals and instead concludes that all animals (all beings capable of sensation) have this capacity to judge the incoming sensory information. All animals are able to identify *this* as a colour, a certain colour, and which hue of that colour. Oresme goes as far as to talk about 'concepts' in this context to refer to that sensory content by which something is perceived as coloured or big or white, noting that this is 'concept' (*conceptu*) taken in a general sense (coloured) and determinate (white) (*Expositio* II.11, 307). That means that we do not need to appeal to any other cognitive powers outside this processing module, if we are talking about a general sensory module, to account for this kind of complex perception (*Expositio* II.11, 306).

If we wish to isolate the different aspects of this processing module, so that the retaining of the information is done by one faculty, the judgment$_1$ is done by one power, judgment$_2$ by another, judgment$_3$ by another still, then we have different modules at the sensory level that operate in coordination but that receive input from the others in order to perform the operation that is proper to themselves. In that case, it is legitimate to ask whether it makes sense to think about the process in modular terms. In other words, medieval thinkers build a system of perceptual powers, which they call internal senses, such that each power is determined, metaphysically, to operate only on content of a given type. But certain functions necessary for the description of experience seem to require the concurrent cooperation of different powers at the horizontal level and at the vertical level. So, the judgment of that thing as *coloured* and as *white* and as *x-white* (where 'x' stands for a hue of white) requires not only the common-sense module, but also the memory module and perhaps even the intellect module – in those judgments that are rational, like those concerning distance and number.[24] The argument is then that if for the judgment of this thing as being snow-white, it does not suffice the operation of

> the external sense [of sight] but with it concurs the internal reasoning sense, and the same applies to the [judgment] of difference between those sensibles, like cognizing the small and big, the many and few, the fast and the slow, the long and short, etc.[25]

No matter what categories are under examination, the important point is that this requires a cooperation that blurs the lines between the different internal senses and thus between the dedicated modules, if we take these in a narrow sense content-determined. This is a further problem in considering the application of the modularity thesis to medieval faculty psychology.

VI. Conclusion

My first concluding suggestion is that the modularity of the mind thesis is an Aristotelian one. Faculties do what they do if they receive the right sort of information and are properly tuned to the environment. They do not require and are even metaphysically prevented from being able to handle information formatted by higher order powers; for instance, the estimative power deals with intentions only, which is sensory-bound content, so it would be unable to handle abstract universal rational content. At the same time, there is a clear and basic separation between the low lever perceptual processes, which have a modular nature, and the higher level cognitive (rational) processes that do not.

My second concluding suggestion is that two challenges were presented to this encapsulated view: the first is the non-innate nature of the rules of operation of each of these modules. According to the authors examined, only the powers themselves exist from the outset but these are empty of content. It remains of course one of the main questions to be asked in this respect, what justifies that animals of certain species react in specific ways to intentional stimulus, like perceiving harmfulness in/from a wolf. The second challenge is the question of the penetration of perceptual processes by reason, for instance in the case of perception of distance. Some authors addressed this concern by explaining this higher order process by a high order *sensitive* power, instead of a rational one. But some have argued for the direct intervention of reason, even if they were unclear in what way this intervention is done: content-wise or guiding-like. In other words, does the higher power direct the lower power to a given conclusion or does the higher power infuse the conclusion into the lower power? In any case, it seems clear that it imposes certain constrains to the modularity thesis.

To conclude on a positive note, one should say that the idea of conceiving the human mind according to the modularity model has proved to be a helpful exegetical tool. Despite clear divergences between the medieval theoretical framework of psychological processes and the contemporary theories of mind, they seem to share this basic Aristotelian idea that things – souls, minds, processes, etc. – are determined (and defined) by what they do and in turn these (types of) activities are determined by what they are about in a specific way. In that sense, modules and psychological faculties are just two versions of that same story, so there are clear benefits of better understanding the shared ground between contemporary and medieval theories of mind.

Notes

1 By horizontal influences, I mean influences from other faculties at the same level of processing, for instance at the level of perception, whether sight is influenced by imagination; and by vertical influences, I mean influences from higher order faculties, like whether visual perception can be influenced by reason. The author would like to acknowledge the funding from the European

Research Council under the ERC grant agreement n.637747 for the project 'Rationality in Perceptions: Transformations of Mind and Cognition 1250–1550'.

2 Jerry Fodor, *The Modularity of Mind* (Cambridge, MA: MIT Press, 1983), pp. 47–101. Fodor's original list includes more items, but here I refer to those that are most relevant for this comparison with medieval sources.

3 See Peter Carruthers, *The Architecture of the Mind* (Oxford: Clarendon Press, 2006), who describes them as 'input-to-output modular processing systems' (p. 7).

4 In this chapter, my focus is on the nature of the mind and its architectonic structure. I do not discuss issues that arise from the relation of the mind and the body, on the one hand, and the mind and the world, on the other. For instance, I do not examine the questions of embodied and extended cognition, neuroplasticity or even the existence of affordances in perceived objects. For careful analyses of these issues, see the chapters by Blud, Onians and Rider (respectively) in this volume.

5 See Aristotle, *De anima* II.4, 415a14.

6 See Pavel Gregoric, *Aristotle on the Common Sense* (Oxford: Oxford University Press, 2011).

7 Two important clarifications about my use of certain terms throughout the article: First, I refer interchangeably to psychological faculties (such as the common sense) as *faculties* and *powers*, and to their activities as *operations*, *functions* or even *processes*. Secondly, I use the expression 'psychological', as in 'psychological faculties' and 'psychological functions', instead of the more contemporary-sounding 'mental' for reasons of accuracy: for ancient and medieval authors, the mind (*mens*) is just a part of the soul (*anima*/*psyche*).

8 Aristotle examines these faculties especially in his works *De anima*, *De memoria et reminiscentia* and *De sensu et sensibilibus*. On this issue, the scholarship is vast but for an accessible introduction in its historical setting, see Klaus Corcilius, 'Faculties in Ancient Philosophy', in D. Perler (ed.), *The Faculties. A History* (Oxford: Oxford University Press, 2015), pp. 19–58.

9 Avicenna Latinus, *Liber De anima seu sextus de naturalibus*, ed. S. van Riet (Louvain-Leiden: Peeters-Brill, 1972), book I, pars I, c. 5, 79–102. On Avicenna, see Dag N. Hasse, *Avicenna's* De Anima *in the Latin West. The Formation of a Peripatetic Philosophy of the Soul 1160–1300* (London and Turin: The Warburg Institute-Nino Aragno Editore, 2000).

10 Thomas Aquinas, *Summa Theologiae*, ed. P. Caramello (Turin: Marietti, 1948–50), I.78.4. On this, see Anthony J. Lisska, *Aquinas's Theory of Perception: An Analytic Reconstruction* (Oxford: Oxford University Press, 2016).

11 On this, see Anselm Oelze, *Animal Rationality. Later Medieval Theories 1250–1350* (Leiden: Brill, 2018), pp. 52–87.

12 Harry A. Wolfson, 'The Internal Senses in Latin, Arabic, and Hebrew Philosophic Texts', *Harvard Theological Review*, 28/2 (1935), 69–133; Simon Kemp, *Cognitive Psychology in the Middle Ages* (Westport, CT: Greenwood Press, 1996); see also Juhana Toivanen, *Perception and the Internal Senses: Peter John Olivi on the Cognitive Functions of the Sensitive Soul* (Leiden: Brill, 2013).

13 'Sensibilis autem cognition est communicata quinque sensibus, et ideo oportet esse unum fontem, ex quo omnis sensus oriatur et ad quem omnis motus sensibilium referatur sicut ad ultimum finem. Et hic fons vocatur sensus communis', Albertus Magnus, *De anima* II.4.7, 156. On Albert the Great, see Pierre Michaud-Quantin, La Psychologie de l'Activité chez Albert Le Grand (Paris: Vrin, 1966); and Nicholas H. Steneck, 'Albert the Great on the Classification and Localization of the Internal Senses', *Isis* 65 (1974), 193–211.

14 Oresme explains this by saying that 'we cognize privation by means of a habit' (*Expositio et Quaestiones in Aristotelis De anima*, ed. B. Patar (Louvain: Peeters, 1995) (hereafter *Expositio* II.27, 300), i.e. by remembering that before there was light – and I take this before to refer to either the previous instant or what was habitual to perceive in such a similar situation.

15 The principle of localisation is pervasive in the medieval period. One question that needs to be systematically considered in these sources is whether the functions performed by a given power can continue to be performed if a lesion appears in the part of the brain when that power is located. I am currently preparing a study on this topic.

16 'Videtur quod sufficiat unus sensus interior, scilicet sensus communis, respectu omnium sensibilium, sicut sufficit unicus intellectus in homine respectu omnium quae intelligit', *Expositio* II.21, 297.

17 See José Filipe Silva, 'Stop making sense(s): Some late medieval and very late medieval views on faculty psychology', in Jacob Fink (ed.), *Medieval Theories of the Internal Senses* (Springer, forthcoming).

18 But even contemporary versions of modularity have been criticised for their domain specificity: see e.g. Jesse Prinz, 'Is the Mind Really Modular?', in Robert J. Stainton (ed.), *Contemporary Debates in Cognitive Science* (Oxford: Blackwell, 2006), pp. 22–36.

19 See Steven Pinker, *How the Mind Works* (London: Penguin Press, 1997); Carruthers, *Architecture of the Mind* (2006).

20 'Ad septimam, cum dicitur quod intellectio est in pede, hoc non est inconveniens, si intellectio ponatur subiective in anima, sicut est', *Expositio* III.4, 340.

21 He denies they have proper reasoning capacities due to their lack of language: 'si possent loqui ratiocinarentur sicut homines' (*Expositio* III.4, 335).

22 *Expositio* II.10, 291. There is not space here to consider possible background influences for this hierarchy of perceptual judgments, but it is clear that Ibn a-Haytham (Alhacen, as he was known in the Latin West) and Roger Bacon are among them.

23 'Patet ergo qualiter sensus habet iudicare; et hoc est universale in omnibus animalibus habentibus sensus', *Expositio* II.10, 291.

24 'Verumptamen ibi concurrit racio', *Expositio* II.12, 321, for distance; and for number: 'Et capiendo numerum isto modo dico quod non est sensibile commune nec per se – quia non potest percipi solo sensu, nec interior nec exteriori. Et ideo hoc non percipient bruta, sed percipitur per intellectum, tamen coadiuvante sensu', *Expositio* II.14, 348. This list is not comprehensive.

25 'Et istud iudicium non fit solo sensu exteriori sed cum hoc concurrit sensus interior discursivus; et similiter quantum ad differencias istorum sensibilium, sicud cognoscendo magnum et parvum, multum et paucum, velox et tardum, longum et breve, etc.', *Expositio* II.12, 316.

Select Bibliography

Carruthers, Peter, *The Architecture of the Mind* (Oxford: Clarendon Press, 2006).

Corcilius, Klaus, 'Faculties in Ancient Philosophy', in D. Perler (ed.), *The Faculties. A History* (Oxford: Oxford University Press, 2015), pp. 19–58.

Fodor, Jerry, *The Modularity of Mind* (Cambridge, MA: MIT Press, 1983).

Gregoric, Pavel, *Aristotle on the Common Sense* (Oxford: Oxford University Press, 2011).

Hasse, Dag N., *Avicenna's* De Anima *in the Latin West. The Formation of a Peripatetic Philosophy of the Soul 1160–1300* (London and Turin: The Warburg Institute-Nino Aragno Editore, 2000).

Kemp, Simon, *Cognitive Psychology in the Middle Ages* (Westport, CT: Greenwood Press, 1996).

Lisska, Anthony J., *Aquinas's Theory of Perception: An Analytic Reconstruction* (Oxford University Press, 2016).

Michaud-Quantin, Pierre, *La Psychologie de l'Activité chez Albert Le Grand* (Paris: Vrin, 1966).

Oelze, Anselm, *Animal Rationality. Later Medieval Theories 1250–1350* (Leiden: Brill, 2018).

Pinker, Steven, *How the Mind Works* (London: Penguin Press, 1997).

Prinz, Jesse, 'Is the Mind Really Modular?', in Robert J. Stainton (ed.), *Contemporary Debates in Cognitive Science* (Oxford: Blackwell, 2006), pp. 22–36.

Silva, José Filipe, 'Stop making sense(s): Some late medieval and very late medieval views on faculty psychology', in Jacob Fink (ed.), *Medieval Theories of the Internal Senses* (Springer, forthcoming).

Toivanen, Juhana, *Perception and the Internal Senses: Peter John Olivi on the Cognitive Functions of the Sensitive Soul* (Leiden: Brill, 2013).

Wolfson, Harry A., 'The Internal Senses in Latin, Arabic, and Hebrew Philosophic Texts', *Harvard Theological Review*, 28/2 (1935), 69–133.

2

An Unrealised Conversation: Medieval Mysticism and the Common Core

RALPH W. HOOD JR

But if nothing is more present than the most absent One,
If nothing is more absent than the most precious One
Is anything more marvelous, anything more incomprehensible?
(Richard St Victor, *The Mystical Ark*)[1]

It is rare to find a textbook on the history of psychology that devotes more pages to medieval thought than it does to the emergence of cognitive psychology that many see as the future of psychology as a science. Daniel Robinson's *An Intellectual History of Psychology* (3rd edition), does just this, seeking a conversation between a psychology of the past richer in scope than that prophesied as the psychology of the future.[2] Robinson forces a conversation between psychologists who would identify cognition and claims to neurological substrates as determinants of not simply thought but experience (a broader term) with those who have yet been persuaded that psychology is, ought, or can be a natural science. His concerns are both metaphysical and metaphorical: the former a caution to the limits self-imposed on cognitive neuroscience, the latter a caution to a secular age in which God and nature have switched positions relative to which is reality and which is metaphor. Robinson asks scholars to reflect on the rhetorical question, 'What effect have psychological hypotheses or findings had on the size and nature of the ontological domain in which all genuinely psychological phenomena are to be found?'[3] Surprisingly, in perhaps the briefest but most reflective of texts summarising the history of psychology, he reveals his opposition to the cognitive turn in psychology and to what he perceives as reductionist strategies that are not merely premature, but finally misguided. This is at best a cautious introduction to psychological science yoked to the 'biologizing of the mind'.[4] Robinson warns that modern psychological science committed to the gold standard of experimental methods based upon natural science is more restrictive than medieval psychology and ultimately of less substance: 'In a wide variety of settings, this method [experimental] has yielded fairly stable functional relationships between dependent and independent variables under conditions generally so unlike the domain of interest as to render generalizations jejune'.[5] Here the invitation to consilience seems to close off any discussion between psychology and the humanities rather than encourage it. Or does it?

Toward Another Cognitive Science of Religion: William James's Common Core

In this welcome and much needed edited text on cognitive science and medieval studies the editors open up the possibility of a conversation between psychology and the humanities, the former less broadly conceived than the latter. One possibility is that modern cognitive neuropsychology and related biosciences have much to contribute to an understanding of medieval Christianity in general, and, for purposes of this chapter, medieval mysticism in particular. But does the reverse hold? Consilience as a unity of knowledge is not restricted to the sciences. Edward Wilson has noted the paradoxical state of psychology, whose soul is split between those who wish to merge it with the biosciences and favor psychological science (hence a BS degree) and those who insist on a merger with the humanities (and hence a BA degree).[6] I teach at a university that recently dropped the BA option in psychology and now only offers the BS degree in a programme tailored more to psychological science than psychology more broadly conceived. The latter may include the former, but the former, as we shall see, tends to exclude the latter. In this chapter we will defend James's turn to a broader view of psychology as he sought a non-reductive explanation of religion in general and mystical experience in particular. We shall argue that William James's views of mysticism endorse a common core view associated with metaphysical realism, a correspondence theory of truth, and religious pluralism.

On Reading William James

The poet W. H. Auden said of Freud: 'To us he is no more a person/Now, but a whole climate of opinion'.[7] No less can be said of William James. He met Freud only once (at Clark University) where he is reported by Ernst Jones, one of Freud's earliest biographers, to have said, 'The future of psychology is yours'.[8] However, this causal comment (if true) must be tempered by James's disdain for the arrogance of emerging 'scientific' psychologies: in a letter to Miss Calkins he cautioned:

> I strongly suspect Freud, with his dream-theory, of being a regular hallucinė. But I hope that he and his disciples will push it to its limits, as undoubtedly it covers some facts, and will add to our understanding of 'functional' psychology, which is the real psychology. The 'function' of Titchener's 'scientific' psychology . . . is to keep laboratory instruments going, and to provide platforms for certain professors. Apart from that it seems to be more unreal than any scholasticism.[9]

Likewise, in his classic text, *Varieties of Religious Experience* (hereafter *VRE*),[10] James echoed what has become a standard critique of classical Freudian theory. In a thinly veiled reference to Freud, James rejected the claim that religious belief could be explained as 'perverted sexuality':

> The plain truth is that to interpret religion one must in the end look at the immediate content of the religious consciousness. The moment one does this, one sees how wholly disconnected it is in the main from the content of the sexual consciousness. (*VRE*, pp. 18–19).

I will discuss the immediate content of the religious consciousness in relation to the common core thesis later in this chapter in terms of an admittedly uncommon reading of James in which what have become common readings are viewed as misguided. However, I am not alone in claiming that James has commonly been misunderstood. Our reading of James supports the dual claim that James's theory of religion is both committed to a correspondence theory of truth and to metaphysical realism. The former has been argued by Levinson and then Putman.[11] Slater has provided the most persuasive argument in defence of the claim that James is committed to *both* metaphysical dualism and a correspondence theory of truth.[12] Elsewhere we have argued that James was committed to a common core theory of mysticism that is congruent with both metaphysical realism and a correspondence theory of truth which also entails, as Slater has argued, a defence of religious pluralism.[13] Obviously many readings of James are possible and as with readings of Freud theories are less committal than the climate of opinion that is at least implicit in any one reading.[14]

Whether or not one accepts Tertullian as the father of Western theology, the question 'What has Athens to do with Jerusalem?' is forever linked to this name. Further, it suggests barriers to consilience, especially if the humanities and the natural sciences are seen as Scylla and Charybdis disguised as *explanans* and *explanandum*. Here we can cite one example from a contemporary, Alvin Plantinga, the noted Christian philosopher and recipient of the Templeton prize in 2017. He is far from a fundamentalist and is even further from enchanted by evolution than most cognitive scientists. Reproductive success, whether individual or group, is not criticised simply as a theory but as a Grand Evolutionary Myth (GEM) that plays a quasi-religious role in contemporary Western culture and as such makes any religious view at odds with scientific naturalism unable to participate in an honest conversation.[15] The GEM simply asserts that life is a contingent fact, has no purpose, and has evolved by purely mechanical means by random processes that selected only for reproductive success. Of course, one can cite Plantinga's Christian commitment here, but that is precisely the point. It is not that Christians are 'medieval' but rather that Christianity as a religion has deep roots in medieval thought and the struggle for universalism (hence, 'catholic') that perhaps was more premature than in error. This is where we might begin to unravel how it is that psychology and religion might exhibit consilience with respect to what shall be the major focus of this chapter, mysticism in light of James's common core theory.

William James and Charles Taylor's Secular Age

A good place to begin our discussion of James's common core thesis is with Charles Taylor's influential book, *A Secular Age*, which in the decade since its publication has led many to look forward to even a post-secular age.[16] The philosopher Jürgen Haberman and bishop Joseph Ratzinger (now Pope Emeritus Benedict XVI) suggest possibilities for consilience relative to dialogue between religion and philosophy in the public square in such an age.[17]

On the psychological side, it is clear that the most empirical of psychologists, William James, is both silenced and a participant in this unrealised conversation. As we have argued elsewhere, his refusal to restrict empirical psychology to naturalism left him abandoned by modern psychology.[18] As has recently been noted, today James is more likely to be read in religious studies programmes, including medieval studies, than by students in psychology.[19] On the other hand, as the architect of 'modern mysticism' focusing on quasi-ontological claims to an experience common across traditions, his is the major voice in the conversation whether being critically rejected for his presumed 'orientalism' or applauded[20] for advancing the empirical study of mysticism even if criticised for 'psychologizing' it.[21] McGinn reviews James's *Varieties* as philosophy, not psychology, and is dismissive of his study of mysticism: 'Mysticism for James is both cognitive and non-cognitive but we are never sure how'.[22] We can briefly address the central issues in James's expansive psychology for which the fault of psychology as an unrealised conversation cannot be upon his shoulders. We will summarise a complex history in an imaginary dialogue Charles Taylor initiated with William James as two Gifford lecturers separated by over a hundred years seek to realise a conversation.

Metaphysical Realism, Correspondence, Religious Pluralism and a Common Core

Recent criticisms of methodological atheism are based upon the fact that insofar as one raises social constructionism to a methodological absolute, reality as empirically investigated is necessarily incapable of referring to anything outside social constructs that may contribute to experience. Ontological issues as to the nature of the 'real' are not simply bracketed but ignored.[23] As Charles Taylor, himself a believer, put it, '[t]he believer is thought to have invented the delusion that beguiles him'.[24] Simply put, the object of religious belief has no reality external to the believer. This is the crux with reductionist critiques of the evolutionary psychology that is the grand metanarrative that frames most cognitive neuroscience. One need but look to William James – a strong admirer of Darwin but no fan of survival theories – to anticipate the problem:

> There is a notion in the air about us that religion is only an anachronism, a case of 'survival,' an atavistic relapse into a mode of thought which humanity in its more enlightened examples has outgrown; and this notion our religious anthropologists at present do little to counteract (*VRE*, p. 387).

Of course, psychologists have done no better. The issue is not whether the psychologist (or anthropologist) is religious, but the obverse/opposite. The psychology of religion like that of anthropology explains religion as an ontological error, but one that has led to reproductive success. In this sense the truth is in dual process theories that make religion 'easy' and natural, while science is hard and requires more than a default to an evolutionary mechanism in which the assumption that intentionality has more survival in ambiguous situations is the better part of nature's built-in Pascal wager. Type II errors (to falsely affirm the absence of what is true) are costlier overall than type I errors (to falsely affirm what is not true). Only truths won by the discursive intellect yoked to science and its methods can provide at least probable estimates as to the improbability of a world in which creation, intentionality and gods or God were once common.[25] The linkage of rich or thick descriptions of conscious experience to sophisticated neurophysiological knowledge of structures and process is likely one of the major factors providing the illusion that causal physiological processes produce the conscious experience of subjectivity by process unavailable to reflection, or what James simply called introspection.[26] Phenomenological description and causal claims need to be carefully distinguished lest the latter be confused with the former.[27] James saw all observation as difficult, whether of subjectivity (mental states) or objectivity (objects revealed to sense). It takes much experience and training to distinguish conscious subjectivity (what is actually experienced) from what is thought to have produced it.[28]

If we take the above more philosophical issues seriously, we can return to a conversation between William James and Charles Taylor made possible by the central question raised by Taylor in an age in which the cognitive neurosciences claim explanatory power relative to central issues that define medieval studies. The view suggests explanatory power in the present that can illuminate what happened in the past. Here is how Charles Taylor summarised his 874-page book following a request from the editors of website *The Immanent Frame:*

> Almost everyone can agree that one of the big differences between us and our ancestors of five hundred years ago is that they lived in an 'enchanted' [medieval] world, and we do not; at the very least, we live in a *much less* 'enchanted' world. We might think of this as our having 'lost' a number of beliefs and the practices which they made possible. But more, the enchanted world was one in which these forces could cross a porous boundary and shape our lives, psychic and physical. One of the big differences between us and them is that we live with a much firmer sense of the boundary between self and other. We are 'buffered' selves. We have changed.[29]

Taylor's well-known appeal to a buffered self contrasts with that of a porous self, one that William James acknowledged as integral to any understanding of religion in his own Gifford lectures delivered more than a hundred years before Taylor's lectures. James's *VRE* has continued to stimulate conversation since it was initially delivered as the Gifford Lectures at the beginning of the twentieth century. Taylor's own assessment is critical. He applauds its 'unparalleled phenomenological insight' and acknowledges 'how little dated it is' but bemoans its lack of treatment of the social aspects of religion.[30]

More than one psychologist has noted that if James were writing today, his lectures would undoubtedly have been titled '*Varieties of Spiritual Experience*'.[31] Fuller holds William James to be the exemplar of what it means to be 'spiritual but not religious'.[32] James ignored doctrine and institutions and focused instead on individual religious experience or spirituality. Likewise, Robert Bellah, in the second best-selling sociological work in American history, *Habits of the Heart*, echoed what we shall see is one of the major concerns of Taylor with William James.[33] In an in-depth interview in *Habits*, one participant, Sheila Larson, gave rise to the term 'Sheilaism' used by Larson to describe her own faith. Yamane has noted that if she had today's language available to her during the interview, she 'surely would have offered up the contemporary mantra, "I'm spiritual, not religious"'.[34] This is precisely one of the critiques Taylor has of James's work. He claims that James succumbs to the individualist (Protestant) view that believers connect to God only through passion and that James's psychology 'hasn't got a place for a collective connection through a common way of being'.[35] To introduce this concern, Taylor used an invitation by The Institute for Human Sciences in Vienna celebrating the centenary of

Hans Gadamer's birth to deliver comments on James's Gifford lectures in preparation for his own that were published as *A Secular Age*. Taylor's Vienna lectures revisited William James's own Gifford lectures and were published under the rubric *Varieties of Religion Today* in 2002. The contrast in titles is deliberate and the emphasis not simply temporal.

Taylor faults James's Protestant bias from his own Catholic perspective. James's psychology, while religious through and through, is admittedly Protestant. In his work on pragmatism James noted that his own position favoured 'an alteration in the "seat of authority" that reminds one almost of the protestant reformation. And ... to papal minds, Protestantism has often seemed a mere mess of anarchy and confusion'. There, James proposed a science of religions that is '"scientific and individualistic" but crucially, not irreligious'.[36] As others have noted before Taylor, James's methodology is to focus on primary documents that are deeply protestant in structure, tone and implicit theology.[37] For Taylor, they ignore the social dimension of religion, and force James, like Sheila, to be spiritual but not religious. Taylor's own position is explicit in that he argues that the personal and collective should be complementary and that he himself is both religious and spiritual.[38]

Religious and Mystical Experience: Pluralism from a Common Core

James's definition of religious experience for the purposes of the Gifford lectures clearly revealed his sympathy for the extreme forms of Protestant religious experience. James defined religion as '*the feelings, acts, and experiences of individual men* [and women], *in their solitude, so far as they apprehend themselves to stand in relation to whatever they may consider the divine*' (*VRE*, p. 34; emphasis in original). James's clarification of what he meant by 'divine' makes the case for the near-universal application of this concept. As he saw it, the divine is 'such a primal reality as the individual feels compelled to respond to solemnly and gravely, and neither by a curse nor a jest' (*VRE*, p. 39). Thus, influenced by James's notion of divinity, religious experience – ultimately, the experience of the solitary individual – is placed at the forefront of the scientific study of religion. James's Gifford lectures minimised both rituals and community, and, while subtitled 'a study in human nature', they refused to engage religious belief. As Alfred North Whitehead, heavily influence by James, noted, 'all collective emotions leave untouched the awful ultimate fact which is the human being, consciously alone with itself, for its own sake'.[39] Slater reminds us that James's rejection of reductive explanations of religious experience in general and mystical experiencer in particular are reduced to natural scientific explanations at the cost of dismissing their content as merely epiphenomenal manifestations of a psychopathic temperament.[40] Madness and mysticism may have similar roots but bear radically different fruits.

As James perceived it, the infinite variety of religious and spiritual experiences can be subsumed under a simple formula: discontent and its resolution. James's effort in the *Varieties* was to deny that psychologists must adopt Flournoy's methodological exclusion of the transcendent as the only option for psychology of religion.[41] Both supernaturalism as a belief in disembodied intentionality and supranaturalism as a belief in ultimate reality as a personal being are viable metaphysical options to naturalism. Wildman proposes a spiritual anthropology that avoids dogmatically adopting a naturalism that would reduce views of religious experience to inappropriate anthropomorphic projections of human experience onto a universe that is indifferent to human concerns.[42] In Charles Taylor's terms it is to abandon a porous self in an enchanted world in favour of a buffered self in a secular one. In James's terms the buffered self mistakes a 'deanthroporphization of the imagination' for scientific progress such that if that is all religion is, people 'would have begun with animistic explanations of natural fact and criticized these away into scientific ones, as they actually have done' (*VRE*, p. 388).

Elsewhere we have argued that, despite the deserved reputation of *VRE*, it is wise to read it as partly a response to issues that he alluded to in his monumentally influential *Principles of Psychology* (hereafter *PP*) but refused to address there.[43] James tried to restrict himself in the *PP* to the assumptions of natural science, an appeal that continues to make psychology an agent of secularisation.[44] James's efforts to separate psychology from philosophy (metaphysics) in the *PP* can be seen as an effort to show the limits of a natural science perspective, not to exclude psychological consideration of what is outside those limits.[45] In this sense, after the *PP* James's *oeuvre* can be seen as an effort to start over given the metaphysical limits that psychology must transcend if it is to appropriately confront the totality of experienced reality that need not, indeed cannot, be totally disenchanted. James's refutation is of a materialistic natural science, one that denies that the moral order is eternal. His spiritualism is an affirmation of an eternal moral order (*VRE*, p. 533) and the right to believe in doctrines of hope. In James's abridgement of the *PP*, much of the reduction was accomplished by the exclusion of philosophical material. James concludes the greatly abridged *Psychology*: *The Briefer Course* which his students at Harvard referred to affectionately as '*Jimmy*':

> . . . at present psychology is in the condition of physics before Galileo and the laws of motion, of chemistry before Lavoisier and the notion that mass is preserved in all reactions. The Galileo and the Lavoisier of psychology will be famous men indeed when they come, as come they some day surely will, or past successes are no index to the future. When they do come, however, the necessities of the case will make them 'metaphysical'. Meanwhile the best way in which we can facilitate their advent is to understand how great is the darkness in which we grope, and never to forget that *the natural science assumptions with which we started are provisional and reversible things*.[46]

In his own reading of the *Varieties*, Taylor confesses that he wished his forthcoming Gifford lectures to be a conversation and a confrontation with James.[47] The conversation is not historical but contemporary. Taylor notes that James's *VRE* 'could have been written yesterday, as against almost a hundred years ago'.[48] The confrontation between James and Taylor provides options for how one responds to a secular age which James anticipated and Taylor describes with such remorse. It is more than appropriate that 'metaphysical leaks' is the metaphor James used to describe psychology as a natural science.[48] As Dittes noted,

> He is the liberating Moses who called down a plague on both the house of the religious and medical [scientific] Establishment, and led the psychology of religion into an independent existence. But his recommendations as to how that independent existence should be conducted are ignored as thoroughly as the builders of the golden calf ignored those of the law-giving Moses.[50]

When applied to psychological efforts to confront religion, Taylor's Catholic concerns are ill-addressed. Taylor sees James as devaluing belief, ritual and the attendant collectively shared phenomena associated with 'church' in favour of intense experiences. Taylor fears that the focus is too much misplaced on feeling and the many Protestant streams that at best form various tributaries that flow from and sometimes back into what are the great churched faiths. As Waldenfels notes, 'mystical sidestreams tend to accompany the main stream of unquestionable devotion to law and text, casting a shadow of heterodoxy and anarchy'.[51] Slater documents in how many separate lectures James insists that 'overbeliefs' or interpretation of experience are the most interesting things about individuals and perpetually can become problematic for religious institutions.[52] Clearly James was not fond of religious dogma not freely chosen:

> The religious experience which we are studying is that which lives itself out within the private breast. First-hand individual experience of this kind has always appeared as a heretical sort of innovation to those who witnessed its birth. Naked comes it into the world and lonely; and it has always, for a time at least, driven him who had it into the wilderness, often into the literal wilderness out of doors, where the Buddha, Jesus, Mohammed, St. Francis, George Fox, and so many others had to go (*VRE*, p. 269).

Taylor faults James for his stand on privatised religion as in fact serving the interests of secularisation. Both believers and non-believers in a secular age denounce the religion of churches. It is, at best, a second-hand faith. James traces his own view of the origin of religion in terms of the secularisation hypothesis:

> A genuine first-hand religious experience like this is bound to be a heterodoxy to its witnesses, the prophet appearing as a mere lonely madman. If his doctrine prove contagious enough to spread to any others, it becomes a definite and labeled heresy. But if it then still prove contagious enough to triumph over persecution, it becomes itself an orthodoxy; and when a religion has become an orthodoxy, its day of inwardness is over: the spring is dry; the faithful live at second hand exclusively and stone the prophets in their turn. The new church, in spite of whatever human goodness it may foster, can be henceforth counted on as a staunch ally in every attempt to stifle the spontaneous religious spirit, and to stop all later bubblings of the fountain from which in purer days it drew its own supply of inspiration (*VRE*, p. 270).

Thus James argues that religious belief (*theologica speculativa*) without actual experience (*theologica mystica*) is simply the repeating of beliefs without the existential foundation in actual experience. As we have seen, Teresa made every effort to assure others that her *theologica mystica* was not merely *speculativa*.

Consilience: James's Cognitive Psychology and Medieval Mysticism

McGinn has traced the consensus of contemporary scholars that mysticism is a modern term and notes that the focus upon identifying mystical experience is fraught with difficulties.[53] His own studies document that medieval Christians were involved in mystical theology broadly defined as struggling in diverse ways to live out the sensed presence of God in their individual and collective lives. In a similar vein Wolfson argues there can be no mysticism in the abstract, only historical instantiations of the mystical.[54] Such instantiations are often linked to sacred texts and the obvious fact that insofar as experiences are articulated or communicated in any way they must be contextualised in terms of history, language and culture. The contrast is between contextualists or constructionists, who argue there can be no unmediated experiences, and those who are unity or common core theorists, who argue for a distinction between experience and interpretation, the latter attempting to give expression to an experience that itself is neither totally determined by nor totally constructed.[55] Thus McGinn's ongoing series and Julia Lamin's recent edited volume[56] could easily be seen as varieties of only *Christian* mysticism, but the debate regarding constructivism is broader than one faith tradition.[57] However, if the focus is on mystical experience as expressed throughout the Christian tradition, the experience can be isolated and seen as operating differently and with other interpretations in other traditions, both non-Christian and secular. This seems to be the point of a recent biography of Teresa of Avila, proclaimed the first female Doctor of the Catholic Church in 1970. McGinn has high praise for Teresa 'as among the most significant mystics in Western Christianity'.[58] A popular biographer of her noted that her mysticism was not restricted to the church:

> One of the reasons she was made doctor of the church was that her teaching had bridged ecumenical divisions. Her works are studied not only by Roman Catholics but by those of every denomination and faith, from Lutherans to Calvinists to Buddhists, Hindus, and Shintoists. They even find appreciative readers among atheists and unbelievers, who find in her writings a serious witness to the existence of God.[59]

Tyler's study of Teresa in light of Wittgenstein's own mysticism actually can be seen as supporting the common core thesis and the psychologisation of mysticism he attributes to James and opposes.[60] While granting that Teresa's writing is *theologia*, the question is whether *mystica* or *speculativa.* Tyler correctly notes that Teresa's writing is deliberately subversive precisely to demonstrate that it is based upon her actual experience, not a reflection upon knowledge gained from authoritative writings. Thus, despite cautionary concerns with the phrase 'mystical experience', Howells correctly notes that to ignore the use of this phrase tends to reduce much of Teresa's writings as reporting mere affect or emotionality without any epistemological or ontological warrants.[61] However, by introducing the term 'experience' that both McGinn and Tyler have cautioned against, Teresa's ever deepening sense of the presence of God can be revealed as a noetic experience of the ineffable. This mystical experience is the 'root and centre' of all religion (*VRE*, p. 309). Teresa refuses to talk about *theologia speculativa*. Instead she seeks to evoke mystical experience in others by her writings (*theologica mystica*) based upon her own first-hand experience. Both Teresa and James distinguish knowledge *about* from knowledge *of*, the former useful only if it elicits the latter. Thus James's empiricism is not simply modern, but a means of communication promoting consilience. Consilience is the search for a unified theory of knowledge uniting the sciences and the humanities. Teresa is of importance precisely because her mystical experience awakened in her a seeing of reality that was transformative. Elsewhere we have argued that isolated mystical experiences have all the limits McGinn worries about; but when they become developed as traits rather than simply as discrete experiences, they lead precisely to the *theologia mystica* that he applauds.[62] However, not only does Teresa bypass *theological speculativa* – she subverts by means of language the claim that her own *theologia mystica* is meant to be descriptive or simply another interpretation of an experience which it is meant to evoke. What is evoked is paramount. It is both real (noetic) and ineffable. Thus, a focus on mystical experience integral to the common core thesis allows *theologia* to extend beyond the Christian God and the *theologia speculativa* that McGinn and Taylor so admire in the teaching magisterium of the church. Both James and Teresa find mysticism even in traditions that do not speak of God, and among the unchurched:

> In Hinduism, in Neoplatonism, in Sufism, in Christian Mysticism, in Whitmanism, we find the same recurring note, so that there is about mystical utterances an eternal unanimity which ought to make a critic stop and think, and which brings it about that the mystical classics have, as has been said, neither birthday nor native land. Perpetually telling of the unity of man with God, their speech antedates language, and they do not grow old (*VRE*, p. 332).

Thus, for two reasons, contra McGinn[63] the focus on mystical experience extends the possibility of conversations both among the churched and unchurched. It does not dispute the value of a sense of presence of God for its ability to enhance a dialogue between medieval Christianity and a psychology receptive to the reality whose history McGinn continues to trace masterfully. However, it implies that a distinction can be made between experience and its interpretation that does justice to the interpretation of an experience that remains ontologically present now as then but ineffable and noetic. It thus endorses both a methodological agnosticism advocated by Hood and an ontological agnosticism advocated by Tyler.[64] Second, it suggests that we are not trapped into a contradiction in which we claim that all reality is social constructed.[65] This point can be forcefully made by the translation of the diary of Dag Hammarskjöld by W. H. Auden. Like Teresa, he had an active life of service not in spite of but because of his mysticism. Both mystics had experiences that were transformative. Auden's translation of this diary, written in Swedish, is all the more remarkable given his confession: 'It is no secret that I do not know a single word of Swedish'.[66] Teresa would likely have said it was not needed. In Slater's reading of James, mystical experiences have epistemic force evidenced in transformation of a life in which James's correspondence theory of truth can only be realised by the subjects' participation in the reality they help realise. Thus the epistemic authority of religious experience in general and mystical experience in particular is that they are not merely products of our psychology, history or culture. This is why it is crucial to understand James as a metaphysical realist in which *both* the supernatural and the natural are necessary for understanding religious and mystical experiences. Egan reminds us that the great Catholic mystic, Karl Rahner claims that humans are *homo mysticsus* with an unlimited receptivity to an unthematic awareness of God and repeats the prophetic claim of Rahner that 'The devout Christian of the future will either be a "mystic," one who experiences "something," or he [or she] will cease to be anything at all'.[67] Mysticism is both affirmed in sacred texts and evoked in the reader. It thus becomes not simply an isolated experience, but part of everyday lived reality. Thus, one may properly speak of the commonality of everyday mysticism as central both in Rahner's understanding of mysticism and others.[68] When James's *VRE* are read in this light, Slater correctly notes that James is more akin to Plato than Kant in supporting a sentiment of rationality whose existence cannot be totally captured nor exhausted by any conceptualisation.[69] That said, reality simply is. Overbeliefs and what we say about reality may be true or false and various pluralism need not negate each other's truths (*VRE*, pp. 51–70). A common core bears many fruits.

The Not Uncommon Core and Religious Pluralism

The position that mysticism can be evoked has been most systematically developed by Stace under the rubric of the universal core thesis and is the basis of the most commonly used empirical measure of mysticism, the Mysticism Scale which has been used in numerous studies for more than a quarter of a century.[70] While McGinn claimed Stace's work suffered theoretically and historically from the distinction between experience and interpretation,[71] he failed to appreciate the distinctions made above. Findlay attacked Stace's 'rag bag of empirical features', while Mason and Mason harshly criticised Stace for his selection of popular translations of the sacred texts he used to identify his universal core.[72] However, these criticisms fail to appreciate the phenomenological method by which Stace articulated his universal core. At the root of the confusion is that the linguistic turn in philosophy corresponds to psychologists no longer having their students read James.[73] As Barnard has noted, there has been such a stress on the linguistic nature of experience in recent philosophical thought that lay claims to immediacy or to a knowledge that is not structured linguistically are instantly suspect.[74]

Given my own treatment of James's as an exemplar of the common core thesis, it might sound contradictory to reference Barnard, who argues that James is *not* an advocate of the common core or unity thesis.[75] However, the contradiction between my view and Barnard's is more apparent than real if we but remember that James always spoke and wrote with a particular audience in mind.[76] He criticised narrow and overly technical 'shop-habits' of professionals.[77] Carolyn Dinshaw in a popular, perhaps even fictionalised mixture of academic and amateur assessments of medievalism, makes the point that amateur fascination with all things medieval, nevertheless, can make texts available that continue to have the power to transform lives.[78]

James's own widely quoted definition of mysticism in the *VRE* must be put in context; it was less a definition than an effort to mark off a territory for discussion 'for the purpose of the present lectures' (*VRE*, p. 302, emphasis mine). He knew that despite his own emerging commitment to pluralism, the understanding of mysticism was often in terms of philosophical monism long guided and directed by the teaching magisterium of the church. As McGinn notes, medieval mystics were creating *theologia* defined as true discourse about God.[79] In volume IV of *The Presence of God*, devoted to mysticism in medieval Germany (1300–1500), a central theme is the clash between mysticism and the magisterium of the church in which interpretations of mystical experience are often judged in terms of propositional claims that risk being heretical.

The two primary markers of mystical experience that James employs for his Gifford lectures are that these experiences are noetic and ineffable. His insistence on noetic is crucial, especially when combined with the other primary marker of mysticism, ineffability. Here is the strongest claim to situate James with the common core school of mysticism. Ironically, it is first expressed in a curious quote given James's intent to battle with monism:

'In mystic states we both become one with the Absolute and we become aware of our oneness' (*VRE*, p. 332). James's reference to the Absolute is partly sleight of hand, for he readily admits in the written lectures that his preference is for God since God is (a) a medium of communion and (b) a causal agent (*VRE*, p. 402, footnote 32). Furthermore, that consciousness is not obliterated is crucial for James, for he insists in the written lectures that, as noted above in his criticism of Freud: 'Consciousness of illumination is of us the essential mark of "mystical states"' (*VRE*, pp. 323–4, footnote 28).

Even in the *VRE*, James quickly retreats from a focus upon only introvertive mysticism. He admits to focusing primarily on classical mysticism. On the fringes where a wide variety of mystical experiences exists, the unanimity evaporates:

> The fact is that mystical feeling of enlargement, union, and emancipation has no specific intellectual content of its own. It is capable of forming matrimonial alliances with material furnished by the most diverse philosophies and theologies (provided only that they can find a place in their framework for its particular emotional mood (*VRE*, p. 337).

These remarks need not disturb the common core or unity theorists as they already accept the ineffability associated not only with the expression of mystical experience but with the interpretation of it as well. The role of language and culture in interpreting the state is not challenged but their role in determining the state (experience) is. We always have more than the text to help us and thus even medieval texts can be read today and evoke the experience of transcendence experienced then as now. Copleston notes that Meister Eckhart used 'shock tactics' in which his writings were expressions of his own mystical experience and intended to facilitate similar experiences in others.[80] The text always points within to something transcendent. James referred to this fact as simply evoking an awareness of something 'MORE' (*VRE*, p. 401, emphasis in original). Faith traditions, secular and religious, struggle to interpret this more. James's sub-marginal thesis argues that the more is '*conterminous and continuous with a more of the same quality, which is operative in the universe outside him*' (*VRE*, p. 400, italics in original). Here is sufficient warrant for mystical experience as the awakening of the 'more' in human consciousness. He also notes that, 'It is when we treat of the experience of "union" with it that their speculative differences appear most clearly' (*VRE*, p. 401). Thus, James can accept an aspect of the constructionist position which was articulated at the time of James's *VRE* by Rufus Jones: 'The most refined mysticism, the most exalted spiritual experience is *partly* a product of the social and intellectual environment in which the personal life of the mystic has formed and matured'.[81] Jones's emphasis is crucial, for it allows what James allows, that portions of experience escape cultural influences. Stace notes that self-transcendence (James's 'MORE') is part of the experience and *not* of the interpretation of experience.[82] The issue now is whether such experiences can be measured such that we can determine their occasion and transformation within various religious and even secular traditions.

The Common Core, Mystical Experience and Mystical Traditions

Religion has proven to be difficult to define yet a consensus is that, however defined, religion is multi-dimensional.[83] While many multi-dimensional schemes have been proposed, all include religious belief and experience as identifiable components along with other variations that can differ widely. Further, the search for unique characteristics of religious experience has been challenged with the assertion that religious experience is unlikely *sui generis*, but rather we should seek the conditions under which experiences are deemed to be religious.[84] As we have noted above, this is the dilemma of religion in a secular age where the locus of authoritative interpretation is challenged. Even McGinn notes that both democratisation and secularisation have roots in the medieval period: for instance, by 1200 women's voices were raised as mysticism was no longer a flight from the world into monasticism but could be found in the midst of everyday experiences. His volume III in the *Presence of God* is an effort in his own words to reconstruct 'overheard conversations' between men and women mystics.[85] If we accept the claim of William James (*VRE*, p. 309) that mysticism is the 'root and centre' of religion, or agree with McGinn that mysticism is the sense of the presence of God integral to variations in the Christian tradition (and now, of course, others as well), mystical experience can be isolated. Not only medieval texts but the experience they reference are available to us today. Text and context combine to identify the focal point of the transformation of both individuals and traditions as they confront what is ultimately real.

The reality in James's metaphysical realism is always available while expressed in various cultural and historical forms. This opens the discussion – conceptually and empirically – about how exactly mysticism relates to religious and spiritual experiences. Moreover, from James's account we receive at least two markers creating problems for a measurement-based empirical psychology, regardless of its relation to neuropsychology. If we accept James's claim that mystical experience is both noetic (a source of knowledge) and ineffable, we must not be beguiled by either language of culture. Instead, we must seek a means to look to linguistic reports (textual and others) of how individuals report or express what remains both a source of knowledge and transcends that source as it is expressed in culture, history and language. Measurement is an effort to have individuals report an experience and not a substitute for the experience. For the non-mystic reports are hypotheses to be explored and studied by means akin to *theologica speculativa*. However, innovative methods even with medieval texts using linguistic programmes can lead to a genuine cooperative between the humanities and a psychology not confined to naturalism but open to the possibility of a common core to mystical experience.[86]

Hood's Mysticism Scale

Walter Stace addressed James's issue of a uniformity to mystical experience by selecting from a wide catholicity of evidence descriptions of mystical experience he argued are 'alleged' to be ineffable, but from textual examples representing the Abrahamic faiths, Hinduism, Buddhism, Islam and Taoism he provided a phenomenological model that he argued is a universal core to mystical experience. His solution to the problem of language was to make a distinction between minimally interpreted experience and the linguistic expression of this experience. This allows for the claim that similar if not identical experiences at the phenomenological level may be differently described linguistically due to historical, cultural and inherent language differences. It leaves open the claim that mysticism may be a unique *sui generis* experience that can occur spontaneously or be deliberately cultivated within various faith traditions. Mystical experience need not be religiously motivated although interest in mysticism is unlikely to be sustained by those without at least implicit religious interests.[87]

Hood developed the Mysticism Scale (M scale) based upon operationalisation, which amounts to finding descriptions for each of Stace's proposed universal core items. Over the decades it has become the most widely used measure of mysticism.[88] Hood's scale has proved to be a robust empirical confirmation of Stace's phenomenological model, used in both exploratory and confirmatory factor analytic studies.[89] It provides an empirical operationalisation of mysticism that is both theoretically and empirically driven. Hood's construction of the M scale is not only deeply rooted in James's account of mysticism, but also clearly reflects the phenomenology of mysticism presented by Stace and is the strongest scholarly tradition linking the history of mysticisms, both in terms of their development and variations, but also in terms of contemporary psychology, that allows text and context to be related in ways that allow for universal claims. If change is to be recognised, it must be from a common shared reference point. While McGinn is correct in his concern with 'experience', he tends to confound religious transformation that may or may not follow from mystical experiences with the definition of mysticism. As we have argued with efforts to denote 'Islamic fundamentalism' with violence, such definitional approaches do not allow an empirical determination of the conditions under which fundamentalist (Islamic or other) become violent.[90] McGinn's entire series can be read in light of this distinction, as can the debate between Taylor and James on mysticism in a secular age. The empirical question is, under what conditions does mystical experience transform lives?

While the initial analysis by Hood in 1975 discovered indeed two factors related to mystical experiences (the first factor including the *introvertive* and *extrovertive* dimensions, the second including *interpretation*), further confirmatory factor analysis has demonstrated a three-factor solution that has been replicated in several cultures.[91] The three-factor model includes:

a. *introvertive mysticism* as first factor consists of items related to the aspects (facets) *timelessness and spacelessness, ego loss and ineffability*;
b. *extrovertive mysticism* is the second factor, which consists of items related to *inner subjectivity and unity*;
c. the third factor, *interpretation*, consists of items associated with *sacredness* and *noetic quality*.

This is not the place to review purely empirical studies of biological processes associated with both spontaneous and cultivated reports of mystical experience as measured by the M scale.[92] The point to be made here is that we can empirically distinguish mystical experience in terms of *unio mystica* (whether introvertive or extrovertive) that has troubled and continues to stimulate immense controversy in the Abrahamic traditions in terms of theological debates on identity versus unity.[93] Drawing on the common core thesis,[94] the three-factor model appears to be applicable not only in the US context, but in other cultural and geographic contexts. In their own review of eight traditions across both history and cultures that can be identified with totalising worldviews, Dahlsgaard, Peterson and Seligman have noted that, of seven virtues identified across eight traditions, transcendence of self (mysticism) is explicitly mentioned in the Abrahamic faith traditions of the West (Christianity, Islam, Judaism) and in the two explicit faith traditions of the East (Hinduism, Buddhism).[95] Here we emphasise not only did Stace develop his phenomenological analysis from texts representative of all these traditions, but Hood's three-factor solution has been replicated in all these traditions as well.[96]

While the emphasis on text and context in the study of mysticism remains important, we also have access to the reality through contemporary empirical psychology. Copleston has noted modern scholars often poke fun at medieval philosophers for their subtle distinctions.[97] James did the same in *VRE* (pp. 340–60). The M scale simply reflects that continuing controversy. It is no less so today in modern psychology, where, as we have noted above, neurophysiology ignores distinctions at the phenomenological level that remain open, perpetually available to all. Cognitive neuropsychology is itself, as argued above, limited if its only metaphysical option is naturalism. Copleston has emphasised that both empirical data and arguments are needed to defend theism or monism but, regardless, the conceptual point remains that, 'in regard to the existence of a reality which is transcendent in the sense that it cannot be identified with the physical world about us or with the individual self, mystical experience in East and West provides evidence which is more reasonable to accept as evidence than not to do so'.[98] In this sense the conversation between psychology and the humanities can be a genuine dialogue. McGinn's suspicions regarding empirical psychology centres on the continuing impasse between empiricism and transempirical epistemology.[99] However, Vörös argues that cognitive science is on the verge of re-discovering that the conscious self, uncovered in laboratory studies, is but an illusion.[100] As embedded cognition, it is linked to neurological process not accessible to conscious reflection. Outside the laboratory, when placed in the dynamics of lived reality and exemplified in mystics across cultures and often dismissed as mere folk psychology, embedded cognition is mysticism fully fleshed out in lives transformed by this experience. The increasing acknowledgement of a common core to mystical experience allows us to study the contextualised record not as fossils of an historic past, but also as experiences available to all now. It also suggests that a genuine dialogue between medieval studies and psychology is possible but under the penumbra of humility. As Vörös has so nicely asked, 'Could it be the greatest gift that mysticism could give cognitive science is to save us from some of its own metaphysical spectres that haunt it – and help demystify itself?'[101]

Notes

1 Cited in Bernard McGinn, *The Presence of God: A Western History of Christian Mysticism: Vol III, The Flowering of Mysticism* (New York: Crossroad, 1998), p. 421.

2 Daniel N. Robinson, *An Intellectual History of Psychology*, 3rd edn (Madison, WI: University of Wisconsin Press, 1995).

3 Ibid., p. 332.

4 Daniel N. Robinson, *A Student's Guide to Psychology* (Wilmington, DE: ISI Books, 2002), pp. 47, 51.

5 Ibid., p. 332.

6 Edward O. Wilson, *Consilience: The Unity of Knowledge* (New York: Vintage, 1999), p. 12.

7 W. H. Auden, 'For Sigmund Freud', *The Kenyon Review*, 2, 30/234 (1940), p. 33.

8 Robert D. Richardson, *William James: In the Maelstrom of American Modernism* (Boston: Houghton Mifflin, 2006), p. 514.

[9] Cited in R. B. Perry, *The Thought and Character of William James: Volume II, Philosophy and Psychology* (Westport, CT: Greenwood Press, 1935), p. 123.

[10] William James, *The Varieties of Religious Experience: A Study in Human Nature (1902)* (Cambridge, MA: Harvard University Press, 1985).

[11] Henry S. Levinson, *The Religious Investigations of William James* (Chapel Hill: University of North Carolina Press, 1981); H. Putman, 'The Permanence of William James', *Bulletin of the American Academy of Arts and Sciences*, 46/17 (1992).

[12] M. R. Slater, *William James on Ethics and Faith* (Cambridge: Cambridge University Press, 2009).

[13] Ralph W. Hood Jr, 'The Common Core Thesis in the Study of Mysticism', in Patrick McNamara (ed.), *Where God and Science Meet*, vol. 3 (Westport, CT: Praeger, 2006), pp. 119–38; idem, 'Methodological Agnosticism for the Social Sciences? Lesson from Sorokin's and James's Allusions to Psychoanalysis, Mysticism, and Godly Love', in Matthew T. Lee and Amos Yong (eds), *The Science and Theology of Godly Love* (DeKalb, IL: NIU Press, 2012), pp. 121–40; M. R. Slater, 'William James's Pluralism', *The Review of Metaphysics*, 65 (2011), 63–90.

[14] Martin Halliwell and Joel D. S. Rasmussen (eds), *William James and the Transatlantic Conversation* (New York: Oxford University Press, 2014).

[15] Alvin Plantinga, 'Methodological naturalism?', in *Origins and Design*, 18/1 (1997), 18–27; 'Methodological naturalism? Part 2', *Origins and Design*, 18/2 (1997), 22–34.

[16] Charles Taylor, *A Secular Age* (Cambridge, MA: Harvard University Press/Belknap Press, 2007).

[17] Jürgen Haberman and Joseph Ratzinger, *The Dialectics of Secularization* (San Francisco: Ignatius Press, 2006).

[18] Hood, 'The Common Core Thesis in the Study of Mysticism' and 'Methodological Agnosticism for the Socials Sciences?'.

[19] F. Vandenberghe, 'Experiments With Truth. A Sociological Variation on William James's *Varieties of Religious Experience*', *Journal for the Theory of Social Behaviour*, 48 (2018), 31–47.

[20] Peter Tyler, *The Return to the Mystical: Ludwig Wittgenstein, Teresa of Avila and the Christian Mystical Tradition* (London: Continuum, 2011), pp. 8–16 and Hood, 'The Common Core Thesis in the Study of Mysticism', respectively.

[21] Tyler, *The Return to the Mystical*, p. 8.

[22] Bernard McGinn, *The Presence of God: A History of Christian Mysticism: Vol I: Origins to the Fifth Century* (New York: Crossroad, 1991), p. 293.

[23] Hood, 'Methodological Agnosticism for the Social Sciences?'; Douglas V. Porpora, 'Methodological atheism, methodological agnosticism and religious experience', *Journal for the Theory of Social Behavior*, 36 (2006), 57–75.

[24] Taylor, *Varieties of Religion Today*, p. 55.

[25] R. W. Hood Jr, P. C. Hill and B. Spilka, *The Psychology of Religion: An Empirical Approach*, 5th edn (New York: Guilford, 2018).

[26] William James, *The Principles of Psychology (1890)* (Cambridge, MA: Harvard University Press, 1981).

[27] Evan Thompson, 'Neurophenomenology and Contemplative Experience', in Philip Clayton (ed.), *The Oxford Handbook of Religion and Science* (Oxford: Oxford University Press, 2008), pp. 226–35.

[28] James, *The Principles of Psychology*; Sebastjan Vörös, 'Demystifying Consciousness with Mysticism? Cognitive Science and Mystical Traditions', *Interdisciplinary Descriptions of Complex Systems*, 11 (2013), 391–9.

[29] Charles Taylor, 'Buffered and Porous Selves' (2 September 2008), *The Immament Frame: Secularism, Religion and the Public Sphere* (blog), *https://tif.ssrc.org/2008/09/02/buffered-and-porous-selves/*.

[30] Taylor, *Varieties of Religion Today*, pp. 22, 3.

[31] R. L. Gorsuch and W. R. Miller, 'Assessing Spirituality', in W. R. Miller (ed.), *Integrating Spirituality into Treatment* (Washington, DC: American Psychological Association, 1999), pp. 47–64.

32 Robert C. Fuller, *Spiritual But Not Religious: Understanding Unchurched America* (New York: Oxford University Press, 2001), p. 130.

33 Robert N. Bellah, Richard Madsen, William M. Sullivan, Ann Swidler and Steven M. Tipton, *Habits of the Heart: Individualism and Commitment in American Life*, rev. edn (Berkeley: University of California Press, 1996).

34 David Yamane, 'Introduction: *Habits of the Heart* at 20', *Sociology of Religion*, 69 (2007), 179–187 (p. 183).

35 Taylor, *Varieties of Religion Today*, p. 24.

36 William James, 'Pragmatism' (1907), in *William James's Writings 1902–1910* (New York: The Library of America, 1987), p. 540.

37 D. A. Hollinger, 'Damned for God's Glory: William James and the scientific vindication of scientific culture', in Wayne Proudfoot (ed.), *The Cambridge Companion to William James* (New York: Cambridge University Press, 2004), pp. 9–30.

38 Taylor, *Varieties of Religion Today*, p. 8.

39 A. N. Whitehead, *Religion in the Making* (New York: Meridian Books, 1926), p. 16.

40 Slater, *William James on Ethics and Faith*, p. 123.

41 T. Flournoy, 'Les principles de la psychologie religieuse', *Archives de Psychologie*, 2 (1903), 33–57.

42 Wesley Wildman, *Science and Religious Anthropology: A Spiritually Evocative Naturalist Interpretation of Human Life* (Farnham: Ashgate, 2009).

43 Ralph W. Hood Jr, 'The Soulful Self of William James', in D. Capps and J. L. Jacobs (eds), *The Struggle for Life: A Companion to William James's* The Varieties of Religious Experience (Newton, KS: Mennonite Press, 1995), pp. 209–19; idem, *Dimensions of Mystical Experiences: Empirical Studies and Psychological Links* (Amsterdam and Atlanta: Rodophi, 2002).

44 Hood, 'Methodological Agnosticism for the Social Sciences?'; Slater, *William James on Ethics and Faith.*

45 G. William Barnard, *Exploring Unseen Worlds: William James and the Philosophy of Mysticism* (Albany, NY: State University of New York Press, 1997); Ralph W. Hood Jr, 'Self and Self Loss in Mystical Experience', in T. M. Brinthaupt and R. P. Lika (eds), *Changing the Self* (Albany: State University, New York Press, 1994), pp. 279–305; idem, 'The Soulful Self of William James'; C. H. Seigfried, *William James's Radical Reconstruction of Philosophy* (Albany, NY: State University of New York Press, 1990).

46 William James, *Psychology: The Briefer Course* (New York: Henry Holt, 1892), p. 468, emphasis added.

47 Taylor, *Varieties of Religion Today*, p. vi.

48 Ibid, p. v.

49 James, *Psychology: The Briefer Course*, p. 467.

50 J. E. Dittes, 'Beyond William James', in C. Y. Glock and P. E. Hammond (eds), *Beyond the Classics? Essays in the Scientific Study of Religion* (New York: Harper & Row, 1973), p. 329.

51 Bernhard Waldenfels, *Phenomenology of the Alien*, trans. Tanja Stähler and Alexander Kozin (Evanston, IL: Northwestern University Press, 2011), p. 10.

52 Slater, *William James on Ethics and Faith.*

53 Bernard McGinn, 'Mystical Consciousness: A Modest Proposal', *Spiritus: A Journal of Christian Spirituality*, 8 (2008), 44–63.

54 Elliot R. Wolfson, *Venturing Beyond: Law and Morality in Kabbalistic Mysticism* (New York: Oxford University Press, 2006).

55 Ralph W. Hood Jr, 'Conceptual and Empirical Consequences of the Unity Thesis', in J. Belzen (ed.), *Mysticism: Some Psychological Considerations* (Amsterdam: Rodopi, 2003), pp. 17–54; idem, 'The Common Core Thesis in the Study of Mysticism'.

56 *The Wiley-Blackwell Companion to Christian Mysticism*, ed. Julia Lamin (New York: Oxford University Press, 2013).

57 Adam Tyson, 'The Mystical Debate: Constructivism and the Resurgence of Perennialism', *Intermountain West Journal of Religious Studies*, 4 (2012), 77–92.

58 Bernard McGinn, *The Presence of God: A History of Western Christian Mysticism*: *Vol. VI Part 2. Mysticism in the Golden Age of Spain 1500–1650* (New York: Crossroad, 2017), p. 206.

59 Shirley du Boulay, *Teresa of Avila: An Extraordinary Life* (New York: Blue Bridge, 2004), p. 269.

60 Tyler, *The Return to the Mystical.*

61 Edward Howells, *John of the Cross and Teresa of Avila: Mystical Knowing and Selfhood* (New York: Herder and Herder, 2002), p. 182.

62 Ralph W. Hood Jr, 'Mysticism and the Paranormal', in J. Harold Ellens (ed.), *Miracles: God, Science, and Psychology in the Paranormal: Vol. 3, Parapsychological Perspectives* (Westport, CT: Praeger, 2008), pp.16–37.

63 Bernard McGinn, *The Presence of God: A Western History of Christian Mysticism: Vol II. The Growth of Mysticism* (New York: Crossroad, 1994); idem, 'Mystical Consciousness: A Modest Proposal'.

64 Hood, 'Methodological Agnosticism for the Social Sciences?'; Tyler, *The Return to the Mystical*, p. 50.

65 Wolfson, *Venturing Beyond*; Hood, 'Conceptual and Empirical Consequences of the Unity Thesis' and 'The Common Core Thesis in the Study of Mysticism'.

66 W. H. Auden, 'Foreword', in Dag Hammarsköld, *Markings* (New York: Alfred A. Knopf, 1978), p. xxii.

67 H. D. Egan, 'The mystical theology of Karl Rahner', *The Way*, 52/2 (2013), 43–62 (p. 54).

68 Ben-Ami Scharfstein, *Mystical Experience* (New York: Bobbs Merrill, 1973).

69 Slater, *William James on Ethics and Faith*, p. 136.

70 W. T. Stace, *Mysticism and Philosophy* (Philadelphia, PA: Lippincott, 1960); Ralph W. Hood Jr, 'The construction and preliminary validation of a measure of reported mystical experience', *Journal for the Scientific Study of Religion* 14 (1975), 29–41; idem, 'The Empirical Study of Mysticism', in B. Spilka and D. N. McIntosh (eds), *The Psychology of Religion* (Boulder, CO: Westview Press, 1997), pp. 222–32.

71 McGinn, *The Presence of God: A Western History of Christian Mysticism: Vol. II*, pp. 315–17.

72 John N. Findlay, *Ascent to the Absolute: Metaphysical Papers and Lectures* (London: Allen and Unwen, 1970), p. 170; J. Masson and T. C. Masson, 'The Study of Mysticism: A Criticism of W. T. Stace', *Journal of Indian Philosophy*, 4 (1976), 109–25.

73 Richard Rorty, *Philosophy and Social Hope* (London: Penguin, 1999), p. 24.

74 Barnard, *Exploring Unseen Worlds*, p. 120.

75 Hood, 'Conceptual and Empirical Consequences of the Unity Thesis' and 'The Common Core Thesis in the Study of Mysticism', Barnard, *Exploring Unseen Worlds*, p. 135.

76 Seigfried, *William James's Radical Reconstruction of Philosophy*; Richardson, *William James*.

77 William James, 'A Pluralistic Universe' (1909), in *William James's Writings 1902–1910* (New York: The Library of America, 1987), p. 677.

78 Carolyn Dinshaw, *How Soon Is Now?: Medieval Texts, Amateur Readers, and the Queerness of Time* (Durham, NC: Duke University Press, 2012).

79 McGinn, 'Mystical Consciousness: A Modest Proposal', p. 45.

80 Frederick Copleston, *Religion and the One: Philosophies East and West* (New York: Crossroad, 1982), pp. 128–9.

81 Rufus Jones, *Studies in Mystical Religion* (New York: Russell & Russell, 1909), p. xxxiv, italics in original.

82 Stace, *Mysticism and Philosophy*, pp. 153–4.

83 Hood, Hill and Spilka, *The Psychology of Religion.*

84 Ann Taves, *Religious Experience Reconsidered: A Building Block Approach to the Study of Religion and Other Special Things* (Princeton, NJ: Princeton University Press, 2009).

85 McGinn, *The Presence of God: A Western History of Christian Mysticism: Vol. III*, p. 17.

86 Hood et al, *The Psychology of Religion.*

87 Copleston, *Religion and the One.*

88 Hood, 'The construction and preliminary validation of a measure of reported mystical experience'; D. Lukoff and F. G. Lu, 'Transpersonal Psychology Research Review Topic: Mystical Experience',

Journal of Transpersonal Psychology, 20/2 (1988), 161–84; H. Streib, H. Klein, B. Keller and R. W. Hood, 'The mysticism scale as a measure for subjective spirituality. New Results with Hood's M-scale and the development of a short form', in L. Ai, K. A. Harris and P. Wink, *Assessing Spirituality and Religion in a Diversified World: Beyond the Mainstream Perspective* (New York: Springer, in press).

89 Hood, 'The Common Core Thesis in the Study of Mysticism'.

90 R. W. Hood Jr, P. C. Hill and W. P. Williamson, *The Psychology of Religious Fundamentalism* (New York: Guilford, 2005).

91 Hood, Hill and Spilka, *The Psychology of Religion.*

92 See Lukoff and Lu, 'Transpersonal Psychology Research Review Topic'; Ralph W. Hood Jr, 'Chemically Assisted Mysticism and the Question of Veridicality', in J. Harold Ellens (ed.), *Seeking the Sacred with Psychoactive Substances: Chemical Paths to Spirituality and God. Volume I: History and Practices* (Santa Barbara, CA: Praeger, 2014), pp. 395–410; idem, 'Methodological Issues in the Use of Psychedelics in Religious Rituals', in J. Harold Ellens (ed.), *Seeking the Sacred with Psychoactive Substances: Chemical Paths to Spirituality and God. Volume II: Insights, Arguments, and Controversies* (Santa Barbara, CA: Praeger, 2014), pp. 179–99.

93 Copleston, *Religion and the One*; McGinn, *The Presence of God: A Western History of Christian Mysticism: Vol II*; T. L. Putthoff, *Ontological Aspects of Early Jewish Anthropology: The malleable self and the presence of God* (Leiden: Koninklijke Brill, 2017).

94 Hood, 'The Common Core Thesis in the Study of Mysticism'.

95 K. Dahlsgaard, C. Peterson and M. E. P. Seligman, 'Shared Virtues: The Convergence of Valued Human Strengths Across Cultures', *Review of General Psychology*, 9 (2005), 203–13.

96 Stace, *Mysticism and Philosophy*, pp. 41–133; Hood, Hill and Spilka, *The Psychology of Religion.*

97 Copleston, *Religion and the One*, p. 162.

98 Ibid., p. 212.

99 McGinn, *The Presence of God: A Western History of Christian Mysticism: Vol II*, p. 343.

100 Vörös, 'Demystifying Consciousness with Mysticism?'

101 Ibid., p. 398.

Select Bibliography

Barnard, G. William, *Exploring Unseen Worlds: William James and the Philosophy of Mysticism* (Albany, NY: State University of New York Press, 1997).

Copleston, Frederick, *Religion and the One: Philosophies East and West* (New York: Crossroad, 1982).

Findlay, John N., *Ascent to the Absolute: Metaphysical Papers and Lectures* (London: Allen and Unwen, 1970), p. 170.

Fuller, Robert C., *Spiritual But Not Religious: Understanding Unchurched America* (New York: Oxford University Press, 2001).

Halliwell, Martin and Joel D. S. Rasmussen (eds), *William James and the Transatlantic Conversation* (New York: Oxford University Press, 2014).

Hood Jr, Ralph W., Peter C. Hill and Bernard Spilka, *The Psychology of Religion: An Empirical Approach*, 5th edn (New York: Guilford, 2018).

Hood Jr, Ralph W., 'The Soulful Self of William James', in D. Capps and J. L. Jacobs (eds), *The Struggle for Life: A Companion to William James's* The Varieties of Religious Experience (Newton, KS: Mennonite Press, 1995), pp. 209–19.

Howells, Edward, *John of the Cross and Teresa of Avila: Mystical Knowing and Selfhood* (New York: Herder and Herder, 2002).

James, William, *Psychology: The Briefer Course* (New York: Henry Holt, 1892) .

James, William, *The Principles of Psychology (1890)* (Cambridge, MA: Harvard University Press, 1981).
James, William, *The Varieties of Religious Experience: A Study in Human Nature (1902)* (Cambridge, MA: Harvard University Press, 1985).
James, William, *William James's Writings 1902–1910* (New York: The Library of America, 1987).
Jones, Rufus, *Studies in Mystical Religion* (New York: Russell & Russell, 1909).
Levinson, Henry S., *The Religious Investigations of William James* (Chapel Hill: University of North Carolina Press, 1981).
McGinn, Bernard, *The Presence of God: A History of Christian Mysticism: Vols I–VII:* (New York: Crossroad, 1991–2017).
Richardson, Robert D., *William James: In the Maelstrom of American Modernism* (Boston: Houghton Mifflin, 2006).
Robinson, Daniel N., *An Intellectual History of Psychology*, 3rd edn (Madison, WI: University of Wisconsin Press, 1995).
Rorty, Richard, *Philosophy and Social Hope* (London: Penguin, 1999).
Scharfstein, Ben-Ami, *Mystical Experience* (New York: Bobbs Merrill, 1973).
Slater, Michael R., *William James on Ethics and Faith* (Cambridge: Cambridge University Press, 2009).
Stace, W. T., *Mysticism and Philosophy* (Philadelphia, PA: Lippincott, 1960).
Streib, Heinz, Constantin Klein, Barbara Keller and Ralph W. Hood, 'The mysticism scale as a measure for subjective spirituality. New Results with Hood's M-scale and the development of a short form', in L. Ai, K. A. Harris and P. Wink, *Assessing Spirituality and Religion in a Diversified World: Beyond the Mainstream Perspective* (New York: Springer, in press).
Taves, Ann, *Religious Experience Reconsidered: A Building Block Approach to the Study of Religion and Other Special Things* (Princeton, NJ: Princeton University Press, 2009).
Tyler, Peter, *The Return to the Mystical: Ludwig Wittgenstein, Teresa of Avila and the Christian Mystical Tradition* (London: Continuum, 2011).
Whitehead, Alfred North, *Religion in the Making* (New York: Meridian Books, 1926).
Wildman, Wesley, *Science and Religious Anthropology: A Spiritually Evocative Naturalist Interpretation of Human Life* (Farnham: Ashgate, 2009).
Wilson, Edward O., *Consilience: The Unity of Knowledge* (New York: Vintage, 1999).

3

Questions of Value: Brain Science, Aesthetics and Art in the Neurohumanities

MATTHEW RAMPLEY

In the third edition of his *Practical Phrenology*, published in 1850, Orson Fowler makes the following assertion:

> Location. – Self-[esteem] is located on the mesial line of the head, about half an inch above the union of the lamboidal sutures, and directly back of firm[ness]; or, in the middle of the superior-inferiour [*sic*] portion of the head, at an angle of about forty-five degrees with the plane of the base of the skull. [Love of] Approbat[ion] is located on the two external sides of it, and cautious[ness] beyond [love of] approbat[ion] in the same range.

> The existence of this faculty demonstrates the position, that the feeling or principle of liberty and of equal rights, is inalienable, and inherent in the very nature and constitution of man; that, therefore, it can no more be destroyed than hunger, or love; that a purely republican and democratick form of government is the *only* one adapted to the nature of man . . .[1]

Fowler's central claim, therefore, is that since there is a locatable module for self-esteem, the political system based on self-esteem – namely, democracy – is rooted in human biology and therefore a natural and inevitable feature of human social life. All sorts of questions arise out of this. For example, Fowler identified other modules, such as wonder, veneration or combativeness; does this mean that fascism or any other political system based on authoritarian government and veneration of the leader is also 'inalienable'?[2] Phrenology does not really help when it comes to debating whether democracy or fascism is more 'natural' or 'inalienable'. It also offers no guide when we try to choose between *types* of democracy (representative? participatory? parliamentary? presidential?). They might be all equally inalienable.

Phrenology has since fallen into disrepute, but it is an object lesson in the dangers that arise when descriptive findings from one domain of knowledge are used to make normative claims in another. This chapter is not a historical study of phrenology but rather of issues that emerge from parallel attempts to apply insights and methods from brain science to the understanding of art and culture. This approach has gained a remarkable foothold in the last 20 years, giving rise to new fields such as neuroaesthetics, neuroarthistory, neurogeography, neuroeconomics, neurocognitive poetics, neuroarchaeology and even neurotheology – the study of the brain processes that dispose individuals to foster religious belief.[3] This volume is concerned with the application of neuroscience to medieval studies, and the ideas explored in this essay should be conceived of as being in an implicit debate with those of the other contributions.

Despite the diversity of interests evident in what one might term the neurohumanities, certain tenets are common, and the unifying theme is the notion that since humans constitute a single biological species, social and cultural practices can be understood by reference to human biology and, specifically, the brain as the seat of cognition. Understood thus, the idea has obvious appeal, and contributors to this volume demonstrate some of the creative insights and conclusions that it can generate. Daniel Lord Smail, for example, argues for the need to overcome the nature–culture divide by highlighting the co-evolution of culture and the brain; Jeff Rider, drawing on Gibson's theory of affordance, explores how engagement with medieval material culture 'enhances our neurocognitive abilities because it helps us form new motor and visceromotor representations of actions we could perform and feelings we could feel'; Godelinde Perk suggests that if we attend carefully to the rhetorical qualities of Julian of Norwich's *Revelation*, we see a rich interweaving and looping of themes (Perk terms it 'knitting') that indicate different cognitive processes at work and might entitle us to talk of the distinctively medieval brain.

The approach has the obvious appeal in its promise to bridge the traditional divide between the sciences and the humanities. A central argument of this chapter, however, is that the interdisciplinary ambitions of the neurohumanities suffer from various methodological and theoretical difficulties. Others have expressed similar caution over the claims made on behalf of neurohumanities, some even regarding them as a latter-day phrenology.[4] This chapter focuses on these issues as they relate specifically to aesthetic experience and the visual arts. It considers, first, what neuroscientific data can actually tell us about the brain, and then how that might be translated into an aesthetic theory. In terms of the latter, it analyses in closer detail the question of mirror neurons, that have underpinned many attempts to establish the neural correlates for aspects of aesthetic experience. I then expand outwards from the question of *individual* engagement with artworks to the wider question of how neuroscience may help inform our understanding of art as a *social* practice. The guiding preoccupation of the discussion is, ultimately, not merely the *validity* of the insights of brain science, a concern shared with all the contributors to this volume, but also the *added value*. As such, analysis of neuroscientific approaches can cast light more generally on the value but also the pitfalls that can await research that attempts to bridge the traditional divide between the arts and the natural sciences.

The Science of the Brain

Phrenology may have long since been dismissed, but the idea that specific cognitive functions are localised in different areas of the brain is now unquestioned, based on the results of brain scanning experiments. Exploration of the brain has been revolutionised by the invention of different techniques for observing brain activity, including functional magnetic resonance imaging (fMRI), positon emission tomography (PET) and single-photon emission computerised tomography (SPECT). Invented in the early 1990s, fMRI in particular has attracted the attention of researchers in the humanities, who have used experimental data to advance claims about the neurological locations of a range of different cognitive operations, including the focusing of aesthetic attention.[5] Caution needs to be exercised, however, when we consider what fMRI scans actually tell observers about the brain; the first step in a critical analysis therefore needs to examine the scope and limits of the technology.

It is commonly assumed that fMRI measures neural activity, but it in fact offers only an *indirect* measure of the activity of neurons. As its name indicates, it is a measurement of magnetic resonance; specifically, it measures blood flow to the brain (haemodynamic changes) based on the different magnetic properties of oxygenated and deoxygenated blood. Thus fMRI serves as a proxy measurement of neural activity: when neurons 'fire,' they metabolise oxygen, which then has to be replenished by the inflow to the brain of fresh (oxygenated) blood.[6] The blood oxygen level-dependent (BOLD) signal thus helps the observer to *infer* neural activity but not measure it. Further caveats have to be applied when considering its use. Specifically, because it is an indirect measure, there is a delay between the neural activity and the measurable signal, sometimes of up to 6 seconds.[7]

The fMRI scan is thus a picture of the effects of an event that occurred in the past. Adjustments can be made to compensate for this in the design of experiments and in the interpretation of data, but it must also be noted that, while the highest resolution scan can narrow down the detectable blood flow in the brain to an area of only 1 mm^3 – the smallest unit that can be represented by a three-dimension pixel or *voxel* – this is still, in neurological terms, a crude measure. To understand how crude, one should note that 1 mm^3 contains more than 1,000,000 neurons.[8] A BOLD signal is thus the delayed representation of blood flow in an area in which *some* neurons with which it is associated *may* be the neurological seat of a specific cognitive operation.

The fMRI scans present further interpretative challenges. Their use as a proxy measure for neuronal activity is based on the presumption that measurable BOLD signals are proportional to the level of increased (or decreased) neural responses, but important neurological research has indicated that may not be the case.[9] Therefore, fMRI data may not be precise and predictable indicators of actual levels of neuronal activity. For example, as Heeger and Ress have suggested, blood flow increases in proportion to the level of brain activity, but only to a certain point; beyond this, additional neuronal operations are not matched by higher blood flows. Hence, fMRI scans may well not capture further changes, even though there may still be additional neural activity.[10]

Experimental research also suggests that a large part of the BOLD signal captures the effects not of neurons but of astrocytes. The latter are important non-neural brain cells that play a crucial part in supplying neurons with oxygen.[11] Further, as Singh argues, the term 'neuronal activity' is poorly specified and results in a simplistic picture of what is actually happening in the brain.[12] For example, fMRI scans measure responses to external visual, auditory or other stimuli, but it is also necessary to take into account brain activity in response to such stimuli from other *intracortical* activity that may be unrelated, or only indirectly related, to the stimulus response. Finally, it has been demonstrated that fMRI scans register not only the haemodynamic changes related to stimulus response, but also those related to the *anticipation* of carrying out tasks, specifically, 'a novel anticipatory brain mechanism' that plays 'the role of preparing the cortex for anticipated tasks by bringing additional arterial blood in time for task onsets'.[13]

Such correctives have been made possible by the use of alternative brain scanning technologies that capture other kinds of data. The advantage of fMRI is that it is non-invasive whereas these other techniques are not, and hence they report on experiments that have been conducted on animals but which cannot be used on human subjects. New techniques may well be developed that overcome such barriers; at present, however, it is nevertheless the case that fMRI provides a partial picture of the brain's operation; the data it produces may be of limited significance, and some of the most cautious voices are those within the neuroscientific community.

From Neurons to the Mind

A central aspect of neurological research has been the attempt to correlate various cognitive functions with particular areas in the brain. There have been enormous medical benefits from such experiments, and they have proven especially successful when examining the relation between physical brain damage and cognitive impairment. The medical and psychological insights generated by this kind of research have been highly significant, but translating such work into the concerns of the humanities is rather less straightforward, and for a number of reasons.

A preliminary example might illustrate the kinds of issues encountered. Informed by the numerous studies that have associated the amygdala with negative emotions, John Onians has suggested that Michelangelo's well-known drawing (Figure 3.1) that turns the base of a column into the profile of a turbaned Turk can be traced back to the amygdala, reflecting the anxiety prompted by the thought of the Ottoman Empire in sixteenth-century Europe.[14] This may be true but, equally, it is open to all sorts of questions. For example, do we know that Michelangelo always associated the idea of the Ottoman Empire with fear? Given the extensive cultural and commercial links between Italy and the Ottoman Empire, the latter might have conjured up a host of different associations, such as admiration, curiosity or indeed disdain. Fear might not have been the predominant emotion. It may also be that the drawing is just a playful visual pun, rather than an evocation of primeval fear of 'the Turk'. In other words, even before we try to connect an image to a particular neural base, we have to be certain that it is not open to alternative interpretations. Onians may well be right to note that the amygdala is the neurological seat of fear, but research has also suggested it may be associated with other more positive emotions.[15] Hence, even if the amygdala is, in some way, the locus of the image's identity as a representation of fearful emotions, this is not a sufficient explanation in itself. Onians's claim, illustrative of a wider approach, thus raises an important methodological issue, for it assumes an unambiguous correlation between localisable brain activity and specific cognitive and other mental operations. There are good reasons for doubting whether such unequivocal correlations can be found.

A much-discussed theory of moral judgement provides a similar example of the difficulties that the neurohumanities approach runs into. Joshua Greene and others have claimed to be able to identify the different locations in the brain of distinct kinds of moral judgement.[16] Specifically, they argue that deontological judgements (i.e. those motivated by adherence to basic moral principles), differ from consequentialist ones (i.e. those motivated by concern for the consequences of a particular course of action).

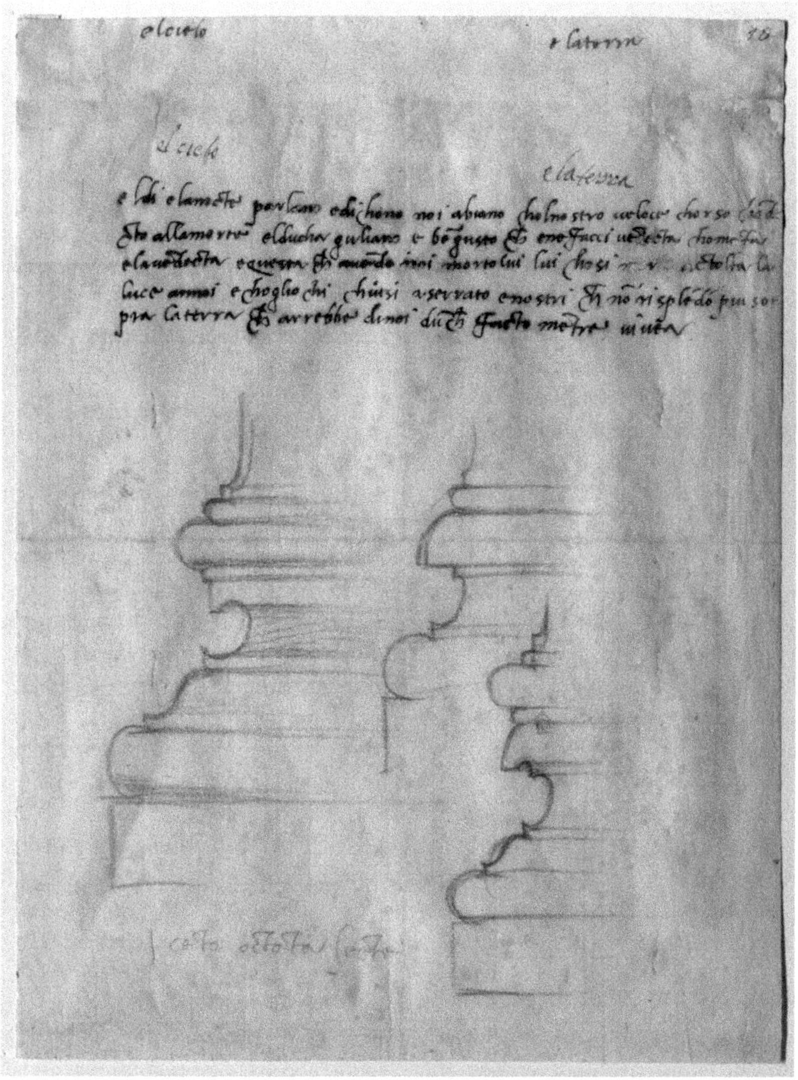

Figure 3.1: Michelangelo, drawing for the Medici tombs in the New Sacristy of San Lorenzo, Florence. Casa Buonarroti, Florence, A10r, *c.*1523.

Following an experiment in which subjects were presented with a series of different kinds of moral dilemmas, Greene and his associates advanced the thesis that 'deontological judgments are driven by emotional processes, whereas characteristically consequentialist judgments are driven by "cognitive" processes'.[17]

When subjects are asked to respond to dilemmas that compel either deontological or consequentialist reasoning, different parts of the brain appear to be involved. According to this argument, the making of decisions in response to different kinds of moral dilemma rests either on impulsive emotional (deontological) reactions, or on slow, 'cognitive' (consequentialist) processes that demand abstract reasoning. In the experiments conducted by Greene et al, the former are apparently associated with areas of the brain such as, but not only, the medial prefrontal cortex, the posterior superior temporal sulcus/inferior parietal lobe and the amygdala, while the latter have been associated with the dorsolateral prefrontal cortex and the parietal lobe. The implication of the argument is that deontological moral judgements, in other words, reactions based on the normative role of basic ethic principles, are not *judgements* at all, but rather, post-hoc rationalizations of emotional responses to certain situation. However, as with the ambiguity of the amygdala, the difficulty with this conceptually neat division between consequentialist and deontological moral stances is that areas associated by Greene et al. as associated with impulsive emotional responses have also been identified in other experiments with language use, which might be regarded as underlying the careful deliberation associated with consequentialist moral reasoning.[18] Although the logical distinction between the two may be clear, attempts at linking them to distinct parts of the brain are inconclusive.

It may also be objected that, contrary to the impression given by such studies, the brain is not so easily divided into neatly demarcated regions.[19] Identification of distinct 'areas' of the brain is a crude representation that may serve heuristic purposes, but little more; unlike different organs of the body, brain areas are not discrete entities with definable boundaries. Conversely, even if there were no insuperable technical obstacles to such mapping, there is still no general consensus as to how to arrange a taxonomy of cognitive processes, or even if mental functions can be organised into 'modules' traceable to neurological events. There is also no generally agreed view as to the optimal level of neuroscientific analysis. While some have argued that the single neuron should be the basic unit of observation, others have operated with the metaphors of the field or the network, all of which involve different levels of analysis, as well as different techniques of observation.[20]

More generally, one can argue that neurohumanistic research is prone to what Amir Raz has termed 'reverse inferencing': in other words, assuming that because a particular behaviour or cognitive process can be correlated in fMRI scans with a localisable neural event or set of events, the reverse also holds, namely, that a mental event can be inferred from an observed haemodynamic change.[21] Yet, given that even the highest level resolution is still crude, in neurological terms, the possibility has to be entertained that fMRI is not sufficiently refined to be able to distinguish between different mental events that might *appear* to occur in the same place. It might be countered that higher resolution scanning technology *in the future* might be able to pinpoint their location with greater accuracy, and this may be correct, but for the present, caution needs to be exercised over the conclusions that can currently be drawn from neurological scans.

It might be objected that such criticisms are not decisive, but merely methodological quibbles. Perhaps, it might be claimed, they point merely to the need for further investigation and experimental research. Perhaps, too, it may be argued, while fMRI is a limited and coarse tool, future technologies may be invented that enable a much more fine-grained analysis of the brain that will be able to distinguish operations *within* the crude landscape of voxels, including, for example, differentiating between the activity of neurons and astrocytes. The criticism of reverse inferencing may thus well turn out to be misplaced.

This much can be conceded, but it does not invalidate the basic call for caution when interpreting the result of fMRI scans.

Mirror Neurons

If the relation between observed neural events and cognitive processes is still a problematic issue, doubly problematic are the claims surrounding the discovery of mirror neurons, which have taken on a particular significance in neuroaesthetics. Some twenty-five years ago, a team of researchers at the University of Parma conducted research on macaques that demonstrated the existence of a class of neurons – 'mirror' neurons – that were activated not only when a subject performed a specific action, but also when they observed another performing the same action.[22] These findings have been taken up by many proponents of the neurohumanities and underlie explanations of a variety of behaviours related to art; their presence, it is claimed, explains the impulse towards mimesis in art, as well as the aesthetic capacity for empathic projection. As Gallese has argued: 'To observe objects is therefore equivalent to automatically evoking the most suitable motor program required to interact with them. Looking at objects means to unconsciously "simulate" a potential action'.[23] Looking at a work of art is thus equivalent to an imaginative projection, and mirror neurons are the neural basis of aesthetic experience. They ensure that paintings and sculptures evoke a physical involvement, a kind of embodied simulation in the spectator.[24]

Mirror neurons have had a particular attraction for some art historians since they appeared to cast new light on a feature of aesthetic experience that had preoccupied some of the leading art theorists of the late nineteenth century, including Aby Warburg, Heinrich Wölffin and Robert Vischer – namely, aesthetic empathy.[25] Contemporary commentators like David Freedberg went as far as to suggest that when we view artworks we imaginatively recreate the gestures that went into their original making: observing the brushstrokes of an artist such as Franz Kline activates the same neural networks that were involved in the original act of painting.[26] In other studies, too, the action of mirror neurons has been taken as explaining basic aspects of human cultural practice. In *Getting Inside your Head: What Cognitive Science Can Tell Us About Popular Culture*, Lisa Zunshine postulates that literary fictions and the avidness with which they are read are attributable, in part, to the operations of mirror neurons, which make us cognitively 'hungry'.[27] Specifically, we project ourselves eagerly into the minds of others in literary works, in order to imagine the intentions of both authors and fictional characters, for 'we must have neural circuitry that is powerfully attuned to the presence, behaviour and emotional display of other members of our species . . . the functioning of mirror neuron systems underlies everyday mind attribution'.[28]

This is at first sight a compelling argument, but it assumes that we mimic the actions of others without granting them any significance, or that we *implicitly* grasp their meaning (what the team responsible for the original research have referred to as 'action understanding').[29] Each of these is questionable. As Gilbert Ryle famously illustrated with the example of contracting eyelids, an identical observable action may be one of many possible gestures.[30] It may be a blink, or it may be an involuntary twitch. Equally, however, it may be a wink, with numerous different possible meanings; it may be a patronising gesture, or a conspiratorial sign, or have some other significance according to some agreed code. It may be a satirical or ironic performance, for example, or a cruel imitation of a third party suffering from an involuntary twitch. The possibilities multiply.

Ryle's decades-old argument poses challenges for the thesis of mirror neurons, which rests on the idea of a univocal neurological equivalence between a behaviour and the 'action understanding' of the observer. For since a single observable action may be the consequence of many different neurological states, depending on its meaning, simply *observing* an action (let alone repeating it) cannot be a guarantee that one's own brain replicates the brain state that underlay the original performance, for one first has to decide *which* performance one is observing. It is always possible to interpret the gesture otherwise. This distinction is frequently blurred in the literature on mirror neurons, which attributes to them the ability to decode the intentions of others. As Fogassi has claimed, 'the parieto-premotor mirror neuron circuit may involve a primitive form of intention understanding that occurs automatically without any type of inference process'.[31] In other words, individuals can decode the intentions of others because, when observing their behaviour, 'they can reproduce it internally'.[32] The problem with this argument is that 'intention understanding' is never defined nor distinguished from the drawing of inferences. It is simply asserted on the basis of the metaphor of coding, which presumes the operation of a neural cryptographic 'key' that can reverse engineer from observed behaviour to neurological cause.

The mirror neuron theory has nevertheless become commonplace. One author asserts, for example, that 'representation of the other's action by means of mirror neurons is direct and immediate and does not require any intervening symbolic code or a mental language, as there is an instantaneous mapping from self to other and from other to self'.[33] This putative capacity for instantaneous mapping underlies the capacity for mimicry and may cast light, it is argued, on an earlier 'mimetic' stage in the evolution of human culture in which metaphorical gesture was a predominant mode of expression. Such theories are accompanied by a systemic erasure of the concept of representation, or rather, by a theory of representation *without* representation; as such, they offer a provocative challenge to the orthodoxies of literary and cultural studies, for they run counter to *any* semiological theory, for even putatively 'natural' signs – Peircean indices – are understood on the basis of inference.

The idea of a primary mimetic stage of human development has a long history; it was first posited by Vico, and has enjoyed many advocates, from Gottfried Herder and Edward Tylor to Walter Benjamin and Theodor Adorno.[34] It has enjoyed a renewed level of interest since the early 1990s, when the evolutionary psychologist Merlin Donald proposed it in his influential theory of cognitive and cultural evolution.[35] Mimicry is of course an important part of the repertoire of human behaviour, but, as theorists of learning have argued, it is parasitic on other, *observed*, behaviours and it is highly improbable that it could be the basis of some putative 'stage' of cultural evolution.[36] At stake, once more, is the question of inference. To take one example that may be indicative of the wider issue, namely, language acquisition, even at the earliest stage of the development of language, speakers cannot merely have 'copied' the utterances of others, for those primitive utterances had to have had meanings attributed to them, starting with the basic distinction between utterance and arbitrary, random noise. This applies not only to *Hmmmmm*, the primordial music-language posited by Steven Mithen and others, but also to language forms with greater structural complexity.[37] For whatever simple syntactical and grammatical rules there may have been, they could never have been learnt inductively on the basis of imitation alone; rules had to be *inferred* from linguistic interaction with other speakers.

Speculation about origins may seem removed from theoretical debates about the present, but the theory of mirror neurons links the two, and is of direct pertinence to accounts of aesthetic response. If we return to an earlier example, David Freedberg's argument about the parallels between painting and observing the painter at work, the same objections can be made. Indeed, Freedberg goes further, arguing that the painting itself, as an *index* of the act of painting, mobilises the same neurons as viewing the painter at work, in this case, Franz Kline. Yet viewing the painting and artistic production are different cognitive acts, since one has first to *infer* the gestures that went into the work's making from their trace. And even if viewing the painting and the act of painting fire the same neurons, picking up the brush and applying paint to the canvas very clearly differs from viewing the outcome of that action and copying it. Observing and repeating an action (actually or in the imagination) consist of at least *two* separate actions: inferring and imitating.

One might finally note that the claims regarding mirror neurons were first made in relation to experimental work with macaques, and the applicability of such results to human subjects is open to question for a number of reasons. First, the idea of 'action understanding' implies that macaques have a theory of mind, in other words, recognition of the intentionality of others and an ability to infer the intentions of others from their actions. Whether or not some animals have a theory of mind is a much debated topic, but even those who have suggested that higher level primates and corvids *do* possess theory of mind have acknowledged that it may be limited in scope.[38] Specifically, it may amount to no more than what Saidel has referred to as 'minimal mind-reading', that is, the ability to recognise goal-directed behaviour in others, as opposed to 'substantive mind-reading', which relies on the ability to identify propositional attitudes in others, in other words, their mental states, a skill that is dependent on the possession of language.[39] If we accept this limitation, it would suggest that the mirror neuron activity in macaques is related to much lower level behavioural observation than is involved in human interactions. Linking this to mimicry is a further unwarranted step, for while adult macaques observe others, they do not imitate; the conclusion that detection of mirror neurons in macaques can explain mimetic action in humans seems, at the very least, premature.[40]

The Brain and Aesthetic Experience

Arguments about the relation between observing, mimicry and the brain rely on minimising the importance of inference and representation, and a similar problem is evident in experiments that purport to illuminate the question of aesthetic experience. An example that illustrates the kinds of issue encountered is the attempt by Gerald Cupchik et al. to find the distinctive neural structures underlying aesthetic attention.[41] At the heart of their investigation is the attempt to pinpoint the neurological difference between aesthetic viewing and normal everyday cognitive reasoning.

It is important, of course, to establish what is meant by the idea of 'aesthetic viewing'. In this case it is derived from the Kantian aesthetic tradition, more specifically, perhaps, Schopenhauer's aesthetics, for Cupchick et al. place special emphasis on the idea of the active suspension of everyday cognition in order to 'overcome the automatic cuing of semantic categories and to reinvest attention in sensory experience elicited by the stylistic properties of artworks'.[42] This recalls Schopenhauer's notion of the suspension of the principle of sufficient reason, and is grounded in a similar initial idea, namely, the idea of everyday cognition ('object identification') as the default mode of perception.[43] The objective of the experiment Cupchick et al. conduct is then to determine the extent to which these theoretical postulates are borne out by neurological data, and, hence, the extent to which subjects exercise conscious cognitive control when they direct attention to the purely aesthetic properties of a stimulus. The research seeks to identify where such control takes place.

For the experiment, a group of sixteen subjects, intentionally selected for their lack of formal training, were shown a series of representational paintings. They were instructed, first, to approach them 'in an objective and detached manner to obtain information about the content of the painting and visual narrative' and then 'to approach the paintings in a subjective and engaged manner, experiencing the mood of the work and the feelings it evokes, and to focus on its colours, tones, composition, and shapes'.[44] Other aspects of the study included presenting the subjects with a range of abstract paintings, specifically, examples of hard-edged abstraction and others referred to as 'soft edge' in order 'to test whether soft edge paintings facilitate aesthetic experience', in contrast to hard-edged images, which function as visual analogues of the process of categorisation and the drawing of conceptual boundaries and distinctions.[45] fMRI scanning indicated that the bilateral insula were more associated with the exercise of the aesthetic attitude, whereas the right fusiform gyrus was more associated with 'pragmatic' viewing, but there was also interaction between areas of the brain involved in both types of viewing. As a result, the conclusion drawn was that 'aesthetic experience is a function of the interaction between top-down orienting of attention and bottom-up perceptual input'.[46] In Kantian terms one might describe it as the combination of intuition and pure reason.

A number of observations are pertinent here. The first is that the experiment was dependent on prior acceptance of a specific concept of the aesthetic. In other words, the experiment assumed the character of aesthetic experience to be settled, and that was also embedded in the instructions given to the subjects. This clearly means the significance of the experiment would be limited to an examination of the supposed neural bases of aesthetic experience *as already described* by a specific philosophical tradition. In addition, verification as to whether the subjects were indeed attending to the images in purely aesthetic or purely pragmatic ways relies entirely on reassurance from the subjects that they had behaved as instructed, for their mental experience is empirically inaccessible.[47] Hence, if, as is initially contended, suspension of the conceptual apparatus of 'pragmatic judgement' requires no small effort of will, there is no guarantee that they were viewing the images in the prescribed manner. Moreover, even if the test subjects *are* treated as reliable, the experiment hinges on the assumption that aesthetic and non-aesthetic judgement can be disentangled from each other, when a central debate in aesthetics has been precisely the question as to whether this is possible. To take one much debated issue, the relevance of moral to aesthetic judgements has been a central topic of discussion, and there is a powerful school of thought that argues that the moral features of a work of art are relevant to the assessment of its aesthetic properties.[48] The idea, too, that the difference between soft- and hard-edged abstract paintings is of significance is open to interrogation; there is no *a priori* reason to assume that soft-edged abstract paintings are any more ambiguous, and thus liable to prompt aesthetic viewing, than the hard-edged paintings of, for example Ellsworth Kelly, Piet Mondrian or Terry Frost.

Finally, there is the question of the sample subjects, chosen deliberately so as to exclude those with any expert knowledge. This is common practice in such experiments, designed to avoid bias in the result and to render the sample more typical of humans in general. But it would be almost impossible to select subjects who had *not* had *some* kind of experience of artworks and the culture of art, such is its ubiquity; the notion that the set would provide some kind of unbiased sample is open to challenge. Indeed, one could go further and argue that since discussion in the philosophy of art often centres on the distinction between 'appropriate' and 'inappropriate' aesthetic judgements it could be that unschooled test subjects are the *least* suitable group to choose. If adopting the aesthetic attitude involves a suspension of habitual patterns of perception, and if this may require training and exercise, there is no way of knowing whether the subjects in the test even knew *how* to adopt an aesthetic attitude, or, again, whether, when they were being scanned, they were doing so. Such arguments do not necessarily invalidate the experiment, but they do problematise its working assumptions and suggest, at the very least, that the results have to be treated with care.

I have focused at length on this example, but it typifies much neuroaesthetics research, which glosses over and simplifies important conceptual problems. A parallel instance is the work by Boccia et al. on responses to the famous allegorical portraits by Arcimboldo.[49] At the core of the investigation was the question of the ambiguity of the painter's works, which derived from their richly allegorical character. Subjects were asked to express aesthetic like or dislike of the portraits, which were also set alongside other, 'realistic', Renaissance portraits which were, supposedly, non-ambiguous. The results showed an inverse relation between aesthetic appreciation and face recognition. Specifically, 'ambiguous artworks eliciting a negative esthetic experience lead to more pronounced activation of regions of face processing, while ambiguous artworks eliciting a positive esthetic experience lead to reduced activation of these areas'.[50] Pleasure in the ambiguity of Arcimboldo's allegorical paintings is accompanied by suppression of those areas of the brain responsible for the conceptual ordering and categorising of the contents of perception.

In one sense this may be an uncontentious conclusion, but it rests on precarious suppositions, such as the meaning of the term 'ambiguity'. For in one sense there is nothing at all ambiguous about Arcimboldo's portraits; they are unmistakeably facial representations and their allegorical references are not, in fact, difficult to decode, especially for the educated viewer for whom they were originally painted. They present, admittedly, striking visual puns, but these do not tax the interpretative efforts of the viewer. Conversely, one might argue that many 'realistic' Renaissance portraits can be highly ambiguous, if we are not quite sure how to read the facial expressions of the sitter, for example, or if we are not sure of their identity. One could cite one of the most 'ambiguous' portraits of all: van Eyck's Arnolfini portrait, which is 'realistic' in the manner assumed by the experiment, but which has been the object of hundreds of varying and opposed interpretations. There are many other examples of what James Elkins has termed 'monstrously ambiguous paintings', such as Botticelli's *La Primavera*, Giorgione's *La Tempesta* or *Las Meñinas* by Velázquez, all of which would be 'realistic' in the terms of the experiment.[51]

Whether aesthetic response can be summed up as a matter of merely 'liking' or 'disliking' a picture is obviously open to debate, especially as the meaning of both terms is not straightforward. One can 'like' a work of art for many different, and occasionally contradictory, reasons; indeed one can 'like' and 'dislike' one and the same picture in light of different aspects. Yet this formulation is recurrent in much neuroaesthetic literature. A notable example is Herbert Lindenberger's argument that since aesthetic enjoyment of music appears to be associated with the same regions of the brain as more basic bodily pleasures, 'Art thus becomes the creation not so much of those lofty figures whom we seek to honor with the term genius but simply of those skilled enough in their various crafts to manipulate their consumers' brains to produce particular effects. Producing and consuming art, in short, becomes an activity as "natural" as, say, having sex or cooking and enjoying food'.[52] Lindenberger's suggestion, which evokes the empirical aesthetics of turn of the century thinkers such as Theodor Lipps, may well demystify the process of creation, but its equation of carnal pleasure and aesthetic judgement represents a simplification.[53] The clue lies in the term itself, since aesthetic judgement consists of a *judgement* open to scrutiny by others, whereas pleasure is an entirely subjective, inscrutable phenomenon. This is a basic tenet in Kant's aesthetics, and Lindenberger provides no grounds for disputing it.

Culture and the Brain

Discussion of these representative examples suggests that the programme of neuroaesthetics in particular, and neurohumanities more generally, encounters significant hurdles. However, critical unease might be expressed not over the existence of such hurdles, but rather over the tendency for them to be ignored or dismissed. Instead, much neurohumanities literature confidently advances a range of sweeping claims about the neurological basis of art and culture. Some examples illustrate this:

- 'The participatory imagination employed in the act of meditating upon the Passion of Christ relies heavily on a brain activity that is automatic, namely, the mirror neuron system'[54]
- 'the sense of beauty derives from a joint activity of neural cortical populations responsive to specific elementary or high order features present in works of art and neurons located in emotion controlling centers'[55]
- 'Supported by recent experimental studies, I claim that abstract art frees our brain from the dominance of reality, enabling the brain to flow within its inner states, create new emotional and cognitive associations and activate brain-states that are otherwise harder to access'[56]
- 'One of the hopes of a cognitive neuroscience of cultural transmission is to illuminate mechanisms of cultural transmission while also providing an adaptive explanation for catchy memes and migratory mannerisms . . . A good way of beginning this endeavor would be to ask: "What neurophysiological factors can influence the likelihood that an observed action will be repeated by the observer?"'[57]

These are bold assertions, but, as this paper argues, there are grounds for scepticism about their methodological and theoretical foundations. Of course healthy scepticism should accompany any such project, but the concern here is that proponents of neurohumanities research proceed as if these questions were settled, and as if there were not still a lively debate about them.

Much neurohumanities literature relies, too, on an individualistic model of the brain, conceived in terms of the solitary human subject responding to stimuli in the artificial environment of the laboratory. Informing this latter approach is also a conflation of aesthetics, defined as the study of aesthetic response, with the philosophy (and history) of art and culture. This is evident not only from the design of individual experiments but also from the general summation of neuroaesthetics by some of its leading exponents.[58] An illustration of this can be found in the work of Semir Zeki, one of the earliest advocates of the field, whose primary point of reference was Clive Bell's concept of 'significant form', and who treated this highly contested notion as a basic axiom.[59] The significance accorded to Bell is consonant with Zeki's contention that 'all truths are subjective', a stance that informs the basic question posed by his work, namely: 'to what extent is the structured order, or the ordered structure, of the Universe in which we have evolved reflected in the organization of our brains and to what extent is the experience of beauty a pointer to that structure?'[60] However, this view has been much criticised as leading to a narrow conception of the scope of aesthetic thought.[61] Indeed, the formalist theory of aesthetic experience on which it relies has long ceased to have philosophical currency. Aesthetic judgements in general as well as those specifically about art are coloured by socio-cultural factors and are hard to disentangle from other kinds of judgements. Pierre Bourdieu's analysis of the way taste expresses social status and ambition, for example, is just one particularly well-known example of the broader critique of earlier formalist aesthetics.[62] Anglo-American philosophy of art has reached similar conclusions, although without a concern for the political and ideological resonance of art. Kendall Walton's classic discussion of categories exemplifies this approach, arguing that it is not even possible to discern the aesthetic properties of a work until one has established 'extrinsic' historical and art-historical considerations that help *categorise* it and thus determine which features have aesthetic salience.[63]

William Seeley has attempted to construct a neuroscientific account of aesthetic experience that forestalls such criticisms by arguing that the wider social-cultural determinations shaping the response to works of art can themselves be accounted for by reference to neurological functions and structures.[64] In other words, an expanded neuroaesthetics might compensate for the flaws in the work of Zeki and others. Defining works of art as 'attentional engines', Seeley argues that neuroscience can identify 'how we use semantic content to disambiguate artworks from similarly structured non-art artifacts' using 'biased competition' theories of selective attention. These have shown the ways in which 'top-down, fronto-parietal, and cortico-fugal attentional networks' lie behind our capacity to match 'abstract diagnostic cues both to category knowledge in object recognition and knowledge of the stylistic conventions regulating artistic production in a category of art'.[65]

This has the merit of recognising the need to address the complex socio-cultural context within which art is encountered, but it still reduces that encounter to a matter of the personal appreciation of works of art. It thereby collapses philosophical investigation of art into a theory of aesthetic response (aided by the tendency to refer to both as 'aesthetics'), whereas aesthetic response often plays no role in many philosophical questions to do with art. Equally, many debates in the philosophy of art concern normative issues, which neuroaesthetics is not equipped to answer. Examples drawn from prominent discussions in recent literature illustrate the gulf between the two. They include questions such as:

Is a morally defective work of art necessarily *aesthetically* compromised? Can two incompatible interpretations of a work of art both be true? Are sentimental responses to a work of art always subject to criticism? Should a work once thought to be a masterpiece always be devalued once discovered to be a forgery? Have the aesthetic properties of a work of art that has visibly altered over time also changed? It is difficult to envisage how the study of blood flow to the brain helps discussion of these issues.

At this point one might object that criticising an approach for not being able to answer questions it was never designed to address is equally problematic. Certainly, many exponents of neurohumanities, including contributors to this book, would also recognise the limits of the paradigm. Nevertheless, these and other questions are not so easily dismissed as not relevant. We can take the example of incommensurable interpretations, to which the earlier discussion of mirror neurons may be pertinent. Two observers watch an artist making marks on a canvas with paint. Based on the ideas put forward earlier, one would conclude that an instantaneous mapping of the self onto the other was taking place, thanks to the action understanding enabled by the mirror neurons. Except that the two observers have entirely different impressions (or internal representations) of what they are observing. For one of them, the artist is covering the surface with childish daubs in a random, meaningless, manner, whereas, for the other, the artist is covering the surface with expressive abstract marks that conjure up profound emotions and unconscious thoughts. For the one, the artist is regressing into an infantile behaviour that illustrates the moral and intellectual bankruptcy of 'modern' art, whereas, for the other, the artist is demonstrating the liberating power of raw creative energy. I have stretched this hypothetical case to make the elementary point that the distinction between mere observation and interpretation is not so easy to make, but also, and mainly, to remind us that we have two conflicting interpretations, *both* of which would be based on the functioning of the mirror neurons. It may be that the mirror neurons of both observers form the basic neurological structural apparatus for such observing, but this does not seem to explain what we may find most important. Equally, which of these two might we opt for? Is the one the view of a philistine and the other the view of someone with an informed understanding of Abstract Expressionist (or indeed Neo-Expressionist) practice? Or has the first observer in fact landed on some aspect of the pretentions of the avant-garde? Should we pay more attention to the neural functioning of the informed observer, or are the mirror neurons of the philistine a more valuable source of information? Scientific research into the neurological mechanisms of the brain does not answer these questions.[66] One might think of the parallel case of using knowledge of the human skeleton-muscular system as a means of understanding the creative process. It might provide useful insights into the limitations of human anatomy and their impact on the practice of carving or modelling in certain historical forms of art, into what could and could not be done. It might even make us more alert to the technical sophistication of certain artists, once we know what the limit cases might be, in terms of what anatomically modern humans can do with certain kinds of material. But, as with neuroscience, its findings would be of limited use for the normative concerns guiding our theoretical enquiries into art, much less aesthetic judgements about, for example, Michelangelo's *Dying Slave* or *David*.

Neurohumanities have been repeatedly criticised for their ideological motivations. Critical theorists and the sociologists of science have pointed to the convergence of the metaphor of the network in neuroscience and discourses of modern capitalism, the extent to which exponents of the neurohumanities contribute to the naturalisation of social categories and the biologisation of power.[67] These are important observations, although, since such criticisms are themselves politically motivated, they may not be decisive. Nevertheless, we can put them to one side and still argue that the outcomes of research in neurohumanities have often tended to be disappointing. There are numerous examples of this problem, such as the conclusion that 'art experts classify examples of modern art initially in respect to an art, style or artists. Lay people with no expertise make no such classification'.[68] Or, to take a formulation from neuroeconomics:

> . . . different neuronal representations of value in different parts of the brain contribute to distinct computational processes. In sensory areas, value-related modulation in neuronal activity might promote selective processing of high-value stimuli by attention. In the frontal cortex, neurons representing abstract value could contribute directly to the selection of one among multiple available goods based on subjective preference. Finally, in sensory motor areas, value modulations might promote the selection of one particular action among many to achieve a behavioural goal.[69]

In other words, value judgements involve different parts of the brain depending on the context. There is a danger that, as one commentator has argued, neuroaesthetics 'does little more than provide a more precise quantitative measure of facts about artworks, and our engagements with artworks, that are already widely acknowledged in more qualitative terms within the artistic and critical community'.[70] Indeed, it is sometimes difficult to decide what is meant when reference is made to the brain, and how much analytic work it is meant to perform.

For example, when Nadia Pawelchak asserts, in this volume, that the 'period eye' or 'cognitive style' of an era or culture have their roots in brain activity, it is difficult to decide what conceptual labour is being performed. Clearly, *something* is going on in the brain of the medieval viewer (and user) of an ivory mirror. But until the significance of this observation becomes clearer, until it makes a *difference* to how we interpret the mirror, even *changes* our prior understanding of the mirror, there is the danger that invocation of the brain provides just additional background, contextual, insight. Likewise, when Godelinde Perk talks of the medieval brain, this is clearly not literally meant to imply that the European medieval brain was in some sense different from the 'modern' brain. The pace of biological evolution is too slow for the temporal gap of seven hundred or so years to make any difference. It means, rather, that the brain processes information in different ways, much as the brains of speakers of different languages process linguistic structures and meanings in different ways depending on the character of the language. However, unless the exact nature of the differences in processing can be observed, and the *implications* of those differences demonstrated, the art historical significance of these and other similar observations may be limited.

The ultimate question we have to ask, therefore, relates to the *value* of neurohumanities research. We do not need to look far for an answer. As Herbert Lindenberger has stated:

> the great artists and critics of the past knew what they were doing, that science simply helps corroborate what they (and we) knew all along . . . Do we need the confirmations of science to tell us what artists and critics of the past already understood, albeit in the languages of their own time? It may well be that the high prestige of science in today's culture, especially in comparison

> with the declining prestige of the humanities, enables these confirmations to validate the importance of art in our lives.[71]

In other words, scientific observation validates art. Ironically, however, Lindenberger also indicates just how limited this validation goes, when he states: 'Although neuroscientists cannot (and ordinarily choose not to) explain why a particular abstraction is "great," or even "better" than others, they can show with considerable precision how the visual system creates certain illusions for viewers'.[72] Neuroscientists can thus legitimate our concern for artworks, but they are unable to say why.

Conclusion: What Is To Be Done?

This paper has argued that while neurohumanities draw on generally accepted wisdom concerning the role of the brain as the organ of the mind, considerable difficulties arise once attempts are made to craft more specific correspondences between the mind and the brain. Many critical observers of the neurohumanities have nevertheless tried, despite their misgivings, to be conciliatory towards a programme into which increasing amounts of intellectual and political capital have been invested. The analysis in this chapter is rather less optimistic about the prospects of the enterprise. The barrier it encounters in the face of normative questions may not be the most problematic aspect, but it is perhaps the most striking, because it marks it out from all other methodological innovations in the study of art and culture. For the latter, from examples in recent decades such as new historicism, queer studies and post-colonialism, to older instances, such as marxism, iconology, Freudian and Lacanian psychoanalysis, new criticism, feminism and formal analysis, embedded the reading of individual works of art and literature in broader theories of culture. This is not to endorse any of them in particular, but they did provide answers to the question as to what is of value and merits closer critical attention. The rediscovery of individual works as well as the recovery of the entire oeuvre of specific artists and writers, as well as disputes about the canon, indeed the critique of the very idea of the canon, for example, have all been motivated by debates about the value of art and literature. On these issues neuroaesthetics and neurohumanities are silent because their empirical foundations do not enable them to do anything else.

Engagement with neurohumanities nevertheless brings many important issues into sharp relief. Much of the attraction of neurohumanities research lies in its interdisciplinary reach; under the wider rubric of consilience, it represents perhaps the most radical kind of cross-disciplinary working, bringing together ideas and themes from the most disparate fields of inquiry.

The celebrated biologist Edward Wilson has claimed: 'there is intrinsically only one class of explanation. It traverses the scales of space, time, and complexity to unite the disparate facts of the disciplines by consilience, the perception of a seamless web of cause and effect'.[73] Herein lies perhaps the greatest challenge for the neurohumanities, for the very idea that knowledge is a single enterprise is one that many would contest. Proponents of interdisciplinarity have tended to focus on the institutional barriers they face as well as the difficulty of overcoming 'domain specificity', understood as the restriction to a narrow class of objects and methods of inquiry.[74] Such criticisms are necessary, but disciplines are not defined solely by domains or by methods, but also by the questions they ask, and those are in turn motivated by interests and values. It is on this issue that the neurohumanities are most open to criticism, since the 'data' they produce, the 'disparate facts' they gather together, do little to address the normative dimension of the study of art and literature.

Despite the scepticism expressed in this paper, it would be premature to dismiss the neurohumanities out of hand, for they are part of a broader investigation of a basic issue, namely, the role of universals in human culture and, more specifically, their consequence for the theory of art. The very idea of universals would be rejected out of hand by many, yet the notion has enjoyed a renaissance in recent years, from the biological essentialism of Steven Pinker to the more sophisticated formulations of Maria Kronfeldner.[75] With regard to art, the philosopher Noel Carroll has argued:

> Although every known culture appears to possess art, it is improbable that this can be explained in terms of art's originating in a single location at one time and then being disseminated gradually therefrom. Rather, art seems to have sprung up independently in different locales and at different times, often apart from outside influences. But if the world-wide distribution of art cannot be explained by cultural diffusion, then the alternative that recommends itself is that art has its origins in something common to humankind, something bred in the bone, so to speak.[76]

Neurohumanities research is an attempt to take that notion of universality seriously, grounding the understanding of cultural practices in an understanding of human biology. The danger, however, is that grounding analysis in awareness that aesthetic experience is the culmination of a long process of biological evolution merely produces background noise of little consequence for the exploration of *particular* works of art. Many works may well dazzle viewers by challenging the biological constraints of vision and the ability of the brain to process complexity, by manipulating the perception of colour or the impact of scale on the embodied spectator's experience of the work. It may be, too, that the brains of our medieval forebears really were different. What still needs to be demonstrated, however, is how knowledge of the biological parameters of cognition and perception might *transform* our conception of the phenomenology of viewing, or our capacity for critical judgement of works of art. Exponents of neurohumanities thus need to be able to demonstrate how their work leads to what Gregory Bateson once described as a 'difference which makes a difference'.[77] Above all, this means articulating how their insights might challenge our assumptions about what it is we value in art and literature, and lead us to rethink our answers to the normative questions that motivate our engagement with them.

Notes

1 Orson S. Fowler, *Fowler's Practical Phrenology giving a Precise Elementary View of Phrenology* (New York: Fowler & Wells, 1850), p. 118.

2 Fowler concludes that phrenological analysis of Africans explains their 'proverbial politeness, urbanity, excellence as waiters, love of ornament, swelling and swaggering propensities, timidity, eye-service, fondness for and patience with children, and consequent excellence as nurses, garrulity, and sometimes eloquence, and superior musical passion and talents'. Fowler, *Hereditary Descent: Its Laws and Facts Applied to Human Improvement* (New York: Fowler & Wells, 1848), p. 134.

3 See, for example, Andrew Newberg, *Principles of Neurotheology* (Farnham: Routledge, 2010).

4 William Uttal, *The New Phrenology: The Limits of Localizing Cognitive Processes in the Brain* (Cambridge, MA: MIT Press, 2003). See, too, John Hyman, 'Art and Neuroscience', in Roman Frigg and Matthew Hunter (eds), *Beyond Mimesis and Convention: Representation in Art and Science* (Dordrecht: Springer, 2010), 245–61.

5 Joshua D. Greene, R. Brian Sommerville, Leigh E. Nystrom, John M. Darley and Jonathan D. Cohen, 'An fMRI Investigation of Emotional Engagement in Moral Judgment', *Science*, 293 (2001), 2105–8; Joshua D. Greene, Leigh E. Nystrom, Andrew D. Engell, John M. Darley and Jonathan D. Cohen, 'The Neural Bases of Cognitive Conflict and Control in Moral Judgment', *Neuron*, 44 (2004), 389–400; Gerald C. Cupchik, Oshin Vartanian, Adrian Crawley and David J. Mikulis, 'Viewing artworks: Contributions of cognitive control and perceptual facilitation to aesthetic experience', *Brain and Cognition*, 70 (2009), 84–91.

6 Richard Buxton, 'The Physics of Functional Magnetic Resonance Imaging (fMRI)', *Reports on Progress in Physics*, 76/9 (2013).

7 G. K. Aguirre, E. Zarahn and M. D'Esposito, 'The variability of human BOLD hemodynamic responses', *NeuroImage*, 8 (1998), 360–9.

8 Brea Chouinard, Carol Boliek and Jacqueline Cummine, 'How to Interpret and Critique Neuroimaging Research: A Tutorial on Use of Functional Magnetic Resonance Imaging in Clinical Populations', *American Journal of Speech-Language Pathology*, 25 (2009), 269–89 (p. 272).

9 Nikos Logothetis, 'Neurophysiological Investigation of the Basis of the fMRI Signal', *Nature*, 412 (2001), 150–7.

10 David J. Heeger and David Ress, 'What Does fMRI Tell Us about Neuronal Activity?' *Nature Review of Neuroscience*, 3/2 (2002), 142–51 (p. 146).

11 James Schummers, Hongbo Yu and Mriganka Sur, 'Tuned Responses of Astrocytes and their Influence on Hemodynamic Signals in the Visual Cortex', *Science*, 320 (2008), 1638–43.

12 Krish D. Singh, 'Which "Neural Activity" Do You Mean? fMRI, MEG, Oscillations and Neurotransmitters', *NeuroImage*, 62/2 (2012), 1121–30.

13 Yevgeniy Sirotin and Aniruddha Das, 'Anticipatory Haemodynamic Signals in Sensory Cortex Not Predicted by Local Neuronal Activity', *Nature*, 457 (2009), 475–9 (p. 478).

14 John Onians, *European Art: A Neuroarthistory* (New Haven, CT and London: Yale University Press, 2016), p. 249.

15 Stephan B. Hamann, Timothy D. Ely, John M. Hoffman and Clinton D. Kilts, 'Ecstasy and Agony: Activation of the Human Amygdala in Positive and Negative Emotion', *Psychological Science*, 13/2 (2002), 135–41.

16 See the articles cited in note 5.

17 Selim Berker, 'The Normative Insignificance of Neuroscience', *Philosophy and Public Affairs*, 37/4 (2009), 293–329 (p. 301).

18 Greg Miller, 'Neurobiology: The roots of morality', *Science*, 320 (2008), pp. 734–7.

19 Uttal, *The New Phrenology*, p. 154.

20 William Uttal, *Neural Theories of Mind* (New York: Psychology Press, 2005).

21 Amir Raz, 'From Neuroimaging to Tea Leaves in the Bottom of a Cup', in Suparna Choudhury and Jan Slaby (eds), *Critical Neuroscience: A Handbook of the Social and Cultural Contexts of Neuroscience* (Oxford: Wiley, 2012), pp. 266–7.

22 G. di Pellegrino, L. Fadiga, L. Fogassi, V. Gallese and G. Rizzolatti, 'Understanding motor events: a neurophysiological study', *Experimental Brain Research*, 91 (1992), 176–80.

23 Vittorio Gallese, 'The Inner Sense of Action: Agency and Motor Representations', *Journal of Consciousness Studies*, 7 (2000), 23–40 (p. 31).

24 David Freedberg and Vittorio Gallese, 'Motion, Emotion and Empathy in Esthetic Experience', *Trends in Cognitive Science*, 11/5 (2007), 197–203.

25 On this historic connection see Matthew Rampley, *The Seductions of Darwin* (University Park, PA: Penn State University Press, 2017), pp. 83–7.

26 Beatrice Sbriscia-Foretti, Cristina Berchio, David Freedberg, Vittorio Gallese and Maria Allesandra Umiltà, 'ERP Modulation during Observation of Abstract Paintings by Franz Kline', *Plos One*, 8/10 (2013), 1–12.

27 Lisa Zunshine, *Getting Inside Your Head: What Cognitive Science Can Tell Us about Popular Culture* (Baltimore, MD: Johns Hopkins University Press, 2012).

28 Zunshine, *Getting Inside Your Head*, p. 4. See, too, Christian Keysers, *The Empathic Brain: How the Discovery of Mirror Neurons Changes Our Understanding of Human Nature* (Amsterdam: Social Brain Press, 2011).

29 V. Gallese, L. Fadiga, L. Fogassi and G. Rizzolatti, 'Action recognition in the premotor cortex', *Brain*, 119/2 (1996), 593–609 (p. 606).

30 Gilbert Ryle, 'The Thinking of Thoughts: What is Le Penseur Doing?' in Ryle, *Collected Essays 1929–1968* (London: Routledge, 2009), pp. 494–510.

31 Leonardo Fogassi, 'Shared Meaning, Mirroring and Joint Action', in Michael A. Arbib (ed.), *Language, Music and the Brain: A Mysterious Relationship* (Cambridge, MA: MIT Press, 2013), p. 93.

32 Ibid.

33 Arnold H. Modell, *Imagination and the Meaningful Brain* (Cambridge, MA: MIT Press, 2003), p. 185.

34 Vico first posited the notion that the earliest stage of human culture was 'poetic' rather than 'logical', and Victorian anthropologists promulgated the idea based on their observations of the tendency of 'primitive' peoples to imitate the behaviour of European observers.

35 Merlin Donald, *Origin of the Modern Mind: Three Stages in the Evolution of Culture and Cognition* (London and Cambridge, MA: Harvard University Press, 1991).

36 See, for example, Michael Tomasello, *A Natural History of Human Thinking* (Cambridge, MA: Harvard University Press, 2014).

37 Steve Mithen, *The Singing Neanderthals: The Origins of Music, Language, Mind and Body* (Cambridge, MA: Harvard University Press, 2006).

38 See, for example, Amanda Seed and Michael Tomasello, 'Primate cognition', *Topics in Cognitive Science*, 2 (2010), 407–19; Richard Byrne and Lucy Bates, 'Primate social cognition: Uniquely primate, uniquely social, or just unique?' *Neuron*, 65 (2010), pp. 815–30.

39 Eric Saidel, 'Attributing Mental Representations to Animals', in Robert Lurz (ed.), *The Philosophy of Animal Minds* (Cambridge: Cambridge University Press, 2009), pp. 35–51.

40 Gregory Hickok, 'Eight Problems for the Mirror Neuron Theory of Action Understanding in Monkeys and Humans', *Journal of Cognitive Neuroscience*, 21/7 (2009), 1229–43.

41 Cupchik et al, 'Viewing artworks'.

42 Cupchik et al, 'Viewing artworks', p. 85.

43 Arthur Schopenhauer, *The World as Will and Representation* (Cambridge: Cambridge University Press, 2011), I, p. 201.

44 Ibid.

45 Ibid., p. 88.

46 Ibid., p. 90.

47 As Uttal argues, 'all our interpretations of mental processes are indirectly inferred from what are the presumed effects of some set of stimuli or from what we construe a given overt behaviour to signify about covert mental processes'. Uttal, *Neural Theories of Mind*, p. 256.

48 See, for example, Noel Carroll, 'Moderate Moralism', in *British Journal of Aesthetics*, 36 (1996), 223–37; Berys Gaut, 'The ethical criticism of art', in Jerome Levinson (ed.), *Aesthetics and Ethics: Essays at the Intersection* (Cambridge: Cambridge University Press, 2008), pp. 182–203.

49 M. Boccia, F. Nemmi, E. Tizzani, C. Guariglia, F. Ferlazzo, G. Galati and A. M. Giannini, 'Do You Like Arcimboldo? Esthetic Appreciation Modulates Brain Activity in Solving Perceptual Ambiguity', *Behavioural Brain Research*, 278 (2015), 147–54.

50 Ibid., p. 152.

51 James Elkins, *Why Are Our Pictures Puzzles? On the Modern Origins of Pictorial Complexity* (London: Routledge, 1999), pp. 123–54.

52 Herbert Lindenberger, 'Arts in the Brain: or, What might Neuroscience Tell Us?', in Frederick Aldama (ed.), *Toward a Cognitive Theory of Narrative Acts* (Austin, TX: University of Texas Press, 2010), pp. 13–35 (p. 23).

53 See, for example, Theodor Lipps, *Ästhetik: Psychologie des Schönen under der Kunst* (Hamburg and Leipzig: Voss, 1906).

54 Mayumi Taguchi, 'Imitating Christ as a Meme', *Postmedieval: a journal of medieval cultural studies*, 3/3 (2012), 315–27 (pp. 316–17).

55 Cinzia Di Dio, Emiliano Macaluso and Giacomo Rizzolatti, 'The Golden Beauty: Brain Response to Classical and Renaissance Sculptures', *PlosOne*, 11 (2007), 7.

56 Vered Aviv, 'What Does the Brain Tell us About Abstract Art?' *Frontiers in Human Neuroscience*, 8/85 (2014), p. 3.

57 India Morrison, 'Mirror Neurons and Cultural Transmission', in Maxim Stamenov and Vittorio Gallese (ed.), *Mirror Neurons and the Evolution of Brain and Language* (Amsterdam and Philadelphia: Benjamins, 2002), pp. 333–43 (p. 335).

58 See, for example, Semir Zeki, *Inner Vision: An Exploration of Art and the Brain* (Oxford: Oxford University Press, 1999); Anjan Chatterjee, *The Aesthetic Brain: How We Evolved to Desire Beauty and Art* (Oxford: Oxford University Press, 2015); G. Gabrielle Starr, *Feeling Beauty: The Neuroscience of Aesthetic Experience* (Cambridge, MA: MIT Press, 2015).

59 Semir Zeki, 'Clive Bell's "Significant Form" and the Neurobiology of Aesthetics', *Frontiers in Neuroscience*, 7 (2013), p. 730.

60 Semir Zeki, 'Neurobiology and the Humanities', *Neuron*, 84 (October 2014), 12–14 (p. 14).

61 See, for example, Steven Brown and Ellen Dissanayake, 'The Arts are More than Aesthetics: Neuroaesthetics as Narrow Aesthetics', in Martin Skov, Oshin Vartanian, Colin Martindale and Arnold Berleant (eds), *Neuroaesthetics* (New York: Routledge, 2009) pp. 43–57.

62 Pierre Bourdieu, *Distinction: A Social Critique of the Judgement of Taste*, trans. R. Nice (London: Routledge and Kegan Paul, 1984).

63 Kendall Walton, 'Categories of Art', *The Philosophical Review*, 79/3 (1970), 334–67.

64 William Seeley, 'Art, Meaning, and Aesthetics: The Case for a Cognitive Neuroscience of Art', in Joseph P. Huston, Marcos Nadal, Francisco Mora, Luigi F. Agnati and Camilo José Cela Conde (eds), *Art, Aesthetics and the Brain* (Oxford: Oxford University Press, 2015), pp. 19–39.

65 Seeley, 'Art, Meaning, and Aesthetics', p. 31.

66 As David Davies notes, 'where a normative question is raised as to how we should proceed in a given kind of endeavour, and where the alternatives between which we are asked to choose represent alternatives represent alternatives which are clearly "live" for us in the sense that they involve the exercise of capacities that we demonstrably possess, the issue cannot be resolved by citing empirical research on the psychological mechanisms involved in one of the alternatives'. Davies, 'This is Your Brain on Art', in Greg Currie, Matthew Kieran, Aaron Meskin and Jon Robson (eds), *Aesthetics and the Sciences of Mind* (Oxford: Oxford University Press, 2018), pp. 57–74 (p. 63).

67 See, for example, Martin Hartman, 'Against First Nature: Critical Theory and Neuroscience', in Suparna Choudhury and Jan Slaby (eds), *Critical Neuroscience: A Handbook of the Social and Cultural Contexts of Neuroscience* (Oxford: Wiley, 2012), pp. 67–84; Roger Cooter, 'Neural Veils and the Will to Historical Critique: Why Historians of Science Need to Take the Neuro-Turn Seriously', *Isis*, 105/1 (2014), pp. 145–54.

68 Helmut Leder, Benno Belke, Andries Oeberst and Dorothee Augustin, 'A model of aesthetic appreciation and aesthetic judgments', *British Journal of Psychology*, 95 (2004), 489–508 (p. 496).

69 Michael Platt and Camillo Padoa-Scioppa, 'Neuronal Representations of Value', in Paul W. Glimcher, Colin F.Camerer, Ernst Fehr and Russell A. Poldrack (eds), *Neuroeconomics: Decision Making and the Brain* (London: Elsevier Academic Press, 2009), pp. 441–62 (p. 459).

70 David Davies, 'This is Your Brain on Art', in Currie et al, *Aesthetics and the Sciences of Mind*, p. 65.

71 Herbert Lindenberger, 'Arts in the Brain', p. 22.

72 Ibid., p. 26.

73 Edward O. Wilson, *Consilience: The Unity of Knowledge* (New York: Albert Knopf, 1998), p. 291.

[74] See, for example, Harvey J. Graff, *Undisciplining Knowledge: Interdisciplinarity in the Twentieth Century* (Baltimore, MD: Johns Hopkins University Press, 2015), especially 'The Problem of Interdisciplinarity in Theory and Practice over Time' (pp. 1–19).

[75] Steven Pinker, *The Blank Slate: The Modern Denial of Human Nature* (Harmondsworth: Penguin, 2003); Maria Kronfeldner, *What's Left of Human Nature: A Post-Essentialist, Pluralist and Interactive Account of a Contested Concept* (Cambridge, MA: MIT Press, 2018).

[76] Noel Carroll, 'Art and Human Nature', *Journal of Aesthetics and Art Criticism*, 62/2 (2004), 95–107 (p. 95).

[77] Gregory Bateson, *Steps to an Ecology of Mind* (Northvale, NJ: Jason Aronson, 1987), p. 321.

Select Bibliography

Aviv, Vered, 'What Does the Brain Tell us About Abstract Art?', *Frontiers in Human Neuroscience*, 8/85 (2014), *https://doi.org/10.3389/fnhum.2014.00085.*

Berker, Selim, 'The Normative Insignificance of Neuroscience', *Philosophy and Public Affairs*, 37/4 (2009), 293–329.

Brown, Steven and Ellen Dissanayake, 'The Arts are More than Aesthetics: Neuroaesthetics as Narrow Aesthetics', in Martin Skov, Oshin Vartanian, Colin Martindale and Arnold Berleant (eds), *Neuroaesthetics* (New York: Routledge, 2009), pp. 43–57.

Chatterjee, Anjan, *The Aesthetic Brain: How We Evolved to Desire Beauty and Art* (Oxford: Oxford University Press, 2015).

Davies, David, 'This is Your Brain on Art', in Greg Currie, Matthew Kieran, Aaron Meskin and Jon Robson (eds), *Aesthetics and the Sciences of Mind* (Oxford: Oxford University Press, 2018), pp. 57–74.

Donald, Merlin, *Origin of the Modern Mind: Three Stages in the Evolution of Culture and Cognition* (London and Cambridge MA: Harvard University Press, 1991).

Elkins, James, *Why Are Our Pictures Puzzles? On the Modern Origins of Pictorial Complexity* (London: Routledge, 1999).

Freedberg, David and Vittorio Gallese, 'Motion, Emotion and Empathy in Esthetic Experience', *Trends in Cognitive Science*, 11/5 (2007), 197–203.

Graff, Harvey J., *Undisciplining Knowledge: Interdisciplinarity in the Twentieth Century* (Baltimore, MD: Johns Hopkins University Press, 2015).

Keysers, Christian, *The Empathic Brain: How the Discovery of Mirror Neurons Changes Our Understanding of Human Nature* (Amsterdam: Social Brain Press, 2011).

Kronfeldner, Maria, *What's Left of Human Nature: A Post-Essentialist, Pluralist and Interactive Account of a Contested Concept* (Cambridge, MA: MIT Press, 2018).

Mithen, Steve, *The Singing Neanderthals: The Origins of Music, Language, Mind and Body* (Cambridge, MA: Harvard University Press, 2006).

Modell, Arnold H., *Imagination and the Meaningful Brain* (Cambridge, MA: MIT Press, 2003).

Newberg, Andrew, *Principles of Neurotheology* (Farnham: Routledge, 2010).

Onians, John, *European Art: A Neuroarthistory* (New Haven, CT and London: Yale University Press, 2016).

Pinker, Steven, *The Blank Slate: The Modern Denial of Human Nature* (Harmondsworth: Penguin, 2003).

Rampley, Matthew, *The Seductions of Darwin* (University Park, PA: Penn State University Press, 2017).

Schopenhauer, Arthur, *The World as Will and Representation* (Cambridge: Cambridge University Press, 2011).

Starr, G. Gabrielle, *Feeling Beauty: The Neuroscience of Aesthetic Experience* (Cambridge, MA: MIT Press, 2015).

Uttal, William, *Neural Theories of Mind* (New York: Psychology Press, 2005).

Zeki, Semir, *Inner Vision: An Exploration of Art and the Brain* (Oxford: Oxford University Press, 1999).

Zunshine, Lisa, *Getting Inside Your Head: What Cognitive Science Can Tell Us about Popular Culture* (Baltimore, MD: Johns Hopkins University Press, 2012).

II

Histories of Neuroscience, Psychology and Mental Illness

4

Neuroscience and the Dialectics of History

DANIEL LORD SMAIL

History and neuroscience make strange bedfellows. The past cannot easily offer neuroscientists a set of hypotheses or research questions to be tested via brain imaging experiments. Historians, in turn, have been disinclined (and for good reason) to deal with behavioural or psychological patterns that have the appearance of being universal or hard-wired. In addition, there are problems of relevance, for on what grounds can we legitimately borrow the findings of a science based largely on the study of sea slugs and mice and the like, and project those findings willy-nilly onto the study of the Middle Ages, or indeed any era in the human past? Finally, neuroscience may have something to offer fields that focus on the present day: what goes on in the nervous systems of people who are shopping or dancing or engaging in devotional exercises, for example, or whether music contributes to healing.[1] But how can any study of the brain and the nervous system be drawn into explanations about how and why things have *changed*, the question at the heart of the historical enterprise?[2]

In this contribution, I offer an architecture of historical understanding that may allow us to bring aspects of neuroscience into the conversations we have about change in the human past. I borrow much of this architecture from the field of environmental history, though I will place certain features of the human brain–body system in the role that 'nature' typically plays in environmental history. The key feature of the environmental approach is that it does not treat either humans or the environment as the sovereign partner in the relationship; the model does not assume a simple Aristotelian pattern of cause-and-effect, where influence flows from a prime mover toward an object that is moved. Instead, following the systems approach of Actor-Network Theory and fields such as the New Materialism, which are fundamentally related to the bodies of theory introduced very effectively in Victoria Blud's chapter in this volume, the patterns of influence are understood to be cross-cutting, mutual, and contingent.[3] Rather than offering a solipsistic history, as if humanity is the only agent in creating change, the environmental approach assumes that change emerges from a complex relationship between humans and something else, in this case the environment.

But what, exactly, is 'the environment'? We can, in a narrow sense, think of the environment as nature, in the form of water, climate, sources of energy and disease. Yet it does not violate the architecture of the approach to treat something other than nature as the partner in the relationship. By way of example, it has become possible to argue that human society and sociability have constituted an important element of the environment in which humanity itself has evolved. This argument has been developed most fully in the literature on the social intelligence hypothesis, which suggests that the human brain developed its qualities not simply in response to nature – the dangers of predation; the difficulty of the hunt; the challenge of living in the changeable climate of the Pleistocene – but also in response to other humans.[4] To navigate the complex world of human sociability, early hominins had to learn how to read and infer the intentions of others so as to build support groups or coalitions.[5] The argument also pertains to the modern world of the last five or ten thousand years, where we continue to respond to a constantly changing social niche through adaptations that are cultural in nature or take the form of changes in physical and psychological phenotypes, for example through epigenetic or developmental down-regulation of testosterone.[6]

Given the fact that the 'environment' in environmental history does not have to consist of nature, it takes just a small leap of the imagination to treat our own nervous system as an adaptive environment that has subtly shaped evolving patterns of human culture or human society. At first blush, this sounds like a very peculiar thing to say, but it is not hard to come up with examples that illustrate how a quality of the human nervous system helps explain an emergent feature of human culture. Most historical societies, for example, have found ways to incorporate psychoactive substances – alcohol, qat, opium, marijuana, coca, peyote, and so on – into their rituals or their marketplaces. By virtue of their ability to stimulate or alter the production of neurotransmitters such as dopamine or serotonin, these substances help create distinctive cultural forms, such as the religious trance, that otherwise would not exist in the quite the same way.[7] Neural pathways also help explain why pets are cute and why music has a beat, among many other things. The point that must be borne in mind here is that the science of the nervous system cannot explain the particular details of historical trends. It cannot explain why, for example, the United States has criminalised marijuana, cocaine and other drugs, but has not criminalised nicotine, alcohol, or for that matter other addictive practices like Facebook and shopping.[8] Trends like this are the result of the accidents of history; they cannot be explained by cognitive neuroscience. The nervous system offers a context in which patterns or practices *can* evolve, but it does not insist that those patterns *must* evolve, nor does it guarantee that patterns will endure once they *have* evolved. This is the architecture of a neurohistorical approach to the past.[9] It is an architecture of explanation that abandons the idea of a transfer of sovereignty from nature to culture that is so dominant in history, the humanities, and some of the social sciences like cultural anthropology. It offers instead a model where the nervous system itself is involved in a complex, never-ending dialectic with the cultural formations of the human past, and where the distinction between biology and culture collapses.[10]

In the first section of this chapter, I seek to elaborate on this model by exploring some of the evolutionary principles that help explain how it works, including the principle of coevolution and the idea of a niche. These concepts, borrowed from evolutionary theory, are rather rudimentary components of much larger theoretical constructs, namely, the actor networks, entanglements or meshworks that have figured in recent literature.[11] A key feature of the model is that it does not treat the nervous system of any individual as hard-wired or genetically determined. Virtually no one in the neurosciences these days understands the brain–body system in the simple manner once proposed by pop sociobiology and evolutionary psychology. Part of the reason for this lies in the failure of the human genome project to find a one-to-one relationship between genes and phenotypic traits, at least where behavioural patterns are concerned. This, it turns out, was an immensely productive failure. Gene expression is far more complicated and far more interesting than once imagined, in part because it is subject to developmental and epigenetic influences.[12] The point here is that a neurohistorical model assumes that the nervous system, consisting of synapses and receptors, is like any ecosystem: it can be shaped by the organisms that inhabit it. In practical terms, this means that individual or cultural circumstances help determine features of the practical architecture of the nervous system itself. Translated into history, this means that in the same way that there is a continuous dialectic of influence between humans and their natural environment, so too is there a dialectic of influence between humans and their own nervous systems.

Abstract reasoning, all too often, is an obstacle to understanding. For this reason, I seek to develop in the second part of this essay a brief case study based on the neurobiology of stress, which draws on some of my own work on the patterns of violence in later medieval Europe.[13] Like most neurobiological states, stress is not something we can explore directly via the historical record: we cannot test the saliva or urine of historical actors for the presence of stress hormones, nor can we measure the activity of stress receptors in the hippocampus. This is not even remotely a problem for the practice of history. No historian ever assumes that facts emerge in a simple and uncomplicated way from the record of the past. Historical epistemology is necessarily inferential and inductive; it proceeds by way of strategic comparison and plausible supposition. At their best, historical arguments are based on a consilience of observations drawn from independent bodies of evidence. Historical claims are never assumed to be true; instead, corroborating research allows claims to grow ever more robust and plausible. Thus, although we cannot 'see' stress hormones in the historical record, we can plausibly infer the presence of stress in situations involving violence, humiliation and poverty. Stress is interesting as a historical subject because it allows us to write a human history framed in the context of an ongoing dialectic between the stress-response system on the one hand and human institutions, practices and patterns of behaviour on the other.

The Coevolution of Culture and the Brain–Body System

The dialectical pattern characteristic of environmental history is not unique to that field, for the philosophy of dialectical systems has a deep pedigree within the philosophy of history as theorised by Hegel and Marx. The work of Hegel, who did so much both to clarify and to obfuscate the practice of history, is of special relevance here, in part because of the paradoxes it generates. On the one hand, the Hegelian philosophy of history was instrumental in dividing the realm of biology from the realm of history.[14] Biology, to Hegel, could not describe a historical process of change; it described instead the never-ending cycle of daily existence, revolving around birth, death and the search for food. History, in the Hegelian view, described a non-cyclical or directional pattern of time, in which the presence of a political order, the State, offered humanity a release from the sterile cycling of the biological condition. The State allowed humans to transcend nature by softening and taming it. The memory of the past, that is to say historiography, created the possibility of a moral system, since the desire to be remembered well by the historians of the future encouraged rulers to be beneficent.

The idea that history was founded on a break with nature cast a very long shadow over the practice of history. In the wake of the Darwinian revolution, this break took on special significance. If humans were once animals, after all, they must have once lived in a biological and therefore historyless condition. 'The beast lives ahistorically', wrote Nietzsche, thereby putting his finger on the very nub of the paradox of deep human time – for if humans were beasts and lived without history, where did history come from?[15] And when did it start? By the 1930s, the answer to this conundrum had become clear: history sprang into being during the Neolithic revolution, when some humans, by virtue of the invention of agriculture, civilisation and writing, escaped the grip of nature and embarked upon a new path, the path that Hegel, a century earlier, had described as the path of the State. If this story has a familiar ring to it, that is because it is simply the secular transposition of a story long told by Judeo-Christian sacred history, where history began with the expulsion from Eden.

Hegel, like Leopold von Ranke, Henry Sumner Maine, and Oswald Spengler after him, was partly responsible for the belief that human history can be divided into a historyless period and a period of history. This school of historical philosophy did not simply project historylessness onto the deep past of human existence. To the European observers of the nineteenth century, historylessness seemed to be all around them, not just in the so-called primitive tribes but also in great civilisations like China that, to Europeans, never seemed to be going anywhere. Only Europe, in European historiography of the nineteenth century, was pregnant with historicity.

The paradoxical feature of Hegel is this: not only did he help create the original break in the fabric of history, he also conceived of a philosophy of historical change that now makes it possible to transcend that break. Historical change, to Hegel, is a dialectical process. Absent in nature (or so he thought), the dialectical pattern becomes activated by the presence of the State, and its presence explains the directionality and ceaseless change that marks historical societies. In Hegel's day, of course, Charles Darwin and A. R. Wallace had not yet published their theory of natural selection. Writing when he did, Hegel could not know that natural history, like human history, is thick with dialectics. This is the pattern we now call Darwinian evolution.

As a biological concept, Hegelian dialectics maps well onto a process that some biologists call *coevolution.*[16] The idea of coevolution is that organisms do not evolve in response to a hard and unyielding set of selection pressures. Instead, there is always some sort of dialogue between an organism and its environment. In Hegel's philosophical vocabulary, this was the dialogue between a thesis and its antithesis, but that is just an abstract way of describing the dialogue between an organism and another organism, an organism and its niche, and even between an organism and its own genes.

Coevolutionary patterns share some unusual or interesting features. Some herbivores, for example, can get locked into spiralling relationships with the plants on which they feed, for as plants gain toxins to avoid being eaten, the animal or insect develops the capacity to metabolise those toxins. The competitive one-upping of these coevolutionary relationships describes well how the dyad can go haring off in wild directions. Relative to each other, for example, the cheetah, like its ancestors, has always been just a tiny bit faster than the gazelle or the pronghorn and their ancestors. That ratio, arguably, has not changed over the long evolutionary relationship between the species involved. But even though cheetahs and gazelles stand still in their relationship to one another, both species have become spectacularly swift relative to *other* animals. In his path-breaking 1973 article, Leigh van Valen described this as the 'Red Queen' hypothesis, where Alice and the Red Queen dance furiously but never go anywhere.[17] Following a different metaphor, Richard Dawkins and J. R. Krebs described these evolutionary processes as a kind of 'arms race', where an arms build-up by one party entails a similar build-up by the opponent.[18] Where historical explanation is concerned, what is significant about the evolutionary arms-race is the way in which it describes a trend that seems to spiral off in wild new directions. This is apt description for how historians have understood the dramatic patterns of historical change in the wake of revolutions like the Neolithic Revolution, the Scientific Revolution, the French Revolution, and so on.

Coevolutionary relationships do not have to be antagonistic arms-races. Where human history is concerned, perhaps the most obvious example is offered by the agricultural transition starting some 10,000 years ago. It used to be thought that humans domesticated plants and animals, turning them to do their bidding and creating new breeds or strains in the process. Agriculture, however, is now understood as a process of mutual domestication, with all parties concerned acting as equal partners in a relationship that changed humans just as much as it changed plants and animals.[19]

Recently, the principle of coevolution has been extended to the niche itself, though in a sense this was always understood to be the case.[20] Organisms are adapted not to the entirety of an ecosystem but instead to one particular corner, that is to say a niche. This stands to reason: a snake is largely invisible to an elephant, and is far less entangled in the life of an elephant than, say, an acacia tree. Thus, the genus *Homo* was adapted to exploit a foraging, scavenging and hunting niche that came into being in the savannahs of East Africa with the onset of the drier conditions of the early Pleistocene around 2.6 million years ago. Niches have a number of interesting properties. Among them is the fact that there are only a limited number of solutions to the challenges inherent in exploiting the resources and evading the predators within a given niche. This constraint is what lies behind the principle of convergence, namely, the pattern whereby the phenotypes of plants and animals that inhabit similar niches can converge toward similar solutions.[21] Convergence explains why both the placental and marsupial lineages produced a sabre-toothed cat with teeth designed to kill large prey through puncture wounds that cause them to bleed to death, and why the niche occupied by small mammalian insectivores, as found in both Madagascar and England, has produced two animals, the tenrec and the hedgehog, that are nearly identical in body plan and behaviour despite being separated by tens of millions of years of evolutionary time.

Older models of Darwinian evolution imagined that organisms typically follow a step behind changes in their ecological niches. Thus, human evolution *followed* the pattern of climate change that made the East African savannahs. In a vivid recent example, elephants in certain parts of Africa are now increasingly likely to be born without tusks, a trait that probably developed in response to predation by human ivory hunters.[22] The principle of niche construction, however, suggests that organisms do not simply lie passively within their niche. Instead, to greater or lesser degrees, they are continuously engaged in constructing their own niche. In her study of sheep-raising in colonial Mexico, the environmental historian Eleanor Melville described a process whereby the action of millions of tiny hoofs over a period of decades gradually compacted the soil and removed texture, thus discouraging water retention and fundamentally changing an agrarian landscape to a landscape consisting of an eroded scrubland suitable only for pasture.[23] In the same way that there is a coevolutionary dialogue between two organisms, so too is there a dialogue between an organism and its niche. This is, in fact, the best way to think about the Neolithic transition: as humans found ways to extract calories, power, fibres and a range of secondary products from the plants and animals in their environment, they transformed the niche they occupied, but at the same time were transformed in response to the new niche.

In his seminal early study of patterns of coevolution in the human past, William Durham argued that genes and culture can get tangled up in a coevolutionary relationship.[24] The habit of drinking fresh milk in a few early pastoral societies, to take the best known example, created a selection pressure that favoured the retention into adulthood of the ability to digest milk sugar. As the necessary alleles spread in central Europe, Africa, and perhaps other milk-drinking areas, dietary patterns were changed. Selection pressures generated by cultural changes, in other words, can be felt in the genome, even over relatively short spans of time. Much the same pattern works for features of the brain and the nervous system, though in this case we are not necessarily dealing with genetic changes. The genotype builds neurons and neurons create synapses, and thus the basic architecture of the systems like the stress-response system and the reward system are sketched out by the genome. But epigenetic patterns and developmental experiences determine how these systems actually work in practice by creating, maintaining and in some cases destroying receptors and synapses.

The epigenetic revolution of the last two decades allows us to abandon the idea that in the relationship between culture and the brain, one of the two must be sovereign. Pop sociobiology and certain fields of evolutionary psychology (discussed in this volume by Silva) have insisted that cognitive modules, designed by natural selection, are sovereign in their ability to define behavioural traits. Anthropology and history, in contrast, have insisted that culture is sovereign. Yet despite the illusion of antagonism, these two stances are two halves of the same coin. They share the Hegelian supposition that biology and culture can be placed in an imaginary historical timeline where biology was in the past and culture in the present. Evolutionary psychologists and culturalists differ only on the issue of whether behavioural sovereignty has been handed off from biology to culture. The insights of epigenetics allow us to transcend this utterly sterile debate by treating the nervous system and culture as equal partners in an ongoing and never-ending coevolutionary relationship.

Violence and Chronic Stress in Medieval Europe

To explore how this dialectical model might work in practice, let us consider the neurobiology of stress. As Robert Sapolsky, the leading figure in the study of stress, has pointed out, stress is good for you in limited doses.[25] It primes the system to respond quickly and efficiently to temporary or sudden challenges. Stress generates a number of adaptive responses in the body, ranging from dilated eyes and elevated heart rate to loss of appetite and sexual desire.

As the contributions by Wendy Turner and Juliana Dresvina in this volume point out, however, chronic stress is clearly bad for you, and the effects of chronic stress can begin to erode the ability of the nervous system to handle stress. For this reason, stress works well as a social or political tool. Among certain baboons, for example, dominant females systematically terrorise their subordinates to ensure unfettered access to resources, and one of the effects of stress is that the fertility of lower-ranking females is reduced or diverted toward the production of male offspring who will not compete with the offspring of dominant females. Stress, in other words, is a neurobiological correlate of social rank or position. The experience of stress also implicates the reward system. Consider, in this vein, an experiment involving mice, an animal that shares the stress-response system common to all mammals.[26] If a mouse is handicapped in such a way as to be the loser in a series of fights with other mice, it enters a condition of stress marked by chronically high levels of stress hormones. The mouse loses initiative and becomes listless and compliant.[27] Mice who suffer repeated social defeat begin to self-medicate themselves with cocaine, a dopamine agonist, at a higher rate than other mice. Stress, finally, is heritable in an oddly Lamarckian way that has considerable implications for history. Experiments with rats conducted by Michael Meaney and his associates have shown than the maternal licking of pups leads to a greater density of stress receptors in the hippocampus, which in turn allows the young rats to handle stress more easily.[28] If rat pups are not licked, their ability to handle stress is reduced; what is more, female rats who were not cared for as pups are less likely to lick their own offspring, leading to several generations in which a situation similar to chronic stress is transmitted epigenetically from mother to offspring.

As this rapid survey suggests, the stress-response system is one of many candidates for the dialectical model of neurohistory sketched out above. Because chronic stress can have social or political consequences, it is easy to imagine how human behavioural patterns could have evolved, albeit unconsciously, in ways that allowed powerful or dominant individuals or institutions to exploit the latent quality of chronic stress. The stress-response system, in other words, acts as a niche in which human patterns and institutions take shape. At the same time, the stress-response system has a significant degree of plasticity – not in its structure, but in the way in which it works in given individuals. That plasticity can produce a pattern whereby stress can be an inherited feature of certain class or status groups, which may help explain a pattern that figures like Marx and Gramsci sought to explain through ideas such as false consciousness and hegemony. Chronic stress cannot explain why peasants, workers and revolutionaries have, on occasion, chosen to rebel against the systems that have oppressed them, but it might help explain why they have done so less often than the conditions of their abuse would have suggested. In the example of the mice that experience social defeat, note that the self-medication with a dopamine agonist, although seen as a symptom of defeat by the scientists who have conducted the studies, could just as well be seen as a symptom of resistance.

Let me now bring the neurobiology of stress to bear on patterns of violence in Europe during the later Middle Ages, the period that is the subject of much of my own research. Violence is interesting in part because violence can be stressful to the victims; arguably, this is one of the reasons that violence has proven to be so adaptive for humans, other primates, and other animals. Violence as a stress-delivery system works well if it inflicts non-lethal and humiliating violence on the bodies of others, or if it acts in a context of publicity that allows the message to be conveyed to a wider audience. Far from being irrational, in other words, violence is adaptive by virtue of the stress it induces. Surveying the primatological literature, for example, Randolph Roth has pointed out that the chronic stress to which lower-ranking male chimpanzees are often subjected lowers their testosterone level and discourages them from challenging the position of higher-ranking chimpanzees.[29]

In the records from later medieval Europe, violence can take many different forms.[30] One omnipresent form is the violence inflicted by one person on another. Some of this violence shows up in contests sparked by a sense of honour or justice; such fights often lead to bloodshed, insults and threats. Other violent behaviours include spousal abuse, child-beating, or the abuse of servants and slaves. A second type is the violence that sovereign bodies, including lords, kings, and city-states, chose to inflict upon their subjects. This violence takes the form of public spectacles, such as humiliating punishments and public executions arising from crime, treason, witchcraft, and the like. Even more common if less spectacular are spectacles of private debt collection supervised by the courts of law; these spectacles sometimes involved shaming rituals and also countless acts of highly publicised and potentially violent seizures of goods from the households of debtors.[31]

Relatively uncommon before 1250 or 1300, state-on-subject violence begins to accelerate in the fourteenth and fifteenth centuries, and remains a significant feature of the European scene until the eighteenth century and beyond, when the flow of violence and stress in European states starts to take on new qualities. We can write this history in a conventional Weberian way. That is to say, we can argue that newly emerging states were seeking to develop a monopoly on the exercise of coercive force, and sought to criminalise illicit forms of person-on-person violence in the process. Violence, according to this argument, is permitted only in contexts like sports, where it is sanctioned by the state.[32] The history of violence has long been plotted as a history of declining rates of homicide and everyday acts of aggression, where the state and the civil or courtly institutions that it fosters play a major role in the 'civilising' of a violent instinct. This argument tends to assume that violence is a feature of humanity's evolved psychology. In the recent work of Steven Pinker, for example, violence, like a continental plate in a subduction zone, has largely disappeared underneath the weight of the Leviathan and the emergence of reason or self-control.[33] Like volcanoes or hot water springs, it might occasionally punch through the weight of the plate that lies atop it, but otherwise person-on-person violence has been largely repressed.

There is a lot to be said for this model, since it provides a relatively parsimonious explanation for what appears to have been a general per capita decline in death by violence in Western Europe and the United States. It certainly conforms to a folk reason according to which people in the largely ungoverned Middle Ages were violent and grew progressively less violent over the ensuing centuries. Once we look at violence using some of the perspectives of neuroscience, however, things begin to look a little different.[34]

To begin with, let us consider the nature of testosterone. The history of violence has assumed a steady supply of testosterone, which is one of the hormones that can be associated with violence.[35] But supposing that the production of testosterone itself has been 'down-regulated' or diminished in societies that have less violence? This is at least theoretically possible. Roth has already pointed out that stress might play a role in this, since stress can lead to the down-regulation of testosterone production in socially subordinate chimpanzees.[36] Another study has shown that testosterone production is typically down-regulated in human males who engage in three or more hours of care-giving per day.[37] This process, which is described in the study as a life-cycle issue, is also a historical or cultural one, since the down-regulation of testosterone does not happen automatically with fatherhood. It depends, instead, on the prior existence of a family and work environment that allows or promotes regular contact with infants. The genotype certainly defines the parameters of testosterone production, and it may define a probability spectrum in the testosterone phenotype of any given male, but the actual phenotype is determined in large part by developmental or epigenetic circumstances and by cultural patterns. To put this differently, it is uninteresting to say that males are predisposed to violence if the neurobiological hardware for violence is shaped to a large degree by cultural or historical circumstances.

What this emerging literature suggests is that we ought to look for the decline of violence not just in the rise of state-level policing and crime control but also in other institutional factors, including patterns of chronic stress or social defeat and, perhaps more positively, in transformations in family forms and work patterns that have encouraged greater paternal care-giving. Other potential factors may well come to light, and we can look to see whether they have any historical correlates.

How, then, might we reinterpret the history of violence in later medieval and early modern Europe through the perspectives of the neurobiology of stress? As noted above, we have a strong inclination to contrast person-on-person violence with state-on-person violence, and to assume that the latter emerged only for the purpose of restraining the former. But we can think of this process without the assumption that states are benevolent. In light of the neurobiology of stress, it is possible to think of states as organisations that have an interest in controlling the circulation of stress in society. States criminalised illicit violence, in this view, not for the stated purposes of preventing the sinful or uncivil shedding of blood, but instead to develop a monopoly on the production and distribution of stress in European society. Person-on-person violence, in this model, was interpreted by the new authority figures as an illicit 'stress transaction' that needed to be repressed or taxed via criminal fines. These stress transactions, in other words, were not criminalised because states had an interest in eliminating violence and stress. Far from it: this is exactly the period during which states were perfecting their own systems for delivering stress, in the form of pillories, shaming rituals, public spectacles, and, as I have argued elsewhere, the institutional shaming and humiliation of debtors.[38] Where debt is concerned, the stress transaction still involves two individuals, a creditor and a debtor, but state sovereignty arises from the fact that the transaction necessarily flowed through the civil courts, a medium controlled by the state. The state profited monetarily from the transaction, and also benefited from the monopoly it was developing on the flow of stress in human societies.

Writing about the dialectical process, Hegel supposed that every thesis generated its own antithesis. In this case, it is possible to imagine the antithesis to an emerging state desire to develop a monopoly on the circulation of stress in European society. In our analyses of violence, we tend to sympathise with the victims, and lose sight of the fact that violence is a major element of the tournament of prestige where the humiliations inflicted on the losers are counter-balanced by the pleasures and satisfactions experienced by the winners. State-level restrictions on person-on-person violence motivated by concerns for honour and justice, thus, arguably reduced a significant source of pleasure and self-satisfaction. In this light, one of the most striking features of early modern and modern Europe has been the development of a significant array of new dopamine agonists, ranging from psychopharmacological substances to cultural practices such as theatre, music and consumption. Modern global capitalism, in a sense, can be seen as an enormous dopamine-delivery system. It may be plausible to suggest that when state-level restrictions reduced the prevalence of violence-based tournaments of prestige, citizen-subjects found new sources of reward, and shifted their tournaments of prestige into the realm of competitive consumption and taste.

This, of course, is a vague and insubstantial set of arguments. The value of this sketch, if any, lies in its potential to suggest new research questions. Rather than a vision based on the civilisation of manners and the decline of violence, this neurohistorical perspective suggests a transformation in the ways in which prestige and stress were and are transacted in European societies. Historians, in general, like to generate grand narrative structures, such as 'the birth of Western Civilisation,' 'the rise of the state', 'the creation of patriarchy' or 'the decline of violence'. These narratives are neither true nor false; they are useful only because they help to organise historical work. With any given narrative, you are either for it or against it, and that choice determines how you, as a historian, approach your teaching and your research. The complex history of stress, when viewed from a deep historical perspective, is at least as interesting as any of the usual narratives. Like any deep historical narrative (and unlike conventional historical narratives), the dialectical history of stress does not have a beginning or an end. Put differently, it is not a history defined by the *telos* – civilisation; the state; the patriarchal condition; a peaceful utopia – toward which it is heading. In *1984*, George Orwell hinted at just such a *telos*, where history ends with a system of government that has perfected a pattern of governance based on the exploitation of the stress-response system.[39] Perhaps it is too optimistic to say that this cannot happen, but for now, we can proceed from the assumption that the future is probably not so grim.

Notes

1 Harvey Whitehouse, *Mind and Religion: Psychological and Cognitive Foundations of Religiosity* (Walnut Creek, CA: AltaMira Press, 2005); Aniruddh D. Patel, *Music, Language, and the Brain* (Oxford: Oxford University Press, 2007); Michael Kyrios et al., 'Behavioral Neuroscience of Buying-Shopping Disorder: A Review', *Current Behavioral Neuroscience Reports*, 5/4 (1 December 2018), 263–70, *https://doi.org/10.1007/s40473-018-0165-6.*

2 With respect to emotions, see the important observations on this point by Barbara H. Rosenwein, 'Problems and Methods in the History of Emotions', *Passions in Context: International Journal for the History and Theory of Emotions*, 1 (2010); Jan Plamper, *The History of Emotions: An Introduction*, trans. Keith Tribe (Oxford: Oxford University Press, 2015).

3 Bruno Latour, *Reassembling the Social: An Introduction to Actor-Network-Theory* (Oxford: Oxford University Press, 2005); Diana H. Coole and Samantha Frost (eds), *New Materialisms: Ontology, Agency, and Politics* (Durham, NC and London: Duke University Press, 2010); Timothy LeCain, *The Matter of History: How Things Create the Past* (Cambridge: Cambridge University Press, 2017).

4 Richard W. Byrne and Andrew Whiten, *Machiavellian Intelligence: Social Expertise and the Evolution of Intellect in Monkeys, Apes, and Humans*, Oxford Science Publications (Oxford and New York: Clarendon Press and Oxford University Press, 1988); Daniel Goleman, *Social Intelligence: The New Science of Human Relationships* (New York: Bantam Books, 2006).

5 R. I. M. Dunbar, *Grooming, Gossip and the Evolution of Language* (London and Boston: Faber & Faber, 1996); Sarah Blaffer Hrdy, 'Evolutionary Context of Human Development: The

Cooperative Breeding Model', in Catherine A. Salmon and Todd K. Shackleford (eds), *Family Relationships: An evolutionary Perspective* (Oxford: Oxford University Press, 2008), pp. 39–68; Sarah Blaffer Hrdy, *Mothers and Others: The Evolutionary Origins of Mutual Understanding* (Cambridge, MA: The Belknap Press of Harvard University Press, 2009).

6 Richard W. Wrangham, *Demonic Males: Apes and the Origins of Human Violence* (Boston: Houghton Mifflin, 1996); Clark Spencer Larsen, *Bioarchaeology: Interpreting Behavior from the Human Skeleton*, Cambridge Studies in Biological Anthropology 21 (New York: Cambridge University Press, 1997); Gregory Cochran and Henry Harpending, *The 10,000 Year Explosion: How Civilization Accelerated Human Evolution* (New York: Basic Books, 2009).

7 Harvey Whitehouse and Luther H. Martin, *Theorizing Religions Past: Archaeology, History, and Cognition, Cognitive Science of Religion Series* (Walnut Creek, CA and Lanham, MD: AltaMira Press, 2004).

8 A point that has been addressed by Hermann Herlinghaus, 'From Transatlantic Histories of "Intoxication" to a Hemispheric "War on Affect": Paradoxes Unbound', in Melissa Bailar (ed.), *Emerging Disciplines: Shaping New Fields of Scholarly Inquiry in and beyond the Humanities* (2010), *http://cnx.org/content/m34250/1.4/*.

9 For some recent overviews, see Jeremy T. Burman, 'Bringing the Brain into History: Behind Hunt's and Smail's Appeals to Neurohistory', in Cristian Tileagă and Jovan Byford (eds), *Psychology and History: Interdisciplinary Explorations* (Cambridge: Cambridge University Press, 2014), pp. 64–82; Rob Boddice, 'Neurohistory', in Marek Tamm and Peter Burke (eds), *Debating New Approaches to History* (London and New York: Bloomsbury Academic, 2019).

10 For some perspectives on approaches known as postgenomics and the extended evolutionary synthesis, see Sarah S. Richardson and Hallam Stevens (eds), *Postgenomics: Perspectives on Biology after the Genome* (Durham, NC and London: Duke University Press, 2015); Massimo Pigliucci and Gerd B. Müller (eds), *Evolution, the Extended Synthesis* (Cambridge, MA: MIT Press, 2010); Manfred D. Laubichler and Jürgen Renn, 'Extended Evolution: A Conceptual Framework for Integrating Regulatory Networks and Niche Construction', *Journal of Experimental Zoology* Part B: Molecular and Developmental Evolution, 324/7 (1 November 2015), 565–77, *https://doi.org/10.1002/jez.b.22631*.

11 In addition to the works cited in note 3, see Tim Ingold, *Being Alive: Essays on Movement, Knowledge and Description* (London and New York: Routledge, 2011); Ian Hodder, *Entangled: An Archaeology of the Relationships between Humans and Things* (Malden, MA: Wiley-Blackwell, 2012).

12 Eva Jablonka and Marion J. Lamb, *Evolution in Four Dimensions: Genetic, Epigenetic, Behavioral, and Symbolic Variation in the History of Life*, Life and Mind (Cambridge, MA: MIT Press, 2005); Jörg Niewöhner, 'Epigenetics: Embedded Bodies and the Molecularisation of Biography and Milieu', *BioSocieties*, 6/3 (13 June 2011), 279–98; Randolph A. Roth et al., 'Introduction: Roundtable: History Meets Biology', *The American Historical Review*, 119/5 (1 December 2014), 1492–9, *https://doi.org/10.1093/ahr/119.5.1492*; John L. Brooke and Clark Spencer Larsen, 'The Nurture of Nature: Genetics, Epigenetics, and Environment in Human Biohistory', *The American Historical Review*, 119/5 (1 December 2014), 1500–13, *https://doi.org/10.1093/ahr/119.5.1500*.

13 For another case study involving compulsive hoarding, see Daniel Lord Smail, 'Neurohistory in Action: Hoarding and the Human Past', *Isis: an International Review Devoted to the History of Science and Its Cultural Influences*, 105/1 (2014), 110–22.

14 Thomas Trautmann, Gillian Feeley-Harnik and John C. Mitani, 'Deep Kinship', in Andrew Shryock and Daniel Lord Smail (eds), *Deep History: The Architecture of Past and Present* (Berkeley: University of California Press, 2011), p. 160.

15 Friedrich Wilhelm Nietzsche, *The Use and Abuse of History*, 2nd rev. edn, The Library of Liberal Arts; 11 (Indianapolis: Bobbs-Merrill Educational Publishing, 1957), p. 1.

16 William H. Durham, *Coevolution: Genes, Culture, and Human Diversity* (Stanford, CA: Stanford University Press, 1991).

17 L. Van Valen, 'A New Evolutionary Law', *Evolutionary Theory*, 1 (1973), 1–30; Matt Ridley, *The Red Queen: Sex and the Evolution of Human Nature*, 1st American edn (New York: Macmillan, 1994).

18 R. Dawkins and J. R. Krebs, 'Arms Races between and within Species', *Proceedings of the Royal Society of London. Series B, Biological Sciences*, 205/1161 (1979), 489–511.

19 Michael Pollan, *The Botany of Desire: A Plant's Eye View of the World* (New York: Random House, 2001).

20 F. John Odling-Smee, Kevin N. Laland and Marcus W. Feldman, *Niche Construction: The Neglected Process in Evolution* (Princeton, NJ: Princeton University Press, 2003); Kevin Laland, Blake Matthews and Marcus W. Feldman, 'An Introduction to Niche Construction Theory', *Evolutionary Ecology*, 30/2 (1April 2016), 191–202, *https://doi.org/10.1007/s10682-016-9821-z*.

21 S. Conway Morris, *Life's Solution: Inevitable Humans in a Lonely Universe* (Cambridge and New York: Cambridge University Press, 2003); Richard Dawkins, *The Extended Phenotype: The Gene as the Unit of Selection* (Oxford and San Francisco: Freeman, 1982); Geerat J. Vermeij, 'Historical Contingency and the Purported Uniqueness of Evolutionary Innovations', *Proceedings of the National Academy of Sciences of the United States of America*, 103/6 (2006), 1804–9, *https://doi.org/10.1073/pnas.0508724103*.

22 H. Jachmann, P. S. M. Berry and H. Imae, 'Tusklessness in African Elephants: A Future Trend', *African Journal of Ecology*, 33/3 (1995), 230–5, *https://doi.org/10.1111/j.1365-2028.1995.tb00800.x*.

23 Elinor G. K. Melville, *A Plague of Sheep: Environmental Consequences of the Conquest of Mexico*, Studies in Environment and History (Cambridge and New York: Cambridge University Press, 1994).

24 Durham, *Coevolution*.

25 Robert M. Sapolsky, *Why Zebras Don't Get Ulcers*, 3rd edn (New York: St Martin's Griffin, 2004).

26 Jasmine J. Yap and Klaus A. Miczek, 'Social Defeat Stress, Sensitization, and Intravenous Cocaine Self-Administration in Mice', *Psychopharmacology*, 192/2 (June 2007), 261–73, *https://doi.org/10.1007/s00213-007-0712-4*.

27 Jason S. Snyder et al., 'Adult Hippocampal Neurogenesis Buffers Stress Responses and Depressive Behaviour', *Nature*, 476/7361 (2011), 458-U112, *https://doi.org/10.1038/nature10287*.

28 Doug Liu and Michael J. Meaney, 'Maternal Care, Hippocampal Glucocorticoid Receptors, and Hypothalmic-Pituitary-Adrenal Responses to Stress', *Science*, 277/5332 (1997), 1659–62, *https://doi.org/10.1126/science.277.5332.1659*.

29 Randolph Roth, 'Biology and the Deep History of Homicide', *British Journal of Criminology*, 51/3 (2011), 535–55, https://doi.org/10.1093/bjc/azr029.

30 I have explored some of the extensive literature on medieval violence in Daniel Lord Smail, 'Violence and Predation in Late Medieval Mediterranean Europe', *Comparative Studies in Society and History*, 54 (2012), 7–34. Important overviews include William Ian Miller, *Humiliation: And Other Essays on Honor, Social Discomfort, and Violence* (Ithaca, NY: Cornell University Press, 1993); Guy Halsall, *Violence and Society in the Early Medieval West* (Rochester, NY: Boydell Press, 1998); Mark D. Meyerson et al., *'A Great Effusion of Blood'?: Interpreting Medieval Violence* (Toronto and Buffalo, NY: University of Toronto Press, 2004).

31 Daniel Lord Smail, *Legal Plunder: Households and Debt Collection in Late Medieval Europe* (Cambridge, MA: Harvard University Press, 2016).

32 Norbert Elias, *Quest for Excitement: Sport and Leisure in the Civilizing Process* (Oxford: Blackwell, 1986).

33 Steven Pinker, *The Better Angels of Our Nature: Why Violence Has Declined* (New York: Viking, 2011).

34 See my critique of Pinker in Daniel Lord Smail, 'The Inner Demons of The Better Angels of Our Nature', *Historical Reflections-Reflexions Historiques*, 44/1 (2018), 117–27, *https://doi.org/10.3167/hrrh.2018.440112*.

35 On the complexity of the relationship between testosterone and violence, see Robert M. Sapolsky, *Behave: The Biology of Humans at Our Best and Worst* (New York: Penguin, 2017).

36 Roth, 'Biology and the Deep History of Homicide'.

37 Lee T. Gettler et al., 'Longitudinal Evidence That Fatherhood Decreases Testosterone in Human Males', *Proceedings of the National Academy of Sciences*, 108/39 (27 September 2011), 16194–99, *https://doi.org/10.1073/pnas.1105403108*.

[38] Daniel Lord Smail, 'Debt, Humiliation, and Stress in Fourteenth-Century Lucca and Marseille', in Bénédicte Sère and Jörg Wettlaufer (eds), *Shame between Punishment and Penance* (Florence: Micrologus, 2013), pp. 247–62.

[39] George Orwell, *Nineteen Eighty-Four* (New York: Harcourt, Brace & Company, 1949).

Select Bibliography

Boddice, Rob, 'Neurohistory', in Marek Tamm and Peter Burke (eds), *Debating New Approaches to History* (London and New York: Bloomsbury Academic, 2019).

Cochran, Gregory and Henry Harpending, *The 10,000 Year Explosion: How Civilization Accelerated Human Evolution* (New York: Basic Books, 2009).

Conway Morris, Simon, *Life's Solution: Inevitable Humans in a Lonely Universe* (Cambridge and New York: Cambridge University Press, 2003).

Dawkins, Richard, *The Extended Phenotype: The Gene as the Unit of Selection* (Oxford and San Francisco: Freeman, 1982).

Durham, William H., *Coevolution: Genes, Culture, and Human Diversity* (Stanford, CA: Stanford University Press, 1991).

Goleman, Daniel, *Social Intelligence: The New Science of Human Relationships* (New York: Bantam Books, 2006).

Halsall, Guy, *Violence and Society in the Early Medieval West* (Rochester, NY: Boydell Press, 1998).

Hodder, Ian, *Entangled: An Archaeology of the Relationships between Humans and Things* (Malden, MA: Wiley-Blackwell, 2012).

Hrdy, Sarah Blaffer, *Mothers and Others: The Evolutionary Origins of Mutual Understanding* (Cambridge, MA: The Belknap Press of Harvard University Press, 2009).

Ingold, Tim, *Being Alive: Essays on Movement, Knowledge and Description* (London and New York: Routledge, 2011).

Jablonka, Eva and Marion J. Lamb, *Evolution in Four Dimensions: Genetic, Epigenetic, Behavioral, and Symbolic Variation in the History of Life*, Life and Mind (Cambridge, MA: MIT Press, 2005).

Laubichler, Manfred D. and Jürgen Renn, 'Extended Evolution: A Conceptual Framework for Integrating Regulatory Networks and Niche Construction', *Journal of Experimental Zoology Part B: Molecular and Developmental Evolution*, 324/7 (1 November 2015), 565–77, *https://doi.org/10.1002/jez.b.22631*.

LeCain, Timothy, *The Matter of History: How Things Create the Past* (Cambridge: Cambridge University Press, 2017).

Meyerson, Mark D., et al., *'A Great Effusion of Blood'?: Interpreting Medieval Violence* (Toronto and Buffalo, NY: University of Toronto Press, 2004).

Miller, William Ian, *Humiliation: And Other Essays on Honor, Social Discomfort, and Violence* (Ithaca, NY: Cornell University Press, 1993).

Patel, Aniruddh D., *Music, Language, and the Brain* (Oxford: Oxford University Press, 2007).

Pinker, Steven, *The Better Angels of Our Nature: Why Violence Has Declined* (New York: Viking, 2011).

Plamper, Jan, *The History of Emotions: An Introduction*, trans. Keith Tribe (Oxford: Oxford University Press, 2015).

Smail, Daniel Lord, *Legal Plunder: Households and Debt Collection in Late Medieval Europe* (Cambridge, MA: Harvard University Press, 2016).

Tileagă, Cristian and Jovan Byford (eds), *Psychology and History: Interdisciplinary Explorations* (Cambridge: Cambridge University Press, 2014).

Shryock, Andrew and Daniel Lord Smail (eds), *Deep History: The Architecture of Past and Present* (Berkeley: University of California Press, 2011).

Whitehouse, Harvey and Luther H. Martin, *Theorizing Religions Past: Archaeology, History, and Cognition*, Cognitive Science of Religion Series (Walnut Creek, CA and Lanham, MD: AltaMira Press, 2004).

Whitehouse, Harvey and Robert N. McCauley (eds), *Mind and Religion: Psychological and Cognitive Foundations of Religiosity* (Walnut Creek, CA: Altamira Press, 2005).

Wrangham, Richard W., *Demonic Males: Apes and the Origins of Human Violence* (Boston: Houghton Mifflin, 1996).

5

Medieval English Understanding of Mental Illness and Parallel Diagnosis to Contemporary Neuroscience

WENDY J. TURNER

Scholars of historic and present disability studies use models to help describe who is or is not mentally or physically disabled, impaired, or ill. Many of these models, though, do not work for both historic and contemporary persons with physical or mental impairment, and, as such, scholars end up talking past one another about the same issue. Several years ago, I developed a new way of envisioning, of modelling, disability studies which I called the 'environmental model'.[1] I arrived at this title after reading a line in the World Health Organization report of 2001 that said, a 'key finding is that human behaviour is partly shaped through interactions with the natural or social environment'.[2] I used this model to describe impaired individuals' interactions with their lived environments, which change drastically over time and with technology. This is not the same model to which Daniel Smail refers (see his chapter in this volume), and yet these two environmental models have several things in common. I did not want to treat humans or the environment *or the impairment* 'as the sovereign partner in the relationship' (Smail, p. 83), and the core of my theory is the relationship between humans and the environment. The impaired individual is most comfortable and confident as a person in the most familiar environment, growing exponentially more uncomfortable and, in the case of physical impairment, less abled, further from home or closer to any unknown public audience, such as a court, which in the Middle Ages often travelled. Furthermore, having written on the cultural dimensions of the medieval brain,[3] I wanted to test my conclusions in these two works that medieval constructions of mental health categories run parallel to ideas about mental health today.

The ways in which people of the Middle Ages and those of the contemporary world communicate about health are quite different. For one thing, only a few medieval physicians trained to treat the ill and injured (as opposed to those who taught theory in an academic setting) kept case records or reported their findings to other physicians. In terms of medieval mental function, there were a variety of theories, each with its own audience: physicians and surgeons understood the *mind* to be located in the brain and wrote about the physiological care of this organ (which already sounds much like contemporary neuroscience), but medieval medical personnel had yet to work out the details correctly; ecclesiastics were not yet sure that thinking and feeling were located in the brain and postulated that they might be functions of the heart, writing in abstract terms about possible connections between thinking, feeling and the soul; and, like our contemporary legal system, medieval legal opinion focused on *intent* more than the inner workings of the heart or brain. Yet, these concepts – thinking, feeling, the soul, the heart, the mind, and the brain – are connected both in terms of human will and mental and emotional function, and, with the exception of the heart and the brain, which are tangible objects as organs, the other concepts are all intangible, and, while definable, they can be expressed in a host of different ways depending on the author (such as a poet or philosopher) or authority (as in medical, legal or ecclesiastical records).

For the purposes of this chapter, two areas offer enough evidence to support an attempt to compare roughly medieval mental illness and contemporary neurobiology and neuropsychology: stress disorders and psychoses. The reason for choosing these two areas is that medieval people experienced traumatic events just like individuals do today – the death of a loved one, war, natural disasters, health calamities, and many other such events – and some experienced noticeable breaks from reality, envisioning things that did not exist and also, at times, not comprehending things that were real. These reactions followed a moment of stress, shock or illness. Other categories among the twenty-two covered in the *Diagnostic and Statistical Manual of Mental Disorders* (DSM-5)[4] could be relevant to this discussion; for now, though, two will suffice to shed light on the similarities and differences in the granularity of medieval terminology for mental health, and to look for parallel conditions with those seen in contemporary neurosciences.

The methodology of this chapter is limited by these two phenomena and the sources stemming from administration and the royal courts in late medieval England, since it is in those records that actual lived experience is discussed, categorised and, at times, described. Other sources – medical and encyclopaedic information from physicians or natural philosophers (from England as much as possible, to stay consistent in terms of location) – are brought in to augment these core case studies. Ecclesiastical and literary concerns are left aside altogether because, while these discourses also deal with trauma and stressors, I want to examine real lives and get as close as possible to the experiential elements of these pathologies. Medieval English clerks, juries and judges described defendants and plaintiffs with mental health conditions as part of the official records of court; their descriptions could include functionality, appearance and general demeanour.[5] Physicians also designated conditions for patients with similar symptomologies, but, unlike contemporary physicians, they do not share their findings. Therefore, this discussion will have to rely on court records for medieval terminology and descriptions of mental health patients for the most part. The medieval legal profession and the administrative arm of the crown used terminology that identified various mental health concerns, and the question here is whether some of these conditions parallel modern ones.

The mentally impaired in the medieval English legal tradition, which was generally written in either Latin or Legal French (Norman) and was heavily influenced by Roman law, were divided into categories based on a combination of behaviour and intellectual ability. There were tests for perception, cognition and memory.[6] Medieval society had a general knowledge that conditions like epilepsy, already known as being a condition of the meninges, were quite separate from 'mental illness' and 'impairment'. There were no umbrella terms for 'disability', 'mental illness', 'impairment', and so on, and in order to discuss these conditions as a group, I will use the modern collective of 'mental health' and other terms that are as close to 'neutral' as I can get. Those medieval persons with intellectual impairment issues were normally either an *idiota* (possibly an intellectually disabled person: more on that condition below), or a *fatuus* (a person with mental deficiency) but could also be *non intellectus* (without intelligence), *ignorans* (ignorant), *non sane memoria* (without a healthy memory), or just simply *non compos mentis* (without mental ability). The term *idiota* in earlier Latin referred to an 'uneducated and common' person; later it took on the more nuanced meaning of 'unaware' or even 'inward looking' in medieval England, often with the descriptor of *naturalis* (natural or congenital) or *a nativitate* (from birth).[7] Those persons without the ability to discern – who either could not tell the difference between right and wrong or reality and fantasy – were a *demens* or *amens* (a delusional person), *insanus* ('without health', meaning a mentally unhealthy individual), a *freneticus* (a 'frenzied' person, meaning someone without physical or mental control), a *lunaticus* (a lunatic; an individual with 'phases' like the moon, moving in and out of sanity), or someone that *sciens nec bonum nec malum* (knew neither good nor bad). Erratic and dangerous individuals with the mental affliction of *furiosus* (a person suffering from *furor*, uncontrollable rage or anger; in Greek, *mania*) were watched closely, often accompanied by a *custos* (keeper).[8] Most medieval crimes were committed by mentally ill persons categorised as having this condition. This is to say that there were many categories and some understanding of differing mental conditions.

Some of these terms appear to be akin to our contemporary categories and pathologies, others have no apparent connection to contemporary terminology or are now slang terms for conditions contemporary scholars would position as much more discrete disorders. While terms like *dementia* and *mania* continue to be employed today, others like *idiota* would be quite frowned upon in today's parlance. Still, terminology evolves, and today's post-traumatic stress disorder (or PTSD) might fall to the same overuse in flippant public discussion and need replacing to clarify meaning in future scholarship, which is what happened to the medieval terms *idiota* and *fatuus* as well as later terms such as *moronic* or, recently, *handicapped*.[9]

This study will not attempt to diagnose medieval mental health complaints using terminology of today.[10] That would both be impossible and unhelpful. Rather, this chapter will introduce the theory of *parallel diagnosing*. In parallel diagnosing, similar symptoms are compared using 'neutral' terminology when possible, while at the same time acknowledging that interviewing and actual diagnosis is impossible, given the time and distance to the subjects. Furthermore, it must be acknowledged that the medieval terminology comes from the legal record, whereas the contemporary terminology is from psychological-neuroscientific scholarship. All that said, the work here is intended to shine a light on the terminology used in medieval legal and medical records (as available) in an effort to simultaneously understand their complex set of terminology for symptoms and tease out how those words and descriptions differed, as well as locating parallel symptomology that might give us clues as to how and when medieval officials discussed conditions similar to recognised conditions today. Any commonalities would provide a better standing from which to understand the past and inform the future of mental health and historic neuroscience.

Comparing Contemporary Terms to Medieval Ones

Twenty-first century definitions, while completely different from those of the Middle Ages, are worth reviewing for purposes of comparison. The myriad terminology for various disorders and conditions in the DSM-5 can be overwhelming to the non-specialist.[11] The two areas here under investigation – stress disorders and psychoses – both now and in the past speak of individuals without the health (mental or physical) to cope with abnormal levels of trauma.

Reactions to stress – the most well-known today being PTSD – are described in contemporary popular print and medieval records as having serious levels of stress (different in every patient), resulting in responses that might include such reactions as depression, anxiety, obsessive behaviour or hypochondria. Yet some of these reactions, both today and in the past, could also lead to psychosis, such as the PTSD patient who has a break from reality and attacks someone believing he or she is still in combat.[12] Other psychoses – profound disconnects from reality – might have symptoms of incoherent speech, sleep issues, social withdrawal, and a lack of motivation to complete day-to-day tasks.[13] Aside from PTSD, other conditions considered to have psychotic elements today include bipolar disorder, schizophrenia, certain types of dementia, postpartum psychosis, and various mood disorders.[14] While this list is incomplete, these particular conditions have symptoms, such as hallucinations, delusions and false beliefs, that appear similar to medieval descriptions of individuals with mental health problems.

In the Middle Ages none of these terms – psychosis, stress, bipolar, schizophrenia – appear. Yet, while some terms were the same – trauma, postpartum, anxious, dementia, incoherent, etc. – care should be used when comparing terms as their definitions were not always the same. For example, '*depressus*' is used in a case study below, yet the individual probably did not mean that he was 'depressed' in a modern sense, but rather that he felt 'held down' or 'pressed', as if under a ton of rock. While this *might* mean that he felt mentally pressed flat, he might also mean that he felt physically immobile or incapable of action or that he had trouble breathing, all of which would be different conditions. If care is used to honour the meanings and terminology of different periods, a meaningful dialogue could result in old medications made new, or a new understanding of an old disease, now treated quite differently. This chapter examines the legal, administrative and medical terminology and descriptors for medieval parallels of stress disorders, including accounts of *idiota*, *lunaticus*, *furor*, *demencia* and *frenesis*, some of which exhibit possible elements of contemporary neuroscientific and neuropsychiatric psychoses.

Mental Health in Medieval English Law and Medicine

Medieval English royal law was conducted primarily at three courts: King's Bench, Common Pleas and the Exchequer. All of these entities conducted business for the crown – collecting fees, fines, and issuing punishments as well as payments. Trials for crime most often appeared at the King's Bench, those for disputes over land or other minor issues were seen at the court of Common Pleas, and fees and fines were paid at the court of the Exchequer.[15] Most trials remained at these courts, but a few transferred or appealed to Parliament or the King's Council. Some trials were allowed to appeal from a local court, such as a manor or hundred court, to the appropriate higher court of Common Pleas or King's Bench. At all levels, judges and juries satisfied themselves as to the mental state of the individual on trial because of their need to understand the individual's culpability – especially if on trial for a crime – and, if mentally impaired at the time of the crime, to explain any necessity for pardon.[16] Quite differently, if in wardship because of poor mental health, the guardian would have paid a fee (from the income of the lands of the mentally disabled individual) at the court of the Exchequer.[17]

The medieval English legal community knew that individuals with mental health issues might not have understood what they were doing at the time of a crime and, therefore, should not be punished; most were pardoned.[18] Furthermore, legal experts made distinctions between various conditions, observing peculiarities in behaviour and testimonies about an accused individual. The legal community's use of criteria and categories – quite a different lens than that used today – might inform and provide new perspectives on the often still tentative categorisation of mental health in the twenty-first century.

Medieval physicians and scholars conceptualised mental health conditions as having physical causes (although many of their physiological theories were quite wrong), not possession or demonic interference or, for that matter, metaphysical or psychological ones.[19] Physicians noted that infections or injuries to the anterior brain might interfere with a person's ability to discern reality from fantasy, react with appropriate emotions, remember, think clearly, or sense correctly (smell, taste, etc.). In medieval terms, the front of the brain controlled the senses, including common sense and imagination, with consideration and cogitation in the middle part of the brain, and memory in the back.[20] Physicians theorised that certain infections in the brain could also cause disruptions or loss to its activities, providing clues as to what might be wrong. Furthermore, a blow to the head could cause changes in the way the victim sensed, thought, or remembered, depending on where the blow landed and how hard the impact. Physicians knew that a blow to one side of the head affected the opposite side of the body. They looked for slurred speech, vision troubles, unexplained numbness or tingling, as well as changes in behaviour, unwarranted shifts in emotions, and reported visions or hallucinations.[21]

Idiota *and Stress*

In medieval courts, judges and juries looked for cause in mental health cases; contemporary neuroscientists might say the 'stressor' for a shift or change in behaviour. Anxiety or trauma could be the stressor in several of the following cases.[22] Yet, while stress played a part in medieval illness, including mental health, it is never discussed as 'stress' but rather a more tangible occurrence. For example, Margery Anlatheby was described as an *idiota* (intellectually disabled), but specifically 'not from her birth'.[23] Margery became an *idiota* when her husband died nine years before the writ of *certiorari*, an order to review her case, described her condition in 1289. This could indicate any of a number of issues, and, as contemporary psychiatrists and trauma specialists have shown, 'Exposure to traumatic stressors can happen at any time in a person's life'.[24] Margery could have been an *idiota* from earlier in her life, with her husband as her caregiver. She might have been slowly entering into an age-related dementia, which accelerated with the death of her spouse. Or else the stress of his death became the catalyst for a profound depression or mood disorder (in today's terms).[25] It would be difficult to dismiss the first two possibilities since the investigator used the term '*idiota*', which was normally reserved for individuals who had intellectual impairments. Yet the documentation points so clearly to the moment of her husband's death that a connection between this and her mental health condition must be considered.[26] If this was the stressor,[27] which from the record seems likely, contemporary studies on bereavement-related depression point out that most individuals will not become psychotic, but rather pass through several stages of grief.[28] Nevertheless, in a study on age and grief, one team omitted individuals with mental health complications because that population were 'most vulnerable to complicated grief reactions, functional impairments, or bereavement-induced psychosis'.[29] This is important when considering parallel diagnosis of Margery; contemporary neuroscientific studies of grief in mentally ill patients demonstrate that patients with already weak mental health are vulnerable to having their mental state devolve into much more serious conditions, including psychosis. This population is often unable to handle the stress of bereavement.[30] Perhaps Margery, then, could have been both intellectually disabled *and* unable to cope with the death of her husband because of her mental condition; the death of her spouse only exacerbated her already poor mental health.

In a second case from a later medieval English patent (public) roll, John Berton's expression of '*depressus*' after his father's death points more clearly to some sort of stress reaction. The investigators conclude that John:

> . . . from his infancy until his completion of the age of twenty-one years and more was of sound mind, having no kind of idiocy, but, because of a great fright and excessive grief because of his father's death, he afterwards sustained almost total loss of memory and remained in that state for three years, although with occasional lucid intervals, after which he recovered and his memory was restored and remained so for more than five years before the date of the said inquisition . . .[31]

John was in court fighting to have his guardian removed, to have his life restored. After a three-year grieving process,[32] he became 'capable' again. Finding himself under a guardian, as if incapable of functioning as a cognisant and sane individual, it took him a while to figure out how to get his case heard, since everything he did as a ward needed to go through his guardian. John could have had some other underlying condition that caused his loss of memory, but 'a great fright and excessive grief' indicates that something more happened, perhaps a traumatic moment that led to a stress-related condition. The court officials used the term *idiota* to describe John's condition, as they had with Margery, since apparently his condition affected his intellectual abilities; perhaps he, too, suffered a bout of depression or from a mood disorder in current terms.[33] Yet looking once more at contemporary scholarship on stress disorders, it seems that among PTSD survivors of the Sichuan earthquake, for example, 65 per cent of those who lost a close family member (spouse or child) developed depressive psychopathologies.[34] These neuroscientific ideas parallel John's description of being 'held down' or '*depressus*', which is fascinating. This could be the first use of this term to mean precisely what we mean today: depressed. Though the parallel will never be confirmed, John's word was aptly chosen and proved to the court that he was quite sane and no longer in need of a guardian.

In most legal and administrative documents, an *idiota* is qualified as 'congenital' by the use of *naturalis* (a natural *idiota*) or *a nativitate* (an *idiota* from birth). In the cases above, though, these individuals clearly *became idiota.* Either the stresses they endured *caused* them to take on *idiota* traits, or they *highlighted* an underlying condition already present in the person. Revisiting other examples of persons who *became* an *idiota*, I am struck by how often a moment of change – possible trauma or stress – is mentioned, even if it is not so clearly spelled out. For example, John Heton was 'in good sense and quite sane' until he was 24 years old, then suddenly on 'the feast of St. James, 22 Edward III', John became an *idiota.*[35] Such precision in recording this date. Why mention the feast, unless something happened that changed John? The questions are endless. Was he injured? Did he eat something poisonous? He could have had a stroke or some other physical change, or it could be possible he experienced something akin to the onset of schizophrenia, which according to Armand Loranger is rarely over 30 years old in men.[36] In a similar case, Robert Corbrigge 'left Corbrigge for Oxford of sound mind and memory, and when he returned [a year later] … he was an *idiota*'.[37] Again, the specifics are intriguing, but not enough to draw any conclusions. He could have gone to Oxford for work or something other than education. This record was from seventeen years later, but the mention of his trip to Oxford and that he was only away from Corbrigge for a year before returning as an *idiota* is significant. Clearly his mental health changed swiftly: perhaps there was a traumatic event in Oxford, or his condition might parallel a contemporary disorder, such as (again) schizophrenia,[38] but potentially other types of disorder, such as anxiety, mood, conduct or substance abuse disorder, oppositional defiant disorder (ODD), or attention deficit hyperactivity disorder (ADHD).[39]

Lunaticus *and the Powerless Mind*

The term *idiota,* a person with an intellectual disability, was regularly used in English legal and administrative records, but is not found in medical treatises (though the Latin term *fatuus* is). Instead, medical records use the terms *torpor* (Latin, 'forgetful') or *lethargus* (Latin, 'forgetful' or 'lethargic', having a slow mind/memory and at times slow movement as well) or *litarge* (Middle English, lethargy); these terms appear occasionally in legal or administrative accounts. In both medical and legal records we also find the term *lunaticus*, roughly defined as a person with a cyclical disorder (with cycles like the moon).[40] Medieval physicians located the condition of *lunaticus* in the front of the brain, which in their theories control perception and imagination, while the condition of *lethargus* was in the back, the seat of memory. *Idiota*, then, must be somewhere between, since both lethargy and lunacy were associated with the condition of *idiotsy* but not with each other.[41] I have previously argued that *idiotsy* was a condition of the back of the brain because it seemed to me that all references to *idiota* involved an inability to understand and memory loss, and that these individuals had 'quiet' disorders, meaning that persons with *idiota* were not frightening or breakers of the law.[42] Now, as I have argued more recently,[43] I believe that *idiotsy* must be an intellectual disability affecting the medieval medial brain, either a singular pathology or part of a more complex pathology that also affected perception (*lunaticus*), including both the anterior and medial brain, or also affected the memory (*lethargus*) including both the posterior and medial brain.

The term *lunaticus* later became the word 'lunatic', but even that does not define what the medieval physician or court officer meant when he wrote that the patient or accused was *lunaticus*. For example, Andrew Buriton 'while lunatic' stalked and killed his '*custodiam*' (guardian).[44] Does this mean that Andrew was 'powerless of mind' or 'under the moon's influence' when he killed his guardian? More examples might help clarify. When a relative asked if he might take over the lands of Ralph de la Halt, he told the court, '*lunaticus est et impos mentis sue*' (he [Ralph] is a lunatic and his mind powerless).[45] This conjecture might be exactly what was meant by *lunaticus*: that it was a person with a 'powerless mind'. The neighbour of another man labelled a '*lunatic*' mistook him for a burglar, and killed him when he tried to make a hole in her door.[46] Perhaps this man had a powerless mind, unable to realise what he was doing or to recognise the danger.

The influence of the moon was rarely mentioned in court records, but not absent. Thomas Wulmer, for example, was found guilty (and probably later pardoned) because he became *lunaticus* at the 'time of the moon'.[47] The moon also affected Goda Arcebek. She killed her children while '*furiosa . . . die lune*' (in fury [madness] . . . on the day of the [full] moon).[48] These illustrations associate the moon more closely with being *lunaticus* and also provide more evidence that the condition was periodic. Bartholomaeus Anglicus, a Franciscan friar from England working in Paris, writes:

> *Sub luna . . . unde morborum mutationem medicus perfecre non discernit qui luna res effectus in corporibus non cognouit, unde Hypocras in principio pronosticorum de luna loquens ait.*

> Under the moon . . . where diseases change, [even] the perfect physician does not perceive that the effect of the moon on the body is not known, which Hippocrates says about the moon in the Principio Prognosticorum [*Liber Prognosticorum*, or *Prognostica*]).[49]

Bartholomaeus makes the point that the moon has an effect on the body, but only to say that the extent of that influence is unknown, even by Hippocrates. In the popular *mentalité* of the Middle Ages the moon affected the behaviour of some people, who were locked up during the full moon for their own safety. Another connection should be drawn here with Daniel Smail's chapter in this volume, and the idea of the environment dictating the ideas of connection between cycles and conditions and humans. The lunar cycles, clearly visible before today's urban lights, would have changed the night-time environment and, for those with *lunaticus*, changed the way they interacted with their environment – both natural and social. Locking up a friend, parent or child could not have been easy. Still, in the Middle Ages, the image of the *lunaticus* was closely connected with the moon and this natural and environmental object seems to have been considered a partner in the '*lunations*' (hallucinations) of the lunatic person during a full moon, just as the socio-religious environment gave rise to his or her cravings during Lent.

These environmental elements – the moon, Lent – allowed for social constraints to be placed on those persons considered *lunaticus* at particular times of the month or year. If there was a reaction or change in behaviour during those moments, the shift would indicate without doubt to the medieval community that the individual had *impos mentis* (a powerless mind) and *lunacy*. This may signify that part of the definition of *lunaticus* included a cyclical or periodic 'powerlessness' of the mind, perhaps something like contemporary bipolar disorder.[50] Conceiving of environment as part of the diagnosing process gave the medieval community the sought-after explanation for drastic swings in personality or presence. Many people today, as in the past, believe the moon can influence human behaviour.[51]

Richard Thurbern of Brent might have suffered with something like this in medieval England. He was found guilty of stealing a fowl but had his sentence reduced because he had been '*in furore tempore quo fuit lunaticus*' (in furor [a mad fury] at the time [of the crime] when he was lunatic).[52] A *lunaticus*, then, could be a person who had periodic episodes (*tempore*) of fury (*furore*), possibly suffering from a cyclical ailment such as bipolar disorder, depression or a mood disorder.[53] This association between the conditions of *lunaticus* and *furor* might be cyclical or temporary, with bouts of anger or outbursts, as they are for some contemporary people with bipolar disorder or individuals with developmental disabilities. Today, aggressive behaviour like Richard's might be treatable with anti-aggression medication or, depending on other underlying causes, psychotropic, anti-psychotic or even antiepileptic drugs.[54] In another example, Robert Dura stole a horse, and the record reads '*lunaticus est et in furiositate sua*' (he is a lunatic and he was in a state of fury).[55] Here, it is almost an excuse for a *lunaticus* stealing – as if Robert was powerless against his 'furor'. Once more the neuroscientific conceptualisation of lacking self-control comes to mind – especially in contemporary cases of severe aggression and anger.[56] Contemporary cognitive theories of the abstract concepts of self and social behaviour, such as Jerry Fodor's 'Representational Theory of Mind', could account for why certain individuals react more aggressively than others. If they become 'hard wired' to act in particular patterns, Foder would say within the parameters of a 'modular' system (see José Silva's chapter in this volume), then the environment in which they developed may be in part to blame.[57]

Having a powerless mind would be disabling both today and in the past. Without the ability to think abstractly how to get where he was going, an individual could get lost.[58] The medieval community considered wandering away without explanation part of the condition of being *lunaticus*. For example, Simon Vineter, '*lunaticus*' (a lunatic), wandered into the park of Northampton where he was arrested for poaching. His relatives and neighbours were supposed to watch over him and claimed that, while he had been caught with his dogs and a bow and arrows, 'he took nothing there [the park], and was not sent by anybody's procurement', he was only lost.[59] In other words, he was not out hunting on behalf of a community that knew the mentally impaired Simon might get away with poaching when they could not. In another example, when Thomas Cordereye inherited 'la Ropsled' and other properties, other family members immediately challenged his right to those lands. During the ensuing arguments, Thomas 'became lunatic' and wandered away.[60] Once officials located Thomas, they 'confined [him] as a lunatic (*lunaticus*) in Bristol Castle'.[61] Later the chancellor ordered Thomas released, his lands and person now under the king's protection. The question remains: did these court officials label the mental health conditions of Simon and Thomas as *lunaticus* because they wandered, or did they wander because they had the condition of *lunaticus*? Either way, this condition was closely associated with the loss of abstract thinking.

In several of these cases – Goda Archebek, who killed her children; Richard Thurbern, who stole a fowl; and Robert Dura, who stole a horse – the individual was described as *furore* (or some derivative of that term) and *lunaticus*. Just as physicians preferred the term *lethargus* and lawyers the term *idiota*, the same is true for the terms *furiosus* (or *furore*) and *mania*. I still have questions about whether these terms are fully interchangeable, but the connection seems probable, as there was at least an overlap between the meanings of medical term *mania* and the legal term *furore.* Gilbertus Anglicus, a thirteenth-century physician, describes the condition of *mania*:

> [I]f it comeþ of blood, þe greuauce is with lawghing. And if it be of coler, it is with a fers wode/-nes. And if it be of malencoly, it is with moche drede. And if it is of coler and malencoly medlid togedir, he lawgheþ and fiȝteþ togedir.[62]

Both his phrases 'fierce madness' and 'laughing and fighting together' are nearly the same as definitions of *furore* in legal manuscripts, especially those explanations of persons '*in furore*' (in fury) at the time they committed murder. These descriptions all sound like pieces of contemporary definitions of various psychoses, most closely like bipolar disorder but also personality flaws, stress and mood disorders, and, at times, schizophrenia. Mania, while that is what Gilbertus was discussing, in a contemporary sense is more about the 'high' point of bipolar disorder, someone who is frantically creative and exuberant. In Gilbertus's 'mania', the first line – 'if it comes of blood, the grievance is with laughing' – sounds far more like a psychotic patient than a manic one. The rest of his passage could be parallel to bipolar disorder, or the disorders mentioned above – personality, stress or mood – but this is still a stretch to make this particular medieval term of 'mania' fit the contemporary image of 'mania'. The descriptions for '*furore*' seem far more parallel to contemporary concepts of 'mania', as in bipolar disorder as well as psychotic and other disorders.

Demencia *and Hallucinations*

Just as examples of complex medieval pathologies were explained or characterised using multiple terms – *idiota* and *lunaticus*, or *impos mentis* and *lunaticus* – *lunaticus* was also used in combination with *demencia. Demencia* literally means 'without a mind' or 'mindless' and seems in certain circumstances to indicate a person with delusions or hallucinations who is also, as such, uncontrollable. For example, Henry Yuehust admitted to theft while he was '*demencia . . . quia lunaticus*' ([demented] without a mind . . . because he is a lunatic) and stole when '*amens tempore*' ([lit. 'amented'] without a mind at the time/temporarily).[63] If we think of what is meant today by dementia (memory decline, especially of recent events; confusion; personality or behaviour changes; apathy and/or depression; loss of ability to do everyday tasks; hallucinations),[64] is that at all similar to what *demencia* was in the Middle Ages? If so, what does *lunaticus* mean? In the example of Henry, though, he seems to be quite able to do things – after all, he's caught stealing – and while he might be confused, perhaps thinking the animal was his, there is no indication that he knew what he was doing at the time of his crime because he was '*demencia*' and otherwise mentally unwell.

Other cases include more clues as to what the medieval courts meant by '*demencia*'. Emma Hereward was '*demenciam*' (without a mind) and '*furia*' (in a fury) when she killed her neighbour's daughter, three-year old Maud Wolurich.[65] Emma appears to have been both delusional and in an uncontrolled rage when she killed the child, but, with so little to go on, it would be impossible to make any sort of parallel diagnosis. The use of *demenciam* (*in* dementia) with *furia*, rather than *lunaticus*, might be important. This woman seems to have lost control of her temper while 'without a mind', rather than having a 'powerless' mind. In another example, Edith Rogers died '*de sua propria negligencia et insania*' (by reason of her own negligence and insanity)[66] when she drowned in a well. The record makes it clear that Edith's neighbours and family knew she had mental health issues. Court officers reviewed her past, writing that '*Editha Rogers de Wyke demens et insanis submersa fuit in parvo puteo impleto cum aqua pluviali in alta via vocata Rosestrete in Wyke et invent a fuit mortua*' (Edith Rogers of Wick was delusional [demented] and insane; she drowned in a little well filled with rain-water in the highway called Rose Street in Wick and was found dead).[67] The term '*insania*' (insanity) was used by both physicians and lawyers as a neutral term meaning 'unhealthy', specifically unhealthy in mind. Edith could have been intellectually disabled but something about her demeanour indicated to the court that she was not an *idiota* but rather '*demens et insanis*', delusional or 'without a mind' and (mentally) unhealthy. Underscoring the breadth of *demencia*, the example of John Faytour illustrates both the condition and the symptoms. He killed his father while he was '*demens*', in dementia or in a state of mindlessness, and '*amens existit* [. . .] *in tali demencia et furore*' (exists in amentia [insanity] [. . .] in such dementia and furor) that officials had to bind him with a '*manica*' (handcuff) for safety.[68] As yet, and this case is a good example, scholars (including myself) have made no clear distinction between *amencia* and *demencia*; however, there seems to be a slight difference in the medieval usage here, which I translated as 'insanity' (*amencia*) and 'without a mind' or 'delusional' (*demencia*). The court record described John with both terms, using one almost as if to define the other. He 'exists in *amentia*' and as such became '*demencia*' to the point the court officials restrained him. Still, for the purpose of the argument here, John's *demencia* left him without the ability to know what he was doing.

Bartholomaeus Anglicus includes a section on *dementia* (a variant spelling of *demencia*), which he defines as causing loss of perception, control and sensation. He writes, '*De amentia. Dementia "idem est quod insania". Est autem insania secundu pla. Infection anterioris cellule capitis cum privation imaginationis*' (Of amentia. Dementia 'is the same as insanity'. It was insanity by convention. [This is an] infection of the anterior cell of the head with the privation of the imagination).[69] He, too, uses the term *dementia* to define *amentia. Demencia* was quite similar to how we define dementia today, and individuals could also have slight *demencia*, as with age-related disorders, that included confusion, time-slippage, anger, and general memory loss.[70]

Frenesis, *Agitation and Violence*

While *idiota* and *furore* were favoured by the legal community and *lethargus* and *mania* by the medical community, the terms *demencia* and *frenesis*, like *insania*, appear in both legal and medical records. *Frenesis* was the condition of medieval medical *frenesi* (frenzy), a pathology whereby the patient seemingly loses physical restraint as well as mental control. It might have been a type of delirium, with the individual frenzied in both movement and thinking, or a form of autism. For example, Sergerus Chippenham, who '*sciens nec bonum nec malum*' (knows neither good nor bad), stole a bone during his '*frenesi et quod per septem annos ante sint freneticus*' (frenzy and [during] the previous seven years he was a frenetic).[71] Sergerus became a thief, but the record does not explain if he understood his actions, only that he did not know right from wrong. Contemporary neuroscience might look at Sergerus for disorganised thinking, negativity, mood swings, or psychotic behaviour.[72] Several other examples illustrate how a person with *frenesis* could become violent – not knowing what they were doing at the time, perhaps not knowing their own strength. These first examples all hint at the possibility of something like contemporary hyperactive delirium, characterised by wild excitement, restlessness, rapid mood changes, hallucinations and/or incoherence; or the *freneticus* could have a parallel condition to delusional disorder or depression.[73] Contemporary neuroscience traces these behaviours to severe illness, changes to metabolic balance (such as low sodium), infection, medication or intoxication.[74]

In another example, John Beneit killed his wife, Alice, and his two daughters, Mariota and Alice. Officials confirmed that he killed them '*racione ... frenesimus morbo acuto laborans et non pro feloniam aut maliciam*' (by reason of … frenzy while labouring under acute disease and not by felony or malice).[75] In other examples, individuals with *frenesi* also became violent. For example, after a red dog came into the house and jumped on Agnes Burley, Agnes became '*frenesis*' (frenzied) and killed her daughter Rose.[76] Walter Makepays became '*frenesis unde freneticus*' (frenzied from being in a state of franticness) and killed Adam Grenhamerton.[77] Henry Brumman, '*dum in frenetica passione*' (while suffering with frenzy) and '*sciens nec bonum nec malum*' (knowing neither good nor bad) killed Hugh Faucumbe.[78] Richard de Upton, son of Reginald, '*freneticus percussit seipsum in ventre cum cultello suo ita quod tercia die post inde obit*' (being in frenzy stabbed himself in the stomach with his knife so that he died three days later).[79] Richard Pessoner beat his roommate, Brother Walter, to death (and later told the authorities what happened while 'laughing'). Richard was ill and had become '*freneticus et furiosus de toto*' (a completely frenzied and [mentally] furious person).[80] In all of these cases, the person with *frenesis* killed while in a state of frenzy and did not show signs to the court that they knew what they were doing at the time. Much the same is true in studies of contemporary persons incarcerated for murder. Many of these subjects suffered from mood disorders, schizophrenia, or psychotic conditions; most of them killed intimate partners or family members while enraged or angry using a firearm or sharp object.[81] Other than the firearms, these people do not sound terribly different from persons in the medieval cases cited above.

By at least the thirteenth century, Gilbertus Anglicus wrote that frenzy was a mental condition of the anterior ventricle of the brain: 'Comen signes þat folowen [i.e. manifest because of] þis sikenes is: moche waking, and lacking of good witt, wreeþ and wodenes, and doneyn risinggis vp, and sodeyn fallinggis dovne'.[82] Bartholomaeus Anglicus agreed with Gilvertus, writing in *De proprietatibus rerum* of *frenesis*: '*Percutier re furiose et amentia et stupor etc. furiosem vocat frenesum quam sic describit est an*' (Those stricken with furor or amentia or stupor, etc. called *furiosi* [delirious], are described as *frenesis*).[83] He describes a variety of symptoms:

> *Signa vero frenesis: sunt urine discoloratio; mathimatice febris insania. uigiliorum instancia, oculorum nobilitas et extensio dissoluta; manuum proiectio, capitus commotio, dentium frendor et collisio. Semper uolunt surgere de lecto, modo cantant, modo rident; modo plorant se custodientem; et medicantem libentem mordent atquam lacerent. raro silent. multum clamant. hii [sic] periculosissime egrorant et tamen se egrorare tunc ignorant.*

> The signs in truth of frenzy: they are urine discoloration, a measured (mathematical) fever of insanity (being mentally unhealthy); insistent waking, noble of (shining?) eyes and extensive weakness; projecting of hands, upset of the head, gnashing and grinding of teeth. Always they will to rise out of their bed, now they sing, now they laugh, now they weep the more [and] keep to themselves; and they will readily bite and tear at their physician. Rarely quiet. They yell a lot. These are the most perilously sick and yet they do not know they are sick.[84]

The movement and agitation of the patient is clear from the passage. According to medieval physicians, therefore, if a humoral imbalance or injury affected the anterior of the brain, the imbalance or injury might become *frenesis*, *demencia*, or *amencia*, causing a loss of perception, control and sensation. Contemporary psychologists might suggest that such a patient was having hallucinations, delusions, thought disorder, catatonia, a manic episode, or had a complete absence of affect.[85] In any of these symptoms or combination of them, contemporary psychiatrists might suggest antipsychotic medications.[86] In all cases, both medieval and contemporary physicians would recognise this patient as having either a serious illness, like encephalitis, or psychosis.

Sciens nec Bonam nec Malum, *Immorality and Psychosis*

These four concepts – *lunaticus*, *furore*, *demencia* and *frenesis* – all are associated in medieval records of those with a 'powerless mind', a cyclical or temporary condition. To add to this mix, another element appeared in some of the cases mentioned above, such as that of Sergerus Chippenham – the concept that the individual '*sciens nec bonum nec malum*' (knows neither good nor bad). At a Hundred Court (a local court), for example, Isabell, wife of Dick le Fader, was found to be a '*lunatica*'. She admitted her guilt in stealing a goose and a chicken during '*furor*' (a fury).[87] The record went on to explain that the accused also '*sciens nec bonum nec malum*' (knows neither good nor bad). In other words, she did not know right from wrong, could not discern the difference, and would be in contemporary terms immoral. In another case of theft, Roger Thurl who also '*sciens nec bonum nec malum*' (knows neither good nor bad) could not be held accountable.[88] While Roger might be a thief, Richard Russel killed his spouse. Richard 'acted from *insania*' (insanity; [mentally] unhealthy) and '*sciens nec bonum nec malum*' when he murdered his wife Isota.[89] In another case of killing, Richard del Boche '*sciens nec bonum nec malum*' and '*non fuit compos mentis sue*' (he was not of sound mind) when he killed his wife Almarica.[90] This lack of ability to judge right from wrong was also determined to be a mental condition that affected the individual's ability to understand his actions. This could be parallel to contemporary studies on mental health and immorality,[91] perhaps even the so-called 'Dark Triad' of Machiavellianism, narcissism and psychopathy.[92]

Other medieval cases either blend terms or speak directly of a disconnection from reality. For example, in 1212, an interesting, albeit brief, entry submitted by a gaoler to the court, expressed concern for a prisoner; a medieval gaol was something between a jail and a prison and used to incarcerate both the accused and prisoners. The manager of the gaol was asking the court to consult with the king about '*quodam stulto qui est in prisona eo quod per demenciam congnoscit se esse latronem sed non est culpabilis*' (a certain fool who is in prison because in his madness he believes [lit. 'knows'] he is a thief, but he is not guilty).[93] It is possible that he was lying – in theory hoping to protect a guilty party – yet the man with *demencia* seems to have lost his hold on reality, since even when told he was not '*culpabilis*' (culpable), he refused to leave the gaol. These types of entries are rare, but in this case, certainly it could be hypothesised that this individual was possibly afflicted with something akin to the modern concept behind psychosis. What exactly was wrong and why he believed himself *so* guilty that he wished to remain in a medieval gaol – likely on starvation rations and in unsanitary conditions, not to mention the potential cold – will remain a mystery. Still, the description the gaoler sent provides clues to medieval legal thinking about mental health and guilt. The man in this case was not guilty, yet was in gaol because he *believed* himself guilty. He must have turned himself in, confessing to a theft, and only later did the sheriff, gaoler or other royal official learn he was not guilty; he had to have ended up in the gaol somehow. Someone else must have been caught and punished for the crime, or others have testified to the gaoled man's innocence; otherwise, how did the gaoler know the man was '*non* [...] *culpabilis*' (not guilty)?

In the Middle Ages, while they did not use the term 'psychotic', individuals who could not fully comprehend reality did exist, such as the man in gaol, above. Another man, Geoffrey Riche suffered from the condition of '*furor*' (fury). Geoffrey killed Agnes Fuller when he was in '*demencia*'. Agnes had spurned his sexual advances and Geoffrey cut off her head. For a while he hid under a pig trough and told a neighbour he was a pig. His later actions – including trying to sew Agnes's head back on – illustrate how completely divorced from reality this man was.[94] Obviously, Geoffrey had some sense of responsibility – or, at least, his attempt to make things right by reattaching the woman's head, however gruesome, demonstrates that he did not like the outcome of his actions. Yet the idea that a grown person would think this would either hide the deed or reanimate the dead confirms that either he was quite intellectually disabled or in some way divorced from reality, possibly something a physician today might describe as psychotic.[95]

Conclusions

A patient with an inability to control herself, with a loss of imagination or inability to discern, would have medieval physicians searching for causes that might have affected her behaviour or injuries that might have impeded the workings of the brain. Quite differently, court officers would not have investigated reasons for the individual's affliction, but rather would have acted to protect the person and her community from harm and, possibly, directed someone to become her keeper. The court would have described her disconnection from reality or immorality and named the mental health condition as they interpreted it. They might have given the condition as the cause for a crime or inability to fulfil her responsibilities to society.

If she were unable to explain where she was or how to get home, had poor recall, and lacked imagination, she might be referred to in administrative records as having *demencia* (or *amencia*). This would parallel contemporary diagnosis of dementia patients.[96] If she wandered away from family or friends, court officials likely said that she had the condition of *lunaticus* (a lunatic) and might have *impos mentis* (a powerless mind), which contemporaries might also investigate as dementia, if not an intellectual disability.[97] If, along with an inability to demonstrate knowledge of her surroundings, she also became out of control and unrestrained, the officials would call her *freneticus* (a frenzied person), or if she lacked all control and perhaps became violent, a *furiosus* (a person with fury) or *in furore* (in fury). Neuroscientific scholars might look for underlying causes for this person to have a stress disorder, personality flaw, substance abuse disorder, paranoia or psychosis.[98] If she were at times *furiosa* (in fury or madness), the medieval court might check to see if she had a history of being affected by the phases of the *lune* (moon), or if she were known to be immoral, that she *sciens nec bonum nec malum* (knows neither good nor bad). These dissociative symptoms might have contemporary psychologists looking for bipolar disorder, borderline personality disorder or considering forms of schizophrenia.[99]

Medieval judges and juries did not investigate illness per se, only crime and property issues (such as inheritances) and the responsibilities associated with such properties. When illness was mentioned in court records, it was done so as part of the argument of the court – either by the plaintiff's attorney or the jury as part of the case against the perpetrator, or by the defence attorney as part of the justification of the crime. Those persons found guilty but mentally incapable of crime were pardoned.[100]

Medieval theories of the mind incorporated elaborate schemes of mental health and the working of the brain, mostly issues of senses – including perception and discernment associated with the anterior brain, cognition in the middle, and memory in the posterior. *Demencia*, for example, could be because of a loss of sense (common sense), an anterior brain issue; but it could also be because of a loss of memory, a posterior brain condition.[101] Some conditions, like *frenesi* and *furore* could present in each patient differently, according to medieval medical and scholarly texts, depending on what part of the brain was affected. The medical term *mania*, though, would not have paralleled what contemporary psychiatrists mean by 'mania' or 'hypomania' but rather part of contemporary bipolar disorder or other conditions that manifest euphoria, delusions, or overactivity for periods of time.[102] Medieval physicians used the term *mania* to indicate far more aggressive, perhaps psychopathic personalities and illnesses.[103]

Those persons suffering from trauma in the Middle Ages are even more difficult to pin down. Many of these individuals only enter the records once they have committed a crime or neglected their responsibilities. People with mental illnesses who were violent were sometimes kept in gaol or bound, tied or handcuffed to the bed, floor or wall for undefined amounts of time or until they stopped raging, although they would not otherwise have been corporally punished for their crimes.[104] A person known in the community as *lunaticus* or who *sciens nec bonum nec malum* was often watched more closely or even locked up during the days of the full moon, just in case he lost control.

Medieval physicians considered it a serious condition to have an '*apostume*' (infection or pooling of humours) interfere with the senses, including common sense and the imagination. And, while they did not use the term 'psychotic', physicians clearly described symptoms that parallel what twenty-first century physicians might call psychotic behaviour – erratic movements, delusions, hallucinations, and breaks with reality. These medieval concepts are mirrored in descriptions of contemporary patients with mood and anxiety disorders, PTSD and other stress-related disorders, depression, schizophrenia, and personality disorders.

Those conditions with the greatest similarities to post-modern stress disorders include '*idiota*' or '*lethargus*' and some '*lunaticus*'. The descriptions of those medieval persons with these conditions parallel many of the contemporary symptoms of PTSD, other stress disorders, depression, and perhaps schizophrenia. Medieval conditions with various elements that parallel psychoses (in contemporary terms) include '*furore*', '*demencia*', '*frenesis*' and '*sciens nec bonum nec malum*'. These might be medieval terms, and yet they offer interesting elements of diseases named 'fury' or 'without a mind' or 'franticness' or 'immoral'. This loss or lack of ethics and morals – not knowing how to tell good from bad or having a mind powerless to know the individual's own will – resonates with contemporary forensics and psychological studies. As scholars continue to study the mind through behaviour and individual responses are measured through tests based on one metric for psycho-socio-economic behaviour, there will continue to be inequalities. If, instead, scholars looked for a balance among individuals, their mental health and their environments – as is shown by this nascent study of parallel diagnosis – people and their mental health conditions change little over time. We still have stress, trauma, pressures of daily life: red dogs inviting moments of psychological disorder into our kitchens, things seen or unseen that give us real mental trouble functioning within the boundaries of our natural or social environment. Mental health in the Middle Ages parallels contemporary studies of mental health and, while we will never know exactly what was wrong with particular individuals, we know that those that adjudicated their cases knew they were seeing a mentally ill person and that those collective cases parallel the conditions of contemporary neuroscience.

Notes

1 'The Environmental Model', in C. Nolte, B. Frohne, U. Halle and S. Kerth (eds), *Dis/ability History der Vormoderne* (*Pre-Modern Dis/ability History*) (Affalterbach: Didymus, 2017), pp. 63–7. I introduced this in a keynote address in 2014 to the Creative Unit: *Homo Debilis* at the University of Bremen, 'Public-Environment: A Working Model for the History of Disability', after reflection on the social model put forth by Michael Oliver (see: M. Oliver and B. Sapey, *Social work with disabled people* (London: Palgrave Macmillan, 2006)) and theories on socio-cultural ideas of disability in Sharon L. Snyder and David T. Mitchell's book, *Cultural Locations of Disability* (Chicago: University of Chicago Press, 2006). See also Irina Metzler's work on the social model in *Disability in Medieval Europe: Thinking about Physical Impairment in the High Middle Ages, c.1100–c.1400* (Abingdon: Routledge, 2006). The religious model for medieval disability studies is suggested by Edward Wheatley in *Stumbling Blocks before the Blind: Medieval Constructions of a Disability* (Ann Arbor: University of Michigan Press, 2010); and the cultural model by Joshua R. Eyler in *Disability in the Middle Ages* (Farnham: Ashgate, 2010). All of us agree that the medical model does not work for the past and often is problematic in the present.

2 *The World Health Report 2001. Mental Health: New Understanding, New Hope* (Geneva: WHO, 2001), p. 12.

3 Wendy J. Turner, 'The Medieval Mind and Brain', in Iona McCleery (ed.), *A Cultural History of Medicine: vol. 2 Medieval* (London: Bloomsbury, forthcoming 2020).

4 American Psychiatric Association, *Diagnostic and Statistical Manual of Mental Disorders: Fifth Edition* (Arlington, VA: American Psychiatric Association, 2013), *https://www.psychiatry.org/psychiatrists/practice/dsm* (accessed 18 September 2018); hereafter: DSM-5.

5 I have written extensively on mental health in the medieval English court system. In particular see: *Care and Custody of the Mentally Ill, Incompetent, and Disabled in Medieval England*

(Turnhout: Brepols, 2013), pp. 63–6; 'Defining Mental Afflictions in Medieval English Administrative Records', in C. J. Rushton (ed.), *Disability and Medieval Law: History, Literature, Society* (Newcastle upon Tyne: Cambridge Scholars, 2013), pp. 134–56; 'Mentally Incapacitated Persons Tried for Crimes: Incarceration, Protection, Care, Pardon in Medieval England', in Cordula Nolte et al. (eds), *Dis/ability History der Vormoderne*: *Premodern Dis/ability History* (Affalterbach: Didymus, 2017), pp. 333–8; and Turner and Aleksandra Pfau, 'Legal Norms and Legal Practice/ Rechtsnormen und Rechtspraxis' (pp. 262–5) and 'Legal Landscapes: France and England in Comparison' (pp. 256–61), in C. Nolte et al. (eds), *Dis/ability History der Vormoderne.* For information on Continental treatment of mental illness, see the work of Cordula Nolte, such as *Disability History der Vormoderne – Umrisse eines Forschungsprogramms* (Affalterbach: Didymus 2013); Bianca Frohne, *Leben mit 'kranckhait'. Der gebrechliche Körper in der häuslichen Überlieferung des 15. und 16. Jahrhunderts. Überlegungen zu einer Disability History der Vorderne* (Affalterbach: Didymus, 2014); Aleksandra Pfau, 'Protecting or Restraining? Madness as a Disability in Late Medieval France', in Joshua R. Eyler (ed.), *Disability in the Middle Ages: Reconsiderations and reverberations* (Farnham: Ashgate, 2010); and Vesa Hirvonen, 'Late medieval philosophical and theological discussions of mental disorders: Witelo, Oresme, Gerson', *History of Psychiatry*, 29/2 (2018), 165–86.

6 Turner, *Care and Custody*, pp. 64–6.

7 Turner, 'Defining Mental Afflictions', p. 135.

8 Turner, 'Defining Mental Afflictions', pp. 134–56.

9 This term continues to be used in the United States to a limited degree but is seen in the UK and much of Europe as hurtful to the disabled community, meaning something akin to 'beggar', as in 'cap-in-hand'.

10 Diagnosing really cannot be done without interviewing and/or examining the patient, which in the case of medieval people is impossible. Still, we can draw parallels, and we can with some certainty see descriptions that resonate similarly to conditions of today. For example, in a recent work I researched a brutal crime in which the victim was beaten up (and raped) so badly that she died four days later. While the event could be said to be traumatic, I argue that it is highly likely that she suffered from the trauma of the event, which accounted in part for her 'madness' until her death. The courts at the time agreed, outlawing the primary culprit for homicide and executing the secondary for aiding and abetting. See: Turner, 'The Leper and the Prostitute: Forensic Examination of Rape in Medieval England', in Wendy J. Turner and Christina Lee (eds), *Trauma in Medieval Society* (Leiden: Brill, 2018), pp. 122–47.

11 See a longer list in the DSM-5.

12 There are numerous articles and books on this topic. For examples, see: Julian D. Ford, Damion J. Grasso, Jon D. Elhai and Christine A. Courtois, 'Epidemiology of PTSD', *Posttraumatic Stress Disorder*, 2nd edn, Scientific and Professional Dimensions (Cambridge, MA: Academic Press, 2015), pp. 133–82; and Charles W. Hoge, Carl A. Castro, Stephen C. Messer, Dennis McGurk et al., 'Combat Duty in Iraq and Afghanistan, Mental Health Problems, and Barriers to Care', *New England Journal of Medicine*, 351 (July 2004), 13–22.

13 For examples of articles on this topic, see: P. A. Garety, E. Kuipers, D. Fowler, D. Freeman et al., 'A cognitive model of the positive symptoms of psychosis', *Psychological Medicine*, 31/2 (Feb 2001), 189–95; P. A. Garety, T. K. J. Craig, G. Dunn, M. Fornells-Ambrojo et al., 'Specialised care for early psychosis: Symptoms, social functioning and patient satisfaction: randomised controlled trial', *The British Journal of Psychiatry*, 188/1 (Jan 2006), 37–45; Hélène Verdoux and Jim van Os, 'Psychotic symptoms in non-clinical populations and the continuum of psychosis', *Schizophrenia Research* 54.1–2 (March 2002): 59–65.

14 DSM-5.

15 For more on English trials and forensic investigation, see: Thomas A. Green, *Verdict According to Conscience; Perspectives on the English Criminal Trial Jury, 1200–1800* (Chicago: University of Chicago Press, 1985); and T. Oldon, 'Of Enchantment: The Passing of the Ordeals and the Rise of the Jury Trial', *Syracuse Law Review*, 50 (2000), 109–96.

16 Sara M. Butler, *Forensic Medicine and Death Investigation in Medieval England* (New York: Routledge, 2015); Greg Eghigian (ed.), *The Routledge History of Madness and Mental Health* (London: Routledge, 2017).

17 Wendy J. Turner, 'Town and Country: A Comparison of the Treatment of the Mentally Disabled in Late Medieval English Common Law and Chartered Boroughs', in Wendy J. Turner (ed.), *Madness in Medieval Law and Custom* (Leiden: Brill, 2010), pp. 17–38; and *Care and Custody*.

18 Elsewhere I have investigated how modern treatment of the mentally impaired compares to medieval treatment. In particular see: Wendy J. Turner, 'Mental Health and Homicide in Medieval English Trials', *Open Library of Humanities*, 4(2) (2018), 11, *http://doi.org/10.16995/olh.295*. See also: Elizabeth Papp Kamali, '*Felonia Felonice Facta:* Felony and Intentionality in Medieval England', *Criminal Law and Philosophy*, 9 (2015), 397–421; and Sara M. Butler, 'Representing the Middle Ages: The Insanity Defense in Medieval England', in Wendy J. Turner and Tory Vandeventer Pearman (eds), *The Treatment of Disabled Persons in Medieval Europe* (Lewiston: Mellen, 2010), pp. 117–33.

19 These concepts differed over time and place, but generally physicians in the high and later Middle Ages looked for physical causes for most mental health conditions. Ecclesiastics, however, often blamed a person's mental sin (lust, jealousy, blaspheme, or disrespect of ecclesiastics) as having caused God to lift his protection, allowing demons to inhabit the person and causing loss of mental function. See Karen Louise Jolly, *Popular Religion in Late Saxon England: Elf Charms in Context* (Chapel Hill: University of North Carolina Press, 1996); and Sylvia Huot, *Madness in Medieval French Literature: Identities Found and Lost* (Oxford: Oxford University Press, 2003).

20 Mary Carruthers, *The Book of Memory: A Study of Memory in Medieval Culture* (Cambridge and New York: Cambridge University Press, 2008); and Mary Carruthers (ed.), *Medieval Craft of Memory: An Anthology of Texts and Pictures* (Philadelphia: University of Pennsylvania Press, 2002).

21 For more on memory and emotion, see: Carruthers, *Book of Memory*; Carruthers, *Medieval Craft*; and Patrick J. Geary, *Phantoms of Remembrance: Memory and Oblivion at the End of the First Millennium* (Princeton, NJ: Princeton University Press, 1996); Esther Cohen, *The Modulated Scream: Pain in Late Medieval Culture* (Chicago: University of Chicago Press, 2010); Wendy J. Turner, 'Silent Testimony: Emotional Displays and Lapses in Memory as Indicators of Mental Instability in Medieval English Investigations', in Wendy J. Turner (ed.), *Madness in Medieval Law and Custom* (Leiden: Brill, 2010), pp. 81–95; Peter King, 'Emotions in Medieval Thought', in Peter Goldie (ed.), *The Oxford Handbook of Philosophy of Emotion*, Oxford Handbooks Online (2010) (Oxford: Oxford University Press, 2009), online: *http://www.oxfordhandbooks.com/view/10.1093/oxfordhb/9780199235018.001.0001/oxfordhb-9780199235018* (accessed 20 June 2017); Stephen Pender, 'Subventing Disease: Anger, Passions, and the Non-Naturals', in Jennifer C. Vaught (ed.), *Rhetorics of Bodily Disease and Health in Medieval and Early Modern England* (Farnham: Ashgate, 2010), pp. 193–218; and Barbara H. Rosenwein (ed.), *Anger's Past: The Social Uses of an Emotion in the Middle Ages* (Ithaca, NY: Cornell University Press, 1998).

22 For more on stress, see Smail in this volume.

23 Turner, *Care and Custody*, esp. pp. 76–81; Christopher F. Goodey, *A History of Intelligence and 'Intellectual Disability': The Shaping of Psychology in Early Modern Europe* (Farnham: Ashgate, 2011), and W. J. Turner, 'The Conceptualization of Intellectual Disability in Medieval English Law', in P. McDonagh, C. F. Goodey and T. Stainton (eds), *Intellectual Disability: A Conceptual History, 1200–1900* (Manchester: Manchester University Press, 2018), pp. 26–44.

24 Ford et al., 'Epidemiology of PTSD' (2015), p. 133.

25 For more on mood disorders, especially cultural-specific diagnoses, see: Peter Guarnaccia and Igda Martinez Pincay, 'Culture-Specific Diagnoses and Their Relationship to Mood Disorders', in Sana Loue and Martha Sajatovic (eds), *Diversity Issues in the Diagnosis, Treatment, and Research of Mood Disorders* (Oxford: Oxford University Press, 2008), pp. 32–53.

26 *Calendar of Inquisitions Post Mortem and other Analogous Documents Preserved in the Public Record Office*, Public Record Office, 20 vols (London: HMSO, 1904–70) (hereafter CIPM), vol. III, no. 728.

27 Mary L. S. Vachon, 'Grief and Bereavement Following the Death of a Spouse', *The Canadian Journal of Psychiatry*, 21/1 (Feb 1976), 35–44. This is a review article that summarises much of the work on spousal bereavement from 1944 until the mid-1970s.

28 These stages are outlined in many places. One excellent overview is in S. R. Shuchter and S. Zisook, 'The Course of Normal Grief', in M. S. Stroebe, W. Stroebe and R. O. Hansson (eds), *Handbook of Bereavement: Theory, research, and intervention* (Cambridge: Cambridge University Press, 1993), pp. 23–43.

29 Holly G. Prigerson, Ellen Frank, Stanislav V. Kasl, Charles F. Reynolds et al., 'Complicated Grief and Bereavement-Related Depression as Distinct Disorders: Preliminary Empirical Validation in Elderly Bereaved Spouses', *American Journal of Psychiatry*, 152/1 (Jan 1995), 22–30.

30 For example, I. J. McLoughlin and M. S. Bhate, 'A Case of Affective Psychosis following Bereavement in a Mentally Handicapped Woman', *The British Journal of Psychiatry*, 151/4 (Oct 1987), 552–4; and Cindy J. Grief and David D. Myran, 'Bereavement in Cognitively Impaired Older Adults: Case Series and Clinical Considerations', *Journal of Geriatric Psychiatry and Neurology*, 19/4 (Dec 2006), 209–15.

31 *Calendar of the Patent Rolls Preserved in the Public Record Office, 1216–1509*, Public Record Office, 52 vols (London: HMSO, 1891–1901) (hereafter CPR), vol. 1354–58, 44–5.

32 *Calendar of the Fine Rolls*, Public Record Office, 22 vols (London: HMSO, 1911–62) (hereafter CFR), vol. 5, 410.

33 For more information on adolescent psychiatric mood disorders, see: James B. McCarthy, Shira R. Weiss, Kristin T. Segovich and Baptiste Barbot, 'Impact of psychotic symptoms on cognitive functioning in child and adolescent psychiatric inpatients with severe mood disorders', *Psychiatry Research* (25 July 2016), *http://dx.doixorg/10.1016/j.psychres.2016.07.049.*

34 Cecilia L. W. Chan, Chong-Wen Wang, Andy H. Y. Ho, Zhi-Yong Qu et al., 'Symptoms of posttramatic stress disorder and depression among bereaved and non-bereaved survivors following the 2008 Sichuan earthquake', *Journal of Anxiety Disorders*, 26/6 (Aug 2012), 673–9.

35 The National Archive, Kew, UK (hereafter TNA), Chancery manuscript (hereafter C) C 135/125, m 25 and TNA C 66/245, m 13. See also: Calendar of Inquisitions Post Mortem, v. 10, Ed III, no. 142 (p. 132).

36 Armand W. Loranger, 'Sex Difference in Age at Onset of Schizophrenia', *Archives of General Psychiatry* 41 (Feb 1984), 157–61, *doi:10.1001/archpsyc.1984.01790130053007.*

37 CIPM Ed III, v. 7, no. 491, p. 349.

38 Loranger, 'Sex Difference', p. 157.

39 Robert E. Roberts, Catherine R. Roberts and Wenyaw Chan, 'One-year incidence of psychiatric disorders and associated risk factors among adolescents in the community', *The Journal of Child Psychology and Psychiatry*, 50/4 (25 Mar. 2009), 405–15, *https://doi.org/10.1111/j/ 1469-7610.2008.01969.x.*

40 Turner, *Care and Custody*, p. 80.

41 Turner, 'The Conceptualization of Intellectual Disability in Medieval English Law'.

42 Turner, *Care and Custody,* pp. 78–80.

43 Turner, 'Mind and Brain'.

44 TNA manuscript of the Justices Itinerant, Eyre Assize and other Plea rolls, JUST 1/300, m 23.

45 TNA manuscript of the King's Bench, 'Curia Regis Rolls', KB 26/171, m 11d.

46 TNA JUST 1/463, m 4d.

47 TNA manuscript of the Justices of Gaol Delivery, JUST 3/106, m 5.

48 TNA JUST 3/125, m 10. There might be more here about gender that needs to be teased out. The WHO found that many women could not escape their stress because of pressure in traditional roles from social, economic or religious pressure to stay, and this does not begin to take into account abusive relationships, which could be a whole other discussion. WHO 2001, p. 42.

49 Bartholomaeus Anglicus, *De proprietatibus rerum* (Nuremberg: Anton Koberger, 1483), *https:// archive.org/stream/deproprietatibu00anglgoog#page/n0* (accessed 18 September 2018), section 8, 175.

50 M. M. Ryan, H. E. Lockstone, S. J. Huffaker, M. T. Wayland et al., 'Gene expression analysis of bipolar disorder reveals downregulation of the ubiquitin cycle and alterations in synaptic genes', *Molecular Psychiatry*, 11 (2006), 965–78, *https://doi.org/10.1038/sj.mp.4001875*.

51 While in the mid-twentieth century many articles and books wrote believable studies that confirmed what hospitals had reported – during a full moon, there is more crime and poor decision-making. D. E. Campbell and J. L. Beets, 'Lunacy and the moon', *Psychological Bulletin*, 85/5 (1978), 1123–9, *https://doi.org/10.1037/0033-2909.85.5.1123*; and A. L. Lieber, *Lunar Effect: Biological Tides and Human Emotions* (Garden City, NY: Doubleday: 1978). Since that time, there has been some evidence to debunk these theories. J. Rotton and I. W. Kelly, 'Much ado about the full moon: A meta-analysis of lunar-lunacy research', *Psychological Bulletin*, 97/2 (1985), 286–306, *https://doi.org/10.1037/0033-2909.97.2.286*. Yet, some scholars point to a cultural environment that 'believes' that the moon can influence people. David E. Vance, 'Belief in Lunar Effects on Human Behavior', *Psychological Reports*, 76/1 (Feb. 1995), 32–4.

52 *Select Pleas of the Crown*, ed. F. W. Maitland, Selden Society 1 (London: Selden Society Publications, 1888), no. 187 (p. 119).

53 Roberts Roberts and Chan (2009). In a very few medieval sources, the term 'lunatic' was also used to describe epilepsy, even though physicians quite clearly understood the difference between the two conditions. This can be in part accounted for because of a mistranslation of Matthew 17: 15–20 and Luke 9: 38–43 in which the 'epileptic demoniac' was translated as 'lunatic' in the Vulgate.

54 Nirbhay N. Singh, Robert G. Wahler, Angela D. Adkins and Rachel E. Myers, 'Soles of the Feet: a mindfulness-based self-control intervention for aggression by an individual with mild mental retardation and mental illness', *Research in Developmental Disabilities*, 24/3 (May–June 2003), 158–69; and M. S. Stanford, N. E. Anderson, S. L. Lake and R. M. Baldridge, 'Pharmacologic treatment of impulsive aggression with antiepileptic drugs', *Current Treatment Options in Neurology*, 11/5 (2009), 383–90, *doi: 10.1007/s11940-009-0043-3*.

55 TNA JUST 1/244, m 27.

56 H. G. Kennedy, 'Anger and Irritability', *The British Journal of Psychiatry*, 161/2 (Aug. 1992), 145–53, *https://doi.org/10.1192/bjp.161.1.145*.

57 Richard M. Eisler, Jay R. Skidmore and Clay H. Ward, 'Masculine Gender-Role Stress: Predictor of Anger, Anxiety, and Health-Risk Behaviors', *Journal of Personality Assessment*, 54/1 (10 June 1988), 133–41, *https://doi.org/10.1207/s15327752jpa5201_12*; and Singh et al., 'Soles of the Feet'.

58 Turner, *Care and Custody*, 130–1.

59 TNA C 145/331, m 12 and *Calendar of Inquisitions Miscellaneous (Chancery), Henry III–Henry V*, 8 vols (London: HMSO, 1916–2003) (hereafter *CIM*), v. 2, no. 2093, p. 526.

60 His inheritance also included a messuage in Bristol that had been his mother's dower land, 'held of the king in chief by the yearly service of a pair of gilt spurs'. TNA C 145/69, m 17 and *CIM*, v. 2, no. 47, p. 13.

61 TNA C 54/129, m 22. In this manuscript he is called Thomas de la Ropsled. See also: *Calendar of the Close Rolls Preserved in the Public Record Office: Edward II*, 4 vols (London: HMSO, 1892–98) (hereafter *CCR Ed II*), vol. 1307–13, p. 382.

62 Gilbertus Anglicus, in Gaye Marie Getz (ed.), *Healing and Society in Medieval England: A Middle English Translation of the Pharmaceutical Writings of Gilbertus Anglicus* (Madison: University of Wisconsin Press, 1991), p. 13.

63 TNA JUST 1/775, m 18 (1236).

64 There are many types of dementia, including the most well-known Alzheimer's Disease. For general information see: Gustavo C. Román, Thomas K. Tatemichi, T. Erkinjuntti, J. L. Cummings et al., 'Vascular dementia: diagnostic criteria for research studies: report of the NINDS_AIREN International Workshop', *Neurology*, 43/2 (1 Feb. 1993), 250, *https://doi.org/10.1212/WNL.43.2.250*; Didier Leys, Hilde Hénon, Marie-Anne Mackowiak-Cordoliani and Florence Pasquier, 'Poststroke Dementia', *The Lancet: Neurology*, 4/11 (Nov. 2005), 752–9, *https://doi.*

org/10.1016/s1474-4422(05)70221-0; and Vladimir C. Hachinski, Linnette D. Iliff, Elias Zilhka et al., 'Cerebral Blood Flow in Dementia', *Archives of Neurology*, 32/9 (Sept. 1975), 632–7, *doi:10/1001/archneur.1975.00490510088009*.

65 TNA C 66/62, m. 6; and *CPR*, vol. 1247–1258, p. 100.

66 *Select Cases from the Coroners' Rolls 1265–1413*, Charles Gross (ed.), Selden Society Publications 9 (London: Bernard Quaritch, 1896), 50.

67 *Select Cases from the Coroners' Rolls 1265–1413*, p. 49.

68 TNA JUST 3/158, m 11d.

69 Bartholomaeus Anglicus, section 7, p. 120.

70 Román et al. (1993).

71 TNA JUST 3/103, m 3.

72 Susan K. Schultz, Del D. Miller, Susan E. Oliver, Stephan Arndt et al., 'The life course of schizophrenia: age and symptom dimensions', *Schizophrenia Research*, 23/1 (17 Jan. 1997), 15–23, *https://doi.org/10.1016/S0920-9964(96)00087-4*.

73 V. Geberth and R. Turco, 'Antisocial Personality Disorder, Sexual Sadism, Malignant Narcissism, and Serial Murder', *Journal of Forensic Sciences*, 42/1 (Jan. 1997), 49–60, *https://doi.org/10.1520/JFS14067J*. See also the white paper from the Office of Research and Public Affairs at the Treatment Advocacy Center, on Mass Homicides, 'Serious Mental Illness and Mass Homicide' (June 2018).

74 Mayo Clinic: Patient Care and Health Information, 'Delirium', *https://www.mayoclinic.org/diseases-conditions/delirium/symptoms-causes/syc-20371386*; DSM-5, 'Delirium'.

75 TNA C 66/109, m. 6; *CPR*, 1281–92, p. 390; and Turner, *Care and Custody*, pp. 120, 136–7.

76 TNA C 260/16, m 24.

77 TNA C 260/34, m 29; C 260/35, m 9; C 260/37, m 5.

78 TNA C 260/11, no. 1A; and *CCR*, vol. 1279–88, p. 143.

79 *The Roll of the Shropshire Eyre of 1256*, Alan Harding (ed.), Selden Society 96 (London: Selden Society Publications, 1981), no. 798.

80 TNA C 145/44, m 40; *CIM*, vol. 1, no. 2279; and Turner, 'Silent Testimony', 81–96.

81 Jason C. Matejkowski, Phyllis L. Solomon and Sara W. Cullen, 'Characteristics of Persons with Severe Mental Illness who have been Incarcerated for Murder', *Journal of the American Academy of Psychiatry and the Law*, 36 (Mar. 2008), 74–86.

82 Gilbertus Anglicus, p. 10.

83 Bartholomaeus Anglicus, section 7, p. 120. See also, Rolf Brüggemann and Gisela Schmid-Krebs, *Verortungen dear Steele – Locating the Soul: Psychiatriemuseen in Europe's – Museums of Psychiatry in Europe* (Frankfurt am Main: Mabuse-Verlag, 2007).

84 Bartholomaeus Anglicus, section 7, p. 120.

85 Michael S. Zandi, Sarosh R. Irani, Bethan Lang, Patrick Waters et al., 'Disease-relevant autoantibodies in first episode schizophrenia', *Journal of Neurology*, 258/4 (Apr. 2011), 686–8.

86 Singh et al. 'Soles of the Feet'.

87 TNA JUST 1/62, m 5.

88 TNA JUST 1/62, m 5.

89 TNA C 260/2, m 30.

90 TNA C 260/11, m 27.

91 Reinout E. de Vries and Dirk van Kampen, 'The HEXACO and 5DPT Models of Personality: A Comparison and Their Relationships with Psychopathy, Egoism, Pretentiousness, Immorality, and Machiavellianism', *Journal of Personality Disorders*, 24/2 (2010), 244–57, *https://doi.org/10.1521/pedi.2010.24.2.244*.

92 Delroy L. Paulhus and Kevin M. Williams, 'The Dark Triad of Personality: Narcissism, Machiavellianism, and Psychopathy', *Journal of Research in Personality*, 36/6 (Dec. 2002), 556–63.

93 *Placita corone, or La corone pledée devant justices*, J. M. Kaye (ed.), Selden Society Publications 4 (London: Selden Society, 1966), pp. 66–7.

94 TNA JUST 1/1109, m 18; see also: Naomi D. Hurnard, *The King's Pardon for Homicide before A.D. 1307* (Oxford: Clarendon Press, 1969), pp. 166–7; and Turner, 'Homicide'.

95 Ford et al. (2015).

96 Román et al. 1993.

97 A. Strydom, G. Livingston, M. King and A. Hassiotis, 'Prevalence of dementia in intellectual disability using different diagnostic criteria', *British Journal of Psychiatry*, 191 (Aug. 2007), 150–7.

98 Ford et al. (2015).

99 Dagna Skrzypińska and Barbara Szmigielska, 'Dream-reality confusion in borderline personality disorder: a theoretical analysis', *Frontiers in Psychology: Psychopathology* (15 Sept. 2015); *https://doi.org/10.3389/fpsyg.2015.01393*.

100 Turner, 'Mental Health and Homicide'.

101 Turner, *Care and Custody*, 66–90; Turner, 'Silent Testimony', 81–95.

102 Ryan et al., 'Gene expression analysis of bipolar disorder'.

103 For more information on contemporary psychopathy, see: J. Blair, D. Mitchell and K. Blair, *The Psychopath: Emotion and the Brain* (Oxford: Blackwell, 2005).

104 Turner, 'Mental Health and Homicide'.

Select Bibliography

American Psychiatric Association, *Diagnostic and Statistical Manual of Mental Disorders: Fifth Edition* (Arlington, VA: American Psychiatric Association, 2013).

Blair, J., D. Mitchell and K. Blair, *The Psychopath: Emotion and the Brain* (Oxford: Blackwell, 2005).

Butler, Sara M., *Forensic Medicine and Death Investigation in Medieval England* (New York: Routledge, 2015).

Cohen, Esther, *The Modulated Scream: Pain in Late Medieval Culture* (Chicago: University of Chicago Press, 2010).

Eghigian, Greg (ed.), *The Routledge History of Madness and Mental Health* (London: Routledge, 2017).

Eyler, Joshua R., *Disability in the Middle Ages* (Farnham: Ashgate, 2010).

Geary, Patrick J., *Phantoms of Remembrance: Memory and Oblivion at the End of the First Millennium* (Princeton, NJ: Princeton University Press, 1996).

Goodey, Christopher F., *A History of Intelligence and 'Intellectual Disability': The Shaping of Psychology in Early Modern Europe* (Farnham: Ashgate, 2011).

Jolly, Karen Louise, *Popular Religion in Late Saxon England: Elf Charms in Context* (Chapel Hill: University of North Carolina Press, 1996).

King, Peter, 'Emotions in Medieval Thought', in Peter Goldie (ed.), *The Oxford Handbook of Philosophy of Emotion*, Oxford Handbooks Online (Oxford: Oxford University Press, 2009).

Metzler, Irina, *Disability in Medieval Europe: Thinking about Physical Impairment in the High Middle Ages, c.1100–c. 1400* (Abingdon: Routledge, 2006).

Pfau, Aleksandra, 'Protecting or Restraining? Madness as a Disability in Late Medieval France', in Joshua R. Eyler (ed.), *Disability in the Middle Ages: Reconsiderations and reverberations* (Farnham: Ashgate, 2010).

Rosenwein, Barbara H. (ed.), *Anger's Past: The Social Uses of an Emotion in the Middle Ages* (Ithaca, NY: Cornell University Press, 1998).

Snyder, Sharon L. and David T. Mitchell, *Cultural Locations of Disability* (Chicago: University of Chicago Press, 2006).

Turner, Wendy J., 'Defining Mental Afflictions in Medieval English Administrative Records', in C. J. Rushton (ed.), *Disability and Medieval Law: History, Literature, Society* (Newcastle upon Tyne: Cambridge Scholars, 2013), pp. 134–56.

Turner, Wendy J., 'The Medieval Mind and Brain', in Iona McCleery (ed.), *A Cultural History of Medicine: vol. 2 Medieval* (London: Bloomsbury, forthcoming 2020).

Turner, Wendy J. (ed.), *Madness in Medieval Law and Custom* (Leiden: Brill, 2010).

Turner, Wendy J. and Tory Vandeventer Pearman (eds), *The Treatment of Disabled Persons in Medieval Europe* (Lewiston: Mellen, 2010).

Vachon, Mary L. S., 'Grief and Bereavement Following the Death of a Spouse', *The Canadian Journal of Psychiatry*, 21/1 (Feb. 1976), 35–44.

Wheatley, Edward, *Stumbling Blocks before the Blind: Medieval Constructions of a Disability* (Ann Arbor: University of Michigan Press, 2010).

6

Attachment Theory for Historians of Medieval Religion: An Introduction

JULIANA DRESVINA

Religion as Adaptation?

The past twenty or so years have seen a significant rise in research dedicated to the intersection of evolution and religion, which increasingly engages with an extra ingredient: neuroscience.[1] Many scientists, of whom Richard Dawkins is the most famous but certainly not the first, have advocated the general theory of 'religion as an accidental by-product – a misfiring of something useful'.[2] At the same time, other researchers, most prominently American professor of biology D. S. Wilson in his monograph *Darwin's Cathedral: Evolution, Religion, and the Nature of Society* (2002), have strongly argued in favour of religion as a multi-level adaptive mechanism necessary for our species' survival and well-being, rather than simply a by-product or 'parasite' of evolutionary development. Interestingly, Darwin himself seems to have resisted thinking of religion as an adaptation.[3] There are numerous hypotheses that interpret adaptive functions of religiousness, including the placebo effect, the capacity for trance, promotion of character strengths and cooperation among individuals, and explanatory models that give life meaning and calm the fear of death. Recently, in an important and ambitious three-volume enterprise, *Where God Meets Science*, the participating scholars could not come to an agreement as to whether or not religion is an adaptation. On the one hand, Joseph Bulbulia declares: 'In sum, our recent and deep history suggests that we are a faith-healing primate'. Yet Lee A. Kirkpatrick, in the same volume, argues in favour of the multiple by-products view of religion, i.e. that the development of religion was a side-effect of a variety of psychological mechanisms that evolved for other purposes. In the second volume, Pehr Granqvist calls religion 'a by-product of evolved psychology', following the line of reasoning that religion is not a biological adaptation in its own right and is 'held to emerge indirectly from the operation of evolved psychological mechanisms that did, in turn, fill an adaptive function in the environments in which the human species evolved'.[4] Even a single project may contain several conflicting views; so the debate goes on, with no consensus in sight.[5]

Many scholars nevertheless accept that religions and religiosity *can* be an adaptation and *can* act as a part of collective or individual psychological defence mechanism. It is for this reason that I argue studying the religiosity of the past simultaneously helps us understand current issues.[6] It would be simplistic, of course, to assume that influence always flows in one direction, from nature to culture (see Daniel Smail's chapter in this volume); however, as one aspect of an explanatory model, the adaptation hypothesis is sufficient. It is well known that the defence mechanisms we form early in life in order to adapt to our circumstances become part of our brain circuitry – what fires together, wires together. These defence mechanisms remain part of our neural make-up as automatic responses, even after they are no longer needed for survival.[7] We might bring to mind multiple cases of adaptations that were recorded and sanctified in early texts later but which later became maladaptive: the advocacy of slavery is one such example, along with numerous gender-based restrictions. These practices are often propagated by the very people they harm, precisely because they believe in their divine origin.

Yet seeing religion as a sort of adaptation helps cultural historians better understand periods of heightened, obsessive religiosity, such as we find during the Middle Ages and the Early Modern period in the West. Scholars of medieval affective piety, gendered theology and self-narrative will recognise the often healing effects of such heightened religious states, as exemplified by Julian of Norwich's 'Shewings', in which she interprets God not solely as our Father but also as our Mother, before making a full physical and psychological recovery from her grave illness.[8] These familial interpretations are extremely important for Julian (and, as she saw them, for humankind in general): taking my cue from the prominent role of familial imagery and analogy in certain accounts of heightened religious states, in this chapter I suggest that applying the principles of attachment theory offers a new way to approach studies of past religiosity. Reading and interpreting pre-modern material in this way – especially devotional, (para)liturgical, and broadly (auto) biographical sources – is an interdisciplinary, consilient endeavour, combining evolutionary and cognitive psychology and cultural history. Since classification of adult attachment relies heavily on the balance between the speaker's cognition and affect, narrative sources dealing with experiences of affective piety are particularly useful for examining religiosity through the lens of attachment theory.

Attachment Theory

Since its inception in the middle of the twentieth century, attachment theory has rapidly become one of the most heavily researched and widely used conceptual frameworks in modern psychology.[9] Attachment theory in psychology describes types of interpersonal relationships, focusing on parents (or primary caregivers) and children and then, concentrically, romantic partners, friends or any object that can be perceived as relatable, such as authorities or country, or God, for that matter. One of the main tools of attachment theory, Adult Attachment Interviews (AAI), gauges how a person cognitively and affectively processes the events of their life, especially those connected with danger and subsequent protection and comfort, since information processing (the way we interpret life events) underlies all behaviour.[10] Yet attachment theory has not been applied to the study of the past, including the Middle Ages. While we cannot subject the people of the past to a study involving spontaneous reactions in a semi-structured interaction, or map the AAI questions about attachment figures, dangerous episodes, loss and reflections on one's early experiences directly onto surviving examples of pre-modern discourse, we can still apply its main interpretive technique – that is, discourse analysis informed by cognitive psychology and neuroscience – to a variety of pre-modern examples of life-writing. In the particular case of my own research, reflected in this chapter, coaching in pre-modern literary history and rhetoric provides awareness of the expectations of the genre, and filters the information presented in the sources. At the same time, psychological training in AAI administering and coding allows me to identify the elements of discourse analysis necessary for hypothesising about pre-modern speakers' attachment strategy. Such elements include cognitive or affective organisation, use of flat or animated images in memories, self-reliance, reductionist blaming thought (reducing a person to a problem), triangulation (siding with one person to belittle another), and whether the discourse reflects the person's own perspective or that of others.[11] The purpose of applying this theory is not to demonstrate that it works in historical perspective, as its universality should make it valid for any period of the development of human society, even with the inevitable temporal and cultural variations. Nor is it an argument in favour of superiority or singularity of an Anglo-American scientific approach that boils down complex historical material to a simple classification or even a diagnosis, always privileging the present over the past. One of the areas where I believe attachment theory and its methods are relevant to an understanding of the past is the examination of the forms and types of protective strategies that people of the past developed in response to situations of danger and distress, as well as, to a lesser extent, procreation and sexual impulses, not least because these are the key elements for adaptation and survival which define the main vector of the current development in attachment theory's practical application by clinicians, social services and in forensics.[12] Making sense of the significant events of one's life is essential for human functionality, and attachment theory often takes the 'strengths' approach to maladaptive behaviour, emphasising its functionality rather than seeing it as a deficit – 'if it protects you, it is a right strategy'. It may well be that what the clinicians and social workers of today would classify as a dysfunction was a normative developmental trajectory in the past.

In its basic meaning, attachment is an evolutionarily determined process of seeking proximity to an identified attachment figure in situations of perceived distress or alarm, for the purpose of survival.[13] The first to study attachment in humans from this perspective was British psychiatrist and psychologist John Bowlby; his ideas were later developed by American-Canadian developmental psychologist Mary Ainsworth from the 1950s to the 1990s. Bowlby suggested that attachment behaviours such as proximity-seeking were adaptive responses to separation from a much stronger primary attachment figure that provides care and protection. Of all mammals, human children take longest to gain a degree of independence – unlike many other organisms, who are able to sustain themselves independently within hours of 'birth' – and therefore those infants who were able to maintain proximity to an attachment figure via attachment behaviours would receive the necessary care and make it to maturity. Thus a motivational system gradually evolved through natural selection (in the behaviour of humans and many other advanced animals) to regulate proximity to an attachment figure. Interestingly, John Bowlby's last book was a biography of Darwin – a testimony to the importance of evolution to his work as a psychologist.[14]

Researchers established two main types of attachment. One is *secure* (B-type): securely attached children are ready to explore the world if they know they have a secure base, their primary caregiver(s), to turn to in times of need and achieve a psychological state of 'felt security'; this is perceived as the most adaptive attachment style, which enables individuals to attune their responses to changing circumstances. The other is *insecure*, often divided into two or three subcategories: anxious-avoidant (A-type), or 'dismissive' in adults, who tend to be mostly cognitively organised at the expense of affect, demonstrating generalisations and hypothetical projections rather than concrete episodic memories, and either omit/deny negative affect or replace it with false positive one; anxious-ambivalent/resistant (C-type), or 'preoccupied' in adults, who tend to be predominantly affectively organised and demonstrate either omitted or false cognition in their discourse; and disorganised attachment (AC-type), displaying both cognition and affect but no integration, as opposed to the secure B-type. Currently there are two similar systems of classifying attachment available: one known as ABC+D, and the other as DMM (Dynamic Maturation Model). The latter is in many ways a modification of the former, especially when it comes to adult attachment; it expands the classification of ABC+D and does not allow for 'cannot classify' conclusions.[15] The classification among adults is not about good/bad, normal/abnormal attachment, but about the degree of integration of one's life-experiences, especially those connected with danger, and subsequent psychological comfort and stability derived from these synthesised meanings. In the DMM model especially, normative attachment strategies are those of B-types and the lower subscripts of As and Cs, whereas the higher As and Cs are often found among the clinical sample of the population.

From the late 1980s, attachment research was extended to adults, predominantly to romantic partners. It was suggested that attachment-related affect-regulating strategies are active from cradle to grave, and that acquired attachment styles, like many other early social experiences, produce relatively lasting differences in relationship patterns in adulthood.[16] Obviously, due to neuroplasticity, it does not mean that in their later relationships people who displayed insecure attachment styles as children cannot modify their responses and demonstrate secure attachment patterns (or vice versa), but such scenarios would require some significant change of circumstances as well as consistent effort from the person themselves. In other words, the attachment model formed in one's childhood may predict but does not necessarily determine one's attachment style as an adult, hence many scientists prefer to study children because they present clear-cut examples of primary attachment. Furthermore, in most people the attachment system is less easily activated as they mature, 'and when it is activated at lower levels, a telephone call, a letter, even the mere knowledge that an attachment figure would be available if the situation got worse, may suffice to give the individual a sense of felt security'.[17] Yet dramatic 'life events', such as divorce, serious illness, massive social change or the death of loved ones, will still cause high activation of the attachment system, and proximity of an attachment figure is the most effective way to achieve affect regulation (i.e. a person's ability to modulate their emotional state in order to adapt to the demands of their environment) in such situations.

At this point, it is worth asking if attachment is innate, rather than a constructed, historical concept. It is true that so far attachment theory has predominantly been tested in Western society where it is usually expected that children will have a primary caregiver. Yet it was in Uganda in 1954–5 that Mary Ainsworth came up with her tripartite attachment system while observing infant–mother dyads, later replicating the results of her experiments in Baltimore.[18] Bowlby also emphasised the universality of attachment, as it can also be observed in non-human primates and other species (although not all the ideas stemming from the studies of other species are relevant to the studies of humans);[19] therefore, it is possible to apply attachment theory to human societies that are distant from Western culture both geographically and historically. Indeed, since the beginning of attachment research, the validity of the theory has been demonstrated by multiple studies taking in a wide range of areas and diverse groups, and there is no reason to believe that in the past such attachment categories were drastically different.[20] This universality, however, does not make attachment theory insensitive to cross-cultural differences – it only maintains that 'attachment bonds will be established in any known culture, regardless of childrearing arrangements and family constellations'.[21] This is because attachment theory focuses on how individuals adapt to danger through self-protective strategies: danger is perceived differently in different cultures and circumstances, yet the certain identifiable range of adaptive behaviours is observable in all of them.

So far, most of the data on attachment distribution indeed comes from the West, and especially from North America. The numbers usually suggest that between 60 and 70 per cent of people are securely attached, with roughly equal distribution between the remaining 'insecure' subcategories, which may be divided into either two or three types.[22] This data seems to be consistent overall for both infants and adults, which supports the theory that attachment styles remain stable throughout one's lifetime. While attachment theory describes a global adaptive behaviour, and can accommodate culture-specific influences, at this stage the studies of non-Western attachment are, unfortunately, few and far between. So far, small-sample studies in various parts of the globe suggest that the norm is consistent throughout the world, with the range of between 56 and 72 per cent of securely attached children recorded for most of the studies.[23] Interestingly, intra-cultural variation is rather large compared with cross-cultural variation: for example, some Japanese samples show a higher rate of ambivalent attachment and a lower rate of avoidant attachment compared to global norms, while other Japanese samples demonstrate a lower rate of both.[24] It is therefore very probable that the attachment style distribution in the population of the past, especially the distant past, was very different from the modern picture, but that the actual styles – secure (B), avoidant/dismissive (A), ambivalent/preoccupied (C) and disorganised (AC) – remained the same.

Attachment and Religion

Attachment distributions vary not only internationally, but by other cultural variables that shape interpersonal behaviours, particularly religion. Kirkpatrick and Shaver, pioneers of research into religion and attachment, proposed in 1992 that the relationship with God can be viewed as another attachment bond. They suggested that, since attachment is based on generalised mental models of 'self' and 'other', people with a positive view of others who are securely attached should also have a positive view of God and be more intrinsically religious.[25] However, some studies point to a positive association between religiosity and attachment anxiety. This led to two opposing hypotheses about how individual differences in attachment may relate to religiousness. On the one hand, the *correspondence hypothesis* argues that 'securely attached individuals, who possess positive working models of themselves and others, will come to view God in a similar manner – as a reliable, secure base with whom one can have an enduring personal relationship'. On the other hand, the *compensation hypothesis* theorises that 'insecure individuals may develop an attachment to God or other divine figures as surrogates for unsatisfactory human attachment figures'.[26]

However, not all religions are equal in this regard. Again, the research on variation in attachment style within various Christian denominations is still limited, and within other religions virtually non-existent, but we can already see how there may be a strong correlation between the relationship with God and general adult attachment, suggesting that adherents of religions with a more punitive view of God (e.g. Orthodox Christian or some Protestant denominations) may be less securely attached. Additionally, Christian denominations tend to vary in their doctrine of inherent human sinfulness and the ease with which its adepts can commit grave sins – as well as the nature of such sins. Both of these characteristics (the degree of innate human sinfulness and the range of mortal sins) have been associated with mistrust in others, and could reasonably be associated with higher attachment avoidance. Furthermore, 'endorsement of the doctrinal belief that G-d expects perfection has been linked to general anxiety, and might conceivably relate to higher attachment anxiety'.[27] Research on parenting practices in religious communities also suggests that 'there may be denominational differences in childhood disciplinary measures and in positive parenting, two factors that are thought to influence the development of attachment'.[28] Given the portability of attachment theory, similar observations can be anticipated when looking at religiosity of the past, as we will see in the following sections.

Medieval Implications (1): Medieval Childrearing Practices

These observations on childhood attachment styles are useful for thinking about religiosity as a key part of people's identity within societies with strong organised religions. Surveying medieval childrearing practices in order to hypothesise the attachment styles they likely encouraged is generally not for the fainthearted. Every historic period preserves horror-stories about the treatment of children, often related with habitual nonchalance. Being alive before vaccination and anaesthetics was no fun, and even less for children; early medieval childhood has 'danger' written all over it. Even if one is sceptical of early forays into psychohistory and sees some of the conclusions of Lloyd DeMause (its leading theorist) as over-claims, his volume *The History of Childhood* – subtitled *The Untold Story of Child Abuse* in the second edition – is a powerful read. More recently, the opening titles of the 'Childhood of the Past' monograph series tellingly feature *Childhood and Violence in the Western Tradition* and *The Dark Side of Childhood in Late Antiquity and the Middle Ages*.[29]

To start with, *expositio*, or child exposure or abandonment, was a familiar practice in Antiquity, and one that never waned throughout the Middle Ages, despite some historians' claims for the 'civilising' effect of Christianity. Pre-modern literature, from the legend of Romulus and Remus to numerous heroes of romance, portray a number of 'happy endings' in which abandoned children are rescued, reclaimed or achieve greatness. These, however, are little more than wishful thinking. To quote a recent study, '[m]ost exposed infants died before they were rescued and most who were rescued were enslaved and never reclaimed, just as children in foundling hospitals usually died of starvation and neglect, despite a complex wet-nursing system'.[30] Margery Kempe, a self-made devout English woman of the fifteenth century, reports that her own confessor suspected her of bearing and abandoning a child while on her first overseas pilgrimage. I will return in detail to Margery's experiences in the latter half of this chapter. However, gossip and slander aside, one wonders if someone who knew Margery so well had particular reason (social or personal) to think that an emphatically Christian, married member of his town's elite could have done such a thing and whether, more generally, this indicates that the practice of child abandonment was still thought of as a 'standard option' in fifteenth-century England.[31]

Although the medieval concept of the child did certainly exist, contrary to Philippe Ariès's much-cited and long-criticised claim, the category was less clear-cut than the modern one and very much a response to socio-economic pressures.[32] Thus a man in his twenties who was still serving his apprenticeship could be called a boy, due to his subordinate status, while the need to legitimise a dynastic alliance or secure a property transfer might mean a child was married off before even reaching puberty.[33] The seven ages of man, well known from Jacques's soliloquy in *As You Like It* (Act 2, Scene VII) and numerous late-medieval and Renaissance sources, defined infancy (*infantia*) as the first seven years of one's life, with childhood (*pueritia*), exemplified by the schoolboy, continuing from age seven to age fourteen, the start of *adolescentia*. In the later Middle Ages, childhood was often a time of separation from the primary figures of attachment, with children being sent to schools (including boarding schools) or to become servants, or offered as a child oblate to a monastery (though this practice became less widespread as the Middle Ages wore on). Fourteen was the standard age for beginning an apprenticeship, although it could start as early as ten.[34] Such separation was sometimes dictated by economic need, but was also commonly perceived as good parental practice, since children were believed to acquire skills and learn discipline better by living with comparative strangers for the period between the ages of seven and fourteen years old. Given that even the parents apparently lived by the adage 'he who spares the rod, spoils the child', in these new households children were subject to abuse by beating, malnutrition, overwork and sexual assault. On top of that, there are numerous examples of contract sales, when the child servant or apprentice changed hands several times in a short period.[35]

Such strings of early separations were experienced by all classes. Wet-nurses were popular; they were not necessarily resident in the houses where they were employed (especially in Italy, where urban children were often sent away to a *balia*) but in the absence of formula milk well-off parents were unwilling to use the milk of beasts to suckle the infant, lest it resemble the source when grown up. A chaotic pattern of wet-nursing is well depicted in the case of Florentine twins born in 1385:

> 'Manno' was kept by his mother two weeks, then sent out to a wet-nurse who kept him for two months (until she became pregnant), returned to his mother for eleven days until a second nurse was found with whom he stayed for sixteen months (until she became pregnant). 'Gherardo' stayed with his mother for about five weeks, then went in direct succession to three wet-nurses (the first two became pregnant) for periods of six, nine and three months.[36]

It is not clear how widespread this practice was outside late-medieval Italian towns, nor do we know for sure what happened to the twins as they grew up, but one wonders if the distorted early attachment was at least partially responsible for the ruthless politics and imbalanced emotions observable among the Italian upper classes of that time. Today we know that such erratic patterns of foster care play a key role in the development of attachment patterns of advanced insecurity, frequently resulting in clinical cases.[37]

Separation of siblings from each other and from their parents is also evident in cases of London wardship. After the death of a parent (normally the father), depending on economic priorities there was absolutely no guarantee that the mother would be given guardianship of her children. In fourteenth- and fifteenth-century London between 40 and 50 per cent of cases were judged in favour of the mother alone or the mother and her new husband (given the lucrative marriage market). These figures are relatively low because 'by city law, wardship of minors "ought not to be in the hands of a kinsman to whom the inheritance could descend"'.[38] It was not unusual for the children to be taken away from the mother and sent to live with the executors of the dead father's will or with his guild brothers, while the mother and her new husband would get custody of another small child. Despite the financial incentive to look after such wards, the number of children who died during wardship was 32 per cent.[39] Comparable numbers may have died while away at boarding schools, if Winchester College is anything to go by – in one particularly bad year, twenty out of seventy pupils died, while a number of others left on account of infirmity.[40] Epidemics, other diseases and accidents are certainly the main suspects here, but separation from attachment figures may have contributed to the cases of pupils' deaths and infirmities. We know that Bowlby's thinking about attachment crystallised when he became puzzled by the fact that in post-war UN-run orphanages with good nutrition, hygiene and healthcare, the death rates were significantly higher than among those children given to random poor families, who were often raised in much less materially advantageous conditions, yet with stable attachment figures instead of constantly changing nurses.[41]

Medieval Implications (2): Attachment Styles Encouraged by Medieval Circumstances

From what we have seen, medieval people were more likely to experience loss of primary attachment figures, early separation (physical and emotional), abuse at home, high stress, insecurity and instability of their environment. Certainly, the data is only accessible to us through texts which are not intended to directly reflect on attachment styles, rather reflecting social or economic realities or displaying a devotional aim; achieving precision in their analysis within the proposed terminology is therefore difficult. It is hard to make projections in the absence of reliable statistics, but one might expect that, due to higher degrees of daily danger, culturally normalised separations and fewer opportunities for immediate protection and comfort from attachment figures, the number of insecurely attached individuals in the Middle Ages would have been higher than it is today: today, studies estimate that around 30 per cent of the population display high attachment anxiety, so it might not be unreasonable to speculate that in the Middle Ages, this figure could have been as high as 50 per cent.[42] In turn, these circumstances shaped appropriate cultural responses, for example the affective piety of the late Middle Ages. If, as attachment theory suggests, we are hardwired by evolution to seek proximity even in an environment where attachment figures are in short supply, then, in one theologian's words, 'the idea of God is the idea of an absolutely adequate attachment figure'.[43] At a very basic level, the figure of God did not only promote values that were beneficial for society's survival, such as charity and cooperation (as Wilson repeatedly highlights in *Darwin's Cathedral*), but also provided people with an idea of stability in an unstable environment, thus contributing to both multi-level selection and general mental and emotional well-being. At the more complex level of cultural psychology, the evolution of religion itself was shaped by both securely and insecurely attached individuals, as seen in the sentiments expressed in liturgy, daily prayers, mainstream theology, and religious literature and imagery (some of which are explored below). The struggle to make sense of these internalised, seemingly conflicting messages lies at the heart of Julian of Norwich's *Shewings* in the late fourteenth century, as well as numerous other theological works, both medieval and modern.[44]

We can find evidence in the surviving sources to support the hypothesis that a higher proportion of Western Europeans in the Middle Ages had attachment anxiety compared to their modern counterparts. The methodology for analysing these sources can be drawn from the growing body of research that looks at religion as attachment in modern-day believers, especially since the beginning of the twenty-first century.[45] An attachment system is activated mainly in the context of danger and distress, with the question 'Is an attachment figure available and likely to be responsive to my needs?' If the answer is affirmative, security-based strategies of affect regulation are implemented. They demonstrate 'optimistic beliefs about distress management, trusting beliefs about others' goodwill, and a sense of self-efficacy about dealing with threats'.[46] This optimism is perhaps best seen in Julian of Norwich's famous words 'All shall be well, all shall be well, all manners of things shall be well', which, according to her own confession, she heard from God in a sickbed revelation.[47] Such confidence, however, only applies with *securely attached* individuals. The case of heightened attachment anxiety, where the attachment figure is perceived as unavailable, results in *hyper-activating strategies*. These are indicated by overdependence on attachment figure as a source of protection and perception of oneself as relatively helpless. This fits very well with God (or a special saint) as a primary attachment figure. Many key quotations used in daily devotions confirm this tendency: 'The Lord is my helper' (Hebrews 13:6, with parallels in Psalms); 'Remember, Man, that thou art but dust and unto dust thou shalt return' (Ash Wednesday liturgy); 'For without me you can do nothing' (John 15:5), and so on.[48]

In many ways, traditional Christianity is especially suitable for people with anxious and disorganised attachment style: there, the main attachment figure is notionally ever-present ('I am with you all days, even to the consummation of the world', says Jesus in Matthew 28:20), but in practice unavailable, or available in such a way that the devotee cannot sense this availability (which is perceived his or her own fault). The belief in a figure who is simultaneously loving and punishing mirrors a child's feelings about a 'disorganised' caregiver, because rather than being a solution to fear, such a caregiver is actually part of its source, resulting in an irresolvable dilemma for the person seeking proximity. A disorganised style of attachment is strongly linked to dissociative mental states, such as experiences of loss or dissolution of self, or out-of-body experiences. High attachment anxiety also causes intensified negative emotional response to painful events, keeping them alive in the working memory and causing chronic activation of the attachment system; thus 'psychological pain related to the unavailability of attachment figures is exacerbated'.[49] Here medievalists can readily recognise the familiar longing for Christ and the constant memories of Christ's suffering that inform affective piety. Julian of Norwich reports the beginning of her 'shewings' as follows: 'Than came suddenly to my minde that I should desire the second wounde of our Lords gracious gift, that my body might be fulfilled with minde and felyng of His blissid passion, for I would that His peynes were my peynes, with compassion, and, afterward, longeing to God'.[50] Meanwhile, Julian's junior colleague and fellow countrywoman, Margery Kempe (1373–c. 1440), for many years displayed signs of extreme distress every time she was reminded of Christ's Passion through hearing preaching, being read the Scriptures or devotional literature, viewing religious imagery or even seeing a handsome man or a male child (*BMK*, I: ch. 35).

Another interesting aspect of anxious attachment is that, whereas a securely attached individual responds to a partner's unavailability or perceived negative behaviour by expressing functional anger, an anxiously attached person redirects this anger towards themselves, resulting in shame, self-disgust and depression.[51] As one cannot be angry with God for being unavailable, these affects can only be expressed as culturally normalised self-harm, such as extreme asceticism, flagellation, excessive fasting, drinking pus, and so on.[52] Margery Kempe's dramatic conversion began with a bout of illness, which was caused by her first experience of childbirth and her inability to confess a sin which long bothered her; during this sickness she tried to kill herself or at least became suicidal and, when restrained, bit her own hand so hard that the scar remained there for the rest of her life ('Sche wold a fordon hirself many a tym at her steryngys and a ben damnyd wyth hem in helle. And into wytnesse therof sche bot hir owen hand so vyolently that it was seen al hir lyfe aftyr'). Yet when Christ appeared by her bedside, his question, 'Dowtyr, why hast thow forsakyn me, and I forsoke nevyr the?' (Book I: ch. 1) displays first and foremost not comfort and compassion, but rebuke and blame. In Margery's world, the cause of her problems was not that Christ was absent throughout her pain, distress and demotic temptation – it was her own fault, and her troubles were a consequence of her abandoning him in the first place through her presumably less-than-perfect life (about which we have been told nothing at this stage of the *Book*).

Religiosity Used to Cope with Attachment Anxiety? The Case of Margery Kempe

Margery, whose book can be styled – with many caveats – the first English vernacular autobiography, is an interesting case for testing the significance of attachment style in the choice and expression of the religious practices that helped her maintain basic psychological functionality. As Wendy Turner observes in the previous chapter of this volume, diagnosing medieval mental health complaints is usually both impossible and unhelpful; however, sometimes the information is just about sufficient to suspect either a normative or a clinical background. Judging by her text and its historic context, Margery's problems spread across organic, psychological and social spectrums, usually flowing into each other. Organic problems, even though Margery did not always view them as such, include hallucinations of demonic visions (I: ch. 1), or perceiving sweet smells or celestial melodies (I: chs 35–36), convulsions ('wondyrfully turnyng and wrestyng hir body on every syde', I: ch. 28), and the emotional seesaw that characterises the early part of the *Book*, with Margery cycling through manic exhilaration at her perception of the 'fyer of lofe' before being brought low by bouts of demonic temptation or acute panic. The best example of this transition is described in I: ch. 4, in which Margery goes from dreading 'no devylle in helle' and being on top of her devotional practices, to a complete collapse brought on by believing that 'God had forsakyn hir' only one year (or half a page) later. Alongside these extremes of emotion, Margery goes through multiple pregnancies and births – at least one of which was traumatic enough to warrant special mention in a book that is not concerned with Margery's own childbearing, and in an age where difficult births were common. Margery's *Book* also describes numerous difficulties that we would class as psychological issues, and they are often the flip side of the organic ones. Margery displays a constant need for reassurance, fear of death and damnation, fear of abandonment (she is a very social creature, even by medieval standards), a fixation with males (especially handsome young ones), some difficulty judging time, and massive problems with attachment (more on which in a moment). Her social difficulties, meanwhile, include repeated spousal rape, frustrated expectations regarding her status, authority and agency, and the necessity of negotiating a rapidly changing social climate.

Scholars have previously tried to diagnose Margery Kempe with a range of mental conditions, but most of them accept that, retrospectively, such diagnostics can only be applied fairly loosely.[53] So far, none seem to have observed that reading Margery's account is often reminiscent of going through the narrative of a person with a DID (dissociative identity disorder) who has been through years of therapy.[54] According to modern research, DID develops out of early abuse, abandonment or severe illness, and is characterised by disorganised attachment, impaired social sensitivity, emotional imbalance and multiple inner voices or personalities, combined with very vivid and developed 'pretend world' over which the person often has only a limited degree of control.[55] Once again, these observations are presented here not to issue Margery with a modern diagnosis but, rather, to try and use what we know about DID and its therapy to suggest the sources of both Margery's difficulties and her defences and coping mechanisms.

Many scholars have been puzzled by the fact that Margery did not say anything about her fourteen children outside her reference to her adult son, when he became useful to her during the writing of her *Book*. Even by medieval standards – or by the standards of the specific literary genre in which texts like hers are written, which offer a very skewed representation of the lives they describe – her near-complete blackout concerning her children is disturbing. We can, of course, argue that Margery was modelling herself on Elizabeth of Hungary or similar saints, or compare this with Julian removing the references to her mother in her first Short Text, so as not to distract the reader from her revelations when she came to write the Long Text. Yet these arguments do not seem sufficient. All Margery's frequent early references to marital debt and her pregnancies lead to nothing. At one point, Jesus implies in his speech to her that both her husband and at least some of her children are alive, so it was not the case that all the children simply died in infancy (Book I, ch. 86). Margery is more eager to fantasise about swaddling the infant Christ or to express her over-the-top affection for random male babies she sees on the street than she is to see her own granddaughter, whose birth excites her originally, but whom we do not even know if Margery bothered to visit when she travelled to Germany (Book II, chs 2–4).

One can suspect this emotional dissociation was caused by pain of childbirth and potentially the loss of at least some of her children, but looking at her text from the perspective of attachment theory rather suggests that Margery was displaying sure signs of disorganised attachment. Such attachment style is often generational,[56] and I wonder whether Margery's son and daughter-in-law's decision to leave their only child, an underage daughter, with friends in Germany (as it happened, for over two years, Book II, ch. 2), is a reflection not only of more widespread parental practices, but of damaged attachment. It is also curious that Margery proudly mentioned her father to other people but in her *Book* never reports talking to him directly, even though we know from other sources that he lived in Lynn into his old age and died about the time Margery left on her first pilgrimage, perhaps later. Nor did Margery ever refer to Robert Brunham, who may have been either her brother or uncle and who was also very prominent in Lynn politics – mayor in 1406 and 1408, alderman *c.*1413 – an association that we might expect to hear more of, given Margery's obsession with status. More astonishingly, she never talked about her mother, who lived an even longer life virtually next door to Margery.[57] It is tempting to wonder if these people had anything to do with her early trauma, but it may also be a sign of triangulated relationship, where one parent is idealised and the other is vilified or ignored.

What kind of trauma could Margery have experienced in her early life? As we have seen, some medieval childrearing practices hardly encouraged healthy psychological development, but, even by these standards, Margery seems to have turned out quite unstable. One wonders if the sin she cannot bring herself to confess in the first chapters of the book had anything to do with it. One of Margery's major concerns throughout most of the *Book* is her sexuality, and although she says she never slept with anyone but her husband, it does not exclude the possibility of sexual trauma or abuse. Episodes such as a particularly graphic temptation, replete with images of numerous men flashing their genitalia at her and the Devil urging her to offer herself in public to all these men (I: ch. 59), Margery's constant expectation of rape (spelled out in I: ch. 47 directly, and hinted at in many other places), her uncontrollable sexual craving for a fellow parishioner who makes a pass at her, only to be rejected in a humiliating way when she offers herself to him (I: ch. 4) – all suggest an unresolved trauma in a preoccupied form. The lack of resolution for most of the early stages of the text is evident in the seeming contradiction between Margery's constant fear of rape and putting herself in situations when rape would have been a possibility (such as travelling unaccompanied). Therapeutic literature demonstrates that most sufferers of sexual abuse, especially early in life, develop multiple voices as a result of precisely this sort of early trauma – something we see in Margery's paramystical experiences.[58] The worst part of such abuse for the sufferer is the inability to talk about it with those closest to them; it is that inability (and not the sin itself) which causes Margery's first mental collapse, when her priest cuts short her long-delayed painful confession in the first chapter of her *Book*.

The disintegration of the social world of Margery's childhood and youth may have played a key role in her reimagining her life story. Margery idealised her father, or rather his status, claiming that she married down, and she continues to refer to her father's status after his death. As Michael Myers brilliantly demonstrates, at the time of Margery's marriage, around 1393, John Kempe looked a perfectly worthy match that would secure and assure the future high social status of John Burnham's daughter.[59] However, amid rapidly changing socio-economic circumstances, Margery seems to ignore or be ignorant of her husband's struggle to succeed. 'In a process of transference', Myers argues, 'Margery attributed the loss of her mundane self-image and the accompanying comfort, status, and prestige not to economic and political transitions but to a "bad" marriage'.[60] This is a good example of what AAI coders call 'reductionist blaming thought'. The early chapters of the book depict a conflicting image of Margery's husband: an insensitive, financially inept, sex-driven bore, but also a loyal and obedient companion. This incompatibility of discourse strategies is a feature of individuals displaying disorganised attachment.[61]

By 1410, Margery's mundane social reality – the web of mercantile relationships that provided shared experiences and values for two or three generations – was no longer there, having been 'replaced by an entrepreneurial elite whose realities differed markedly from that of Margery's youth and early marriage'.[62] Myers argues that this new social reality is what Margery rebelled against:

> The early frames of reference and their values continued to influence and mould her persona even as she assumed her spiritual identity, but their reality was becoming increasingly marginal shortly after her marriage to John Kempe. Nor did Margery fail in her kinship and social relations, nor they her, instead as the kinship and social relations of her youth became marginal she replaced them with new webs of meaningful relationships.[63]

And these meaningful relationships were as much 'imaginary' as they were real.

Margery's attempts to return to a stable and promising past may be seen in her modelling of the figure of Jesus. He is certainly the focus of her attachment, but his main role is not of the ideal spiritual lover, despite his famous Song-of-Songs-inspired suggestion that Margery take him to bed with her. Corinne Saunders and Charles Fernyhough observe that his voice

> is deeply practical: the Lord offers advice on where Margery should go, to whom she should speak and what she should say (particularly when it is confrontational), how she should treat her husband, what ascetic practices she should adopt and when, how she should dress, and whether she should write the book. He assures her of her well-being, safety, and health, and those of the people around her, and provides explanations for natural events, for the responses of people to her, and for her own physical states – illness, pain, the affects of vision.[64]

This sounds more like an ideal parent rather than an ideal lover. Never is Margery called 'friend' or 'darling' by her divine spouse – only 'daughter'. At a very basic level, his voice really responds to 'the lowest part of our needs', as Julian of Norwich puts it: health, safety, love, support. It provides explanatory models, it takes responsibility for her life. In a very uncertain world where she has most of the responsibility and does most of the adulting – her husband seems quite a passive party – Margery's initial collapse may be a response to the extreme frustration at her many responsibilities and very few rights (some academic partners and parents will surely sympathise with her). Delegating these cares and responsibilities must have been liberating. Even Kempe's mystical marriage to God the Father, arranged by Jesus (whose hierarchical status within patriarchy is lower), takes place in Rome in 1414 soon after the death of Margery's own father in Lynn (I: ch. 35). One idolised 'status parent' is replaced by another of an infinitely higher status.

But is Margery's Lord like Julian's 'God as mother' (*Long Text*, ch. 57–60)? Not at all. Margery seems to make him in the image and the likeness of her idea of (parental) authority. Margery's God, like a primary caregiver of a child with disorganised attachment, is often inconsistent: after assuring her multiple times that he will never forsake her and that she is saved and all her sins are forgiven, he will punish her for the lack of faith or obedience through withdrawal of his grace and company, or says he will test her love by making her suffer nearly to death.[65] After saying how pleased he is with everything she does and the way she loves him, he suddenly reminds her of her wickedness, sending her on a guilt-trip thinking that she can never repay his love even if she were killed a thousand times a day.[66] Is this how she was punished as a child – by being ignored and isolated? Was she confused by conflicting messages about her significance and her nothingness? All these ideas about a primary caregiver are, again, consistent with modern understanding of insecure (preoccupied or disorganised) attachment. A modern-day psychologist working within the remit of attachment theory, even without any background knowledge of medieval devotional practices, is likely to find Margery's narrative strangely familiar after reading a number of higher-subscript AAIs, just as a medieval historian, trained in the cultural idiom of the fifteenth-century England, sees her as a unique product of many generally recognisable cultural traits.

Yet the tale of Margery's intuitive attempts to counterbalance and amend her preoccupied attachment traits with the help of religion has a happy ending. As the *Book* progresses, the overall tone of Margery's narrative becomes increasingly positive, reassuring, confidence-building. This seems to be partially facilitated through her therapeutic relationships with confessors and spiritual advisers, but also, more broadly, through self-expansion, by trying to achieve her ideal self through para-social as well as social interactions. Psychological research suggests that interactions with 'fictional' characters may offer some advantages, partly because of 'reduced risk of rejection, creating a safer context in which to form relationships'.[67] Of course, from Margery's perspective Jesus, Mary and saints were not fictional characters: in theory, the saints were always accessible, and God was supposed to be everywhere, but in reality one required a fair degree of imaginative power to have a meaningful exchange with these entities, and the fact that they did not speak directly to the vast majority of people resulted in Margery's privileged access being regularly questioned. The advantages of 'absent interaction' might explain why Margery does not talk about her immediate social circle (she habitually falls out with the people she spends more time with on a daily basis) and focuses on the relationships with the 'fictional' characters, such as Jesus and special saints – just as some people now often prefer 'friends' on Facebook or followers on Twitter.[68] For sure, some of them still argue with us, but the virtual reality of social networks allows for significantly better filtration (hiding Margery on Facebook or blocking her on Twitter would have been a much easier job for the Archbishop of York in the twenty-first century).

Given, however, that the Margery of the *Book* has more friends than foes, and even seemingly manages to establish amiable relationships with her husband and her son in the end, her consistent self-expansion through (perhaps imaginary) relationships with spiritual entities like Jesus and Mary seems to have yielded some psychological and social fruit. Margery is terrified of Archbishop Arundel in 1413, worried about Archbishop Bowet in 1417, and is seemingly nonchalant about Archbishop Chichele in 1418, who finally grants her the requested letter to confirm her religious orthodoxy and seal of approval without giving her any trouble. Now she can finally belong and accept that she is all right. Years of almost compulsive confessing to various people and relating them her life 'fro hyr chyldhod as ny as it wolde come to hir mende' (I: ch. 17) allowed her to form attachments and have sessions of pseudo-therapy with male figures of religious authority, as well as gradually construct a coherent life-story. Being eventually able to write it into her own *Book* must have had a healing effect: creating a coherent narrative and making sense of one's past is a key element of mental well-being and earned security, and is particularly important for those displaying traits of disorganised attachment.[69] In attachment terms, if initially Margery displays many signs of the preoccupied attachment style, such as bad temporal order, complaining tone, exalting one parent and ignoring the other, lack of other people's perspective and significant dysfluency, towards the end she may have arrived at what the DMM model calls 'reorganising towards a gained B' – that is, gradually developing a more balanced personality achieved later in life through mental integration and metacognition.

Preliminary Conclusions

In his renowned work *The Future of an Illusion*, Sigmund Freud famously suggests that god(s) were imagined by people as substitute parents and that their 'longing for a father' is a reflection of their need for protection and a 'defence against childish helplessness'.[70] Freud's suggestion, although only covering some aspects of religious experiences, may not be widely off the mark and can be further refined in the light of continuing research. It appears to be justified that in the times of increased danger and subsequent heightened attachment anxiety it was natural for people to latch on to a stable and 'adequate' attachment figure of God; at the same time, the idea of God was also shaped by generations of individuals, whose attachment strategies were formed through trying to make sense of unavailable or unstable caregivers, and who built their vision and expectations of the deity on the foundations of the processing of their life-experiences. Many examples of these adaptive strategies seemingly worked, enabling the degree of functionality that allowed people of the past to continue both biologically and culturally, in the mutual process described by Daniel Smail in this volume (even if epigenetics, and especially genetics, are playing catch-up to the changing natural and socio-cultural environment).

I hope that, methodologically, I have managed to persuade a sceptical reader to give attachment theory a chance in the studies of the past, and especially in the studies of religion. As with neuroaesthetics or 4E cognition, contextual adjustments will have to be made when approaching specifically pre-modern material, but I agree with Pehr Granqvist's argument that a major strength of the attachment approach to religion, ironically, is precisely that attachment theory was not originally coined to understand religiosity, but rather 'to make sense of a very basic but fundamental aspect of mammalian and primate functioning, namely our strong proclivity to form affectional relational bonds'. As he continues, this is, incidentally, or so it may seem – 'also at the core of religion and spirituality'.[71]

As a preliminary conclusion, this may sound very broad, and it is true that the psychologies of the past are nearly impossible to measure. Also true is that attachment theory is just one of the many filters that cultural historians need to take into account. However, I believe that, even with such caveats, all these issues are worth considering. Here we specialise in probing, not proving. Studying the past helps us understand our personal and cultural differences, even today. We know that distorted attachment, continuing past the first two years of human life, leads to irreversible organic changes in the brain, and, even though we may be part of the same genus, our formative experiences, both personal and cultural, make us like Darwin's Galapagos finches, developing different beaks – that is, different brains, adapted for different environments. It is important to remember that in times of high anxiety, instability and adverse childrearing practices, the attachment aspect of religion, however skewed sometimes, was one of very few things that enabled our ancestors to function and eventually facilitated their survival – and our existence.[72]

Notes

1 The most important contribution which fuelled the debate was the monography by David Sloan Wilson, *Darwin's Cathedral: Evolution, Religion, and the Nature of Society* (Chicago and London: University of Chicago Press, 2002). See also Harvey Whitehouse, 'Cognitive evolution and religion: cognition and religious evolution', in Joseph Bulbulia et al (eds), *The Evolution of Religion: Studies, Theories, and Critiques* (Santa Margarita, CA: Collins Foundation Press, 2008), pp.19–29; Paul Bloom, 'Religion, Morality, Evolution', *Annual Review of Psychology*, 63 (2012), 179–99; William Irons and Richard D. Alexander, 'Evolution and Religion', in Kyle Summers and Bernard Crespi (eds), *Human Social Evolution* (Oxford: Oxford University Press, 2013); and notes 4–5 to this chapter.

2 Richard Dawkins, *The God Delusion* (London: Bantam Press, 2006), p. 188.

3 Charles Darwin, *The Descent of Man and Selection in Relation to Sex (1871)* (Princeton, NJ: Princeton University Press, 1981), pp. 67–9.

4 In Patrick M. McNamara (ed.), *Where God and Science Meet: How Brain and Evolutionary Studies Alter Our Understanding of Religion* (Westport, CT: Praeger, 2006). See Bulbulia, 'Nature's Medicine: Religiosity as an Adaptation for Health and Cooperation', vol. 1, pp. 87–121 (p. 91); Kirkpatrick, 'Religion Is Not an Adaptation', vol. 1, pp. 159–79; Granqvist, 'Religion as a By-Product of Evolved Psychology: The Case of Attachment and Implications for Brain and Religion Research', vol. 2, pp. 105–50 (p. 105).

5 For another recent account concerning the complexities of the debate, see Léon Turner, 'Neither Friends nor Enemies: The Complex Relationship between Cognitive and Humanistic Accounts of Religious Belief', in Fraser Watts and Léon Turner (eds), *Evolution, Religion, and Cognitive Science: Critical and Constructive Essays* (Oxford: Oxford University Press, 2014).

6 For a useful review, see Richard Sosis and Candace Alcorta, 'Signaling, solidarity, and the sacred: the evolution of religious behaviour', *Evolutionary Anthropology*, 12/6 (2003), 264–74.

7 A number of examples written in a language accessible for non-specialists can be found in Dean Burnett's *The Idiot Brain: A Neuroscientist Explains What Your Head Is Really Up To* (London: The Guardian Books, 2017).

8 Julian's text was used for many years in training counsellors and psychotherapists, especially in her native Norwich: see especially the works of Brian Thorne, such as *Julian of Norwich: Counsellor for Our Age* (London: Guild of Pastoral Psychology, 1999) and *Counselling and Spiritual Accompaniment: Bridging Faith and Person-Centred Therapy* (Oxford: Wiley-Blackwell, 2012).

9 Mario Mikulincer and Philip R. Shaver (eds), *Attachment in Adulthood: Structure, Dynamics, and Change*, 2nd edn (New York: Guilford Press, 2018), p. 4.

10 The original AAI protocol can be found at *http://www.psychology.sunysb.edu/attachment/measures/content/aai_interview.pdf* (accessed 24 February 2020).

11 For the recent handbook on administering and coding the AAI, see Patricia M. Crittenden and Andrea Landini, *Assessing Adult Attachment: A Dynamic-Maturational Approach to Discourse Analysis* (New York and London: W. W. Norton and Co., 2011).

12 Crittenden and Landini, *Assessing Adult Attachment*, pp. 328–9; 373; Howard and Miriam Steele (eds), *Clinical Applications of the Adult Attachment Interview* (New York and London: Guilford Press, 2008).

13 Mikulincer and Shaver, *Attachment in Adulthood*, p. 31.

14 John Bowlby, *Charles Darwin: A Biography* (London: Pimlico, 1991).

15 The first is based on the work done by Mary Main and her colleagues in the late 1980s and 1990s (e.g. *Clinical Applications of the Adult Attachment Interview*), the second on the research by Patricia Crittenden and her school in the 1990s and 2000s (e.g. Crittenden and Landini, *Assessing Adult Attachment*).

16 See, for example, Jude Cassidy and Phillip R. Shaver (eds), *Handbook of Attachment: Theory, Research, and Clinical Applications*, 2nd edn (New York: Guilford Press, 2008), p. 457.

17 Granqvist, 'Religion as By-Product of Evolved Psychology', 109.

18 M. D. S. Ainsworth, *Infancy in Uganda: Infant Care and the Growth of Love* (Baltimore, MD: John Hopkins University Press, 1967); M. D. S. Ainsworth and B. A. Wittig, 'Attachment and Exploratory Behavior of One year Olds in a Strange Situation', in B. M. Foss (ed.), *Determinants of Infant Behavior* (London: Methuen, 1969), vol. 4, pp. 113–36.

19 John Bowlby, *Attachment and Loss: vol. 1. Attachment* (New York: Basic Books, 1982), 2nd edn, *passim*, especially pp. 38, 183–96.

20 The best testimony to the portability and tenacity of the theory is perhaps Cassidy and Shaver's *Handbook of Attachment*, a hefty volume which gets updated and reissued every few years.

21 For more detailed advocacy of universality of the attachment theory, see Marinus H. van IJzendoorn and Abraham Sagi-Schwartz, 'Cross-Cultural Patterns of Attachment: Universal and Contextual Dimension', in *Handbook of Attachment: Theory, Research, and Clinical Applications*, p. 881.

22 'The first 10,000 Adult Attachment Interviews: distributions of adult attachment representations in clinical and non-clinical groups': Marian J. Bakermans-Kranenburg and Marinus H. van IJzendoorn, cite '23% dismissing, 58% secure, 19% preoccupied attachment representations, and 18% additionally coded for unresolved loss or other trauma' (*Attachment & Human Development*, 11(3), 223–63).

23 'Cross-Cultural Patterns of Attachment', p. 889.

24 Peryl Agishtein and Claudia Brumbaugh, 'Cultural variation in adult attachment: the impact of ethnicity, collectivism, and country of origin', *Journal of Social, Evolutionary, and Cultural Psychology*, 7/4 (2013), 384–405, retrieved online from *http://psycnet.apa.org/fulltext/ 2014-01529-013.html*.

25 L. A. Kirkpatrick, and P. R. Shaver, 'An attachment-theoretical approach to romantic love and religious belief', *Personality and Social Psychology Bulletin*, 18 (1992), 266–75.

26 Pehr Granqvist, 'Religion as Attachment', *Archive for the Psychology of Religion*, 32 (2010), 5–24 (p. 8). For the most up-to-date discussion of the existing research see idem, *Attachment in Religion and Spirituality: A Wider View* (New York: Guilford Press, 2020), especially chapters 5 and 6.

27 Agishtein and Brumbaugh: *http://psycnet.apa.org/fulltext/2014-01529-013.html*.

28 Ibid.

29 Lloyd DeMause (ed.), *The History of Childhood: Untold Story of Child Abuse*, 2nd edn (London: Bellew, 1991); L. W. B. Brockliss and Heather Montgomery (eds), *Childhood and Violence in the Western Tradition* (Oxford: Oxbow Books, 2010); and Katariina Mustakallio and Christian Laes (eds), *The Dark Side of Childhood in Late Antiquity and the Middle Ages* (Oxford: Oxbow Books, 2011).

30 Judith Evans Grubbs, 'The Dynamics of Infant Abandonment', in *The Dark Side of Childhood in Late Antiquity and the Middle Ages*, p. 32.

31 *The Book of Margery Kempe* (hereafter *BMK*), book I: ch. 43. All references to Lynn Staley's edition (Medieval Institute of Kalamazoo, MI, 1996), available online at *http://d.lib.rochester.edu/teams/publication/staley-the-book-of-margery-kempe*.

32 '[I]n medieval society the idea of childhood did not exist', in Philippe Ariès, *Centuries of Childhood: A Social History of Family Life*, trans. Robert Baldick (New York: Vintage, 1962), p. 125.

33 A good overview of the scholarship on medieval childhood can be found in Daniel Pigg, 'Children and Childhood in the Middle Ages', in Albrecht Classen (ed.), *Handbook of Medieval Culture* (Berlin and Boston: De Gruyter, 2015), pp. 149–58.

34 Barbara Hanawalt, *Growing Up in Medieval London* (New York; Oxford: Oxford University Press, 1993), pp. 113, 171.

35 Hanawalt, *Growing Up in Medieval London*, pp. 187, 201, 211. This could partly account for high statistics of crime and violence of the Middle Ages – see Bowlby's classic work on child thieves, many of whom experienced prolonged periods of total separation before the age of five: John Bowlby, 'Forty-four juvenile thieves: their character and home-life', *International Journal of Psychoanalysis*, 25 (1944), 19–52.

36 James Bruce Ross, 'The Middle-Class Child in Urban Italy', in L. deMause (ed.), *The History of Childhood*, p. 188.

37 Manuela Garcia Quiroga and Catherine Hamilton-Giachritsis, 'Attachment Styles in Children Living in Alternative Care: A Systematic Review of the Literature', *Child Youth Care Forum*, 45 (2016), 625–53, *doi:10.1007/s10566-015-9342-x*.

38 Hanawalt, *Growing Up in Medieval London*, p. 93.

39 Ibid., pp. 103, 223.

40 Nicholas Orme, *Medieval Children* (New Haven, CT and London: Yale University Press, 2001), pp. 114–16.

41 It was first formulated in 1951 as a report for the WHO on the homeless and refugee children and then published in a book form as John Bowlby and Margery Fry, *Child Care and the Growth of Love* (London: Penguin Books, 1953).

42 Unfortunately, very little research has yet been done on attachment patterns among believers in the countries where the traditional society is still strong and where social instability is persistent. One comparable result can be cited from the research looking at attachment patterns in modern-day urban Russia, a country with a high level of historic trauma and relatively high nominal religiosity, whose dominant religion (Russian Orthodoxy) is closer to medieval Catholicism, aesthetically and ritually, than modern Catholicism. See Natalia L. Pleshkova and Rifkat J. Muhamedrahimov, 'Quality of attachment in St Petersburg (Russian Federation): A sample of family-reared infants', *Clinical Child Psychology and Psychiatry*, 15/3 (2010), 355–62.

43 G. D. Kaufman, *The Theological Imagination: Constructing the Concept of God* (Philadelphia, PA: Westminster, 1981), p. 67.

44 For recent readings of Julian in the light of cognitive/neuroscience, see Blud and Perk in this volume, as well as my own 'What Julian Saw: The Embodied Showings and the Items for Private Devotion' in a special issue of *Religions: Domestic Devotions in Medieval and Early Modern Europe,* ed. Salvador Ryan (2019), *https://www.mdpi.com/2077-1444/10/4/245/pdf.*

45 Especially the work by Pehr Granqvist, Phillip Shaver, Mario Mikulincer and Lee Kirkpatrik.

46 M. Mikulincer and P. R. Shaver, 'Attachment theory and emotions in close relationships: Exploring the attachment-related dynamics of emotional reactions to relational events', *Personal Relationships*, 12 (2005), 151.

47 *The Long Text*, ch. 27. *The Shewings of Julian of Norwich*, ed. Georgia Ronan Crampton (Kalamazoo, MI: Medieval Institute Publications, 1994), digitised at *http://d.lib.rochester.edu/teams/publication/crampton-shewings-of-julian-norwich*, hereafter cited as *Long Text*.

48 All quotations are takes from the Douay-Rheims Bible.

49 Granqvist, 'Religion as By-Product of Evolved Psychology', pp. 112–14.

50 Julian of Norwich, *Long Text*, ch. 3.

51 Mikulincer and Shaver, 'Attachment theory and emotions in close relationships', p. 155.

52 On the potential role of extreme asceticism in broadly understood mystical experiences, see Jerome Kroll and Bernard Bachrach, *The Mystic Mind: The Psychology of Medieval Mystics and Ascetics* (New York and London: Routledge, 2005). See also Rudolph Bell, *Holy Anorexia* (Chicago: University of Chicago Press, 1985).

53 See Richard Lawes, 'The Madness of Margery Kempe', in Marion Glasscoe (ed.), *The Medieval Mystical Tradition in England, Ireland and Wales: Exeter Symposium VI, Papers Read at Charney Manor, July 1991* (Cambridge: D.S. Brewer, 1999), 147–68; idem, 'Psychological Disorder and the Autobiographical Impulse in Julian of Norwich, Margery Kempe and Thomas Hoccleve', in Denis Renevey and Christiania Whitehead (eds), *Writing Religious Women: Female Spiritual and Textual Practices in Late Medieval England* (Cardiff: University of Wales Press, 2000), pp. 217–43; Nancy P. Stork, 'Did Margery Kempe suffer from Tourette's Syndrome?', *Mediaeval Studies*, 59 (1997), 261–300; Becky R. Lee, 'The Medieval Hysteric and the Psychedelic Psychologist: A Revaluation of the Mysticism of Margery Kempe in the Light of the Transpersonal Psychology of Stanislav Grof', *Studia Mystica*, 23 (2002), 102–26. A number of scholars have rejected this approach altogether: Juliette Vuille, 'Maybe I'm Crazy? Diagnosis and Contextualisation of Medieval Female Mystics', in Naoe Kukita Yoshikawa (ed.), *Medicine, Religion and Gender in Medieval Europe* (Cambridge: D.S. Brewer, 2015), pp. 103–22; Laura Kalas Williams, '"Slayn for Goddys lofe": Margery Kempe's Melancholia and the Bleeding of Tears', *Medieval Feminist Forum: A Journal of Gender and Sexuality*, 52/1 (2016), 84–100. A good summary of the historiography of the question and further bibliography can be found in Alison Torn's chapter 'Margery Kempe: Madwoman or Mystic – a narrative approach to the representation of madness and mysticism in medieval England', in D. Robinson (ed.), *Narrative and Fiction: An Interdisciplinary Approach* (University of Huddersfield), pp. 79–89, or *eadem*, 'Looking back: Medieval mysticism or psychosis?' *https://thepsychologist.bps.org.uk/volume-24/edition-10/looking-back-medieval-mysticism-or-psychosis*.

54 See, for example, Valerie Sinason (ed.), *Attachment, Trauma and Multiplicity: Working with Dissociative Identity Disorder* (Hove: Brunner-Routledge, 2002), and *eadem* (ed.), *Trauma, Dissociation, and Multiplicity: Working on Identity and Selves* (London: Routledge, 2012).

55 E.g. Margaret Wilkinson, 'A Clinical Exploration of the Origin and Treatment of a Dissociative Defence', in Sinason (ed.), *Trauma, Dissociation, and Multiplicity*, pp. 81–93.

56 'Disorganized attachment can be passed from generation to generation, because parents who struggle with unresolved trauma themselves may have trouble tolerating a range of emotions in their child' (*https://www.psychalive.org/disorganized-attachment*). Also Granqvist, 'Religion as By-Product of Evolved Psychology', p. 115; Peter Fonagy, 'Multiple Voices versus Meta-Cognition: An Attachment Perspective', in *Attachment, Trauma and Multiplicity*, p. 79; and Laura E. Kwako, Jennie G. Noll, Frank W. Putnam and Penelope K. Trickett, 'Childhood Sexual Abuse and Attachment: An Intergenerational Perspective', *Clinical Child Psychology and Psychiatry*, 15/3 (2010), 407–22.

57 See Michael D. Myers, 'A Fictional-True Self: Margery Kempe and the Social Reality of the Merchant Elite of King's Lynn', *Albion*, 31/3 (1999), 377–94 (p. 382); also Anthony Goodman, *Margery Kempe and Her World* (Harlow: Longman, 2002), p. 223.

58 See, for instance, Arnon Bentovim, 'Dissociative Identity Disorder: A Developmental Perspective', in *Attachment, Trauma and Multiplicity*, pp. 21–36, esp. pp. 24–6.

59 Myers, 'A Fictional-True Self', p. 380.

60 Myers, 'A Fictional-True Self', p. 388.

61 Granqvist, 'Religion as By-Product of Evolved Psychology', p. 115. This conflicting discourse can also be the result of Margery's son trying to tone down his mother's unflattering portrayal of his father, if it is indeed true that he was her first scribe.

62 Myers, 'A Fictional-True Self', p. 391.

63 Myers, 'A Fictional-True Self', p. 394.

64 Corinne Saunders and Charles Fernyhough, 'Reading Margery Kempe's inner voices', *postmedieval: a journal of medieval cultural studies*, 8/2 (2017), 209–17, published online at *https://link.springer.com/article/10.1057/s41280-017-0051-5*.

65 BMK, I: chs 14, 22, 32, 56, 59, 64, 84.

66 BMK, I: ch. 77 and then the conflicting message in I: chs 85 and 86.

67 Randi Shedlosky-Shoemaker, Kristi A. Costabile and Robert M. Arkin, 'Self-Expansion through Fictional Characters', *Self and Identity* (2014), 556–78 (p. 556).

68 Alexis Elder, *Friendship, Robots, and Social Media: False Friends and Second Selves* (London: Routledge, 2018).

69 *https://www.psychalive.org/disorganized-attachment*, also Granqvist, 'Religion as By-Product of Evolved Psychology', p. 115.

70 Sigmund Freud, *The Future of an Illusion* (London: Hogarth Press and the Institute of Psycho-analysis, 1928), p. 24.

71 Granqvist, *Attachment in Religion and Spirituality*, p. 44.

72 A version of this chapter also appears as an article in *Irish Theological Quarterly* (2020), 1–18, under the title 'Darwin's Cathedral, Bowlby's Cloister: The Use of Attachment Theory for the Studies in Medieval Religion, with the Example of *The Book of Margery Kempe*'.

Select Bibliography

Agishtein, Peryl and Claudia Brumbaugh, 'Cultural variation in adult attachment: the impact of ethnicity, collectivism, and country of origin', *Journal of Social, Evolutionary, and Cultural Psychology*, 7/4 (2013), 384–405.

Brockliss, L. W. B. and Heather Montgomery (eds), *Childhood and Violence in the Western Tradition* (Oxford: Oxbow Books, 2010).

Cassidy, Jude and Phillip R. Shaver (eds), *Handbook of Attachment: Theory, Research, and Clinical Applications*, 2nd edn (New York: Guilford Press, 2008).

Crittenden, Patricia M. and Andrea Landini, *Assessing Adult Attachment: A Dynamic-Maturational Approach to Discourse Analysis* (New York and London: W. W. Norton and Co., 2011).

DeMause, Lloyd (ed.), *The History of Childhood: Untold Story of Child Abuse*, 2nd edn (London: Bellew, 1991).

Granqvist, Pehr, *Attachment in Religion and Spirituality: A Wider View* (New York: Guilford Press, 2020).

Hanawalt, Barbara, *Growing Up in Medieval London* (New York and Oxford: Oxford University Press, 1993).

McNamara, Patrick M. (ed.), *Where God and Science Meet: How Brain and Evolutionary Studies Alter Our Understanding of Religion* (Westport, CT: Praeger, 2006).

Mikulincer, Mario and Philip R. Shaver (eds), *Attachment in Adulthood: Structure, Dynamics, and Change*, 2nd edn (New York: Guilford Press, 2018).

Mustakallio, Katariina and Christian Laes, *The Dark Side of Childhood in Late Antiquity and the Middle Ages* (Oxford: Oxbow Books, 2011).

Myers, Michael D., 'A Fictional-True Self: Margery Kempe and the Social Reality of the Merchant Elite of King's Lynn', *Albion*, 31/3 (1999), 377–94.

Orme, Nicholas, *Medieval Children* (New Haven, CT and London: Yale University Press, 2001).

Saunders, Corinne and Charles Fernyhough, 'Reading Margery Kempe's inner voices', *postmedieval: a journal of medieval cultural studies*, 8/2 (2017), 209–17.

Shedlosky-Shoemaker, Randi, Kristi A. Costabile and Robert M. Arkin, 'Self-Expansion through Fictional Characters', *Self and Identity* (2014), 556–78.

Sinason, Valerie (ed.), *Attachment, Trauma and Multiplicity: Working with Dissociative Identity Disorder* (Hove: Brunner-Routledge, 2002).

Sinason, Valerie (ed.), *Trauma, Dissociation, and Multiplicity: Working on Identity and Selves* (London: Routledge, 2012).

Wilson, David Sloan, *Darwin's Cathedral: Evolution, Religion, and the Nature of Society* (Chicago and London: University of Chicago Press, 2002).

III

Case Studies: Reading Texts and Minds

7

'A Knot So Suttel and So Mighty': On Knitting, Academic Writing and Julian of Norwich

GODELINDE GERTRUDE PERK

In the late fourteenth century, a woman reflects upon the union of God and humanity in startlingly material metaphors that turn God into a crafter. She claims that God wishes us to be aware that the soul was 'knit[ted] to him in the making' by 'a knot so suttel and so mighty' (*Revelation*, 53:50, 51).[1] This woman is the vernacular theologian and earliest known English woman writer, Julian of Norwich (*c.*1343–*c.*1416). Although the verb 'knitted' may merely denote 'to fasten' or 'to tie', and the art of knitting may not have been widely known in England at that time, I argue that Julian of Norwich knits together minds, matter, text, critic and reader and unravels our preconceptions concerning them.[2]

This discussion proposes that the form of *A Revelation of Love* uniquely recalls knitting in the round. In this resemblance, the text both figures and analogises cognitive processes associated with knitting, mysticism and meditative texts. This relation invites reading the form of the text alongside neuroscientific understandings of such mental processes. When reading form as enacting and signifying particular mental processes, these knitting-like formal features in *Revelation* interrogate both medieval and modern conceptualisations of authoritative writing and cognitive processes.

Several critics, such as Maud McInerney, Denys Turner, Caroline Walker Bynum and Elisabeth Dutton, already discern a circular or spiralling quality in Julian of Norwich's Long Text.[3] The current exploration contributes a neuromedievalist dimension to these discussions.[4] It considers how both medieval culture and modern brain sciences would conceive of mental engagement with this particular work. One possibility is reading the text as an 'echo object'. The term 'echo object', coined by art historian Barbara Maria Stafford, refers to how art and images not only illustrate, but also constitute particular mental processes. They mirror mental processes and call them into being.[5] Applying Stafford's framework to Chaucer's *House of Fame*, Ashby Kinch defines echo objects as 'those products of human cognition that emblematize and analogize the completed cognitive process embedded in an object of art'.[6] The echo object participates in the production of the finished mental process it signifies. It symbolises what it accomplishes. I also posit that, when we read *A Revelation of Love* as an echo object, the text invites us to bring Julian's text and her understanding of her writing to bear upon academic writing. Julian critically scrutinises the visions and her own words, a scholarly rigour that led

Barbara Newman to designate her an intellectual.[7] I argue that Julian's text challenges contemporary perceptions of effective, convincing writing. It also interrogates modern assumptions of the relation between critic and text, and impresses upon the reader a more inclusive, compassionate understanding of both the theory and practice of academic writing. Ultimately, I seek to illuminate how the medieval and modern models of thinking, crafting and writing can enrich one another and allow for a 'touch across time', to use Carolyn Dinshaw's oft-cited phrase.[8] How can Julian's knitting of words transform ours?

To answer that question, following a brief introduction and description of relevant contexts, I first investigate the transformative similarities between Julian's text, the literary principles underpinning it, and knitting. I explore how her later work, *A Revelation of Love*, resembles a piece of round knitting, continuously spiralling upward, and thereby suggests that texts and arguments need not be linear to progress. I then examine the importance of the texture of language to Julian, by investigating what Vincent Gillespie and Maggie Ross term her 'word-knots'.[9] These knots continuously oscillate between negating concepts applicable to the relation between God and humanity (*apophasis*) and affirming such concepts (*cataphasis*). In this manner, they question the need for affecting an attitude of dispassionate detachment when writing, and for seeing certain binaries and earlier insights as in conflict. I conclude by considering Julian's understanding of writing and reading. The text's resemblance to knitting calls for a reliance on expertise and intuition when writing but also for adopting an attitude of patient wonder. These attitudes all gesture towards Julian's life-affirmative, compassionate conceptualisation of the creative and analytical process, as well as of the relation between author, critic, text studied and scholarly text produced.

The writings of Julian of Norwich have fascinated academic and religious audiences alike for decades. Two Middle English texts are ascribed to her, the shorter *A Vision Showed To A Devout Woman*, also called the *Short Text*, written in the 1380s, and the longer *A Revelation of Love*, also known as the *Long Text*, written sometime between the late 1390s and Julian's death.[10] Both texts recount a series of visions Julian reportedly experienced in May 1373, when seriously ill and believed to be on her deathbed. Almost four times as long as *Vision* and supplementing numerous reflections, new insights and some new visions, *Revelation* forms an expanded, fully revised *Vision*. It differs in tone, content and audience.[11] *Revelation* has attracted the most attention from critics, who laud its compassionate theology and subversive imagery. The current discussion centres on *Revelation*, but Julian's continuous revising of her text should be kept in mind.

Of equal significance are the anchoritic context in which *Revelation* was produced and the spiritual aim of the anchorite's crafts. At some point during her life and after the visions, Julian became an anchorite, a professional religious living walled in a cell in a church. She likely wrote or dictated *Revelation* in such an anchorhold. As the thirteenth-century anchoritic rule *Ancrene Wisse* prescribes, female anchorites were expected to engage in handicrafts, such as sewing church vestments and clothes for the poor.[12] This occupation will prevent the anchorite's mind from wandering and falling into temptation: '[A]nanrihtes þe feond beot hire his werc þe in Godes werc ne swinkeð . . . For hwil he sið hire bisi, he þencheð þus: "For nawt Ich schulde nu cume neh hire; ne mei ha nawt iȝemen to lustni mi lare."'('[T]he devil offers his own employment straight away to the woman who is not employed in God's business . . . For while he sees her busy, he thinks like this: "It would be useless to approach her now; she can't concentrate on listening to my advice."')[13] By fashioning a piece of clothing, the female anchorite fashions a devout, focused mind. A modern neuroscientist seems to concur with the *Ancrene Wisse* when hypothesising that crafting demands such a meditation-like absorption in the act of creating.[14] This mentally demanding quality of the textile arts and their cognitive benefits will recur at several points in my discussion; Julian's text requires and effects a similarly engrossed attention characterised by a deliberate suspension of interpretative control.

Knitting is a textile art in which subsequent series of loops construct a fabric. The earliest extant English examples of knitting, dating from the late fourteenth century, suggest that circular knitting was the first form of this craft to reach England.[15] Circular knitting or knitting in the round is done on four double-pointed needles, or on one or two circular needles. When knitting in the round, the knitter returns full-circle to the first stitch, thus creating a knitted tube without seams. The knitter constantly adds a new circle of stitches to the previous row, and repeats the same stitch pattern, instead of reversing the pattern, as one would when knitting back and forth. The created work thus circles upward. This circular yet progressive movement also pervades *Revelation*. For instance, it cross-references earlier and later visions, and gradually wraps images in layers of meaning, as I will demonstrate.

This discussion responds to the dialogue between humanities and cognitive and neuroscientific research. Cognitive research, particularly on embodied cognition, informs this discussion; in this focus on cognition, it resonates with the next chapter by Victoria Blud, which similarly reads the cognitive sciences and medieval religious culture through one another. I adopt Elizabeth Hart's definition, in which the adjective 'cognitive' refers to 'the architecture and the contents of the human brain/mind'.[16] As Hart recommends, the current exploration centres on investigating how attending to this architecture and these contents can 'contribute structurally to the writing, reading, and interpretation of texts'.[17] The form and content of the text are read through (our knowledge of) the form and the content of the brain/mind, and vice versa, illuminating both. However, I do not perceive of the medievalist contribution to such dialogues between humanities and brain sciences as static and informed by conclusive bibliography. Rather, I understand neuromedievalism as offering a dynamic conversation that is ever in flux.

While engaging in this conversation, I remain alert to the risks that reading a medieval text and modern brain sciences alongside one another entail, for instance, essentialist or reductionist readings. Such readings assume that medieval and modern brains operate in comparable, analogous or even identical ways (see Silva in this volume for a comparison of medieval and contemporary theoretical models of the brain). In her cognitive analysis of chansons de geste, Paula Leverage cautions against these assumptions: 'If [Wolfgang] Iser and [Mark] Turner are proposing similar theories of mind to Hugh of St. Victor, then should we assume that the mind functions in essentially the same way as it did in the twenty-first century?'[18] The answer to Leverage's question hinges upon the significance of 'essentially'. On the one hand, a comparison becomes reasonably unproblematic when considering that neurobiologists situate the appearance of the 'modern' brain in its current form and function 200,000 years in the past. This appearance followed a brain evolution starting between two and three million years ago. This evolution involved changes in brain size, brain organisation, cortical volume, folding of the cortex, interneuronal connections, and brain volume, among other things.[19] On the other hand, the effects of neuroplasticity and culture complicate such a comparison. Neuroplasticity refers to how input from an external source transforms the brain. It denotes drastic cortical reorganisation and neuronal changes after trauma. However, it also encompasses how new experiences, learning and memory effect changes at neuronal level, which is a common, non-trauma-related phenomenon. This dynamic quality of the brain renders medieval brains substantially different from modern brains.[20] Evidence from cultural neuroscience poses another challenge. These studies show intercultural differences in neural activity (that is, which brain regions are activated) in various processes, including attention, perception and self-reflection.[21] These differences have led scientists to conclude that although there is limited evidence for culture shaping brain structure, culture does shape brain function.[22] Consequently, the medieval brain arguably did not function in a manner identical to that of the modern brain. However, even to juxtapose medieval and modern brains essentialises them. Therefore, Chance's recommendation that neuromedievalist discussions examine 'cognitive alterities' is constructive.[23] Chance nevertheless advocates 'essential . . . reductionism'.[24] Such a perspective potentially involves the danger of reducing medieval brains to mere biology, especially since the adoption of too pluralist an interpretative perspective may lead to less in-depth attention to cultural situatedness and cultural specificities. Although neuromedievalism allows for a powerful cross-temporal connection, this seeming commonality should not tempt the researcher away from the alterity of the Middle Ages.

Spiralling Upwards by Knitting in the Round

Reading *Revelation*'s form as knitting-like and analogous to certain cognitive processes reveals how it challenges medieval and modern assumptions of academic and mystical texts and arguments needing linearity to progress. (The conclusion explores modern presuppositions; the current section focuses on medieval norms.) *Revelation* participates in both medieval religious and literary culture. It deploys literary concepts to think through its literary endeavour and to conceptualise the relation between God and humanity. Although one critic debates whether Julian can be considered a mystic or not, *Revelation* does thematise the union between God and humanity, presenting this union as axiomatic.[25]

In medieval religious and literary culture, linear models for arguments abound, as well as for *ductus*, defined by Mary Carruthers as 'the way by which a work leads someone through itself'.[26] Geoffrey of Vinsauf's influential thirteenth-century poetic guide *Poetria Nova* stresses the need for a 'definite order' in the work. The writer decides on 'a certain point' with which to begin the work's 'course', and 'fix[es] its Cadiz', the endpoint of the journey.[27] Geoffrey envisions work and argument as progressing linearly from beginning to end; what is more, literary texts need to display such linearity to be successful. Likewise, medieval meditational guides jointly offer a veritable garden shed stocked with ladders, frequently with numbered rungs mapped onto Christ's body or days of the week. Linear models for spiritual ascent punctuate these texts in the form of an image, exercise or central organising principle, as titles such as *The Ladder of Monks and Twelve Meditations* and *A Ladder of Eight Rungs* encapsulate.

However, a different set of metaphors would have been available to Julian as well. A long tradition analogises text to textile crafts. The word 'text' derives from Latin *texere*, to weave. Similarly, Middle English *weven* signifies literal weaving and weaving a text or argument out of different elements. In Chaucer's *Boece*, Philosophy promises the narrator that she will 'weve . . . resouns yknyt by ordre' ('weave . . . arguments joined in proper order').[28] Likening texts to tapestry arguably offers a less teleological conceptualisation of writing than the journey or ladder metaphor does. It also highlights the parts' interconnectedness more. It nevertheless still connotes linearity, like Philosophy's reference to arranging arguments in a particular order indicates. Writing as a form of knitting in the round draws on the same tradition, but does not require such linearity.

Revelation creates such circular structures by cross-referencing other visions, sometimes not yet described. Felicity Riddy and Elizabeth Dutton have drawn attention to these frequent cross-references, which are unique to Julian and to *Revelation*. Riddy sees the cross-references as contributing to the recursivity of the long version and allowing Julian to look forwards and backwards simultaneously.[29] Dutton proposes that although evoking devotional compilations, a particular cross-reference 'guide[s] a reading more critical than devotional'.[30] She further claims that the text's structural control makes the text appear to compile itself and prompts a non-sequential reading by revelation rather than by chapter.[31] I would like to add that, by means of the cross-references, the text generates a similar back- and forward-looking perspective in the reader by prompting a circular reading process, allowing *Revelation* to envelop the reader in itself and to develop its argument by spiralling upwards instead of in a linear fashion.

The fifteenth revelation exemplifies how the cross-references knit an argument and text in the round. After describing the majority of her visions, in a reflection foreshadowing her famed meditation on Christ's motherhood, Julian invites readers to leaf back to the first vision only to return them full-circle to where they started:

> And oure saviour is oure very moder, in whome we be endlesly borne and never shall come out of him. Plenteously, fully and swetely was this shewde; and it is spoken of in the furst, wher it saide: 'We be all in him beclosed.' And he is beclosed in us; and that is spoken of in the sixteenth shewing, where he seyth: 'He sitteth in oure soule.' For it is his liking to reigne in oure understanding blissefully, and to sitte in oure soule blissefully, and to wonne [dwell] in our soule endlessly, us all werking into him.(*Revelation*, 57:42–7)

First, the book sends the reader back to the first revelation, either mentally, by thinking back to it, or physically, by turning the page. Then, the reference to the sixteenth revelation enjoins the reader to turn to the sixteenth and final revelation. The reader circles back from the beginning (the first revelation) to the end (the sixteenth revelation). Finally, to grasp the argument about Christ's locutions, the reader needs to return to the starting point of this circular movement, the fifteenth revelation. Such cross-references, then, knit the text around the reader. The text not merely presents Julian and the reader ('we') as eternally dwelling in Christ and vice versa; it also crafts the very wrapping it describes, enclosing the reader in itself.

Reading *Revelation*'s *ductus* as resembling knitting reveals a distinctly Julianic manoeuvre: with this new 'round' or 'row' of rereading the earlier and later revelations, these revelations accumulate a new layer of significance. Julian knits a new stitch on top of a previous stitch, as it were. In doing so, she also elaborates a central argument: she insists that Christ continuously cares for each individual's lived, embodied experience and essence, unceasingly holding the two together. In the first revelation, a spiritual sight prompts Julian to declare that 'God . . . hath us all in himselfe beclosede' (*Rev*. 6.39), the phrase cross-referenced in the fifteenth revelation. That same spiritual sight further reveals that God's loving attention even encompasses guiding human defecation. When the cross-reference redirects the reader to this vision, bodily, seemingly profane aspects of human life signify the seemingly wholly spiritual, mutual indwelling of Christ and humanity as well. Similarly, when leafing forward to the scene from the sixteenth revelation alluded to, the sight of Christ signifies more than how Christ 'ruleth and yemeth [governs] heven and erth and all that is' (*Revelation*, 58:6–8), as Julian glosses the visionary moment in the sixteenth revelation originally. When rereading this scene following the cross-reference, it also signals how Christ gives birth to humanity. Thus, *Revelation* develops several central claims, but circularly rather than linearly: it spirals upwards.

Exploring this circular knitting from several cognitive perspectives unveils how subtly *Revelation* challenges the linear norm. First, by revisiting earlier visions and previewing later ones, Julian consolidates the memory of the original versions and the amplifications. In doing so, she facilitates and diversifies readers' imaginative participation in her visionary experience. Like her contemporary Chaucer, Julian attends carefully to and thematises her own cognitive processes, which expresses itself as a continuous reworking of previous (sequences of) images, a constant translation also traced by Juliana Dresvina.[32] Medieval and modern prisms reveal the effect of this attention. According to medieval faculty psychology and *memoria*, a glance at an object or person already yields a mental image or *species*, but for the image to turn into a memory, individuals actively need to engage with this image in their imagination.[33] According to modern cognitive science, attention brings about repeated activation of neurons consolidating the connections between neurons that seeing any object or person requires, a role of attention similar to that found in medieval optics.[34] This effect extends to imagination. Neuroscientific research by Alvaro Pascual-Leone and his team suggests that visualising learning certain new activities (for instance, playing the piano) reorganises the relevant cortex similarly to physically practising that activity.[35] Reading Julian's meditation alongside both understandings, by revisiting the earlier revelation and foreshadowing the later one, all three moments physically alter the reader's brain significantly. By imprinting themselves more firmly upon the mind, they embody the eternal indwelling that they envisage. They thus transform the matter of the brain into an image of Christ's maternal body.

Secondly, *Revelation*'s cognitive scaffolding makes the reader participate in its spiralling upward and challenging of linear norms. According to several understandings of memory, Julian provides cognitive scaffolding that facilitates remembering and imaginatively engaging with her intricate argument. Drawing on classical mnemotechnics, medieval monastic *memoria* built elaborate memory systems to support the remembering of Scripture, the liturgy, meditational texts and other spiritually edifying works. The practitioner would utilise variations of common mnemonic techniques. For instance, the technique that Carruthers terms the 'architectural mnemonic' consists of imaginatively placing images in particular places against a background (often a familiar space). Another popular mnemonic was the 'the numbered grid', which deploys brief texts instead of images, numbers instead of places and a grid instead of a background.[36] Carruthers discerns a parallel between the latter mnemonic and what neuropsychologists today call 'chunking' information. When chunking information, the individual groups or segments informational units and replaces these groupings by items even richer in information.[37] In the cross-reference cited earlier, Julian deftly combines the numbered grid and the architectural mnemonic. She numbers each revelation clearly and 'chunks' these multi-part revelations as brief locutions. However, instead of mentally situating her new insights in a particular point in space, she places them in a particular moment in time, the earlier moment and the later moment when the reader encounters those two revelations.

Julian's strategy here parallels modern descriptions of effective use of brain space, as do other medieval thinkers and texts. Reading medieval mnemotechnics as instances of 'mindware upgrades', a term coined by cognitive theorist and scientist Andy Clark, Ruth Evans argues that Hugh of St Victor's numbered grid contributes to the extended and scaffolded mind.[38] Kinch extends this claim, positing that mnemotechnics 'offload' cognitive resources, a process hypothesised by modern cognitive scientists.[39] Julian's two-pronged strategy of chunking and temporal placing facilitates the reader's attentive engagement with all three revelations. In this manner, it supports meditation upon the visionary experience and sweeps the reader up into the text's circling upward. From a cognitive perspective, it also transforms the reader's mind to the likeness of Julian's, since the same scaffolding and the same information processing strategies underpin their cognition. Julian's circular knitting thus blurs the distinction between the reader's mind and hers, an extension of minds which Victoria Blud examines at length in the next chapter in this volume.

Delighting in a Knotty Texture

The meditation cited above already gestures towards how meticulous attention to and tangible delight in language suffuse *Revelation*. Previous research also has commented upon this linguistic sensitivity. In her examination of Julian's 'web of metaphor', Ena Jenkins professes that she has 'long read Julian as a poet'.[40] Denys Turner, in his book-length study on Julian as a theologian, declares *Revelation* 'a beautifully composed text'.[41] I will spend the remainder of this chapter exploring Julian's delight in the texture of language, focusing on what Gillespie and Ross term her 'word-knots'. Literature, theology and rhetoric meet in these word knots and their effects, as Gillespie and Ross detail: 'Typically she takes a nucleus word and winds around it strands of homonyms, grammatical variants, near-puns and half-rhymes that constitute the genetic code of her theology'.[42] Like the knitting-like cross-referencing, these word-knots require a transformative dialogue with the text that blurs the distinction between feedback and feedforward. In this dialogue, perfect knowledge is continuously deferred while partial understanding, paradoxically, segues into insight, as Gillespie and Ross observe: 'The lexical and theological relationships that such "word-knots" generate are both playful and profound, but they revealed themselves most fully to us in the interaction between text, reflective silence and speculative gropings for understanding'.[43] Juxtaposing these word-knots and delight in the language texture with knitting and cognitive processes reveals that these word-knots decentre the reader's self and invite suspending interpretative control. They open up the mind to an atemporal, apophatic mental space shared by the reader, the visionary and God.

The intricate 'strands' wrapped around such word-knots as 'matter' indicate that Julian revels in their material associations, yet also unbinds these associations and the word-knots themselves. She moves beyond language, by collapsing all strands into Christ. At first, 'mater' solely refers to the content or subject-matter of the visions and text. This use originates from classical rhetoric and also appears in other medieval discourses, from secular texts such as *The Canterbury Tales* to religious works such as mystery plays and sermons.[44] For instance, Chaucer's Parson assures the other pilgrims that his narrative boasts 'moralitee and vertuous mateere'.[45] The proclamation to the Croxton Play of the Sacrament hails its audience with 'We be ful purposed with hart and thowght/off our mater to tell the entent' ('we fully intend with heart and thought/ to tell the import of our subject-matter').[46] Julian first utilises 'mater' after promising readers that, although the 'marvellous homelyhede' ('wonderful intimacy') with God she just perceived in a vision can only be known by revelations or inner grace, it is accessible to believers by faith (*Revelation*, 7:45–50). Upon first reading, her use of 'mater' assures the reader of the internal consistency and orthodoxy of the visions and by extension that of the text: 'And thus be the shewing: it is none other than the faith, ne less ne more, as it may be seene be our Lords mening in the same matter, be than it come to the end' (*Revelation*, 7:53–4). As the alliterating 'mening' underscores, the significance of 'matter' seems fixed: it consists of a single strand. Julian deploys the term in a traditional, abstract manner redolent of other authoritative discourses, and thereby underlines the orthodoxy of her visions and work.

After several revelations, however, 'mater' metamorphoses into a palimpsest that foregrounds materiality and the body, several of its other denotations, but simultaneously unravels these connotations.[47] After the parable of the Lord and the Servant, Julian outlines her intricate model of the human soul, which encompasses 'substance' (essence) and 'sensuality' ('sensory being', as Barry Windeatt translates it).[48] Julian underscores the unity of God and the human psyche, which results from the soul being made by and from the Divinity: 'mannes soul is made of God, and in the same pointe knite to God' (*Revelation*, 53:34). Julian then deftly binds together the earlier strand of significance and several others, which at first glance seem more material:

> Whan God shulde make mannes body, he toke the slime of the erth, which is a *mater* medeled and gadered of all bodely thinges, and thereof he made mannes body. But to the making of mannes soule, he wolde take right nought, but made it. And thus is the kinde [nature] made rightfully oned to the maker, which is substantial kinde unmade, that is God. And therefore it is that ther may ne shall be right noughte betwene God and mannis soule. And in this endlesse love, mannis soule is kept hole, as *all the mater* [subject matter] of the revelation meneth and sheweth (*Revelation*, 53:35–42; emphasis mine).

The human body, mud (suggestive of 'mater' as 'bodily fluid') and the text are all 'mater' that God and writer form and gather into a signifying whole.[49] In stressing physicality, the first mention of 'mater' overlays the literary term with the material and tangible. Julian's word-knot renders the previously abstract, rhetorical term deeply material. The next reference to 'mater', however, already resists these material associations: Julian unknots the word-knot, and then joins and contracts all strands into one strand, which both describes and dramatises the mysterious manner in which Christ unites substance and sensuality. To Julian, bodily materiality and a text's thematic unity ultimately are an image of the intangible unity of the human soul and God. This unity might even be ineffable, as the references to God's uncreated state and the brevity of the description of the soul's creation suggest. The parallelism, moreover, between the soul's and the body's creation points to God being the ineffable matter of which the soul was made, especially when read alongside the claim about humanity being made from God. For Julian, the 'stuff-ness' of the body gestures beyond language and the body. To use a mystical term, the word-knot develops knowledge by way of *via negativa* or *apohasis*. That is, *Revelation* negates earlier terms and conceptualisations in order to grasp the relation between God and humanity more fully.

Despite this, I would argue that the word-knot does not remain apophatic. I would hazard to respond to Gillespie and Ross's consistently apophatic reading, in which *Revelation*'s 'representational images . . . become springboards for the apophatic'.[50] I would propose a circular movement between *apophasis* and *cataphasis* instead. The reference to the entire visionary experience returns the reader to the materiality and the cataphatic quality of the text. The use of 'all' strengthens this enjoinder, since it resonates with the earlier 'all' containing the material things from which the divinity created the human body. The reader and text return full-circle to where they began. Julian continuously ties, unties and reties her word-knots; the text oscillates, or rather, spirals upwards by circling between *cataphasis* and *apophasis*.

The word-knots and their spiralling upwards between *cataphasis* to *apophasis* demand the reader suspend interpretative control and leave all possibilities open. Analytically fruitful parallels to this mechanism can be found in neuroscientific models of religious experience and mysticism. These parallels bring out how the text's circular knitting prompts the reader to trust the text to unite the apparent tensions in the word-knots. First, cognitive neuroscience would discuss the interplay between what Julian's 'seeking' and 'beholding' with reference to Patrick McNamara's four-step model of religious experience. This model revolves around the development of an integrated self through a process of de-centring. McNamara's model has been applied to *via negativa* by Andrea Hollingsworth, who examines it as an option for neuroscientific explanations of *apophasis*.[51] In the second stage of McNamara's model, the agentive self is put aside in a mental box containing all possible identities for that self.[52] Here, McNamara draws on the 'cognitive architecture' model of pretence hypothesised by Shaun Nichols and Stephen Stich, two cognitive theorists. His 'suppositional space' adapts their 'Possible World Box', a distinct mental space containing pretence representations.[53] (These container metaphors recall *memoria*'s mnemonic buildings.) To embark upon the quest for the more integrated self, the individual is required to place aside the self in that Possible World Box or suppositional space.[54]

A similar never-ending search for more integration fuels *Revelation*, namely, for more strands with which to entwine the word-knots. It builds a comparable 'mental workspace' in the reader's memory of the text.[55] With every new reading, it stores new layers of significance. After all, *Revelation* demands that the reader mentally preserve the different strands, word-knots, apophatic and cataphatic moments, and one's memories of oneself reflecting upon them all. This parallel between *Revelation*'s strategies and cognitive models suggests that *Revelation* cognitively primes its readers to develop the word-knots further.

Revelation and McNamara's model do not fully map onto one another, however. (Elsewhere in this volume, Ralph Hood examines this productive tension between psychology and religion further, especially as it relates to mysticism.) A point of divergence between McNamara's model and *Revelation* makes visible how the knitting in the round discussed earlier supports this priming. Conflict and negatively valenced loss of control crucially drive the quest in McNamara's model. An internal conflict leads the religious individual to experience a diminishing or even loss of volition and agency. It also sets in motion the central search for a more integrated self. Religious practice or rituals spark and highlight this conflict and loss of volition.[56] Instead of conflict, *Revelation*'s circular knitting invokes God's maternal care and the safety of being enfolded, encouraging trust in its circular processes. In addition, as the text is read circularly, the reader re-encounters the same word-knot repeatedly, creating an impression of coherence despite possible tensions within the word-knots. Thus, it encourages the reader to suspend interpretative control and leave all interpretative possibilities open. In contrast to McNamara's model, *Revelation* codes this willing surrender of control positively.[57] This disjuncture between Julian and McNamara intimates that Julian's conceptualisation of the *via negativa* does not call for rejecting of earlier realisations of the self. Rather, it accumulates and includes earlier identities and insights.

Neuropsychological research would describe such willing suspense of interpretative control in terms of the mutually supportive relation between memory, imagination and prediction. Reading *Revelation*'s circling between *apophasis* and *cataphasis* accordingly, the text prompts the reader to expand upon it and to continue this spiralling upwards. Such an interpretation extends earlier claims about the generative role of memory in *Revelation.*[58] Episodic memory, autobiographical memories of events, plays a central role in my earlier interpretation of *Revelation* as accumulative and McNamara's framework. The reader needs to integrate the autobiographical memories of the previous encounters with the word-knots into one's memory of the new encounter. Likewise, in McNamara's model, the memories of the earlier identity must be integrated into the new identity.[59] Scene construction theory offers a neuropsychological model that can help explore this pivotal role of memory. Developed by neuropsychologist Sinead L. Mullally and neuroscientist Eleanor A. Maguire, this model theorises particular neuropsychological and neuroimaging findings, which suggest that a common network of brain regions underpins episodic memory, imagination and prediction.[60] This neural system includes the hippocampus but is not limited to it. Scene construction theory ascribes to the hippocampus a similar interest in creating visual, fictitious scenes as Carruthers attributes to medieval *memoria*. Mullally and Maguire postulate that the hippocampus's primary role is to construct spatially coherent, atemporal scenes.[61] That is to say, these scenes are set neither in the past nor in the future but still display the spatial logic of lived experience. In this manner, it provides a base upon which episodic memory, imagination and prediction of the future can draw for its event details. It provides a central component to recollection, imagination and thinking about the future: it enables the construction of scenes not set in a particular time but still showing spatial coherence.[62]

Reading the word-knots analogously, *Revelation* continuously requires the reader to recollect previous strands and previous untying and retying of the word-knot, and to predict future ones. It consequently prompts the reader's imagination to produce similarly atemporal scenes. In doing so, it returns the reader to that suppositional space in which readers can amplify Julian's word-knots themselves and continue the spiralling upward through *via negativa* and *via positiva*. Promoting trust in the text and suspension of interpretative control, the word-knots fashion an atemporal site for the reader to situate themselves and their adaptations of the word-knots. They bring together Julian and the reader and blur the distinction between these different agents and their contributions to the text. In the final chapter, *Revelation* explicitly demands such active participation: 'This boke is begonne by Goddes gifte and with his grace, but it is not yet performed [completed], as to my sight. For charite we pray together, with Goddes werking' (*Revelation*, 86:1–3). Like a yet-unfinished but substantial knitted garment, the work is open-ended and its stitches 'live', that is, still open to being added to. *Revelation* enfolds the reader's contribution and draws it into its upward movement. Instead of dispassionate detachment, it encourages active engagement and bringing in one's lived experiences to contribute to this all-enveloping text.

When comparing the meditative, knitting-like effects of Julian's lexical sensitivity and word-knots to the meditative effects of knitting, the resemblances indicate that the word-knots create the physiological preconditions for deferring analytical control and building an extensive suppositional space.[63] To begin with, Julian's delight in and attention to the fabric of her work inspire a similar response from the reader. Reading Julian's word-knots and fascination with language texture through knitting, both induce the ideal state for surveying the word-knots, suspending the need for a resolution, and engaging in original reflection. When knitting, paying attention to the texture of the yarn and the work enhances the knitter's mood, as a survey of more than 3,000 knitters indicates.[64] According to cognitive approaches to motivation, this positive mood increases the knitter's intrinsic motivation towards the activity. A two-axis model of motivation and creative drive helps diagram this effect, with 'approach–avoidance' as one axis and 'arousal–satisfaction' as another.[65] Attention to texture increases approach motivation and intrinsic motivation; both consistently correlate with creative drive and creativity, and therefore presumably with more elaborate imaginative constructs as well.[66] Surveying the neuroscience of the creative drive, Alice W. Flaherty reports: 'intrinsic approach motivation robustly produces creative works'.[67] Similarly, by delighting in the texture of its language and its word-knots, *Revelation* equips the reader to adopt the cognitive processes embedded in *Revelation*. It thus supports suspending interpretative control and contributing imaginatively, as outlined earlier. Read in relation to this meditative quality, *Revelation*'s dialogue between text and reader blurs the binary, Cartesian mind–body distinction, as readers' cognitive engagement and physiological response mediate their reading of *Revelation*.

Julian of Norwich, Knitter and Critic

Revelation's challenges to dualist, teleological understandings of texts and cognition unravel several strands of modern critique. The knitting in the round enjoins the modern critic to have confidence in their expertise and intuition. It invites critics to envisage understanding, research and writing as not strictly linear, but as accumulative and as circling upwards. It urges the scholar to keep in mind that each insight and each text builds upon earlier perceptions and earlier drafts. Such trust in one's expertise smudges boundaries between seemingly more cerebral activities such as critical writing and seemingly undemanding activities such as knitting. Discussing the mental health benefits of crafting, neuroscientist Kelly Lambert emphasises that this 'dichotomy between manual work and knowledge work' is inaccurate; manual work (including crafting) is equally or even more cognitively demanding than seemingly more cerebral endeavours.[68] As is the case with knitting, trusting in one's scholarly expertise and understanding one's writing skills as ever spiralling upwards towards greater refinement likely increases emotional and physical well-being. Julian models such behaviour when, despite failing to understand the parable of the Lord and Servant fully, she continues to re-see the other visions. By interpreting *Revelation* as cautioning against an overreliance on linearity, I concur with Gillespie and Ross; they note that reading *Revelation* requires an approach in which 'the linearity of the critical method' does 'not hold primacy' and is 'a servant, not a master'.[69] By impressing this conceptualisation of writing, *Revelation* urges academics and others not to let such an overemphasis on continuous progress dominate them either.

By prompting suspension of analytical control, the word-knots and the delight in texture prime the critic to generalise this attitude towards medieval texts and medieval artworks. They inculcate sensitivity to the otherness of medieval culture, particularly of importance when bringing medieval cultures into dialogue with modern critical theory. In her presidential address to the American Historical Association, Bynum recommends medievalists and students approach medieval culture with a sense of wonder, which she characterises as 'non-appropriative' and 'deeply respectful of the specificity of the world'. Medievalists and students alike 'must . . . gaze in wonder at texts and artifacts, [be] slow to project or to appropriate, quick to assume there is a significance, slow to generalize about it'.[70] By knitting the critic's mind to its own in its 'suttel' knot, *Revelation* promotes such patient wonder and fosters a more attentive engagement with medieval culture. Both Bynum's words and Julian's knitted tactics speak to the recent reassessment of critique. Rita Felski, for instance, advocates moving beyond critique's hermeneutics of suspicion as its 'dominant metalanguage'.[71] Instead, literary studies should embrace a greater diversity of argumentative approaches and attitudes. Felski favours a more affirmative methodology rooted in 'generosity . . . affection [and] hope'.[72] *Revelation* gestures towards one such attitude and approach. Instead of understanding critic and reader as in conflict with the text, it sees them as enclosing and supporting one another, with the text as inexhaustible, always holding a surplus.[73]

When exploring *Revelation*'s union of text and reader as an analogy of the extended mind, we discover how cognitive processes can be 'embedded in a work of art', as Kinch puts it, and how *Revelation* challenges any binary distinctions between the text's and the critic's activity: texts construct their critics. The extended mind is one of the dimensions of '4EA model of cognition', which hypothesises that cognition is embodied, embedded, extended, enacted and affective.[74] Victoria Blud details the 4EA model and its usefulness for the study of pre-modern creativity in the next chapter, and likewise explores the extended mind in *Revelation*. Therefore, suffice it to say that in the 4EA model, 'the extended mind' refers to how cognitive processes extend beyond 'the skin/skull boundary' into the outer world.[75] An example of extended cognition would be an individual suffering from memory loss relying on an annotated kitchen calendar to remember what he or she did that day. The many smartphone apps that structure daily activities (such as reminders to drink water) are another example. The world beyond one's skull naturally includes others and their minds: the extended mind spread out cognition across different subjects. *Revelation* similarly extends cognitive processes to the reader. It deposits insights at particular points in time of the reader's perusal of the text, requires upon the reader to provide the text with closure, and transfers its mnemonic strategies to the reader. In doing so, it also imprints a particular understanding of the relation between text and critic upon the reader's mind.

One word-knot particularly signifies *Revelation*'s union of text and critic and emblematises its extended mind between reader and text. Expressly highlighting its own 'knottiness', the word-knot 'knot' functions as another echo-object: it images and effects the text's extension of its conceptualisation of authoritative reading from itself to the reader. The Middle English noun 'knot' signifies the gist or point of a tale, love knot, mnemonic aid in the shape of a knot, and a mystery or intellectual challenge.[76] It appears only twice in *Revelation*, where it follows the description of the creation of the human soul cited earlier. After maintaining that humanity is the noblest part of creation, and describing Christ's soul as surpassing all souls in power and essence, Julian expounds:

> [God] will we wit this deerwurthy soule was preciously knit to him in the making. Which knot is so suttel and so mighty that it is oned into God, in which oning [unity] it is made endlesly holy. Farthermore, he will we wit [know] that all the soules that shall be saved in heven without ende be knit in this knot, and oned in this oning, and made holy in this holyhede. (*Revelation*, 53:49–54)

Upon first reading, this complex meditation suggests that when Christ's soul was created, it was united with God in a union both enduring and intricate. By means of this union, the souls of all saved human beings are also united with God in the same union. However, when focusing on the role of the word-knot, 'knot' echoes the earlier statement about the human soul being 'knite to God' (*Revelation*, 53:33), as does the etymologically related verb 'knit'. Like the cross-references, the word-knot 'knot' invites a circular reading-process. Since Julian unexpectedly relates the word 'knot 'to Christ's soul first, the text enjoins the reader to retrace the word-knot back to earlier mentions of related words, such as 'knit'. Furthermore, like the other word-knots, the 'knot' begins to unravel. The startling reference to Christ's soul being made holy intimates that 'this deerwurthy soul' also refers to humanity. This mystical assertion, then, already unites humanity with Christ before the next sentence explicitly details that union. The parallel pair that follows, 'knit in this knot', structurally echoes the 'knot' binding together God and the human soul, yet also makes it more abstract, less imagistic. Again, the text moves towards the apophatic. At the same time, however, the rhythmic repetition of 'knit' and 'knot' conveys the intricacy of the knot, retying it once more.

The word-knot 'knot' participates in how *Revelation* challenges linearity and promotes suspension of interpretative control. To begin with, *Revelation* calls for reliance upon expertise and intuition. It conceives of the text and critic as enclosing and supporting one another instead of as distinct and possibly in conflict. According to Julian, the reluctant text does not need to be aggressively forced to speak by the more powerful critic. Such critical violence also underlies the medieval *topos* analogising literary images to a nut, and by extension the whole text. The analyst needs to crack open and destroy the nut to reach the kernel, the truth. The word-knot 'knot' encapsulates Julian's alternative: According to Julian, the knot is 'suttel' ('intricate'), however, it is also 'mighty' ('strong') and 'oned into God'.[77] Thus, text, narrator, reader and critic are united when collaboratively constructing the text, yet remain distinct. The word-knot 'knot' emblematises the union of the reader's, implied author's and critic's minds: the strands of the minds are unified and closely intertwined, but distinct, with each participant contributing in a distinct, individual way. Cognitive research would conceptualise this knot of minds in terms of the implied author's or the text's mind being extended to the medieval reader's and the modern critic's minds. All share in the same cognitive processes as a result of the word-knots and the circular cross-referencing, with shared mental content being spread out across minds and time.

To conclude, the suspension of interpretative control that the word-knots promote also sounds a cautionary note to the critic engaging in a neuromedievalist reading. *Revelation* dares them to relinquish their suspicion, which leaves space for thoroughly historicising the text and minds under investigation. In fact, such an attitude of wonder enables medieval theories of cognition and medieval reflections on cognition to interrogate modern neuroscience to an even larger degree. Doing so opens up new avenues into exploring the alterity of medieval cognition, illuminating how medieval brains functioned differently from modern brains. The knitting-like elements also supply the text with anchoritic, pastoral overtones. The text presents itself as a female anchorite's carefully crafted gift to her community; composing and perusing it likewise fashion a particular, attentive mind. That is to say, Julian's text shapes the reader's cognition, an impression the present researcher and several others, including one of the editors of this volume, have long shared whenever exploring her work. However, it is her skilful joining of text, image, vision and structure that accomplishes this effect, and thus offers the most lasting inspiration to the critic writing an academic text. Knitting critic and text together in one extended mind, *Revelation* invites scholars to delight in their created work as Julian does.

Notes

1. All quotations from *Revelation* are taken from *The Writings of Julian of Norwich: A Vision Showed to a Devout Woman and A Revelation of Love*, ed. Nicholas Watson and Jacqueline Jenkins (University Park, PA: Pennsylvania State University Press, 2006).
2. 'Middle English Dictionary Entry: Knitten (V.)', *Middle English Dictionary*, 2015, *https://quod.lib.umich.edu/cgi/m/mec/medidx?size=First+100&type=headword&q1=knitten&rgxp=constrained* (accessed 13 December 2015). The earliest finds of knitted garments in Britain date from the late fourteenth century, and are therefore too narrowly contemporary with *Revelation* to make any confident claims about this craft being practised in Norwich. Elisabeth Crowfoot, Frances Pritchard and Kay Staniland, *Textiles and Clothing, c.1150–c.1450*, Medieval Finds from Excavations in London (Woodbridge: Boydell & Brewer, 2006), pp. 72–5.
3. Maud McInerney, 'In the Meydens Womb: Julian of Norwich and the Poetics of Enclosure', in John Carmi Parsons and Bonnie Wheeler (eds), *Medieval Mothering*, (New York: Garland, 1996), pp. 157–82 (p. 172); Denys Turner, *Julian of Norwich, Theologian* (New Haven, CT: Yale University Press, 2011), p. 4; Caroline Walker Bynum, *Fragmentation and Redemption: Essays on Gender and the Human Body in Medieval Religion* (New York: Zone Books, 1991), p. 196; Elisabeth Dutton, *Julian of Norwich: The Influence of Late-Medieval Devotional Compilations* (Cambridge: D.S. Brewer, 2008), pp. 50, 157.
4. The term neuromedievalism was coined by Jane Chance and Ashby Kinch to denote a medievalist framework informed by neuroscience; it is the 'judicious use of the conceptual tools and research results of neuroscientific research as a means of constructing an enriched engagement with medieval culture'. Jane Chance, 'Cognitive Alterities: From Cultural Studies to Neuroscience and Back Again', *Postmedieval: A Journal of Medieval Cultural Studies*, 3/3 (2012), 247–61 (p. 256); Ashby Kinch, 'Re-Visioning the Past: Neuromedievalism and the Neural Circuits of Vision', *Postmedieval*, 3/3 (2012), 262.
5. Barbara Maria Stafford, *Echo Objects: The Cognitive Work of Images* (Chicago: University of Chicago Press, 2007), p. 2.

6 Ashby Kinch, '"Mind like Wickerwork": The Neuroplastic Aesthetics of Chaucer's House of Tidings', *Postmedieval: A Journal of Medieval Cultural Studies*, 3/3 (2012), 302–14 (p. 303).

7 Barbara Newman, *God and the Goddesses: Vision, Poetry, and Belief in the Middle Ages*, Middle Ages Series (Philadelphia: University of Pennsylvania Press, 2003), p. 223.

8 Carolyn Dinshaw, *Getting Medieval: Sexualities and Communities, Pre- and Postmodern* (Durham, NC and London: Duke University Press, 1999), p. 3.

9 Vincent Gillespie and Maggie Ross, '"With Mekeness Aske Perseverantly": On Reading Julian of Norwich', *Mystics Quarterly*, 30/3–4 (2004), 126–41 (p. 135).

10 Nicholas Watson, 'The Composition of Julian of Norwich's Revelation of Love', *Speculum*, 68/3 (1993), 637–83.

11 Godelinde Gertrude Perk, *Julian, God, and the Art of Storytelling: A Narrative Analysis of the Works of Julian of Norwich*, Umeå Studies in Language and Literature, 32 (Umeå: Umeå University, 2016); Barry Windeatt, 'Julian of Norwich and Her Audience', *The Review of English Studies*, 28/109 (1977), 1–17.

12 *Ancrene Wisse: A Corrected Edition of the Text in Cambridge, Corpus Christi College, MS 402, with Variants from Other Manuscripts*, ed. by Bella Millett, EETS OS, 325 (Oxford: Oxford University Press, 2005), ch. 8:24.

13 Bella Millett, *Ancrene Wisse/Guide for Anchoresses: A Translation*, Exeter Medieval Texts and Studies (University of Exeter Press, 2009), ch. 8:24.

14 Kelly Lambert, 'DO OR DIY', *RSA Journal*, 161/5561 (2015), 20–3 (p. 22).

15 Crowfoot, Pritchard, and Staniland, *Textiles*, pp. 72–5.

16 Elizabeth Hart, 'The Epistemology of Cognitive Literary Studies', *Philosophy and Literature*, 25/2 (2001), 314–34 (p. 319).

17 Hart, 'Epistemology', p. 319.

18 Paula Leverage, *Reception and Memory: A Cognitive Approach to the Chansons de Geste* (Amsterdam: Rodopi, 2010), p. 127.

19 Thomas P. Schoenemann, 'Evolution of the Size and Functional Areas of the Human Brain', *Annual Review of Anthropology*, 35 (2006), 379.

20 The interdisciplinary application of this neuroscientific concept is not without pitfalls. In his response to several neuromedievalist discussions, neuroscientist Anthony D. Passaro cautions against deploying the term to refer to all changes in the brain, a use he argues 'confuses . . . rather than clarifies' the matter. Passaro recommends restricting its use to cortical remapping during recovery. 'A Cautionary Note from a Neuroscientist's Perspective: Interpreting from Mirror Neurons and Neuroplasticity', *Postmedieval*, 3/3 (2012), 356.

21 Trey Hedden and others, 'Cultural Influences on Neural Substrates of Attentional Control', *Psychological Science*, 19/1 (2008), 12–17; Angela H. Gutchess and others, 'Cultural Differences in Neural Function Associated with Object Processing', *Cognitive, Affective, & Behavioral Neuroscience*, 6/2 (2006), 102–9; Ying Zhu and others, 'Neural Basis of Cultural Influence on Self-Representation', *NeuroImage*, 34/3 (2007), 1310–16.

22 Denise C. Park and Chih-Mao Huang, 'Culture Wires the Brain: A Cognitive Neuroscience Perspective', *Perspectives on Psychological Science: A Journal of the Association for Psychological Science*, 5/4 (2010), 391–400.

23 Park and Huang, 'Culture', p. 247.

24 Park and Huang, 'Culture', p. 257.

25 Kevin J. Magill, *Julian of Norwich: Mystic or Visionary?* (London: Routledge, 2006).

26 Mary J. Carruthers, 'The Concept of Ductus, or Journeying through a Work of Art', in Mary J. Carruthers (ed.), *Rhetoric beyond Words: Delight and Persuasion in the Arts of the Middle Ages* (Cambridge: Cambridge University Press, 2010), pp. 190–213 (p. 80).

27 *Poetria Nova*, trans. by Margaret F. Nims (Toronto, Ont.: Pontifical Institute of Mediaeval Studies, 2010), pp. 20, 21.

28 MED 'weven' (V)'; *Boece*, in *The Riverside Chaucer*, ed. by Ralph Hanna III and Traugott Lawler (Oxford: Oxford University Press, 1988), pp. 395–469 (bk. IV.Pr.6.38).

29 Felicity Riddy, 'Julian of Norwich and Self-Textualization', in Ann M. Hutchison (ed.), *Editing Women* (Toronto: University of Toronto Press, 1995), pp. 101–24 (p. 116); Dutton, *Julian of Norwich*, pp. 50, 157.

30 Dutton, *Julian of Norwich*, p. 84.

31 Dutton, *Julian of Norwich*, pp. 50, 84, 157.

32 Ashby Kinch, '"Mind like Wickerwork"', p. 312; Juliana Dresvina, 'What Julian Saw: The Embodied Showings and the Items for Private Devotion', *Religions*, 10/4 (2019), 245, *https://doi.org/10.3390/rel10040245*.

33 Kinch, 'Revisioning', p. 265; Mary J. Carruthers, *The Craft of Thought: Meditation, Rhetoric, and the Making of Images, 400–1200*, Cambridge Studies in Medieval Literature (Cambridge: Cambridge University Press, 1998), pp. 118–22, 130–3.

34 John Onians, *Neuroarthistory: From Aristotle and Pliny to Baxandall and Zeki* (New Haven: Yale Univ. Press, 2007), p. 137.

35 Alvaro Pascual-Leone and others, 'The Plastic Human Brain Cortex', *Annual Review of Neuroscience*, 28 (2005), 377–401 (p. 380).

36 Mary J. Carruthers, *The Book of Memory : A Study of Memory in Medieval Culture*, Cambridge Studies in Medieval Literature, 70 (Cambridge: Cambridge University Press, 2008), p. 100.

37 Carruthers, *The Book of Memory*, pp. 105, 106.

38 Andy Clark, *Natural-Born Cyborgs: Minds, Technologies, and the Future of Human Intelligence* (Oxford: Oxford University Press, 2003), p. 4; Ruth Evans, 'Our Cyborg Past: Medieval Artificial Memory as Mindware Upgrade', *Postmedieval: A Journal of Medieval Cultural Studies*, 1/1–2 (2010), 64–71 (p. 67).

39 Kinch, '"Mind like Wickerwork"', p. 306.

40 Ena Jenkins, 'Julian's Revelation of Love: A Web of Metaphor', in Liz Herbert McAvoy (ed.), *A Companion to Julian of Norwich* (Woodbridge: Boydell & Brewer, 2008), pp. 181–91 (p. 181).

41 Turner, *Julian of Norwich, Theologian*, p. 37.

42 Gillespie and Ross, '"With Mekeness Aske Perseverantly"', p. 135.

43 Gillespie and Ross, '"With Mekeness Aske Perseverantly"', p. 135.

44 Jocelyn Wogan-Browne, 'Glossary: Middle English', in Nicholas Watson, Andrew Taylor and Ruth Evans (eds), *The Idea of the Vernacular: An Anthology of Middle English Literary Theory, 1280–1520* (Exeter: University of Exeter Press, 1999), pp. 393–446 (p. 419).

45 Geoffrey Chaucer, 'The Canterbury Tales: The Parson's Prologue', in *The Riverside Chaucer*, ed. by Ralph Hanna III, Larry D. Benson and Robert A. Pratt (Oxford: Oxford University Press, 1988), pp. 287–88 (l. 38).

46 Jocelyn Wogan-Browne, '"The Croxton Play of the Sacrament": Banns', in Nicholas Watson, Andrew Taylor and Ruth Evans (eds), *The Idea of the Vernacular: An Anthology of Middle English Literary Theory* (Exeter: University of Exeter Press, 1999), pp. 190–5.

47 MED 'mater(e)' (n.).

48 *Revelations of Divine Love*, trans. by Barry Windeatt, Oxford World's Classics (Oxford: Oxford University Press, 2015), p. xxvii.

49 MED 'mater(e)' (n.), def. 4a.

50 Vincent Gillespie and Maggie Ross, 'The Apophatic Image: The Poetics of Effacement in Julian of Norwich', in Marion Glasscoe (ed.), *The Medieval Mystical Tradition in England: Exeter Symposium V: Papers Read at the Devon Centre, Dartington Hall, July 1992* (Cambridge: D.S. Brewer, 1992), pp. 53–77 (p. 57).

51 Andrea Hollingsworth, 'The Architecture of Apophasis: Exploring Options for a Cognitive Scientific Interpretation of the Via Negativa', *Religion, Brain & Behavior*, 6/4 (2016), 290–306 (pp. 290–306).

52 Patrick McNamara, *Neuroscience of Religious Experience* (Cambridge: Cambridge University Press, 2014), pp. 47, 50.

53 Shaun Nichols and Stephen Stich, 'A Cognitive Theory of Pretense', *Cognition*, 74/2 (2000), 115–47 (pp. 122, 123).

54 McNamara, *Neuroscience of Religious Experience*, p. 50

55 McNamara, *Neuroscience of Religious Experience*, p. 115.

[56] McNamara, *Neuroscience of Religious Experience*, pp. 25, 45, 49, 50.

[57] This reading resonates Dutton's claim that Julian persistently keeps earlier insights on the page alongside later ones, never presenting the latter as transcending, contradicting or invalidating the other (Dutton, *Julian of Norwich*, p. 165.)

[58] E. T. Chandler, 'The Present Time of Things Past: Julian of Norwich's Appropriation of St. Augustine's Generative Theory of Memory', *Rhetoric Review*, 31/4 (2012), 389–404.

[59] McNamara, *Neuroscience of Religious Experience*, p. 189.

[60] Sinead L. Mullally and Eleanor A Maguire, 'Memory, Imagination, and Predicting the Future: A Common Brain Mechanism?', *The Neuroscientist*, 20/3 (2014), 220–34 (pp. 221–6).

[61] Mullally and Maguire, 'Memory, Imagination, and Predicting the Future', p. 227.

[62] Mullally and Maguire, 'Memory, Imagination, and Predicting the Future', p. 227.

[63] Both crafters and researchers frequently compare to meditation because of its soothing, relaxing yet absorbing effect. One discussion expressly declares, 'most stitch patterns, once mastered, are truly meditative': Lisa R. Dittrich, 'KNITTING', *Academic Medicine*, 76/7 (2001), 671 (p. 671). However, I do not mean to suggest that reading *Revelation* is as soothing as knitting, or that the embodied experience of reading *Revelation* is identical to that of knitting. *Revelation* is often quite challenging. Rather, reading it can be meditative in the engrossing manner that the *Ancrene Wisse* ascribes to weaving.

[64] Jill Riley, Betsan Corkhill and Clare Morris, 'The Benefits of Knitting for Personal and Social Wellbeing in Adulthood: Findings from an International Survey', *British Journal of Occupational Therapy*, 76/2 (2013), 50–7 (p. 53).

[65] Alice W. Flaherty, 'Homeostasis and the Control of Creative Drive', in Oshin Vartanian and Rex E. Jung (eds), *The Cambridge Handbook of the Neuroscience of Creativity*, Cambridge Handbooks in Psychology (Cambridge: Cambridge University Press, 2018), pp. 19–49 (p. 24).

[66] Teresa M. Amabile, 'Motivational Synergy: Toward New Conceptualizations of Intrinsic and Extrinsic Motivation in the Workplace', *Human Resource Management Review*, 3/3 (1993), 185–201; Carsten K. W. De Dreu, Matthijs Baas and Bernard A. Nijstad, 'Hedonic Tone and Activation Level in the Mood–Creativity Link: Toward a Dual Pathway to Creativity Model', *Journal of Personality and Social Psychology*, 94/5 (2008), 739–56; Mark A. Davis, 'Understanding the Relationship between Mood and Creativity: A Meta-Analysis', *Organizational Behavior and Human Decision Processes*, 108/1 (2009), 25–38.

[67] Flaherty, 'Homeostasis and the Control of Creative Drive', p. 20.

[68] Lambert, 'DO OR DIY', p. 21.

[69] '"With Mekeness Aske Perseverantly"', p. 130.

[70] 'Wonder', *The American Historical Review*, 102/1 (1997), 1–26 (pp. 24, 26).

[71] Rita Felski, *The Limits of Critique* (Chicago: University of Chicago Press, 2015), p. 5.

[72] Felski, *The Limits of Critique*, p. 27.

[73] I bring Julian further into dialogue with modern critique elsewhere (Perk, *Julian, God, and the Art of Storytelling*, pp. 262–4).

[74] Andy Clark, *Supersizing the Mind: Embodiment, Action, and Cognitive Extension* (Oxford: Oxford University Press, 2008); Andy Clark and David Chalmers, 'The Extended Mind', *Analysis*, 58/1 (1998), 7–19; Richard Menary, *The Extended Mind* (Cambridge, MA: MIT Press, 2010).

[75] Clark and Chalmers, 'The Extended Mind', p. 7.

[76] MED 'knotte (n.)'; Watson and Jenkins, 'Sidenotes', p. 294.

[77] Watson and Jenkins, 'Sidenotes', p. 294.

Select Bibliography

Bynum, Caroline Walker, *Fragmentation and Redemption: Essays on Gender and the Human Body in Medieval Religion* (New York: Zone Books, 1991).

Carruthers, Mary J., *The Book of Memory: A Study of Memory in Medieval Culture*, Cambridge Studies in Medieval Literature, 70 (Cambridge: Cambridge University Press, 2008).

Carruthers, Mary J., *The Craft of Thought: Meditation, Rhetoric, and the Making of Images, 400–1200*, Cambridge Studies in Medieval Literature (Cambridge: Cambridge University Press, 1998).

Clark, Andy, *Supersizing the Mind: Embodiment, Action, and Cognitive Extension* (Oxford: Oxford University Press, 2008)

Crowfoot, Elisabeth, Frances Pritchard and Kay Staniland, *Textiles and Clothing, c.1150–c.1450*, Medieval Finds from Excavations in London (Woodbridge: Boydell & Brewer, 2006).

Davis, Mark A., 'Understanding the Relationship between Mood and Creativity: A Meta-Analysis', *Organizational Behavior and Human Decision Processes*, 108/1 (2009), 25–38.

Dresvina, Juliana, 'What Julian Saw: The Embodied Showings and the Items for Private Devotion', *Religions*, 10/4 (2019), *https://doi.org/10.3390/rel10040245.*

Dutton, Elisabeth, *Julian of Norwich: The Influence of Late-Medieval Devotional Compilations* (Cambridge: D.S. Brewer, 2008).

Gillespie, Vincent and Maggie Ross, 'The Apophatic Image: The Poetics of Effacement in Julian of Norwich', in Marion Glasscoe (ed.), *The Medieval Mystical Tradition in England: Exeter Symposium V: Papers Read at the Devon Centre, Dartington Hall, July 1992* (Cambridge: D.S. Brewer, 1992), pp. 53–77.

Jenkins, Ena, 'Julian's Revelation of Love: A Web of Metaphor', in Liz Herbert McAvoy (ed.), *A Companion to Julian of Norwich* (Woodbridge: Boydell & Brewer, 2008), pp. 181–91 (p. 181).

Leverage, Paula, *Reception and Memory: A Cognitive Approach to the Chansons de Geste* (Amsterdam: Rodopi, 2010).

McNamara, Patrick, *Neuroscience of Religious Experience* (Cambridge: Cambridge University Press, 2014).

Menary, Richard, *The Extended Mind* (Cambridge, MA: MIT Press, 2010).

Newman, Barbara, *God and the Goddesses: Vision, Poetry, and Belief in the Middle Ages* (Philadelphia: University of Pennsylvania Press, 2003).

Pascual-Leone, Alvaro, et al., 'The Plastic Human Brain Cortex', *Annual Review of Neuroscience*, 28 (2005), 377–401.

Perk, Godelinde Gertrude, *Julian, God, and the Art of Storytelling: A Narrative Analysis of the Works of Julian of Norwich*, Umeå Studies in Language and Literature, 32 (Umeå: Umeå University, 2016).

Riddy, Felicity, 'Julian of Norwich and Self-Textualization', in Ann M. Hutchison (ed.), *Editing Women* (Toronto: University of Toronto Press, 1995), pp. 101–24.

Riley, Jill, Betsan Corkhill and Clare Morris, 'The Benefits of Knitting for Personal and Social Wellbeing in Adulthood: Findings from an International Survey', *British Journal of Occupational Therapy*, 76/2 (2013), 50–7.

Stafford, Barbara Maria, *Echo Objects: The Cognitive Work of Images* (Chicago: University of Chicago Press, 2007).

Turner, Denys, *Julian of Norwich, Theologian* (New Haven, CT: Yale University Press, 2011).

8

Making Up a Mind: '4E' Cognition and the Medieval Subject

VICTORIA BLUD

What is a mind and where does it live? For some years now, researchers in the cognitive sciences have been changing their minds. The traditional cognitivist model of computation and head-based cognitive activity is being challenged by one that embraces the body, the organism's environment, and potentially its world and its peers. Contemporary approaches and models engage with a broad range of possibilities, but the set of interconnected theories sometimes called *4E cognition* has gathered a special momentum. In this paradigm, cognition is not restricted by the confines of the brain, the skull or even the whole body – the 'organismic skin-bag', as Andy Clark calls it – but is active in a much wider assembly that may comprise bodily, environmental, organic and even inorganic processes and entities.[1] Advocates of '4E' cognition argue that cognition is *embodied*, *embedded*, *enacted* and *extended*. That is, cognitive activity involves not only the brain but somatic feedback from the body more generally; it is also thoroughly linked with environmental data and conditions, involving not only reaction to stimuli but proactive input, and 'extends' from the organism into the wider environment. While advocates of these positions do not always agree amongst themselves, particularly with regard to the relative strength of the functionalism and cognitivism their theories rest on, the movement is growing in strength and numbers and, as Richard Menary puts it, its adherents are in 'a position of abundance'.[2]

Can we think of cognitive processes in the Middle Ages as embodied, embedded, extended, enactive? What difference does it make when we do? In this chapter, I examine the usefulness of such models for the study of pre-modern intellectual activity and creativity (as Godelinde Perk and Antonina Harbus do elsewhere in the volume), especially with regard to the question of agency and how such a methodology supports detailed engagement and meditation on historical texts. In the second part of the chapter, I focus on the fourth 'E', *extended*: this is partly because it is the most controversial – in some ways, the limit case for 4E cognition becomes the extent to which this theory can be supported. However, it is also because it is especially interesting from the perspective of medieval studies, since the evidence and thinking medievalists encounter is so *often* the result of complex socially integrated processes – is it more powerful to consider the role of scribes, confessors, interlocutors, one's own papers, as part of the same process of extended cognition? This chapter therefore provides a sketch of 4E cognition and how it has changed the landscape of cognitive science, what the '4Es' do for the humanities and medieval studies, and what they in turn can do for 4E cognitive studies.

Remaking the Classical Sandwich: the 'Es'

4E cognition developed in part as a reaction to cognitivist models that cast cognitive activity as computational–representational processes that interpret sensory 'input' and produce behavioural 'output'.[3] Such approaches interpret cognition as a specifically neural activity, which is clearly localised (in the brain). Classical cognitivists conceive of thought as the key process that links *perception* – the apprehension of sensory input into the organism's cognising system – and *action*, or behavioural output. Since a cognitive agent is not simply a receptive creature, registering peripheral sensory information and responding, in order to account for the fact that action is not reducible to reflex in such a creature there must be another determining factor in the sequence. In the classical cognitivist view, the process that determines action or inaction is *representational*, involving the cognitive agent's ability to represent circumstances and possible actions to itself, in order to formulate and evaluate hypothetical outcomes. The sensory input and motor output are thus articulated by the processing of these internal representations: this sequencing of *perception–cognition–action* has been dubbed by Susan Hurley 'the classical sandwich'.[4]

The sandwich model therefore holds that the lower-level processing of sensory, non-neural input is clearly distinguished from the higher-order neural processing that characterises classical cognition. By contrast, in more recent years an alternative stance on the matter of how the mind fits into the world has emerged, one that reconfigures the stages of cognition to argue that the mind is not limited to the computational, representational, neural and local – the body's 'computer' – but, rather, is continuous with the body and with the environment in which that body is living.

This is the stance adopted by advocates of '4E cognition'.[5] The '4 Es' are a set of interconnected theories describing cognition as *embodied* (that is, contiguous with the body as an entity, rather than a controlling impulse that the body mechanistically executes), *embedded* (within its surroundings: cognitive activity does not occur only in the head nor in a vacuum, but is situated in an environment that has already been defined by and adapted for the goals of a particular organism), *enacted* (that is, in a living body whose perception and action are intrinsically linked), and finally *extended* (beyond the boundaries of the brain or the individual body: the activity of a single mind may extend into or be supported by technology, texts, or other cognitive agents – other minds). They emerge in the philosophy of the cognitive sciences from an ancestry shared in part with the theories of learning often referred to as *situated* cognition; while this term originally circulated in educational psychology, its scope has since expanded to a movement in the cognitive sciences more generally.[6] In situated cognition, knowledge is shaped by and interrelated with the activities, contexts and wider culture in which it was acquired, and cannot be separated or abstracted from the agent's environment. Cognition takes place not in advance of or alongside physical action, but is constituted *through* it; and is not simply a matter of projecting meaning onto artefacts and other agents, but happens only through *engaging* with the things and people around us.[7] Situated cognition also offers a familiar model for medievalists in the notion of the 'community of practice', wherein novices undergo a cognitive apprenticeship, acquiring knowledge and expertise not only through instruction but through action in specific tasks, by using tools to support their inexpert practice, by being assessed in situ, and through interaction with and mentoring from more expert members of the community. Indeed, this model has been used as a framework for research on medieval monastic life and learning.[8]

The '4 Es' provide potentially transformative insights into psychological theories that are rooted in evolutionary and classic cognitivist models.[9] To say that cognition is embodied emphasises the role of the body beyond the brain and the physical and biological processes beyond neurological activity. This approach to the question of emotion, for example, argues that the somatic experience of emotion is not a *result* of physical responses to rapid mental processing of sensory information or representations: rather, it is precisely *part* of this cognitive process.[10] Embodied cognition incorporates the flesh in a way that is not only of interest to researchers working on the philosophy of mind, but also medievalists and early modernists who are used to encountering the records of pre-Cartesian bodies and minds. In this context, the idea that somatic feedback in episodes of stress or emotionality is a vital component of rational thought offers a productive lens through which to view the traditional divisions between masculine and feminine intellectual qualities.[11]

The notion of embedded cognition focuses on the importance of the way we interact with the world around us, the specialised structures we create and access in order to offload part of our intellectual activity onto other resources in our immediate environment. This 'E' in particular brings the phenomenological principles of thinkers like Maurice Merleau-Ponty and Martin Heidegger to bear on the questions of how cognition occurs and what the realm of the cognitive actually is. At the same time, embedded cognition incorporates and develops theories from educational psychology, in particular Lev Vygotsky's research, on how memory especially may be scaffolded by environmental resources.[12]

The theory of enactivism, meanwhile, insists not only that cognition is embodied and embedded in the environment, but that knowledge is constituted through interactions in specific environments – in a sense, knowing is doing. This point is eloquently summarised by Varela, Rosch and Thompson in one of the earliest explorations of the embodied approach: cognition 'is not the representation of a pregiven world by a pregiven mind but is rather the enactment of a world and a mind on the basis of a history of the variety of actions that a being in the world performs'.[13] Enactivism thus prioritises the lived body, the ability to act on the world and explore it. Perceiving the world visually, for example, is based on our expectations grounded not in our experience of the world but experience of our own movement and how it realigns sensory information available to us – sensorimotor knowledge that shows us what we can see based on what we can do.[14] (This principle is also theorised the other way around:[15] an alternative paradigm espouses James Gibson's theory of affordances, wherein what we are able to do is based on what we can see.)[16] This dynamic may perhaps be compared with the medieval tradition of affective piety, wherein spiritual experience and connection is not simply visited on a believer but is evoked through the contemplation of images, journeys to places where Christ and the saints once lived or suffered, and in various ways seeking emotional and physical experience that allows the believer to feel compassion, to feel as if they are present in religious scenes.

The final 'E', the notion of the extended mind (*EM*) or, in its modified later form, the hypothesis of extended cognition (or *HEC*) has been the subject of particular debate, which I will return to shortly; the scope of its implications has engendered caution and controversy, but the expansiveness of HEC is precisely the reason it is so fascinating and powerful as a theory.[17] While the study of emotion and cognition often draws on somatic, embodied and embedded theories of mind, and the contemplation of consciousness might draw on enaction, a project with a focus on a community might benefit from a look at the *extended mind*. In its simplest form, the 'extended mind' hypothesis deals with the question, 'Where does the mind stop and the rest of the world begin?'[18]

All of these might be familiar notions to medievalists used to taking into account the significance of the humours, or the physicality of medieval descriptions of emotion; they might also bring a further dimension to studies of scholars' and artisans' concerted combined intellectual efforts, the routine use of texts as prompts for memory, and the medieval appreciation of the body's role in preparing the mind for contemplation and opening it to spiritual revelation. Medievalists are familiar with the varieties of medieval mnemonic scaffolding, comprehensively analysed in Mary Carruthers's classic *The Book of Memory*;[19] as Corinne Saunders has written, they are versed in the fluidity medieval psychology espoused with regard to the mind–body problem, as compared with the dualism that would shape thought on cognition after Descartes.[20] Studies of 4E cognition and distributed cognition have informed analyses of literary texts and other cultural artefacts in numerous periods, perhaps especially the early modern period and the eighteenth century.[21] Mark Rowlands describes the proponents of 4E cognition as 'non-Cartesian';[22] if the '4 Es' describe in a new way phenomena that existed long before the field of cognitive science, what can studying the medieval idea of the mind – another non-Cartesian concept – bring to these notions of the mind and cognition?

'Fulfilled with Mind': Julian of Norwich in 4E

The mind that I have in mind, to begin with, is that of an intelligent, passionate and devout thirty-year-old woman, who we meet at the point she believes she is going to die. Julian of Norwich's 'showings' or visions, which she not only relates but uses to construct a sophisticated account of their insights, are narrated in a way that obliges any reader to reflect on the setting and the circumstances in which she received them.[23] In the previous chapter, Godelinde Perk homed in on the cognitive aspects of physical activity in the anchorhold; here, I begin with how Julian describes her physicality and embodiment.

Having previously related how she wished for three gifts or 'woundes' from God – a vision of Christ's passion, an all but mortal illness, and the gifts of contrition, compassion and longing for God – Julian describes how her second desire is granted at age thirty. She suffers from physical illness for three days and nights, and is given the last rites; three nights later, she notes how she is loath to die, not out of fear but rather because she wishes to live longer to know God better. Yet she understands 'by [her] reason and by the feeling of [her] paines' that she is dying nevertheless, and thus assents to God's will 'with all the will of [her] hart'.[24] We see already how Julian closely aligns her developing understanding with the condition of her body: the pains she suffers are signs that God has heard her prayers. Nor is her resulting determination imagined as a process taking place in her head;

in the cultural idiom of Julian’s experience, her will is associated with her heart, the seat of the medieval Christian soul.

Consider, then, the famous moment in Julian’s text in which she believes herself to be dying. Julian here describes her state – physical, sensory, environmental, social – at the point her visions truly begin:

> My curate was sent for to be at my ending, and by then he cam I had set up my eyen and might not speake. He set the crosse before my face, and said: ‘I have brought thee the image of thy saviour. Looke therupon and comfort thee therwith.’ Methought I was well, for my eyen were set uprightward into heaven, where I trusted to come by the mercy of God. But nevertheles I ascented to set my eyen in the face of the crucifixe, if I might, and so I dide, for methought I might longar dure to looke evenforth then right up.
>
> After this my sight began to faile, and it was alle darke aboute me in the chamber as if it had ben night, save in the image of the crosse, wherin held a comon light, and I wiste not how. All that was beseid the crosse was oglye and ferful to me, as if it had ben mekille occupied with fiendes. (*Revelation*, 3: 131–3).

By this point, Julian is ‘dead from the middes downward’, and apparently unable to talk any longer. The sense that will come to support her vision, however, is as yet unimpaired, so aided by helpers at the sickbed, she is manoeuvred from a prone to an ‘underlening’ position, propped up with support so that she can look on the cross that has been set up before her (*Revelation*, 3: 131).

Julian’s experience prompts her showings, and it is affected and perhaps also *effected* by the somatic feedback she receives from her ailing body: the fact that she is in what she believes to be her deathbed, talking to her spiritual adviser, thoroughly embedded, of course, in a deeply religious culture that conditions self-reflection. All this finds a meaningful focus in the shape of the cross on which she has been invited to gaze. After seeing the cross glow as all else fades to black – a memory, perhaps, that is consistent with the experience of sudden intense focus as much as the sensation of failing physical eyesight? – Julian then feels her pain first increase and then vanish. Feeling no immediate ease because she had set her heart to being delivered of this world, her emotional response culminates in another realisation: ‘Then cam sodenly to my mind that I should desire … that my body might be fulfilled with mind and feeling of his blessed passion, as I had before prayed’ (*Revelation*, 3: 133). Again, her cognisance follows the interpretation of her bodily states: while this description is more coarse-grained than the subtle somatic-neurological feedback loops that inform recent research on embodiment, it shows, writ large, the crucial role of bodily states in cognitive processes. The language with which Julian expresses her desire is also significant here: she does not frame her vision as an image or a representation that will come to mind, but as mind (memory) and feeling that will fill her *body*.

We are given details of Julian’s body in her own voice, but the details of her wider environment are more implicit. What can we know about the enculturation of Julian’s mind? It has been suggested that Julian was a nun at the time of her illness, though it is possible she was a laywoman.[25] But at the time the longer version of her text was most likely written, she was living as an anchoress, as we know from the note added to manuscripts of her text and from surviving wills that refer to a Norwich anchoress called Julian or living at St Julian's church. While the life of a nun was regimented, the anchoress was perhaps even more thoroughly scaffolded for one major cognitive task: prayer. *Ancrene Wisse*, the guide for anchorites, dwells extensively on the routine of the anchoress and how these external actions will support her internal development.[26] Her day is divided by the bells that prompt her to observe the canonical hours; her thoughts – and hands – are to be occupied by plain sewing rather than permitted to wander. The anchoress is also encouraged to read devotional and pedagogic literature to her serving maids, in order to foster their own care for and attention to their behaviour and thereby the safety of their souls, but this activity might also be reasonably expected, not only by the subscriber to enaction theory but the user of *Ancrene Wisse* as well, to serve as a regular support to the anchoress's own contemplation of her external and internal condition. (The *Wisse*-writer permits the anchoress to keep a cat, so perhaps not every directive would be so successful in this endeavour.)

The consideration of community brings us back to extended cognition. Variously called *Extended Mind*, *Hypothesis of Extended Cognition*, *vehicle externalism* and *(socially) distributed cognition*, this theory, or set of theories, intersects with social psychology and anthropology, as well as philosophy of mind.[27] The extended mind is influenced by and exerts influence upon – indeed, is composed in part *from* – environmental resources, objects with which the individual interacts or on which they rely, and other people, other minds. Its originators, Andy Clark and David Chalmers, adopted what they called 'the parity principle': 'If, as we confront some task, a part of the world functions as a process which, *were it done in the head*, we would have no hesitation in recognizing as part of the cognitive process, then that part of the world *is* (so we claim) part of the cognitive process'.[28] They use the example of two people (Otto and Inga) making their way to a museum: Otto, who suffers from Alzheimer's disease, needs a notebook to remember the address, but even though the information in the notebook is not in his memory, it doesn't alter his belief that the museum is at that location. Since it is available to him at the relevant moment, it is able to play a role in his cognitive process to produce the same end result as Inga's non-impaired memory does without a notebook. In its original incarnation, then, the extension thesis depends on a fairly liberal functionalism.

In a closely related vein, anthropologist Edwin Hutchins developed the hypothesis of *distributed* cognition to explain how tasks that are too complex or expansive for a single agent to execute may be achieved by a group of agents whose individual cognitive processes are supported and enabled by the culture in which they occur. Hutchins calls this 'cognition in the wild', and specifies that it is both cultural and systemic in nature: he does not 'make any special commitment to the nature of the computations that are going on inside individuals except to say that whatever happens there is part of a larger computational system'.[29] Evelyn Tribble has argued that such a model may be seen at work in the early modern theatre, whose practicalities and mnemonic demands are supported by the company's organisation and the form and conventions of the play itself. The feats of memory involved in retaining functional knowledge of many parts and plays at once may be better understood if, instead of assuming that 'properties of the system as a whole must be possessed by each individual within it', we view cognition as 'distributed across the entire system'.[30] Making a book, as Julian does, exploits a distribution of skill, since one agent in the system does not have to possess the knowledge that is represented by the entire system: a scribe does not necessarily have an input in the compilation of texts, or intervene in the programme of decoration or illustration; the copyist of one section might not be versed in the language of another; an amanuensis need not be personally familiar with the material they are transcribing. The knowledge of one writer may form the basis of the revelations of another; the style of one author may shape the thoughts of another.

Extending Cognition: Confessing the Limits

The medieval approach to the question of the individual mind, how it relates to the body and to the wider world, what a mind is, where it is, and what it does, brings together medicine, natural philosophy and theology. We do not know what treatment Julian received for her mysterious illness, if any: she was told when she came to her senses that she had 'raved' for much of the day (*Revelation*, 66: 331), and mental ailments were typically treated as imbalances of the humours, in much the same way as any other illness. Whatever treatment she might have received, a late medieval remedy would typically have drawn on the natural philosophy, theology and folk practice that informed medieval thought on medical practice and remedies and which were deeply interconnected. The heavenly bodies were implicated in the movements of the earthly body, which in turn were examined through a person's behaviour, character and emotions as well as the state of their general health. A medieval physician would consult not just the patient but the almanac; when bleeding a patient to restore the balance of their humours, for example, they would make sure that the moon was not in the sign that ruled that body part, for fear the blood flow should be excessive.

Clearly this is not an embodiment or extension into the world that would support the type of scrutiny applied by advocates of 4E cognition. However, we might contrast medieval treatment of mental ailments with another practice for the care of the sick. Consider the mechanism of confession, which all Christians were obligated to perform and whose codification coincided with and to some extent influenced the rise of vernacular literature in Western Europe. While by no means an innovation of the thirteenth century, confession was instituted as an annual obligation in 1215 by the fourth Lateran Council.[31] The logic of confession was to reveal any and all impediments to the penitent's relationship with God, and the confessor was likened to a physician whose duty was to ensure all possible psychic wounds were healed. The confessing subject was thus obliged to consult more than her conscience: as Kisha Tracy emphasises, 'In order to speak sins, a penitent must remember them'.[32] The priest might therefore support this process by enquiring carefully about the nature of the penitent's sin, being prepared to prod her memory with a series of questions drawn from an authoritative summa or manual of confession, before directing her towards the cycle of prayers or perhaps bodily performance of penance that would further transform her thinking about her sin and herself. Confession might be biographical – the procession of sins committed from childhood to the present – or related according to a schema such as the seven deadly sins (with the priest interrogating the parishioner as to whether she had committed a named species of sin), or perhaps recollected with prompting about the deployment of the sensory faculties – sins of speech, of touch, of sensual excess. Once identified, the priest might well press the parishioner on the 'circumstances' of the sin – how long ago, how many times, in what place, in what manner, with whom?

The process by which man became, as Foucault famously put it, a 'confessing animal',[33] has received attention from medievalists, cultural historians and psychologists alike, who variously explore the analogy of confession and therapeutic discourse and the suggestive line of descent from the former to the latter, the interiority and subjective experience foregrounded in the necessity of narrating one's life in confession, and of course the depth and breadth of memory required to do so.[34] In social psychology, these interchanges between penitent and confessor would represent an instance of transactional memory. The narrative emerges from the cooperation of the penitent, who does not have to hold every sin in the various complex schemes in her head, and the confessor, who may reliably consult a manual in order to help the penitent relate her sinful behaviour, and thereby a narrative and systematic consideration of her own life.

As Tentler says, 'A good confession is the work of the penitent': it is the penitent who prepares for confession by recalling sins, consulting her conscience.[35] Yet the setting and significance of confessions placed a heavy cognitive load not only on the penitent but on the priest. As Michael Cornett observes of the 'form of confession' genre – a written aid to auricular confession, in the form of a first-person narrative of all the sins that could be admitted to the priest – 'One can only imagine the immense burden it would be to a parish priest should most of the parish come to confession without any preparation, leaving him to do all the work of prodding their memories'.[36] Indeed, priests complained of parishioners who 'come to confession so lighthearted and merry as if they set no store by it, and when they show up, they have little or nothing to say but ask their confessor, "Ask me, sir"'.[37] In numerous ways, then, a summa had to be a highly practical text: its utility was achieved through tables of contents, indices, cross-referencing, scripted interrogations and various mnemonic devices such as verse. The reader benefited further from the stable numeric frameworks around which the more sophisticated discussions were constructed: ten commandments, seven deadly sins, five senses, seven corporal acts of mercy, nine sins against one's neighbour.[38] As a result of such ingenuity, 'there was much, even in the more sophisticated summas, that a simple parish priest could commit to memory and draw on'.[39]

For the priest, interrogatories and forms of confession supplied frameworks for questioning a reluctant, forgetful, anxious or disorganised penitent. For the penitent, the procedure of confession and the priest's manual helped ensure they could be effectively shriven. The whole set-up of confession scaffolded the cognitive work of memory; can we also see the process as *extended*, for instance if we take the interrogations and the use of manual as part of the penitent's cognitive processes in recall? Did they assist the penitent in accomplishing cognitive acts, here mnemonic, that would otherwise take place by entirely neural processes?

We might say *yes*, which leads us to the limitations of the parity principle. Clark and Chalmers's original criteria for a component of cognitive extension were that it should be: (1) a constant in the person's life; (2) directly available; (3) a repository of information or beliefs that are automatically endorsed; (4) at the time of its use, already consciously endorsed.[40] We might question, therefore: how close and how reliable and the repository of how much belief do the priest and the summa have to be? What if it were badly copied? What would happen if the summa were not there, or if the priest used no manual?

Deeper objections to extended cognition arise since, whatever the process going on inside the penitent's head as she recalls her sins, the priest's book does not itself think. As John Sutton observes, the power of 'extended' minds is due not to their breadth but to the use of closely coupled external resources that enable a division of cognitive work.[41] However, the nature of this coupling and whether the nature of the work they do is 'truly' cognitive has been the subject of considerable debate. Responses to Clark and Chalmers's initial article (and Clark's work thereafter) have sometimes refined these ideas and partly reconsidered this model, while others have challenged the whole concept of EM and the enterprise of HEC.[42] Rowlands effectively summarises the challenges and divides the major objections into four main strands. These are: the 'differences' argument (that is, that the processes taking place in brain and body or world are too different from one another to all be brought comfortably under the single descriptor *cognitive*); the coupling/constitution fallacy (Fred Adams and Ken Aizawa's assertion that to say something like Otto's notebook may be closely *coupled* with the processes happening in Otto's head is not the same as demonstrating that it *constitutes* them); 'cognitive bloat' (a termed coined by Robert Rupert to describe the danger that functionalism theoretically allows far *too* much to be brought into the cognitive process: where does the mind stop, indeed?); and the 'mark of the cognitive' (the insistence that cognitive processes differ from all others).[43] Defenders of extension would reply that the hypothesis does not imply that this is the state of affairs in all circumstances, at all times, but rather in particular cognitive processes. Clark has since modified his original criteria, to reflect that a resource need only be 'reliably available and typically invoked', rather than *constantly* available, and equivalent in terms of trustworthiness with biological memory;[44] Clark and Wilson propose a further criterion of durability.[45] Kim Sterelny, though he does not unreservedly endorse extension, suggests that, as far as physical artefacts are concerned, the *degree* of individualised modification is also significant.[46]

However, the manual of confession here still does not seem to satisfy these criteria for the penitent (though it may for the priest). The priest himself, however, might satisfy the criteria in the specific situation of confession: he is consistently available to his parishioners, and as for trustworthiness, he is endorsed by no less an authority than God. One further resolution to the problem common to extension in cognitive states and extension in cognitive processes (that is, cognitive bloat) is proposed by Rowlands, who advances *ownership* as a criterion: 'Cognitive processes – whether neural, embodied, or extended – belong to me when they disclose the world to me'.[47] The penitent does not literally own the summa, nor is she even likely to have access to it. In the ritual of confession, however, not only is the book part of the system that discloses the world to the penitent, but the priest's obligation to observe the 'seal' of confession means the penitent's disclosures must stop with him, be 'sealed' in his own person. Confession thus brings the priest's own memory and understanding within the compass of the penitent's; in effect, his mind functions as part of her mental processes in making her confession and thereby being disposed to receive absolution. Her secrets become his secrets, but his mind extends her mind.

Extending Julian's Mind

While the manual of confession's role in cognition may be debatable, Julian's text, on the other hand, offers a compelling example of extended and distributed cognition and its powerful role in an individual medieval life. Julian recorded her revelations soon after they took place (that is, 13 May 1373, according to the *Revelation* or Long Text),[48] when she was still 'a simple creature unletterde' (*Revelation*, 2: 125).[49] She relates that as soon as she had received her visions, she meditated on them and desired to know their meaning; this went on 'fifteen yere after and mor' before she was 'answered in gostly understonding' that *love* is the meaning of her visions (*Revelation*, 86: 179). At an earlier point in the Long Text, Julian further specifies that she had 'inward teaching' for 'twenty yere after the time of the shewing, save thre monthes' (*Revelation*, 51: 277). The timeline is not precise, but the scribal note in the earliest witness of Julian's *Vision* (the Short Text), the Amherst manuscript (BL MS Additional 37790), names her – 'Julyan that is recluse atte Norwyche' – and declares that twenty years after her visions, in 'Anno d(omi)ni mill(esi) mo CCCCxiij [1413]', she is 'yitt … onn lyfe'.[50] As far as Julian is concerned, this is still not the whole story; the book was 'begonne by Goddes gifte and his grace, but it is not yet performed, as to my sight' – that is, it is still not completed, even after the Long Text is written. She believes that God sent her vision 'for he will have it knowen more than it is' (*Revelation*, 86: 179). Her writings are to be made available to other readers and listeners who might benefit from the spiritual instruction and the revelations she received.

However, Julian also uses her own initial text as a basis for a wholesale expansion on and sophisticated reworking of her original account, when she comes to author the Long Text.[51] Her recourse to her own work demonstrates a cognitive process that necessarily draws on a resource that is outside both her head and her body, reliably available, endorsed by Julian at the time of writing, created in what we must assume is a sufficiently durable form for Julian to refer to it some years later, and naturally individualised. It is also a resource that, since it discloses the world to her (indeed, in a way that it could to no other person), may safely be called hers.

To take a contrasting case, Margery Kempe's narrative is enabled first by one amanuensis (very likely her son), then by a second amanuensis (a priest, probably Robert Spryngolde, identified as her confessor in the *Book*).[52] That first copy of the *Book* 'was so evel wretyn that he cowd lytyl skyll theron, for it was neithyr good Englysch ne Dewch . . . the prest leved fully ther schuld nevyr man redyn it, but it wer special grace'.[53] The priest attempted to find another amanuensis; failing this, he tried again to read the text, but even a pair of spectacles did not help. In the end, trusting in Margery's prayers, the priest was finally able to read the book, and thus finish and revise it. Here we have a case in which the copy text was not an aid for further cognitive work (in transcribing, organising and transforming the auditory data into legible text), and incidentally a case in which the original text, by the first amanuensis, was neither 'owned' nor, at first, endorsed by the second.

Margery's example also shows the extent to which language is the condition for much of the distribution and/or extension of cognition: Margery's priest cannot use what he cannot understand. Julian, meanwhile, uses her writing to support the cognitive work of making sense of her visions: had she not recorded them, soon after they occurred, would she have been able to return as easily to their substance and recall how they affected her? And had she not written and rewritten her showings over the years, would she have been able to develop her theology? Wilson and Clark give writing systems as prime examples of extended cognitive systems, since they 'are not simply used by agents with given cognitive abilities but significantly augment the cognitive abilities that those agents possess, such as the capacity for short- and long-term memory, the ability to keep track of the relationship between abstract propositions as is often required in reasoning, and the ability to systematically fix and then critique our own ideas'.[54] Kim Sterelny likewise takes writing and notation as paradigmatic of the 'extension' of the agent's intellectual toolkit. His evaluation of extension in cognition draws on an analogy with biology to suggest that this might be regarded as a particular type of niche construction, where human cognition is partly a result of interaction with resources in the cognitive niche. In an example that seems almost custom-designed for medievalists, Sterelny discusses the personalisation of a scholar's book, 'massively individualised with underlining, marginal comments and . . . longer commentaries' until it has all but 'disappeared under a mould of marginalia, of hooks to [the owner's] own thought and work'.[55]

As Margery's example suggests, the paradigm of extended cognition and especially the perspective of socially distributed cognition alters how we might see the rewriting process in another way. It has become a significant point in the literature on Julian, and on other anchorites, that the term *recluse* belies the very strong attachments an anchorite would have to the community for which he or she prayed daily, and the necessary worldly connections (domestic help, donations from lay persons to the upkeep of the anchorhold) that made anchoritic life possible. From the text itself, lacking the clerical ruminations that preface Margery's *Book*, it is difficult to be sure how the material record of Julian's visions came into being, but she may well have employed an amanuensis herself (the surviving witnesses are copies done by later scribes).[56] Felicity Riddy suggests that not only the manual but the intellectual labour of revision – 'numbering the visions and the chapters, devising the contents list, adding chapter headings, inserting cross-references' – may have been collaborative, and, noting that scribes need not always be clerics, even posits a female amanuensis for Julian: her one-time maid, Alice.[57]

Writing the second, longer version of her revelations enabled Julian not only to preserve them but to re-order and make sense of them in a way that would encourage others to do the same. The most interesting evidence that this endeavour was taken up by later readers comes from the convent of Our Lady of Comfort, established in Cambrai in 1623. The nuns' library included old favourites for medievalists such as the *Cloud of Unknowing*, works by Tauler and Suso, the revelations of St Bridget and, most famously, the showings of Julian of Norwich. There are additionally a large number of 'collections' out of these authors which are listed and presumably kept for common use. As a Benedictine house, their property and manuscripts were held in common, but often there is a note of the hand in which a text is copied, or the nun to whom a collection of writings from Tauler, Teresa, Julian or another mystic belongs (and who may have chosen or copied them as part of her devotions).[58] The Cambrai nuns played a vital role in the post-Reformation dissemination and publication of Julian of Norwich's writings: before Serenus Cressy printed Julian's text in 1670, the nuns produced two major witnesses[59] (among several other copies).[60] Alexandra Barratt makes the pointed suggestion that, while earlier editors credited the survival of the text to Cressy and to Augustine Baker, 'perhaps the nuns of Paris and Cambrai, who provided the manual labor at least to copy the manuscripts, deserve some acknowledgment too'.[61] The nuns clearly absorbed Julian's writings while they were copying, but they meditated on her words as they incorporated them into new works, where her impact is clear in the writings of individual nuns. It is recorded in the life of Margaret Gascoigne, for example, that she had a quotation from Julian's *Revelation* – 'intend to me, for I am enough for thee: rejoice in me thy Saviour, and in thy Salvation' – placed where she could gaze upon it in her last illness. Thus, where Julian's text and vision began with the sight of the cross, Gascoigne's final meditations are inspired by the sight of Julian's text.

Conclusions

When we think of how a mind is 'made up', our access to other minds, especially medieval ones, is largely limited to textual and spatial traces – what they wrote, what they read, where they lived. This access comes with caveats. Does mystic writing, with its tendency towards self-abnegation and dissolution, lend itself particularly well to this notion of extending the mind (in that the boundary between self and others, self and the world, is permeable) or is it problematic for the same reasons (in as much as some branches of mysticism seek to transcend the world and its limitations in the longing to be one with the divine)? Is this a useful way of looking at texts from the later medieval period, and their users? It might be objected that the principles here are simply another type of intertextuality. On the other hand, we might equally think of the study of literary interactions as a metaphor for a situated, scaffolded, even extended mind. There are risks and temptations associated with what can be a coarse-grained functionalist approach. However, it is also an approach that seeks to consider the text in the lived circumstances of its composition, paying attention to its influence and wider role not only alongside but by putting it (back) in touch with its human origin.

Not a computer

There is a longer history at stake in the medievalist response to modernity and modern-centric perspectives on how the mind works. One of Hutchins's goals in putting cognition back 'in the wild' is as a response to the traditional cognitivist tendency to focus on computation: 'The computer was not made in the image of the person. *The computer was made in the image of the formal manipulations of abstract symbols. And the last 30 years of cognitive science can be seen as attempts to remake the person in the image of the computer*'.[62] Any broader chronology of 4E cognition likewise relies on this recollection that if human minds are not computers in the twenty-first century, they certainly weren't in the fourteenth – to use such a metaphor would be awkward and anachronistic for most purposes when looking at pre-modern studies. Ruth Evans makes the point that the disparity in medieval and modern technology is not the only or most important factor at play: 'It's not just that medieval people didn't have cochlear and retinal implants, software agents, smart phones, and other forms of ubiquitous computing; it's that they conceived of their relationship to technology in fundamentally different ways'.[63] Theories of embodied cognition likewise demand that we reconceive our contemporary relationship to technology, particularly as a pattern for cognition. Where moderns may have only recently begun to think about this embodiment and extension, embedding and enactivism, for medieval writers the fundamental principles on which these theories rest did not run counter to a computational exemplar, but were part of a more familiar discourse in intellectual culture.

Gender and intersectionality

The possibility of extended or distributed cognition raises more possibilities: if we think of intellectual activity in a way that not only allows for external resources and the input of other cognitive agents, but actually *depends* on it, what might this do for our understanding of collaborative work and the role of otherwise anonymous contributors within this work? What contribution does each actor make to such a community, and what is the pre-modern sense of being part of such an operation? The impact of intersectionality is one of the features of more recent work on 4E cognition and the cognitive sciences more widely.[64] Embodied, enactive approaches focus on the lived body: what is the influence of sex and gender, race, sexuality, and disability, on these approaches and cognitive and perceptual activity in individual cases? The methods of the humanities may also offer a steer in this area.

Approaches that react against cognitivism (and the dualism or traditional mind–body scheme that cognitivism implies) may offer a particularly attractive alternative framework for studies of medieval women in intellectual communities, where the focus of activity is re-situated and potentially takes in those that elite male defaults leave out. For a variety of reasons, not only having to do with literacy rates, women might well be more likely than men to draw on this type of distributed cognition and socially scaffolded skill set when committing their texts to parchment and paper: they might seek permission to write from an ecclesiastical authority or superior, or be more likely to employ an amanuensis. Mason Cash has argued for a less individualistic look at cognition: *extended* in particular implies a single point from which extension occurs, whereas drawing on feminist theory 'encourages us to attend to power relationships, and to the ways that different positions within such relationships shape individuals in different ways, reinforcing patterns of power and privilege, disadvantage and disempowerment, ability and inability'.[65] Such a methodology offers not only insight into these imbalances but the tools with which to redress them.

Cognition that goes beyond the brain-bound can thus offer approaches to women's writing and cultural activity in the medieval and early modern period that keep the focus of intellectual and cognitive activity on the women as agents. Male scribes and amanuenses are drawn into a cognising network rather than acting as potential rivals for the credit (as when John Hirsh declared that 'the second scribe, no less than Margery, should be regarded as the author of *The Book of Margery Kempe*').[66] Meanwhile, the Cambrai community, as copyists and preservationists, and Julian's amanuensis (female or not), are not passive receivers of a 'single-minded' genius, but afforded a role that recognises their active contribution to a shared spiritual and intellectual endeavour.

Non-Cartesians and pre-Cartesians

'Non-Cartesian' cognitive sciences benefit in turn from the examples of a longer history, as Sutton has observed. Medieval and renaissance accounts of cognition being pre-Cartesian, they offer an already-aligned cultural template, whose value is demonstrated in Evelyn Tribble's research. Sensitive to concerns about essentialism and universalism arising from any approach that privileges neurobiological consistency in early modern and modern subjects, but equally determined not to adopt cognitive studies in order to 'correct' the humanities, Tribble foregrounds not only the internal cues of early modern play scripts and the spatial mnemonics of stage directions but also the completely different educational, social and material culture: these plays were designed 'for certain kinds of mindful bodies, bodies trained in disciplines such as fencing, dance and gesture', whereas modern actors, 'embedded in very different institutional practices' as they are, 'cannot simply replicate early modern skillsets'.[67] What Tribble's work suggests is that such case studies support the hypotheses of 4E theorists in an important and unique way, since they make the case even more clearly that specific enculturation is crucial to the type of cognitive feats the actors of the Globe (in this instance) were able to achieve.

Like the confessor's prompts, the principles of 4E cognition oblige us to pay close attention to circumstances. This attention to the ways in which certain behaviours and cognitive expressions are embedded in a specific environment and enacted by living and lived bodies, whose states influence and constitute the mind that we access through artefacts and linguistic traces, might offer a way of reconciling the suspicion of essentialism (in acknowledging that the 'medieval brain' is, in evolutionary terms, virtually identical to the contemporary subject's) with the nuance and contextual insight demanded by the study of the humanities. On the other hand, the embodied cognition approach avoids the temptations of retroactive diagnosis, in which accounts of religious experience, for example, become intelligible to modern psychology only as instances of mental illness or psychological disorder. They may also suggest productive intersections with more familiar theoretical models in the humanities, particularly those that understand concepts such as gender as cultural constructs and not inalienable fact. To attend to the individual's circumstances in cognition and to conceive of the mind as necessarily enacted in a lived body, as part of a dynamic environment and community, enables a view of pre-modern intellectual and psychological subjectivity – perhaps especially religious thought and culture – that is neither primitive, nor undifferentiated, nor reduced to pathology, but ingeniously supported, historically specific, and enduringly relevant.

Notes

* I am grateful to the British Academy/Leverhulme Trust Small Grant scheme for supporting the early research that contributed to this chapter (award SG160391).

1 Andy Clark, *Supersizing the Mind: Embodiment, Action, and Cognitive Extension* (Oxford: Oxford University Press, 2008), p. xxviii.

2 Richard Menary, 'Introduction to the special issue on 4E cognition', *Phenomenology and the Cognitive Sciences*, 9/4 (2010), 459–63 (p. 460). Despite the growing influence of these theories, certain debates among theorists amount to fundamental incompatibilities. The functionalist/enactivist dichotomy divides supporters of extended cognition, which advocates a functionalism that does not always see the material nature of the components of mental processes as relevant, from theorists of enactivism, who take as paramount that biological details matter, that minds emerge in living beings. Champions of the extended mind can additionally see the embedded thesis as weak by comparison. Promoters of extension have sometimes been at odds with theorists of embodiment, who privilege biological processes as the location of 'true' cognition. For an overview, see Menary, above.

Contrasting somewhat with Menary's celebration of abundance, Mark Rowlands's objective in his survey and defence of the 'new science' is to demonstrate how such conflict may be pruned from 4E cognition and other non-Cartesian theories, in order to leave a 'leaner, meaner' method. This involves adopting an approach combining only embodied and extended cognition, which he terms 'the amalgamated mind'. Rowlands, *The New Science of the Mind: From Extended Mind to Embodied Phenomenology* (Cambridge, MA: MIT Press, 2010), pp. 83–4.

3 For a brief overview, see '4E Cognition: Historical Roots, Key Concepts, and Central Issues', in Albert Newen, Leon de Bruin and Shaun Gallagher (eds), *The Oxford Handbook of 4E Cognition* (Oxford: Oxford University Press, 2018), pp. 3–16 (esp. pp. 5–7).

4 Susan Hurley, *Consciousness in Action* (Cambridge, MA: Harvard University Press, 1998); 'Perception and action: Alternative views', *Synthese*, 129/1 (2001), 3–40.

5 Although *embodiment* is one of the four 'Es', these approaches are also sometimes called 'embodied theories of cognition' (as distinct from traditional representational–computational theories).

6 Philip Robbins and Murat Aydede, for example, introduce their survey of situated cognition by specifying that 'situated cognition is the genus, and embodied, enactive, embedded, and distributed cognition and their ilk are species'. See 'A Short Primer on Situated Cognition', in *The Cambridge Handbook of Situated Cognition* (Cambridge: Cambridge University Press, 2009), pp. 3–10 (p. 3).

7 For the development of the 4 'Es' or 'embodied cognition' approaches, see Margaret Wilson, 'Six Views of Embodied Cognition', *Psychonomic Bulletin & Review*, 9/4 (2002), 625–36; Rowlands, *New Science of the Mind*; Dave Ward and Mog Stapleton, 'Es Are Good: Cognition as Enacted, Embodied, Embedded, Affective and Extended', in Fabio Paglieri (ed.), *Consciousness in Interaction: The role of the natural and social context in shaping consciousness* (Amsterdam: John Benjamins Publishing Company, 2012), pp. 89–104; Albert Newen, Leon de Bruin and Shaun Gallagher (eds), introduction '4E Cognition: Historical Roots, Key Concepts, and Central Issues', in *The Oxford Handbook of 4E Cognition* (Oxford: Oxford University Press, 2018), pp. 3–17.

8 See Constant J. Mews and John N. Crossley (eds), *Communities of Learning. Networks and the Shaping of Intellectual Identity in Europe, 1100–1500* (Turnhout: Brepols, 2011); Micol Long and Steven Vanderputten (eds), *Horizontal Learning: Peer to Peer Knowledge Transfer in Medieval Religious Communities* (Amsterdam: Amsterdam University Press, 2019).

9 Dean Petters, for instance, has argued that the embodied, enacted and embedded theses offer additional scope for reconsidering infant attachment. See 'An Encounter Between 4E Cognition and Attachment Theory', *Connection Science*, 28/4 (2016), 387–409, DOI: 10.1080/09540091.2016.1214947. For the insights of medieval studies on attachment theory, see Juliana Dresvina's chapter in this volume.

10 On embodied cognition, see Andy Clark, *Being There: Putting Brain, Body and World Together Again* (Cambridge, MA: The MIT Press, 1997); Shaun Gallagher, *How the Body Shapes the Mind* (Oxford: Clarendon Press, 2005).

11 See Victoria Blud, 'Emotional Bodies: Cognitive Neuroscience and Mediaeval Studies', *Literature Compass*, 13/6 (2016), 457–66. On embodiment in emotion and reasoning, see Antonio Damasio, *Descartes' Error* (New York: G. P. Putnam, 1994); *Looking for Spinoza: Joy, Sorrow, and the Feeling Brain* (New York: Houghton Mifflin, 2003).

12 See Lev Vygotsky, *Thought and Language* (Cambridge, MA: MIT Press, 1962); Alexander Luria and Lev Vygotsky, *Ape, Primitive Man, and Child: Studies on the History of Behaviour* (Cambridge, MA: MIT Press, 1992). For a much-cited exploration of how the way we think is shaped by the world around us, see George Lakoff and Mark Johnson, *Metaphors We Live By* (Chicago: University of Chicago Press, 1980).

13 Francisco J. Varela, Evan Thompson and Eleanor Rosch, *The Embodied Mind*, (Cambridge, MA: MIT Press, 1991), p. 9. New edition published 2017.

14 On this point, see Alva Noë, *Action in Perception* (Cambridge, MA: MIT Press, 2004) and one of Noë's antecedents, D. M. Mackay, 'Ways of Looking at Perception', in Weiant Watthen-Dunn (ed.), *Models for the Perception of Speech and Visual Form* (Cambridge, MA: MIT Press, 1967).

15 For a succinct account of the debates in enactivism, see Ward and Stapleton, 'Es Are Good', pp. 90–8.

16 James J. Gibson, *The Ecological Approach to Visual Perception* (Boston: Houghton Mifflin, 1979). For an account of how affordances present a challenge to representationalism and psychological and cognitive models that proceed on ahistorical terms, see Alan Costall and Ann Richards, 'Canonical Affordances: The Psychology of Everyday Things', in Paul Graves-Brown, Rodney Harrison and Angela Piccini (eds), *The Oxford Handbook of the Archaeology of the Contemporary World* (Oxford: Oxford University Press, 2013), pp. 82–91. For a detailed exploration of affordances as scaffolding for cognitive activity in the past, see Jeff Rider in this volume.

17 This theory was most clearly articulated in the 1990s, in two related but distinct forms, by Edwin Hutchins – looking at 'distributed cognition' in a closely knit, cooperative professional operation (the navigation bridge of a navy vessel) – and Andy Clark and David Chalmers, who proposed

the 'Extended Mind' in a now-classic paper. See Hutchins, *Cognition in the Wild* (Cambridge, MA: MIT Press, 1995); Clark and Chalmers, 'The Extended Mind', *Analysis*, 58/1 (1998), 7–19.

18 Clark and Chalmers, 'Extended Mind', p. 7.

19 Mary Carruthers, *The Book of Memory: A Study of Memory in Medieval Culture* (Cambridge: Cambridge University Press, 1990; 2nd edn 2008). Carruthers's work also underpins John Sutton's exploration of 'historical cognitive science' in 'Exograms and interdisciplinarity: History, the extended mind, and the civilizing process', in R. Menary (ed.), *The Extended Mind* (Cambridge, MA: MIT Press, 2010), pp. 189–225. See also Sutton, 'Body, mind, and order: Local memory and the control of mental representations in medieval and Renaissance sciences of self', in G. Freeland and A. Corones (eds), *1543 and All That: Word and Image in the Proto-Scientific Revolution* (Dordrecht: Kluwer, 2000), pp. 117–50.

20 'Mind, Body and Affect in Medieval English Arthurian Romance', in Frank Bransdma, Carolyne Larrington and Corinne Saunders (eds), *Emotions in Medieval Arthurian Literature: Body, Mind, Voice* (Cambridge: D.S. Brewer, 2015), pp. 31–46 (esp. pp. 32–5).

21 Recent studies and collections include Miranda Anderson, *The Renaissance Extended Mind* (Basingstoke: Palgrave Macmillan, 2015); John A. McCarthy, *Early History of Embodied Cognition, 1740–1920* (Leiden: Brill, 2016); Peter Garratt (ed.), *The Cognitive Humanities: Embodied Mind in Literature and Culture* (Basingstoke: Palgrave Macmillan, 2016); Karin Kukkonen, *4E Cognition and Eighteenth-Century Fiction: How the Novel Found its Feet* (Oxford: Oxford University Press, 2019). For a detailed overview of how the humanities have engaged with embodied cognition, see Miranda Anderson, Michael Wheeler and Mark Sprevak, 'Distributed Cognition and the Humanities', in Anderson, Cairns and Sprevak (eds), *Distributed Cognition in Classical Antiquity* (Edinburgh University Press: Edinburgh, 2018), pp. 1–17.

22 Rowlands, *New Science of Cognition*, pp. 6–7 and passim.

23 On Julian's text and its interaction with the reader's cognition, see Godelinde Gertrude Perk in this volume.

24 Quotations are from Nicholas Watson and Jacqueline Jenkins (eds), *The Writings of Julian of Norwich: A Vision Showed to a Devout Woman and A Revelation of Love* (University Park, PA: Pennsylvania State University Press, 2006), and cited by chapter and page number (here, *Revelation*, 3: 131). Watson and Jenkins's subtitle refers to the Short Text and the Long Text of Julian's vision, so I adopt their usage (rather than *ST* and *LT*), for the sake of consistency. Subsequent references appear in the main text.

25 For this possibility, see Benedicta Ward, 'Julian the Solitary', in Ward and Ken Leech (eds), *Julian Reconsidered* (Oxford: SLG Press, 1988), pp. 11–35; Felicity Riddy, 'Julian of Norwich and Self-Textualisation', in Ann M. Hutchinson (ed.), *Editing Women* (Toronto: Toronto University Press, 1998), pp. 101–24. The view that Julian was a nun is that of, among others, Edmund Colledge and James Walsh in their influential critical edition, *A Book of Showings to the Anchoress Julian of Norwich*, Studies and Texts 35, 2 vols (Toronto: Pontifical Institute of Mediaeval Studies, 1978).

26 See *Ancrene Wisse*, Book VIII, in *Anchoritic Spirituality*, ed. and trans. Anne Savage and Nicholas Watson, Classics of Western Spirituality (Mahwah, NJ: Paulist Press, 1991), pp. 199–207.

27 On the distinctions between EM and HEC, see Zoe Drayson, 'Extended cognition and the metaphysics of mind', *Cognitive Systems Research*, 11 (2010), 367–77 (esp. pp. 376–7).

28 Clark and Chalmers, 'Extended Mind', p. 8 (original emphasis).

29 Hutchins, *Cognition in the Wild*, p. 49. Clark and Chalmers acknowledge Hutchins's distributed theory when they suggest that an interdependent couple might play the role of Otto's notebook for one another. 'Does the extended mind imply an extended self? It seems so' ('Extended Mind', p. 18). For an overview of more recent interpretations, see Shaun Gallagher, 'The Socially Extended Mind', *Cognitive Systems Research* 25–26 (2013), 4–12.

30 Evelyn Tribble, 'Distributing Cognition in the Globe', *Shakespeare Quarterly*, 56/2 (2005), 135–55 (p. 135).

31 On the development of confession through the Middle Ages, see, among others, Thomas N. Tentler, *Sin and Confession on the Eve of the Reformation* (Princeton, NJ: Princeton University Press, 1977); John Bossy, 'The Social History of Confession in the Age of the Reformation', *Transactions*

of the Royal Historical Society, 5/25 (1975), pp. 21–38; Peter Biller and A. J. Minnis (eds), *Handling Sin: Confession in the Middle Ages* (Woodbridge: York Medieval Press, 1998), esp. Biller, 'Confession in the Middle Ages', pp. 1–35.

32 See Kisha G. Tracy, *Memory and Confession in Middle English Literature* (Basingstoke: Palgrave Macmillan, 2017), pp. 7–23 (p. 15). Karma Lochrie discusses the ethical dilemmas of the priest charged with eliciting a full confession in *Covert Operations: The Medieval Uses of Secrecy* (Philadelphia: University of Pennsylvania Press, 1999), pp. 12–55.

33 Michel Foucault, *The History of Sexuality I: The Will to Knowledge*, trans. Robert Hurley (London: Penguin, 1998), p. 59.

34 On confession as a precursor to psychotherapeutic discourse, see John D. Richardson and Destin N. Stewart, 'Medieval confession practices and the emergence of modern psychotherapy', *Mental Health, Religion & Culture*, 12/5 (2009), 473–84, DOI: 10.1080/13674670902761707. On the role of confession in modes of subjectivity in the Middle Ages, see Anthony Low, *Aspects of subjectivity: Society and individuality from the Middle Ages to Shakespeare and Milton* (Pittsburg: Duquesne University Press, 2003).

35 Tentler, *Sin and Confession*, p. 104.

36 Michael E. Cornett, 'The form of confession: a later medieval genre for examining conscience' (doctoral thesis, University of North Carolina, Chapel Hill, 2011), p. 118, n. 106.

37 Siegfried Wenzel (ed. and trans.), *Preaching in the Age of Chaucer: Selected Sermons in Translation* (Washington, DC: Catholic University of America Press, 2008), pp. 90–1. Quoted in Cornett, p. 118.

38 Tentler, *Sin and Confession*, pp. 49–50; 135.

39 Tentler, *Sin and Confession*, p. 50.

40 Clark and Chalmers, 'Extended Mind', p. 17.

41 John Sutton, 'Exograms and interdisciplinarity'.

42 The range and implications of these objections are far beyond the scope of this article, but see especially Fred Adams and Ken Aizawa, 'The bounds of cognition', *Philosophical Psychology*, 14 (2001), 43–64; Adams and Aizawa, 'Why the mind is still in the head', in Robbins and Aydede, pp. 78–95; Robert Rupert, 'Challenges to the hypothesis of extended cognition', *Journal of Philosophy*, 101 (2004), 389–428. On the dangers of too liberal a functionalism, see, for example, Mark Sprevak, 'Extended cognition and functionalism', *Journal of Philosophy*, 106 (2009), 503–27.

43 See Rowlands, *New Science*, pp. 85–106.

44 See Clark, *Supersizing the Mind*, p. 79.

45 Robert Wilson and Andy Clark, 'How to Situate Cognition: Letting Nature Take its Course', in Robbins and Aydede, pp. 55–77.

46 Kim Sterelny, 'Minds: Extended or Scaffolded?', *Phenomenology and the Cognitive Sciences*, 9 (2010), 465–81.

47 Rowlands, *New Science*, p. 216.

48 This is the usual consensus; however, Nicholas Watson, in 'The Composition of Julian of Norwich's *Revelation of Love*', *Speculum*, 68 (1993), 637–83, suggests the Short Text was written significantly later than 1373.

49 On the question of Julian's literacy, see Denise Nowakowski Baker, *Julian of Norwich's 'Showings': From Vision to Book* (Princeton, NJ: Princeton University Press, 1994), pp. 8–11.

50 BL MS Additional 37790, fol. 97r. See Watson and Jenkins, *Vision*, 1/63.

51 On Julian's composition and development of the *Revelation* and its relation to the short text, see Watson, 'Composition'; Baker, *Vision to Book*; Barry Windeatt, 'Julian's Second Thoughts: The Long Text Tradition', in Liz Herbert McAvoy (ed.), *A Companion to Julian of Norwich* (Woodbridge: Boydell & Brewer, 2008), pp. 101–15.

52 Spryngolde is named as Margery's confessor in Book I, chapter 57. For the most significant recent scholarship on both amanuenses, see Sebastian Sobecki, '"The writyng of this tretys": Margery Kempe's Son and the Authorship of Her Book', *Studies in the Age of Chaucer*, 37 (2015), 257–83.

[53] Barry Windeatt (ed.), *The Book of Margery Kempe* (Harlow: Longman, 2000), Long Proem: pp. 47–8.

[54] Robert A. Wilson and Andy Clark, 'How to Situate Cognition', p. 64. See also Muriel E. Wheeler, 'Is language the ultimate artefact?', *Language Sciences*, 26 (2004), 693–715, for a detailed consideration and response to Clark's claims about language and embodied and extended cognition.

[55] Sterelny, 'Minds: Scaffolded or Extended?', p. 476.

[56] See, for instance, Marion Glasscoe's opinion that Julian's text adopts the 'rhythms and inflexions . . . of the speaking voice', in *Julian of Norwich: A Revelation of Love* (Exeter: Exeter University Press, 1976), p. xviii. Lynn Staley Johnson discusses the very different relationships of Julian and Margery to their own authority and the role of scribal helpers, in 'The Trope of the Scribe and the Question of Literary Authority in the Works of Julian of Norwich and Margery Kempe', *Speculum*, 66 (1991), 820–38.

[57] Felicity Riddy, 'Julian of Norwich and Self-Textualization', in Ann M. Hutchinson (ed.), *Editing Women* (Toronto: University of Toronto Press, 1998), pp. 101–24 (p. 109). (Riddy does detect a '"clerical" voice' at one point in the Long Text: p. 108; cf. p. 118). We know from the document of a parishioner's bequest that Alice was living with Julian prior to November 1415: see Appendix B in Watson and Jenkins, *The Writings of Julian of Norwich*, pp. 431–5.

[58] One nun even 'annotates', if such it can be called, a sermon exhorting all those of a religious order that they should behave as though their whole lives were the observance of Lent. The single note, repeated eight times, reads simply, 'I'm sorry'. (Booklet in Lille, Archives Départementales du Nord, 20H 13.)

[59] Bibliothèque nationale, fonds anglais 40, and BL Sloane 2499.

[60] On the copying of Julian's revelations, see Alexandra Barratt, 'How Many Children Had Julian of Norwich? Editions, Translations, and Versions of her Revelations', in Anne Clark Bartlett, Thomas H. Bestul, Janet Goebel and William F. Pollard (eds), *Vox Mystica: Essays on Medieval Mysticism* (Cambridge: D.S. Brewer, 1995), pp. 27–39; Barratt revises her survey in 'Julian of Norwich and Her Children Today: Editions, Translations, and Versions of Her Revelations', in Sarah Salih and Denise N. Baker (eds), *Julian of Norwich's Legacy: Medieval Mysticism and Post-Medieval Reception, The New Middle Ages* (Basingstoke: Palgrave Macmillan, 2009), pp. 13–27.

[61] Barratt, 'Julian of Norwich and her Children Today', p. 15.

[62] Hutchins, *Cognition in the Wild*, p. 363: original emphasis.

[63] Ruth Evans, 'Our cyborg past: Medieval artificial memory as mindware upgrade', *postmedieval: a journal of medieval cultural studies*, 3/3 (2010), 64–71 (p. 67).

[64] On 4E cognition as inflected by studies of gender and sex, see Michele Merritt, 'Queering Cognition: Extended Minds and Sociotechnologically Hybridized Gender' (doctoral thesis, University of South Florida, 2010); Robyn Bluhm, Heidi Lene Maibom and Anne Jaap Jacobson, *Neurofeminism: Issues at the Intersection of Feminist Theory and Cognitive Science*, ed. A. J. Jacobson (Basingstoke: Palgrave Macmillan, 2012); Merritt, 'Making (Non)Sense of Gender', in Massimiliano Cappucio and Tom Froese (eds), *Enactive Cognition at the Edge of Sense-Making* (Basingstoke: Palgrave Macmillan, 2014), pp. 285–306. Perhaps appropriately, given that the whole notion of EM began with a hypothetical study of cognitive impairment, Zoe Drayson and Andy Clark have recently written on 'Cognitive disability and embodied, extended minds', in David Wasserman and Adam Cureton (eds), *Oxford Handbook of Philosophy and Disability* (Oxford: Oxford University Press, forthcoming).

[65] Mason Cash, 'Cognition without borders: "Third wave" socially distributed cognition and relational autonomy', *Cognitive Systems Research*, 25–6 (2013), 61–71 (p. 69).

[66] John C. Hirsh, 'Author and Scribe in *The Book of Margery Kempe*', *Medium Ævum*, 44/1 (1975), 145–50 (p. 150).

[67] Evelyn Tribble, *Early Modern Actors and Shakespeare's Theatre: Thinking with the Body* (London: Bloomsbury, 2017), pp. 147–8.

Select Bibliography

Adams, Fred and Ken Aizawa, 'The bounds of cognition', *Philosophical Psychology*, 14 (2001), 43–64.

Anderson, Miranda, Douglas Cairns and Mark Sprevak (eds), *Distributed Cognition in Classical Antiquity* (Edinburgh: Edinburgh University Press, 2018), pp. 1–17.

Baker, Denise Nowakowski, *Julian of Norwich's 'Showings': From Vision to Book* (Princeton, NJ: Princeton University Press, 1994).

Blud, Victoria, 'Emotional Bodies: Cognitive Neuroscience and Mediaeval Studies', *Literature Compass*, 13/6 (2016), 457–66.

Carruthers, Mary, *The Book of Memory: A Study of Memory in Medieval Culture* (Cambridge: Cambridge University Press, 1990; 2nd edn 2008).

Cash, Mason, 'Cognition without borders: "Third wave" socially distributed cognition and relational autonomy', *Cognitive Systems Research*, 25–26 (2013), 61–71.

Clark, Andy, *Supersizing the Mind: Embodiment, Action, and Cognitive Extension* (Oxford: Oxford University Press, 2008), p. xxviii.

Clark, Andy and David Chalmers, 'The Extended Mind', *Analysis*, 58/1 (1998), 7–19.

Cornett, Michael E., 'The form of confession: a later medieval genre for examining conscience' (doctoral thesis, University of North Carolina, Chapel Hill, 2011).

Damasio, Antonio, *Descartes' Error* (New York: G.P. Putnam, 1994).

Drayson, Zoe, 'Extended cognition and the metaphysics of mind', *Cognitive Systems Research*, 11 (2010), 367–77.

Evans, Ruth, 'Our cyborg past: Medieval artificial memory as mindware upgrade', *postmedieval: a journal of medieval cultural studies*, 3/3 (2010), 64–71.

Gallagher, Shaun, 'The Socially Extended Mind', *Cognitive Systems Research*, 25–26 (2013), 4–12.

Garratt, Peter (ed.), *The Cognitive Humanities: Embodied Mind in Literature and Culture* (Basingstoke: Palgrave Macmillan, 2016).

Hurley, Susan, *Consciousness in Action* (Cambridge, MA: Harvard University Press, 1998).

Hutchins, Edwin, *Cognition in the Wild* (Cambridge, MA: MIT Press, 1995).

Menary, Richard, 'Introduction to the special issue on 4E cognition', *Phenomenology and the Cognitive Sciences*, 9/4 (2010), 459–63 (p. 460).

Newen, Albert, Leon de Bruin and Shaun Gallagher (eds), *The Oxford Handbook of 4E Cognition* (Oxford: Oxford University Press, 2018).

Riddy, Felicity, 'Julian of Norwich and Self-Textualisation', in Ann M. Hutchinson (ed.), *Editing Women* (Toronto: Toronto University Press, 1998), pp. 101–24.

Rowlands, Mark, *The New Science of the Mind: From Extended Mind to Embodied Phenomenology* (Cambridge, MA: MIT Press, 2010).

Sterelny, Kim, 'Minds: Extended or Scaffolded?', *Phenomenology and the Cognitive Sciences*, 9 (2010), 465–81.

Tribble, Evelyn, 'Distributing Cognition in the Globe', *Shakespeare Quarterly*, 56/2 (2005), 135–55 (p. 135).

Tribble, Evelyn, *Early Modern Actors and Shakespeare's Theatre: Thinking with the Body* (London: Bloomsbury, 2017).

Ward, Dave and Mog Stapleton, 'Es Are Good: Cognition as Enacted, Embodied, Embedded, Affective and Extended', in Fabio Paglieri (ed.), *Consciousness in Interaction: The role of the natural and social context in shaping consciousness* (Amsterdam: John Benjamins Publishing Company, 2012), pp. 89–104.

Wilson, Robert and Andy Clark, 'How to Situate Cognition: Letting Nature Take Its Course', in Philip Robbins and Murat Aydede (eds), *The Cambridge Handbook of Situated Cognition* (Cambridge: Cambridge University Press, 2009), pp. 55–77.

9

Cognitive Approaches to Affective Poetics in Early English Literature

ANTONINA HARBUS

Literary texts typically have the capacity both to represent emotional states, and also to trigger emotional engagement and even empathy in audiences. Cognitive approaches offer new ways of approaching a fuller understanding of these affective processes, and also provide new perspectives on interpretation beyond the immediate context of production – for instance, for our own contemporary engagement with texts produced in remote cultures, such as the oldest recorded texts in English (written from around the seventh century CE and beyond), which are treated in this study. Because textual production and reception occur within both cultural and embodied contexts, approaches to textual interpretation that are specifically cognitive are useful in that they focus on the mental processes at work during meaning-making, as well as contextual factors.[1] With this combination, we are able to examine very precisely the logistics of interpretation and affective response in the mind of the recipient, and treat textual transmission and cross-cultural intelligibility. With this information, we can develop a fuller understanding of the durable and flexible functions of literature, both social and personal, in a Cognitive Humanities project that looks back well beyond the present day.

This chapter will use such cognitive insights and techniques to consider how a modern reader can engage emotionally with a text from a temporally remote culture, and the functional logistics of what I call the 'affective poetics' of literary texts. Insights from neuroscientific work on emotion in mental processing, the psychology and history of emotions, and cognitive poetic approaches to the aesthetics of reading, can help us to consider how poetic language use interacts with cognitive structures and processes. Given biological and cognitive stability compared with far-reaching cultural shifts over the span of the last millennium, this study ponders the interaction of culture and biology in our engagement with medieval literature. Specifically, by using a new diachronic perspective, this chapter explores the shared cognitive basis of meaning and feeling in short (translated) elegiac poems written over thousand years ago in Old English, to propose that readerly emotional investment arises from linguistic features, including metaphoric language and affective triggers, to produce a literary effect that is available to us today, and more broadly to suggest that humans' use of literary texts to explore and to express feeling is a notable continuity in cognitive/affective development.

The archaeology of emotions in medieval England, and the capacity of older literature to invite emotional engagement, is under inquiry in the field of the history of emotions,[2] though the rich potential of cognitive approaches to affect is still being opened up fully, as are specifically literary affect studies.[3] Such studies are showing that literary texts from remote cultures can be productively analysed for evidence of how emotional life is apprehended and expressed, and beyond that for detail on how affective response can be triggered by textual encounters. Specifically cognitive methods of analysis can yield data on conceptual and semantic cues for affective response on the planes of content, language, and even narrative structure, making literary texts a particularly rich resource for affective information.[4]

Literary studies and cognitive science can benefit mutually from this potential. Much current interest paid to the subject of emotions by cognitive science is restricted by a lack of interest in the diachronic aspect of the affective life, and a delayed and still only minor interest in affective responses to the arts. Given the distinctly separate nature of these lines of research, a more open consideration of the evidence available in the documents of earlier cultures provides a particularly fruitful potential for more actively interdisciplinary inquiry in a history of the emotions, in which ideas and methods from cognitive science play a role. Because literary texts have the capacity to represent the experiential aspect of emotions (depicting what it *feels* like to be ashamed, for instance), they are well placed to bring something new and otherwise unavailable to scientific investigations of lived experience. As Patrick Colm Hogan explains, literary texts can foster 'a fuller imagination of other people's subjective experiences', especially through their 'particularly complex organizations of ambivalence' achieved through narrative structures and strategies.[5] Texts can thereby express and cultivate multiple points of view, emotional and ethical positions, and derive depth and effect from narrative complexity and lack of resolution – a potential in medieval as well as modern texts. Although there is currently much interest in emotion studies and the history of emotion,[6] the focus has been on the representation rather than the stimulation of affect, an imbalance that attention to the capacity of literary texts to represent, stimulate and cause emotions might address.[7]

Understandings of emotions, as well as definitions of them, remain fluid and field-specific, though in cognitive science an emotion is commonly defined as 'a psychological state or process that functions in the management of goals', a state 'seen to serve important intracognitive and interpersonal functions'.[8] The concept of 'management' in these statements captures the foundational role of emotions in determining the entire quality of lived experience. Many cognitive psychologists, like Keith Oatley, favour this 'appraisal' theory to account for the source of emotions. This essentially functionalist theory holds that emotions are caused not by events, but by 'appraisal of events in relation to goals and plans'.[9] Similarly, in neuroscience, emotions are seen as 'brain states and bodily responses' that act as 'managers of mental life … that relate the flow of daily events to goals and social concerns'.[10] Philosopher Peter Goldie goes even further in the conceptualisation of emotions as having management functions, denying that emotions such as grief are mental states, but rather are processes that have a particularly narrative character, 'a complex pattern of activity and passivity, inner and outer, that unfolds over time'.[11]

Conceptions of emotions as essentially narrative managers, or regulators whose agency goes beyond the mere transience of feelings, are especially interesting to the literary or cultural historian, as they underscore the interpenetration of emotional life with cognitive functions, consciousness, and an enduring sense of self. Research into the emotions from several fields has shown us that though we might recognise apparently separate emotions, such as happiness or anger, emotional experience is complex and interconnected with other aspects of being, sensing and interacting, and it exists on a spectrum, somewhat arbitrarily sectioned by conveniently appointed vocabulary. Thus, while it has become conventional to distinguish universal emotions (fear, anger, disgust, sadness, joy, surprise) from social emotions, subject to cultural variation (shame, guilt, embarrassment),[12] and background emotions (well-being or malaise, calm, tension),[13] narrative, linguistic and cultural concerns are central to understanding the emotional life beyond this simplistic labelling.

A further consideration is the inter-reliance of cognitive functioning and the experience of emotions, an idea popularised by neuroscientist Antonio Damasio, who has shown that emotions register in the body before they do in the mind. So, if emotions are determined biologically, the implication follows that the evolved human brain behaves consistently over time. But, significantly, there is cultural variation and contingency: 'the considerable amount of individual variation and the fact that culture plays a role in shaping some inducers do not deny the fundamental stereotypicity, automaticity, and regulatory purpose of the emotions'.[14] This acknowledgement of the constitutive function of cultural context is widely held. Many sociologists, for instance, have long argued that societies condition how emotions are processed.[15] Similarly, cultural anthropologists have increasingly emphasised that the linguistic resources of a community play a role in the understanding as well as the expression of emotions.[16]

In literary studies, cognitive scholars formulate the biology/culture relationship as both constraining and enabling: 'neurophysiological embodied constraints . . . less limit our creativity than condition its possibility and contextualize its significance'.[17] Recently, affect studies have come to prominence in textual criticism,[18] and, conversely, the interaction of culture and cognition has become a more firmly mainstream view: for instance, the conception of the contribution of the physical body to thinking, with a focus on the embodied mind situated in culture, from a 4E perspective (that the mind is embodied, embedded, enactive and extended) has become a very fruitful line of inquiry, as demonstrated by Victoria Blud's essay in this volume.[19] Scholars of medieval English literature are beginning to engage with these ideas, but there is still a great deal of potential in this area.[20]

Broadening the area of inquiry would certainly permit a fully investigation of the general sense that literary texts could be said habitually to focus on the emotions, so that it is claimed that 'written narrative literature, from ancient times to the present, concentrates on our emotional lives . . . Publicly available stories give members of society common exemplars of action of emotion and of responsibility'.[21] Jenefer Robinson asserts that emotions tag highly salient features of narrative that cumulatively influence reader interpretation.[22] Such studies show how literary texts can themselves embody cognitive structures, can model the interaction between cognitive functioning and affective experience, and, in turn, can capture how cognition is culturally determined, an influence that Damasio acknowledges ('learning and culture alter the expression of emotions and give emotions new meanings').[23] Moreover, 'fiction gives people the chance to practice their emotional connections with other people'[24] and 'may play a role in fostering openness to empathetic response',[25] ideas that can combine with existing understandings of the social functions and rhetorical mechanics of literature, and also accommodate the persistent preoccupation of texts, including medieval English ones, with grief and deeply felt emotions.

This potential of literary texts relies on the cognitive role of narrative in human understanding and self-formation. David Herman extends the psychologist Jerome Bruner's influential idea that all human experience is shaped and organised as narrative, out of a cultural context of shared stories.[26] Herman has developed this idea into the formulation that narrative is a 'tool for thinking'.[27] In turn, Richard J. Gerrig has fashioned a technical way of demonstrating this and other such claims, establishing how we integrate existing knowledge and schemas into the process of interpreting texts.[28] During this process, the reader responds to cues in the texts that trigger, via imagination, the creation and development of provisional and evolving scenarios.[29] These reactions are relational and social. Keith Oatley asserts the creation by readers of a 'simulation of selves in their interactions with others in the social world'.[30] These simulations arise at the level of language. Literary expression, from any time period, can be seen as a form of discursive conceptualisation that invites coherence: 'the negotiation of conceptualizations is built into the narrative structure'.[31] This idea means that 'we attribute emotional meaning to linguistic expressions' precisely because fictional narratives are comprehensible only as a result of our evolved cognitive abilities to create meaning,[32] which is why I have extended Herman's idea to propose that narratives are, beyond tools for thinking, tools for *feeling*.[33]

Integral to this creation of meaning is empathetic engagement, a topic treated in relation to popular culture, especially film, so in turn very little, if any, attention has been paid to medieval texts.[34] Empathy, or 'a vicarious, spontaneous sharing of affect',[35] can be created through character identification and emotional simulation, primarily via the activation of mirror neurons.[36] These embodied reactions to emotional encounters – both real and fictional – involve neural activity that spontaneously follows the perceived emotions of another person, and are understood to function pragmatically to assist in the understanding of the actions and emotions of others. Mirror neurons allow us to experience the emotional meaning of our interpersonal encounters, and perhaps also to experience empathy reflexively.[37] Imagination can produce images in the brain of facial expressions that in turn trigger the same sort of emotive mirroring response, even in an acknowledged fictional encounter.[38] Indeed, as Fritz Breithaupt concludes, 'narrative fiction can only exist because it invites, triggers, channels, controls, and manages empathy'.[39] But, because many of these studies are concerned chiefly with contemporary narrative fiction, they overlook pre-modern literatures, especially poetry, the more dominant early literary form.

But, by looking at the affective poetics of early verse, we can examine how the text cues the reader to select particular fragments, and how those pieces are compiled in the process of creating a coherent scenario, a central component of which is emotional simulation. This affective response during reading (or hearing in the case of medieval oral texts) calls upon not only memories of cultural schemas and their conventional attendant emotions, but also the embodied *feeling* of those emotions at an individual experiential level, regardless of the remoteness of the point of textual creation – how a modern reader can have an emotional reaction to a medieval text, in combination with an intellectual and aesthetic experience produced by that literary encounter. The Anglo-Saxon literary corpus, and in particular its fictional representations of emotional experience, is readable to us, but only via the process of linguistic and cultural relocation that operates through translation into present-day English. Nevertheless, a core degree of intelligibility remains, because we share the human experience of an embodied mind and, apparently, a hard-wired predisposition for narrative, a distinctly 'narrative sense of self', and reliance on narrative structure for memory and imagination. Evolutionary proximity means that the similarity of our embodied emotional experiences with other humans from remote cultures makes cross-cultural intelligibility possible. I take as my examples extracts from the elegiac texts, *The Wife's Lament* and *The Wanderer*.

Many Old English texts express familiar, strong emotions. For example, the female narrator of the short elegy, *The Wife's Lament* (one of the so-called elegies of The Exeter Book, a tenth-century manuscript collection) expresses grief in a cross-culturally comprehensible manner. This text uses first-person narration to express emotional anguish:

> þær ic sittan mot sumorlangne dæg,
> þær ic wepan mæg mine wræcsiþas,
> earfoþa fela; forþon ic æfre ne mæg
> þære modceare minre gerestan,
> ne ealles þæs longaþes þe mec on þissum life begeat.
> (*The Wife's Lament*, ll. 37–41)

> [There I can sit for a summer-long day, there I can weep for my wretchednesses, for many hardships. Therefore I can never rest from my anxieties of mind, nor from all this longing that this life has begotten for me.]

This poetic outpouring of emotion expresses a familiar embodied feeling of anguish, isolation and self-pity. As with most Old English verse, this one uses repetition ('there I'), rhythm and alliteration to cue connections across the syntax, and to drive emphasis, as in 'sit' and 'summerlong', 'weep' and 'wretchednesses' and 'longing' and 'life'. These alliterating pairs invite the reader to cluster associations between broad concepts and individual feeling, thereby universalising the represented sensation of apprehending personal misery in manner that is felt in embodied experience. Because the poetic narrative is sketchy rather than fully detailed, the reader fills the gaps by supplying known information along with their emotional associations from lived experience and other textual encounters. The text thereby invites empathetic engagement from its audience through emotional contagion, made possible through the combination of imagery produced in the mind in the process of making sense, and the recognisability of embodied emotional response to a recognisably affecting scenario. In this brief comment, weeping, anguish and longing are all foregrounded, and grief is represented as active, encompassing and time-consuming. The reader is required to call up not only narrative schema, but also emotional schema, created from memories, personal experience and embodied feeling, to fill out the brief scenario, make sense of the sequence of ideas and account for a potential cause for such extreme abandonment to the emotional life. In doing so, the reader enacts feeling, which is implicated in cognitive processing, and thereby becomes emotionally engaged in the narrative. Because we now know that cognition and affect are mutually reliant, it is possible to see how a reader can respond emotionally to culturally remote, poetically communicated fictional narrative, a process that occurs at both the specific and general levels. The recipient of this text is thereby invited to feel empathy that is not necessarily or not entirely culturally specific, but arises from an embodied human response that is shaped only in part by local context.

The poem invites universal human recognition and provides an exemplification of affective reaction, as expressed in literary form. The speaker generalises typical emotional reactions to particular situations, which are then specified by attributions made to 'my lord':

> A sceal geong mon   wesan geomormod,
> heard heortan geþoht,   swylce habban sceal
> bliþe gebæro,   eac þon breostceare,
> sinsorgna gedreag,   sy æt him sylfum gelong
> eal his worulde wyn,   sy ful wide fah
> feorres folclondes,   þæt min freond siteð
> under stanhliþe   storme behrimed,
> wine werigmod,   wætre beflowen
> on dreorsele.   Dreogeð se min wine
> micle modceare;   he gemon to oft
> wynlicran wic.   Wa bið þam þe sceal
> of langoþe   leofes abidan.
>
> (*The Wife's Lament*, ll. 42–53)

[Ever must the young man be sorrowful, and the thought of his heart harsh. Likewise, he must have a cheerful demeanour, along with the care of the heart, a constant multitude of sorrows. May all his worldly joy be dependent on him alone; may he be outlawed widely in a distant tribal land, since my friend sits under a stony cliff, covered with hoar-frost by the storm, my heart-weary lord, surrounded by water in a dreary hole. He, my lord, experiences great sorrow of mind; he remembers too often a more joyful dwelling. Woe it is for the one who must await the dear one in longing.]

After the personal expression of feeling in the first quotation, the focus moves to an account of the state of mind imagined in the loved one, then proceeds on to a generalised account of feeling and response. This lyric text thereby demonstrates the progression from the recognition of feeling, to imagination and empathy, to universal emotional response. The line 'dreogeð se min wine / micle modceare' both represents enacted theory of mind, and requires the reader to attribute empathetic imagining to the narrator who is recounting this process. To keep up with the rapid traversal of this emotional terrain, the reader needs to engage memory, imagination, empathy and embodied feeling, as well as cognitively processing the shifting focalisation into and beyond the minds of the narrator and the object of her affection.

As these extracts show, a distinction between hidden inner and visible outer lives is conceptualised and represented textually, as is a mind/self division, phenomena familiar in everyday existence, and subject to cognitive theorisation. Moreover, memory can be activated, or managed to create a motivated emotional response, here both negative and positive, producing respectively grief and joy. As Hogan argues, 'grief results from the sharp conflict between reality and spontaneous expectation derived from imagination'.[40] *The Wife's Lament* textually focuses on depicting this disjunction, and typically fits it into a narrative account of the autobiographical self by a female speaker, one that invites an empathetic response. As Goldie argues, grieving is best understood in terms of narrative thinking:

> An emotion . . . is a relatively complex state, involving past and present episodes of thoughts, feelings, and bodily changes, dynamically related to a narrative part of a person's life, together with dispositions to experience further emotional episodes, and to act out of the emotion, and to express that emotion.[41]

This narrative constitution of the self is largely informed by a dynamic interplay among emotion, knowledge and autobiographical memory: 'Our memories are infused with what we now know, and how we now feel about what happened in light of what we now know'.[42] In cases of grieving, this interplay naturally results in a form of communication or expression that enacts the 'special explanatory, revelatory, and expressive powers of narratives, whether just thought through in narrative thinking, or whether publicly expressed to others, in writing or in speech'.[43] This spontaneous combination of memory, narrative and emotion can provide the impetus for the creation of poetry driven by what I have termed 'dynamic affect',[44] uttered by a speaker who is apparently speaking to himself or to an unidentified audience, as in Old English texts such as *The Wife's Lament*. The reader or hearer of this text, even at a distant cultural remove, is invited to engage in narrative thinking and emotional reaction, and to recruit memory, imagination and synthetic reasoning, a process made possible by the shared cognitive basis of meaning and feeling.

The Wanderer similarly enacts the process of emotional remembering, and thereby invites affective engagement – the activation of mirror neurons as a result of the cognitive process of interpreting narrative and poetic imagery – and in turn facilitating emotional contagion from that act of imagination. We are told that

Cearo bið geniwad
þam þe sendan sceal swiþe geneahhe
ofer waþema gebind werigne sefan.
(*The Wanderer*, ll. 55–57)

> [care is renewed for the one who must very often send his weary mind over the shackle of the waves.]

Here, the (probably male) narrator is generalising an experience that invites an emotional and potentially an empathetic response, subject to cognitive analysis. Briefly, the combined mental effort of distinguishing and keeping track of the 'one' and the 'mind', and the processing of the metaphor, 'shackle of the waves', recruits emotional investment and embodied feeling, both of which are subject to biological continuity as well as some cultural specificity. The brain attempts to reconcile the information provided according to emotional experience and narrative schema, resolving questions such as why (repetitive, enforced) remembering creates sorrow, and why social isolation has been imposed. This interpretive process requires the inclusion of provisional information, strategically deployed in response to textual cues, to fill the conceptual gaps, but also the recollection of how it feels to be burdened by strong emotion. The motivated selection of information from memory, imagination and embodied experience is a synthetic process that requires complex cognitive handling. In taking this effort, we read – and feel – across time and location, as a result of the consistency of human emotional arousal, and the reliance on memory and narrative thinking. What is interesting to note here is that the familiar sensation of the self, fragmented by emotional response, is not only captured in poetic language and narrative creation, but is the chief focus of that literary expression, in a text that dramatises cognitive and emotional management in action. As a result, the experience of emotion as the perception of change in the body is evoked through figurative expression and narrative discourse, and the text acquires an emotional pull grounded in recognisable embodied feeling.

Poetic products from remote cultures can, when considered in light of recent findings in cognitive science on the sensation and expression of emotions, provide a deeply diachronic viewpoint on the pervasive, perpetual, traditional or biologically determined character of the affective life. They can also inform us about the durable potential of literary texts as vehicles for exploring and expressing emotion, as well as the value of literary analysis to go beyond the explanatory potential of models and methods available to cognitive science. The contribution of such as cognitive humanities' approach can consider in new ways the representation of emotional experience in literary texts, but also in capacity of those texts to trigger or invite the recollection of such experiences or sensations in the writer and the recipient. Both *The Wife's Lament* and *The Wanderer* appear to rely on the production as well as the representation of emotion, so demonstrate the personal and social functions of literary expression.

These examples represent only a small sample; many types of Old English poetic texts, like other medieval and other poems, portray recognisable human emotions, and in turn invite emotional reactions from readers today, as they presumably did their contemporary audiences. We can distinguish the intense and conflicted emotional texture of *The Wife's Lament* and *The Wanderer* precisely because we are familiar with the way in which emotions function in the management of goals and to stimulate action, and can acknowledge the shaping force of the literary lyric poem in the packaging and expression of those emotions. These texts can arouse intense, involved readings from a modern audience because they model emotional reactions and narratively produce emotional experiences and genuine sensations, notwithstanding their acknowledged cultural remoteness, and even their acknowledged or suspected fictionality. This readerly implication, or emotional investment, arises from rich, textured features within discourse that can be analysed in the context of ideas about emotion that are still emerging from the cognitive sciences. Such subjective investment arises from the evocation of recognisable embodied emotions, producing a spontaneous sharing of affect, in which imagination and memory play a role.

As such examples show, a consideration of the emotional basis of the mental processes activated during textual interpretation provides an explanation for cross-cultural intelligibility, as well as the affective capacity of a fictional narrative. Because cognitive processes grounded in the emotional life determine both individual experience and also literary structure and response, the broad continuities in human emotional experience over time ensure the similarity of the emotional quality of textual creation and reception. Notwithstanding this consistency, emotions are subject at least in part to cultural impact, so can be studied in the context of cultural history. More specifically, the textual capacity both to represent the flux of emotional states and also to trigger an emotional reaction in the reader provides a rich resource for a wide range of studies of the emotional life from the vantage point of cognitive humanities.

Given this inter-reliance of culture, cognition and literary expression, scholars of earlier cultures can and should contribute to a fuller diachronic examination of the affective potential of literary texts, as well as the capacity of these texts to represent human emotional experience that is both embodied (and therefore biologically consistent) and also subject to the localised shaping power of a specific cultural context. Scholars open to these cross-disciplinary currents can thereby take part in motivated and productive analyses of both the textual representation and evocation of emotion, and more precisely consider how a text might invite empathy or understanding via the shared cognitive/emotional basis of meaning-making in embodied textual producers and recipients regardless of contextual proximity.

Notes

1 For a useful early overview, see: Alan Richardson, 'Studies in Literature and Cognition: A Field Map', in Alan Richardson and Ellen Spolsky (eds), *The Work of Fiction: Cognition, Culture and Complexity* (Aldershot and Burlington, 2004), pp. 1–29. A lengthy annotated bibliography by Alan Richardson and Mary Crane appears at: *https://www2.bc.edu/~richarad/lcb/home.html#bib*. See also Mark Turner, *Reading Minds: The Study of English in the Age of Cognitive Science* (Princeton, NJ: Princeton University Press, 1991); David Herman (ed.), *Narrative Theory and the Cognitive Sciences* (Stanford, CA: CSLI Publications, 2003); *Poetics Today*, 23/1 (2002) and *The European Journal of English Studies*, 9/2 (2005).

2 The history of emotions as a field is outlined in William Reddy, *The Navigation of Feeling: Framework for the History of Emotions* (Cambridge: Cambridge University Press, 2001); Susan J. Matt and Peter N. Stearns (eds), *Doing Emotions History* (Urbana: University of Illinois Press, 2014); and Jan Plamper, *History of Emotions: An Introduction* (Oxford: Oxford University Press, 2015). On whether emotions can have a history, see M. Scheer, 'Are Emotions a Kind of Practice (and is That What Makes Them Have a History)? A Bourdieuian Approach to Understanding Emotion', *History and Theory*, 51/2 (2012), 193–220. On medieval histories of emotions, see Barbara H. Rosenwein, *Emotional Communities in the Early Middle Ages* (Ithaca: Cornell University Press, 2006); and *Generations of Feeling: A History of Emotions 600–1700* (Cambridge: Cambridge University Press, 2016). For literary overviews, see Stephanie Downes and Rebecca F. McNamara, 'The History of Emotions and Medieval Literature', *Literature Compass*, 13/6 (2016), 444–56; and Sarah McNamer, 'The Literariness of Literature and the History of Emotion', *PMLA*, 130/5 (2015), 1433–42.

3 See Antonina Harbus, *Cognitive Approaches to Old English Poetry* (Cambridge: D.S. Brewer, 2012).

4 Indeed, according to Patrick Colm Hogan, 'story structures are fundamentally shaped and oriented by our emotion systems' (*Affective Narratology: The Emotional Structure of Stories* (Lincoln, NE and London: University of Nebraska Press, 2011), p. 1).

5 Patrick Colm Hogan, *What Literature Teaches Us About Emotion* (Cambridge: Cambridge University Press, 2011), pp. 68 and 302.

6 An issue of *PMLA*, for instance, was devoted recently to the subject (vol. 130: Oct 2015). The Centre of Excellence in The History of Emotions funded by the Australian Research Council, housed at the University of Western Australia: *http://www.historyofemotions.org.au*. The two other major centres are at the Max Planck Institute in Berlin: *https://www.mpib-berlin.mpg.de/en/research/history-of-emotions*; and The Queen Mary Centre at the University of London: *http://projects.history.qmul.ac.uk/emotions*; see especially McNamer n. 2

7 E.g. Downes and McNamara; Sarah McNamer, *Affective Meditation: The Invention of Medieval Compassion* (Philadelphia: University of Pennsylvania Press, 2010); P. Mack, 'Argument and Emotion in *Troilus and Criseyde*', in S.D. Troyan (ed.), *Medieval Rhetoric: A Casebook* (New York: Routledge, 2004), pp. 109–26; and Jill Mann, 'Falling in Love in the Middle Ages', in Charlotte Brewer and Barry Windeatt (eds), *Traditions and Innovations in the Study of Middle English Literature: The Influence of Derek Brewer* (Cambridge: D.S. Brewer, 2013), pp. 88–110.

8 Keith Oatley, 'Emotions', in R. A. Wilson and F. C. Keil (eds), *MIT Encyclopedia of the Cognitive Sciences* (Cambridge, MA: Harvard University Press, 1999), pp. 273–5, at p. 273.

9 Lalita Pandit, 'Emotion, Perception and Anagnorisis in *The Comedy of Errors*: A Cognitive Perspective', *College Literature*, 33/1 (2006), 94–126 (p. 95). For a challenge to the appraisal view, see Patrick Colm Hogan, 'On Being Moved: Cognition and Emotion in Literature and Film', in Lisa Zunshine (ed.), *Introduction to Cognitive Cultural Studies* (Baltimore, MD: Johns Hopkins University Press, 2010), pp. 237–56.

10 Oatley, 'Emotions', p. 275.

11 Peter Goldie, *The Mess Inside: Narrative, Emotion, and the Mind* (Oxford: Oxford University Press, 2012), p. 56.

12 Damasio includes on this list: embarrassment, jealousy, guilt and shame, and lists six primary or universal emotions, with surprise in the place of guilt and shame in the list above (*The Feeling of What Happens: Body and Emotion in the Making of Consciousness* (Orlando, FL: Harcourt, 1999), p. 51).

13 Damasio, *The Feeling of What Happens*, p. 52.

14 Damasio, *The Feeling of What Happens*, p. 51.

15 Many scholars understand that the experience of emotions is culturally specific, and therefore 'how mistaken it would be to assume that emotions are unproblematically translatable from one culture or historical period to another' (Robert A. LeVine, 'Afterword', in Helena Wulff (ed.), *The Emotions: A Cultural Reader* (Oxford and New York: Berg, 2007), pp. 397–9, at p. 398).

16 E.g. 'The most productive analytical approach to the cross-cultural study of emotion is to examine discourses on emotion and emotional discourses as social practices within diverse ethnographic contexts' (Lila Abu-Lughod and Catherine A. Lutz, 'Introduction: Emotion, Discourse, and the Politics of Everyday Life', in Lutz and Abu-Lughod (eds), *Language and the Politics of Emotion* (Cambridge: Cambridge University Press, 1990), pp. 1–23, at p. 1).

17 Donald R. Wehrs, 'Epilogue', in Mark J. Bruhn and Donald R. Wehrs (eds), *Cognition, Literature, and History* (Abingdon and New York: Routledge, 2014), pp. 243–52, at p. 249.

18 See Donald R. Wehrs and Thomas Blake (eds), *The Palgrave Handbook of Affect Studies and Textual Criticism* (Basingstoke: Palgrave Macmillan, 2017).

19 Peter Garratt (ed.), *Cognitive Humanities: Embodied Mind in Literature and Culture* (London: Palgrave Macmillan, 2016). On the 4E view, see Richard Menary (ed.), special *Issue of Phenomenology and the Cognitive Sciences*, 9(4) (2010), and 'Introduction', 459–63. Here, cognition is viewed as 'incorporating our brains, bodies and environments' (Menary, p. 463).

20 For exceptions, see Bruhn and Wehrs, *Cognition, Literature, and History*; Isabel Jaén and Julien Jacques Simon (eds), *Cognitive Literary Studies* (Austin: University of Texas Press, 2012); Paula Leverage et al. (eds), *Theory of Mind and Literature* (West Lafayette: Purdue University Press, 2011); and Paula Leverage, *Reception and Memory: A Cognitive Approach to the* Chansons de Geste (Amsterdam and New York: Rodopi, 2010). Additionally, I have broached these issues in my own work, on which the current discussion draws and develops: *Cognitive Approaches*, cited above, as well as 'Embodied Emotion, Conceptual Metaphor and the Aesthetics of Reading Old English Poetry', in Michael Champion and Andrew Lynch (eds), *Emotions in the Medieval and Early Modern World* (Leiden: Brepols, 2015), pp. 127–49; and 'Affective Poetics: The Cognitive Basis of Emotion in Old English Poetry', in Jonathan Wilcox, Frances McCormack and Alice Jorgensen (eds), *Anglo-Saxon Emotions: Reading the Heart in Old English Literature, Language, and Culture* (London: Ashgate, 2015), pp. 19–34.

21 Keith Oatley, Dacher Keltner and Jennifer M. Jenkins, *Understanding Emotions*, 2nd edn (Oxford: Blackwell, 2006), p. 401. See also Keith Oatley, 'A Taxonomy of the Emotions of Literary Response and a Theory of Identification in Fictional Narrative', *Poetics*, 23 (1994), 53–74.

22 Jenefer Robinson, *Deeper than Reason: Emotion and Its Role in Literature, Music, and Art* (Oxford: Oxford University Press, 2005): see especially chapter 2.

23 Damasio, *The Feeling of What Happens*, p. 51.

24 Blakey Vermeule, *Why Do We Care About Literary Characters*? (Baltimore, MD: Johns Hopkins University Press, 2010), p. 165.

25 Hogan, *What Literature Teaches Us*, p. 74.

26 Jerome Bruner, 'The Narrative Construction of Reality', *Critical Inquiry*, 18 (1991), 1–21. See the development of this idea in his later work: 'Self-making and World-making', in J. Brockmeier and D. Carbaugh (eds), *Narrative and Identity: Studies in Autobiography, Self and Culture* (Amsterdam and Philadelphia: John Benjamins, 2001), pp. 28–37; and *Making Stories: Law, Literature, Life* (New York: Farrar, Straus and Giroux, 2002).

27 Herman, 'Stories as a Tool for Thinking', in David Herman (ed.), *Narrative Theory and the Cognitive Sciences* (Stanford, CA: CSLI Publications, 2003), pp. 163–92.

28 Richard J. Gerrig, *Experiencing Narrative Worlds: On the Psychological Activities of Reading* (New Haven, CT and London: Yale University Press, 1993).

29 See Keith Oatley, 'Fiction and its Study as Gateways to the Mind', *Scientific Study of Literature*, 1/1 (2011), 153–64 (at p. 160).

30 Keith Oatley, *Such Stuff as Dreams: The Psychology of Fiction* (Chichester: Wiley-Blackwell, 2011), p. x.

31 Barbara Dancygier, *The Language of Stories: A Cognitive Approach* (Cambridge: Cambridge University Press, 2012), p. 20.

32 Dancygier, *The Language of Stories*, p. 29.

33 Antonina Harbus, 'Medieval English Texts and Affects: Narratives as Tools for Feeling', in Donald R. Wehrs and Thomas Blake (eds), *The Palgrave Handbook of Affect Studies and Textual Criticism* (Basingstoke: Palgrave Macmillan, 2017), pp. 545–76.

34 For a good overview on philosophical perspectives on readers' empathetic engagement with fictional narratives and characters, see Amy Coplan, 'Empathetic Engagement with Narrative Fictions', *Journal of Aesthetics and Art Criticism*, 62/2 (2004), pp. 141–52; and Noël Carroll, 'On the Ties that Bind: Characters, the Emotions, and Popular Fictions', in William Irwin and Jorge J. E. Gracia (eds), *Philosophy and the Interpretation of Pop Culture*, (Lanham: Rowman and Littlefield, 2007), pp. 89–116. Both emphasise the power of audiovisual cues, especially facial expressions, as emotional triggers, and come up with different explanations for viewers' responses. Carroll denies that consumers of fiction simulate the emotional experience of characters as some scholars argue, but rather 'mobilize an affective stance' that is distinctly produced in response to a fiction whose content we imagine rather than believe (p. 91). Coplan prefers the theory of 'emotional contagion', whereby an automatic affective response is produced when we observe others experiencing emotion, a phenomenon requiring visual sensory input, as in film viewing; literary fictions can produce reactions that are more cognitive but less affective because they produce experiences more removed from real-world sensations (Coplan, 'Catching Characters' Emotions: Emotional Contagion Responses to Narrative Fiction Film', *Film Studies*, 8 (2006), 26–38 (at p. 35)).

35 Suzanne Keen, 'A Theory of Narrative Empathy', *Narrative*, 14/3 (2006), 207–36 (at p. 208).

36 Keen, 'A Theory of Narrative Empathy', p. 208.

37 Giacomo Rizzolatti and Corrado Sinigaglia, *Mirrors in the Brain – How Our Minds Share Actions and Emotions*, trans. Frances Anderson (Oxford: Oxford University Press, 2008), p. 190.

38 See Graham McFee, 'Empathy: Interpersonal vs Artistic', in Amy Coplan and Peter Goldie (eds), *Empathy: Philosophical and Psychological Perspectives* (Oxford: Oxford University Press, 2011), pp. 185–208.

39 Fritz Breithaupt, 'How is it Possible to Have Empathy? Four Models', in Leverage et al. (eds), *Theory of Mind and Literature*, pp. 273–88, at p. 274.

40 Hogan, *What Literature Teaches Us*, p. 123.

41 Peter Goldie, *The Emotions: A Philosophical Exploration* (Oxford: Oxford University Press, 2000), p. 144.

42 Goldie, *The Mess Inside*, p. 54.

43 Goldie, *The Mess Inside*, p. 75.

44 Antonina Harbus, 'The Long View: Cognitive Poetic Approaches to "Dynamic Affect" in Early English Verse', in Szilvia Csábi (ed.), *Expressive Minds and Artistic Creations*, Studies in Cognitive Poetics (Oxford: Oxford University Press, 2018), pp. 159–79.

Select Bibliography

Abu-Lughod, Lila and Catherine A. Lutz (eds), *Language and the Politics of Emotion* (Cambridge: Cambridge University Press, 1990), pp. 1–23.

Bruner, Jerome, *Making Stories: Law, Literature, Life* (New York: Farrar, Straus and Giroux, 2002).

Damasio, Antonio, *The Feeling of What Happens: Body and Emotion in the Making of Consciousness* (Orlando, FL: Harcourt, 1999).

Dancygier, Barbara, *The Language of Stories: A Cognitive Approach* (Cambridge: Cambridge University Press, 2012).

Downes, Stephanie and Rebecca F. McNamara, 'The History of Emotions and Medieval Literature', *Literature Compass*, 13/6 (2016), 444–56.

Garratt, Peter (ed.), *Cognitive Humanities: Embodied Mind in Literature and Culture* (London: Palgrave Macmillan, 2016).

Gerrig, Richard J., *Experiencing Narrative Worlds: On the Psychological Activities of Reading* (New Haven, CT and London: Yale University Press, 1993).

Goldie, Peter, *The Mess Inside: Narrative, Emotion, and the Mind* (Oxford: Oxford University Press, 2012).

Harbus, Antonina, *Cognitive Approaches to Old English Poetry* (Cambridge: D.S. Brewer, 2012).

Herman, David (ed.), *Narrative Theory and the Cognitive Sciences* (Stanford, CA: CSLI Publications, 2003)

Hogan, Patrick Colm, *Affective Narratology: The Emotional Structure of Stories* (Lincoln, NE and London: University of Nebraska Press, 2011).

Hogan, Patrick Colm, *What Literature Teaches Us About Emotion* (Cambridge: Cambridge University Press, 2011).

Jaén, Isabel and Julien Jacques Simon (eds), *Cognitive Literary Studies* (Austin: University of Texas Press, 2012).

Leverage, Paula et al. (eds), *Theory of Mind and Literature* (West Lafayette: Purdue University Press, 2011).

Matt, Susan J. and Peter N. Stearns (eds), *Doing Emotions History* (Urbana, IL: University of Illinois Press, 2014).

McNamer, Sarah, Affective Meditation: *The Invention of Medieval Compassion* (Philadelphia: University of Pennsylvania Press, 2010).

Oatley, Keith, Dacher Keltner and Jennifer M. Jenkins, *Understanding Emotions*, 3rd edn (Hoboken, NJ: Wiley, 2013).

Oatley, Keith, *Such Stuff as Dreams: The Psychology of Fiction* (Chichester: Wiley-Blackwell, 2011).

Plamper, Jan, *History of Emotions: An Introduction* (Oxford: Oxford University Press, 2015).

Rizzolatti Giacomo and Corrado Sinigaglia, *Mirrors in the Brain – How Our Minds Share Actions and Emotions*, trans. Frances Anderson (Oxford: Oxford University Press, 2008).

Robinson, Jenefer, *Deeper than Reason: Emotion and Its Role in Literature, Music, and Art* (Oxford: Oxford University Press, 2005).

Rosenwein, Barbara H., *Generations of Feeling: A History of Emotions 600–1700* (Cambridge: Cambridge University Press, 2016).
Turner, Mark, *Reading Minds: The Study of English in the Age of Cognitive Science* (Princeton, NJ: Princeton University Press, 1991).
Wehrs, Donald R. and Thomas Blake (eds), *The Palgrave Handbook of Affect Studies and Textual Criticism* (Basingstoke: Palgrave Macmillan, 2017).

IV

Approaching Art and Artefacts

10

Medieval Art History and Neuroscience: An Introduction

NADIA PAWELCHAK

In today's world, people record virtually every thought on Twitter, Facebook and other social media platforms, providing a rich body of content about how they view and interact with their world. Medieval scholars, however, do not have access to the daily confessionals of people who lived in the Middle Ages. This dearth of literary evidence creates a problem for art historians who are interested in the reactions of a removed audience.[1] Absent written records, neuroscientific studies can help modern scholars to understand how medieval viewers interpreted the art objects they encountered. I will use cognitive neuroscience both as a framework for investigating how medieval people perceived the world around them and as a means to explain the biological processes behind cognition. After a discussion of this methodology's usefulness and its parameters, I will conduct a cognitive reading of the scene on a fourteenth-century gothic ivory mirror case from the Metropolitan Museum of Art that features an aristocratic couple engaged in the courtly activity of hunting (Figure 10.1).[2] I selected this object because the position of the man and woman lends well to a cognitive reading of the scene. I cite scientific studies of the human brain's response to body orientation, posture and gaze direction to inform my interpretation of this object. However, I use the evidence gleaned from such studies not to argue for an objective interpretation of this scene, but rather to suggest how a medieval audience may have potentially responded to the mirror case's imagery.

As cognitive neuroscience has both theoretical and physiological dimensions, I use the terms 'cognitive theory' and 'neuroscience' to distinguish between these two modes. Both approaches help to create a holistic picture of how medieval people viewed the world around them. As a methodology, cognitive theory is useful for describing such abstract concepts as 'self', 'audience', 'hypothetical viewer' and 'cognitive map'. Neuroscience, on the other hand, explains the potential biological processes behind artistic reception.[3] Ashby Kinch argues that the fusion of medieval studies and science, what he terms 'neuromedievalism', can provide 'an enriched engagement with medieval culture'.[4] However, Kinch qualifies this suggestion by specifying that a neuromedievalist must make 'judicious use of the conceptual tools and research results of neuroscientific research'.[5] Kinch does not establish specific guidelines for assessing judiciousness in his essay, but scientists interested in the intersection of their fields with humanist disciplines have made suggestions for a successful marriage. On the one hand, medievalists should acknowledge that the reception of visual imagery, including art, is subjective rather than objective.[6] Secondly, any neuroscientific data applied toward understanding reception should be utilised as a tool for explaining how people may have viewed their world rather than as definitive evidence for a particular interpretation.[7] On a final note, medievalists must properly apply scientific data to their readings of images and use clear, correct scientific terminology.[8]

Cognitive Maps and Structures

As it is today, people from the fourteenth century undoubtedly had different responses to art.[9] Even though two people may physically see the same object, their brains interpret it differently since the human brain filters visual data through past experiences and cultural knowledge.[10] These differences in interpretation occur because individuals have unique internal models of their worlds, what anthropologist Peter Wells calls 'cognitive maps', that mediate any sensory data they see.[11] These cognitive maps are shaped from a person's neurological make-up, life experiences and cultural influences and, as such, have both biological and cultural components. On an abstract level, each individual's unique experiences and environmental influences mediate responses to visual stimuli, including artwork. Since the human brain is also neuroplastic, it adapts to its environment by creating new neural pathways to accommodate its needs. These physiological differences in the brain's neural architecture also lead to subjective interpretations of visual data from person to person.[12] Such constraints mean that scholars may therefore only construct *potential* cognitive maps for medieval viewers and that the reception of an object, especially a medieval one, is subjective rather than objective.[13]

For the past few decades, but under the umbrella of reception theory, art historians have been creating audiences to behold their objects of inquiry.[14] As an example, in order to understand how fifteenth-century people saw the paintings around them, Renaissance scholar and early modernist Michael Baxandall identified a specific audience comprised of 'Quattrocentro' men whose particular exposure to religious artwork, geometry and specific mathematical proportions influenced how their brains perceived contemporary art.[15] Baxandall coined the terms 'period eye' and 'cognitive style' to describe the culturally determined lens through which these men understood their world.[16] These hypothetical cognitive structures serve the exact function of Wells's cognitive map. Although Baxandall does not specifically refer to 'cognitive theory' in his book, by creating an audience with a 'cognitive style', he becomes one of the first scholars in the discipline to employ cognitive theory as a method for understanding artistic reception.[17] These cognitive styles and maps, of course, are only useful for the specific culture, audience and context for which they were constructed.

What makes Baxandall's application of cognitive theory particularly effective is that he populates the 'Quattrocentro' man's cognitive map with cultural artefacts relevant to this specific audience.[18] Psychologists Nicolas J. Bullot and Rolf Reber indicate that psychology and art history can work together so long as the theoretical framework that unites them acknowledges the artwork's unique context in relation to the beholder.[19] In other words, each type of constructed audience, even from the same period, would have distinctive components in its respective cognitive map that influenced reception. A lay audience, for example, would possess different cultural markers than a religious one. Other factors such as profession, literacy level, gender identity and social class distinguish one audience from another.[20]

Through the example of a hypothetical sculpture of Mary and Christ with accompanying Latin text, medieval art historian Madeline Caviness illustrates how viewers with different cognitive maps could have arrived at separate understandings of the same piece. More specifically, she argues that a literate viewer would likely have had a different theological understanding of the sculpture than an illiterate because of the information imparted by the written text.[21] As she argues about meaning, 'decoding involves an encoding'.[22] However, this 'encoding' involves more than simply absorbing information and assigning significance. As Kinch explains, the 'visual brain' first 'seeks out confirmation of its existing neural templates'.[23] One expecting a statue to possess religious significance would therefore first look for evidence to confirm this interpretation.[24] Caviness also ties these audiences' cognitive perceptions to traditional medieval hierarchies of understanding (historical, allegorical and tropological), making her use of cognitive theory an effective means of extending our knowledge of medieval reception.[25] In this way, cognitive theory provides modern scholars with an avenue of exploration, another useful tool in a toolbox of many useful methodologies.

Neuroscience, Technology and Art History

When properly harnessed, neuroscience also has the potential to be especially valuable for medieval art historians since they work with the tangible, with what people see. Barbara M. Stafford, John Onians and David Freedberg are among the many art historians who have integrated neuroscience into their readings of art objects.[26] Recent technological advances in the sciences, such as through functional MRI (fMRI) and positron emission tomography (PET) scans, have made it possible for neuroscientists to measure how the human brain responds to various visual stimuli.[27] Some art historians and scientists, however, remain sceptical about how neuroscience is applied to the arts.[28] Critics such as P. O. Folgerø and colleagues first reaffirm that, from a cultural perspective, the cognitive map of a modern human differs from that of someone from a previous era.[29] The differences in the two groups' respective neural architecture could also lead them to interpret visual stimuli in distinct ways.[30] As a result, these critics all agree that modern scientific data cannot function as empirical, objective evidence for how a long-dead audience perceived art.[31]

Scientific studies involving mirror neurons appear to generate the most controversy when they are used by scholars as evidence for the brain's interpretation of art objects.[32] Neuroscientist Vittorio Gallese and art historian David Freedberg have championed the role of mirror neurons in uncovering the mechanisms behind aesthetic response. Gallese and Freedberg both argue that humans do have a mirror system that facilitates embodied innate responses.[33] More specifically, Gallese suggests that mirror neurons enable humans to 'understand' emotion and motion when they see it in others and that this process of mirroring becomes an 'embodied response'.[34] In this context, viewers of a work of art could have an innate empathetic response to the artwork's imagery because their mirroring system allows them to understand the emotion or action being depicted.[35] Mirror neurons and their potential for producing innate, universal responses are therefore attractive to art historians since modern scientific evidence could then, theoretically at least, be transposed to a medieval audience.[36]

Mirror neurons have been directly observed in macaque monkeys, yet cognitive scientist Gregory Hickok debates that humans have an equivalent mirroring system.[37] It remains impossible to confirm their existence in humans since doing so would require an invasive, unethical procedure of probing the human brain to record how a single cell responded to visual stimuli. To compensate, scientists observe neural systems in the human brain and the mirroring actions from multiple cells, later using these data to argue for the existence of mirror neurons.[38] Because of their potential, rather than definite, existence in the human brain, Hickok argues that mirror neurons have been assigned more significance than the studies surrounding them indicate. He further suggests that scientists also presuppose that mirroring systems across species have identical purposes. The limited empirical knowledge about mirror neurons and their functions poses obvious methodological problems when mirror neuron data are broadly applied to the arts, humanities and social sciences.[39]

Although Gallese and Freedberg believe that the embodied responses themselves *may* be innate, they simultaneously acknowledge that cultural influences and personal experience play an important role in how an individual viewer ultimately interprets art.[40] In other words, even if a human mirroring system does indeed produce innate responses, Freedberg and Gallese do not debate that the reception of art is still ultimately subjective.[41] As Jeff Rider argues in this volume, for example, when one views an artistic depiction of an act, for his purposes a medieval dance, the human brain both automatically responds because it understands certain motor movements and fills in any knowledge gaps with its own understanding of the world. Innate biological responses thereby become mediated through subjectively determined lenses. Despite these constraints, Freedberg firmly asserts that neuroscience, especially involving mirror neurons, offers important evidence about how people, even deceased audiences, perceived their world and its art.[42]

A way to resolve the tension between the critics and proponents of mirror neurons is to acknowledge their potential existence and, simultaneously, to ensure that any scientific studies involving mirror neurons are not cited as definitive evidence for universal reception.[43] One successful integration of science to art historical discourse is Pamela Sheingorn's discussion of a viewer's potential empathic response to an image of Mary from an early thirteenth-century manuscript that focuses on the life of the Virgin.[44] Sheingorn suggests that the position of Mary's body, oriented away from a knight who seeks to court her, would encourage viewers to experience embodied, empathetic responses due to their brains' mirror neurons.[45] This reading is successful because Sheingorn presents her interpretation as potential rather than universal. In addition, Sheingorn mentions that the exact mechanisms behind this empathetic response are technically unknown, thereby clearly establishing the limitations of her reading of this image.[46] Neuroscience here explains the potential biological processes behind how medieval viewers empathised with the art they encountered, thereby yielding a more concrete understanding of reception than cognitive theory itself permits.[47]

As Matthew Rampley has suggested in this volume, critics of the marriage between neuroscience and art also argue that problems occur when art historians misunderstand the significance of the scientific data and terminology itself.[48] Scientists may measure the brain's activity in response to certain visual stimuli, but that does not necessarily mean that art historians may co-opt such data as supporting evidence for their own purposes.[49] Neuroscientists Eric Racine, Ofek Bar-Ilan and Judy Illes maintain that the lay public often misconstrues the significance of brain imaging data from functional MRI (fMRI) and positron emission tomography (PET), equating a measured response from a human brain with a response from that person's self, which can easily lead to confusion. For example, even if the brain responds to visual stimuli, this does not necessarily mean that the observer's personality, or self, is similarly responding to the stimuli. The scientists therefore maintain that one's understanding of 'identity' and his or her 'brain' are different entities because identity encompasses more than a mere organ.[50] Art historians should therefore clearly distinguish between the viewer's brain and the viewer's identity, or self, when discussing how viewers perceive art.

Embodiment, the Brain and Conceptions of Self

Such a clear delineation of terms does not imply that the mind and body are separate entities, however. George Lakoff and Mark Johnson dismissed such a Cartesian notion of self when they defined the mind as 'embodied' rather than being a separate entity from the body.[51] An embodied mind, according to the authors, is one where 'the very mechanisms responsible for perception, movements, and object manipulation could be responsible for conceptualization and reasoning'.[52] This definition intimately links the body's physiological responses with the mental perceptions that result from them, creating, in other words, an embodied response. Hence, an embodied response, per Freedberg and Gallese, is one where the 'the actions, emotions, or sensations we see activate our own internal representations of the body states that are associated with these social stimuli, as if we were engaged in a similar action or experiencing a similar emotion or sensation'.[53] These definitions of the embodiment process suggest that viewers of a work of art could arrive at a conceptual understanding of the piece through their physiological responses to the work's imagery or visual properties.[54]

Just as there exists an embodied mind, there is also an embodied understanding of self. Although Racine, Bar-Ilan and Illes argue that the 'brain' and 'identity' are distinct terms with vastly different implications, this does not mean that one does not inform the other.[55] In lieu of a dualistic model of self with a distinct mind and body, neuroscientist Emily Postan argues in favour of a 'narrative identity', wherein biology informs one's understanding of self and, simultaneously, identity transcends biology to exist as a more holistic entity.[56] In this way, identity indeed remains embodied rather than a construction determined solely by biological constraints.[57] This abstract understanding of an embodied self aligns with V. S. Ramachandran's definition of the brain's 'body image' as a 'stable internal mental construct of a unitary corporeal self that endures in time and space'.[58] This 'internal mental construct' is informed by the body's sensory systems and is 'malleable' rather than static, changing as new information is gathered via new experiences.[59] Therefore, just as the brain is mutable via its neuroplasticity, so is one's abstract understanding of self.[60]

When art historians create hypothetical viewers for medieval objects, they should take into account the self's fluid nature. Kinch states that the 'dynamic reciprocity – between a brain theorised as an open system with remarkable hardware and a cultural context filled with new stimulus – provides a crucial theoretical framework for any neuroscientific approach to the humanities, medieval or otherwise'.[61] Kinch here refers to a dynamic brain, which is of course not the exact same as the self. However, Postan's idea of a narrative identity and Ramachandran's description of a self correlate well with Kinch's idea of the brain as an 'open source' entity. In essence, therefore, since one's brain, cognitive map and understanding of self change as a result of interacting with the world, a hypothetical viewer is a permeable construction defined by ever-shifting boundaries. Such a model differs slightly from Caviness's defined audiences, which are constructed primarily with historical context in mind. Conversely, for a 'neuromedieval' viewer, to borrow Kinch's terminology, scientific data could be filtered through this hypothetical viewer's cognitive map. Historical context is still important because, in this neuroscientific model, context still determines the cognitive map's defining elements just as it does in a historically based model of artistic reception.[62]

A Potential Reading of a Gothic Ivory Mirror Case

To sum up, neuroscientific data still holds value for art historians so long as they recognise its limitations, apply the science correctly, and properly distinguish between the physical brain and abstract constructions such as identity and self. These parameters are necessary for a 'judicious' reading of the scene in Figure 10.1. This object dates to the mid-fourteenth century, and it hails from France.[63] The mirror case is small, with a diameter of 10.1 centimetres, and it is constructed from elephant ivory. Ivory was an expensive commodity in the Middle Ages, indicating the wealth of the patron, and its secular imagery points to a lay aristocratic owner.[64] Like many contemporary secular ivory mirror cases, Figure 10.1 features an aristocratic couple engaged in a courtly pastime. Due to their prominent location in the centre of the ivory, the man and woman represent the focal point and main action of the scene. The man precedes the lady, orienting his body towards her instead of looking at the path ahead of him. Although the man's attention is focused on the woman's face, the woman's gaze remains enigmatic since a viewer is unable to determine if she is looking straight ahead or at her lover. It is clear, however, that the woman does not deliberately avoid her lover's gaze by looking downward or behind her.

Beyond their obvious utilitarian function, mirrors had a variety of purposes. On one hand, they conveyed personal romantic intentions from the giver to the recipient.[65] As luxury items, mirrors and their cases also communicated status and wealth, especially when women wore them secured to their belts.[66] Both Alexa Sand and Susan Smith argue that, on a deeper level, the mirror additionally provided a template for divine revelation or engagement with the larger medieval world. For example, viewers could enter the performative space of a mirror case's scene when they assessed their reflections against the figures carved upon it.[67]

In Figure 10.1, the couple is hunting, but on similar objects, the figures also play board games such as chess, they joust, and they storm castles of love.[68] These activities were reserved for people who could afford leisure time, and they also figure prominently in contemporary courtly literature.[69] For this audience, comprising both male and female viewers, courtly literature would have informed their understanding of the world, and it

Figure 10.1: *Mirror Case with Falconing Party*, ivory (1350-75). New York. Metropolitan Museum of Art (Acc. 41.100.160, gift of George Blumenthal). *https://www.metmuseum.org/art/collection/search/467733*

would therefore have been a component of their cognitive maps.[70] Rather than representing specific tales, however, scenes on gothic ivory mirror cases refer to popular themes and tropes of courtly love, making such a scene relevant to multiple stories.[71] Viewers would therefore associate the imagery with tales they were most familiar with or recognise the motif as a traditional representation of the courtly milieu.[72] Owners of these mirrors would also have understood that games of chance, hunting, storming the castle of love, and other courtly pastimes symbolised the shifting dynamics of control between men and women, the conquest for love, and the rules of the courtly world itself.[73]

Because these mirrors depict a moment before the final result of the conquest has been decided, Sand argues that these activities visually manifest a sexual and narrative tension, and that it is precisely this tension that engages the viewer.[74] It would therefore remain for the viewers themselves to resolve this narrative ambiguity by interpreting the gender dynamics and the success – or failure – of the conquest for love on this mirror case. Their ultimate interpretations would be informed by their knowledge of specific courtly tales, their personal experiences with love itself, and the physiological cues they read between the man and woman in the scene. Referring back to Freedberg and Gallese's definition of an embodied response, where the body's physiological reactions to visual imagery help to influence the viewer's conception of the artwork, medieval viewers would have had an embodied response when they interpreted the scene in relation to themselves.[75]

Freedberg and Gallese argue that mirror neurons would enable viewers innately to understand a figure's body position and its significance because they would comprehend the action through their ability to reproduce it by virtue of an embodied, automatic response.[76] If we accept that mirror neurons exist in the human brain, it is possible for medieval viewers to have interpreted the relationship between the hunter and his companion in Figure 10.1. Even without mirror neurons, viewers may still have had embodied responses to the man and woman in the hunting scene. Hickok argues that, in essence, embodied cognition means that human cognition is often intertwined with the body's sensory and motor systems.[77] He proposes that, instead of a simple mirroring-system located in Broca's area, action-understanding involves a more complex and layered mechanism of action primarily in the brain's posterior temporal lobes. This area is neurologically responsible for conceptual knowledge. More specifically to Figure 10.1, the posterior superior temporal sulcus (STS) region of the human brain allows one to decode social actions involving eye gaze direction and human bodily actions.[78]

Freedberg and Gallese, as well as Hickok, provide different models for how viewers may have had embodied responses to the man and woman in Figure 10.1. I do not argue in favour of either mirror neurons or a complex series of actions in the STS as the mechanisms through which medieval viewers understood the gender dynamics on the hunting scene. Either biological process could be responsible, yet the important point to note is that react they most likely did. In order to propose a medieval viewer's potential interpretation of the relationship between the man and woman in Figure 10.1, I cite scientific studies investigating the significance of gaze direction, body orientation and posture in human interaction. I argue that medieval viewers would likely have perceived the man's romantic interest in the woman. At the same time, I suggest that these same viewers would have interpreted the woman as either interested or uninterested in her companion, depending on their preconceived notions and their interpretation of the significance of her gaze direction, body orientation and posture. Although the human subjects in the experiments I cite are far removed from a medieval audience, there is evidence that third parties can decode the romantic intentions of a couple based upon this couple's non-verbal interactions, a phenomenon that can occur across cultures.[79] Perhaps time would also not present a barrier to this understanding.

The artist of the scene in Figure 10.1 has rendered the man so that his gaze is explicitly oriented to the woman, but also so that the woman's gaze focuses both on the man and on the road ahead of her. When one's gaze is oriented to someone, it indicates that person's object of focus.[80] Often, a direct gaze and eye contact also signify romantic interest.[81] Eye contact is an important aspect of communication in humans, so a direct gaze facilitates eye contact while an averted one impairs it.[82] Accordingly, viewers of the mirror case may have interpreted the woman as being either engaged or disengaged with her male companion depending upon whether they perceived her to be looking at him or straight ahead. Beyond indicating focus and attention, gaze direction and eye contact also help to facilitate emotional responses among humans. In 2016, Folgerø et al. conducted a study to determine whether human subjects expressed preferences for paintings with faces that directly face the viewer, ultimately discovering that their subjects did indeed respond more positively to faces directly facing them and rated them as more trustworthy.[83] The findings of Jari K. Hietanen, Terhi M. Helminen, Helena Kiilavuori, Anneli Kylliäinen, Heidi Lehtonen and Mikko J. Peltola confirm that humans innately respond positively to a direct gaze, at least in a 'neutral context'.[84] The authors, however, also acknowledge that human interactions rarely occur absent of context. Other physiological cues, personal experiences or cultural factors can change an initially positive response into a negative one.[85]

The participants in the experiments conducted by Folgerø et al. and Hietanen et al. are removed from a medieval audience, so in order to gauge how medieval viewers may have interpreted the man's and woman's gaze in Figure 10.1 more effectively, we must look at what the gaze signified, culturally speaking, in the medieval world. Existing medieval scholarship has used a theoretical assessment of 'the gaze' between figures to discuss each character's agency, the amount of power held in the situation, and his or her possible degree of domination or submission.[86] Charles T. Little argues that the man's direct gaze toward the woman in Figure 10.1 indicates his romantic interest.[87] Susan Smith further suggests that, through his gaze, the man has initiated his conquest of the woman.[88] There is an order to the conquest of courtly love, according to Jean Markale. A man first signals his intentions by gazing upon the female form. Next, the woman either accepts or rejects the man's affections via her own gaze.[89] Smith notes that, for secular courtly images, the woman's reciprocal gaze is an indicator that she was acquiescing to the man's advances because it is ultimately her decision to accept or reject her lover.[90] This understanding that mutual gazes symbolised a shared romantic interest would likely have been part of a medieval viewer's cognitive map; therefore, any innate physiological responses to the ivory would have been filtered through this cultural lens.

But how individual viewers characterised the woman's receptiveness to the man's advances would also depend upon their own life experiences and beliefs. Sarah Stanbury, for example, argues that a woman's direct gaze upon her male companion characterises her as dominant, aggressive and someone in the pursuit of sex.[91] As the dominant force controlling the interaction, she both actualises her desire through her sexual choice and submits to the man's desires through her gaze.[92] On the other hand, a woman who withholds her gaze from a man maintains her modesty, thereby conforming to the medieval ideal of a submissive and chaste woman.[93] In some cases, too, a woman's averted gaze can signal a loss of male agency.[94] To summarise, in the medieval world, a woman withholding a gaze often reveals an imbalance of power and unrequited affection between a man and a woman. Conversely, mutual gazes suggest that a man has won a woman's affections and, thus, her eye contact through his successful romantic conquest.[95]

This is not to say that all humans respond positively to a direct gaze.[96] Although many people interpret direct gazes as romantic interest or simple engagement, gazes rarely happen absent of other social cues.[97] For example, a 2017 study conducted by Elise Holland, Elizabeth Baily Wolf, Christine Looser and Amy Cuddy concluded that humans tend to avert their gazes from those displaying both a direct gaze and dominant 'expansive' postures.[98] In addition to looking directly at the woman on the ivory mirror case, the hunter in Figure 10.1 explicitly orients himself toward the woman and places his arm around her shoulder, therefore bringing her into an embrace. The hunter does not display an expansive posture as Holland et al. assessed, but this study is still relevant because it demonstrates how the meaning of a gaze direction can change when assessed in conjunction with other physiological cues or contexts. A direct gaze from a lover differs greatly from that of an unwelcomed pursuer, for instance.[99]

Even though context can change the meaning of physiological cues, the body orientations and postures of the man and woman in Figure 10.1 can still inform potential readings of the scene. A 2015 study conducted by Sabrina Brugel, Marie Postma-Nilsenová and Kiek Tates indicates that people often feel engagement and perceived empathy from others who are directly facing them rather than in a stance averted from them.[100] The findings of Brugel et al. are supported by earlier studies that assess the link between body orientation and engagement.[101] In modern neutral or positive relationships, an open posture and close physical proximity are also signs of interpersonal engagement.[102] The male hunter on the ivory conveys his interest in the woman through his open body posture and by how he brings his body close to hers. An assessment of the woman's interest in the man, based upon body orientation or posture, is more challenging, however, as her body is both facing the man's and naturally positioned for her own activity. The woman does not turn away, yet her hands grasp the falcon and her horse's reins tightly. The position of her hands creates a protective barrier in front of her body. Overall, the woman on the ivory is definitely not mirroring his actions and thus not explicitly confirming her interest via her posture or gesture.[103]

The ambiguity of the woman's body position leaves room for individual viewers to interpret the scene according to their knowledge of what posture signified in the medieval world as well as their personal experiences. According to Little, the man's placement of his arm on his companion's shoulder clearly indicates his romantic interest.[104] Smith reinforces this interpretation, classifying such caresses or embraces as 'active behavior'.[105] Although Little does not comment on the woman's potential interest or disinterest, Sand suggests the woman holds her falcon 'pensively', perhaps suggesting her hesitancy or disinterest.[106] This interpretation is supported by Smith, who notes that, for secular courtly images, the woman's body position also indicates whether or not she is accepting or rejecting her lover's advances.[107]

The falcons these hunters carry would likewise influence the interpretations of this scene's dynamics. In this context, a viewer's unique understanding of the falcon functions as a likely component of his or her hypothetical cognitive map. On a literal level, of course, falcons signify the hunt and the conquest associated with courtly love itself.[108] However, these birds also symbolised both the male and female sex organs.[109] The male hunter in Figure 10.1 holds his falcon out in front of him, which means a viewer could believe he is leading his companion on a sexual quest with his penis. Conversely, one could also interpret the scene as one where the hunter's falcon signifies that he is being led by his desire to conquer his companion through a successful sexual conquest. The woman's falcon also has multivalent interpretations. At one level, if she holds the falcon 'pensively', she is then reluctant to submit to the man's advances. Simultaneously, however, if the falcon represents his sexual organ, she is grasping it quite firmly.[110] All of these interpretations of the birds' meaning have equal merit because each individual viewer would interpret the falcon uniquely. In addition, because the human brain first looks to confirm its expectations, one's pre-existing understanding of the falcon would also inform one's deeper reading of the scene.[111] One who perceived the falcon as erotic would likely therefore interpret the biological cues between the couple through an erotic lens as well.

Based upon an analysis of the body orientation, posture and gaze direction of the couple in Figure 10.1, the man has demonstrated his interest, and the woman is either accepting or rejecting his advances. Although the scene does not offer a definite interpretation, medieval viewers were engaged via their own resolution of this couple's dynamic. As Sand argues, 'the deferral of the lovers' desire in these images cuts to the core of the purpose of these objects: to stimulate, through the visual sense, the imagination, and through imagination, the body's sensual awareness and anticipation'.[112] While Sand characterises this response as erotic, this eroticism is both of the body and of the mind and, as such, conforms to Freedberg and Gallese's definition of an embodied response. Even though the reception and interpretation of an object would differ from one person to the next, neuroscience allows medieval art historians to understand, with more concrete and tangible means than before, how these viewers likely arrived at their various interpretations.

Notes

1 Madeline Caviness, 'Reception of Images by Medieval Viewers', in Conrad Rudolph (ed.), *A Companion to Medieval Art* (Oxford: Blackwell, 2006), p. 66. Caviness comments that before the late fourteenth century, few literary sources record how medieval audiences responded to art.

2 *Mirror Case with Falconing Party*, ivory (1350–75). New York. Metropolitan Museum of Art (Acc. 41.100.160, gift of George Blumenthal), *https://www.metmuseum.org/art/collection/search/467733*.

3 Ashby Kinch, 'Re-visioning the Past: Neuromedievalism and the Neural Circuits of Vision', *postmedieval: a journal of medieval cultural studies*, 3 (2012), 262. See also Perk's chapter in this volume, referencing Kinch's definition of 'echo objects'.

4 Kinch, 'Re-visioning the Past', p. 262.

5 Kinch, 'Re-visioning the Past', p. 262. Although Kinch does not explicitly define what constitutes 'judiciousness', he does conclude on p. 269 that neuromedievalism 'will not probe brains and it will insist on the unique cultural formations in which a given system of signs generates meaning for readers. But it will also attend closely to the specific biological mechanism that makes this meaning-making possible: the embodied and embedded brain, both our own, and those of bodies long since decomposed'.

6 Alva Noë, *Strange Tools: Art and Human Nature* (New York: Hill and Wang, 2015), p. 122; P. O. Folgerø, L. Hodne, C. Johansson, A. E. Andresen, L. C. Sætren, K. Specht, Ø. O.Skaar and R. Reber, 'Effects of Facial Symmetry and Gaze Direction on Perception of Social Attributes: A Study in Experimental Art History', *Frontiers in Human Neuroscience*, 10 (2016), 9–11. Both Noë and Folgerø et al. argue that artistic reception is ultimately subjective.

7 Jenell M. Johnson and Melissa Littlefield, 'Lost and Found in Translation: Popular Neuroscience in the Emerging Neurodisciplines', in Martyn Pickersgill and Ira Van Keulen (eds), *Sociological Reflections on the Neurosciences: Vol. 13. Advances in Medical Sociology* (Bingley, UK: Emerald Group Publishing, 2011), pp. 282–8. The authors critique how neuroscientific data is improperly universalised and used to support purely theoretical arguments.

8 Eric Racine, Ofek Bar-Ilan and Judy Illes, 'fMRI and the Public Eye', *Nature Reviews Neuroscience*, 6/2 (2005), 160.

9 Folgerø et al., 'Effects of Facial Symmetry', pp. 9–11.

10 Eric R. Kandel, *Reductionism in Art and Brain Science: Bridging the Two Cultures* (New York: Columbia University Press, 2016), pp. 19–22. On p. 20, Kandel states that 'any image projected onto the retina of the eye has countless possible interpretations'. He cites neuroscientist Chris Frith, who poetically explains: 'What I perceive are not the crude and ambiguous cues that impinge from the outside world onto my eyes and my ears and my fingers. I perceive something much richer – a picture that combines all these crude signals with the wealth of past experience . . . Our perception of the world is a fantasy that coincides with reality.' See Chris Frith, *Making Up the Mind: How the Brain Creates Our Mental World* (Oxford: Blackwell, 2007).

11 Peter S. Wells, *Image and Response in Early Europe* (London: Duckworth, 2008), pp. 31–2. Wells specifically defines a cognitive map as 'the essential model of the world we have in our brains and with what we compare everything we see' (pp. 31–2).

12 Norman Doidge, *The Brain That Changes Itself: Stories of Personal Triumph from the Frontiers of Brain Science* (New York: Penguin Books, 2007), p. 300.

13 Noë, *Strange Tools*, 122; Folgerø et al., 'Effects of Facial Symmetry', pp. 9–11.

14 Caviness, 'Reception of Images', pp. 65–85; Cynthia Hahn, '*Visio Dei*: Changes in Medieval Visuality', in Robert S. Nelson (ed.), *Visuality Before and Beyond the Renaissance* (Cambridge: Cambridge University Press, 2000), pp. 169–96; Michael Camille, 'The Image and the Self: Unwriting Late Medieval Bodies', in Sarah Kay and Miri Rubin (eds), *Framing Medieval Bodies* (Manchester: Manchester University Press, 1994), pp. 62–99.

15 Michael Baxandall, *Painting and Experience in Fifteenth-Century Italy* (Oxford: Oxford University Press, 1972), pp. 29–31.

16 Baxandall, *Painting and Experience*, pp. 29–30.

17 See also: John Onians, *Neuroarthistory: From Aristotle and Pliny to Baxandall and Zeki* (New Haven, CT: Yale University Press, 2008).

18 Baxandall, *Painting and Experience*, pp. 29–31.

19 Nicolas J. Bullot and Rolf Reber, 'The Artful Mind Meets Art History: Toward a Psycho-Historical Framework for the Science of Art Appreciation', *Behavior and Brain Sciences*, 36 (2013), 123–6. Bullot and Reber attempt to reconcile empirically driven neuroscience and art history's contextually driven 'historical approach'. Also see: Viren Swami, 'Context Matters: Investigating the Impact of Contextual Information on the Aesthetic Appreciation of Paintings by Max Ernst and Pablo Picasso', *Psychology of Aesthetics, Creativity, and the Arts*, 7/3 (2013), 285–95. Swami's investigation confirms Bullot and Reber's conclusion that a viewer's contextual knowledge does influence how he or she aesthetically perceives a work of art. Although Swami's study focuses on modern art, it does highlight how a viewer's contextual knowledge, or components of a 'cognitive map', influences his or her ultimate perception of the piece.

20 Caviness, 'Reception of Images', pp. 66–72.

21 Caviness, 'Reception of Images', p. 71.

22 Caviness, 'Reception of Images', p. 71.

23 Kinch, 'Re-visioning the Past', pp. 266–7. The author explains how the process of understanding concepts

> is organized at the neural level by specialized cells that respond to certain visual inputs – horizontality, verticality, movement – by a means of 'selective orientation' that generates a 'feedforward' stimulus, which aggregates the reactions of individual cells to specific stimuli. The architecture of the visual cortex creates a bias in the visual brain toward confirmation of the 'expected' sensation over the mechanical feedforward of the stimulus. When a stimulus is inactivated at a lower level, it is inactive at all subsequent levels, which provides a mechanism to account for how the brain filters out irrelevant stimulus and focuses attention on the perception of the 'new' stimulus.

Also see: Henry Kennedy and Kenneth Knoblauch, 'Imagery, Art and Biological Aspects of Visual Consciousness', *Word and Image*, 21/2 (2005), 124–35.

24 Ashby Kinch, '"Mind like Wickerwork": The Neuroplastic Aesthetics of Chaucer's House of Tidings', *postmedieval: a journal of medieval and cultural studies*, 3/3 (2012), 308. Also see: J. P. Changeux, *Du Vrai, Du Beau, Du Bien: Une Nouvelle Approche Neuronale* (Paris: Odile Jacob, 2008), pp. 279–82, 495–7.

25 Caviness, 'Reception of Images', p. 71. See also the collaboration between neurobiologist Y. Dudai and Mary Carruthers, 'The Janus Face of Mnemosyne', *Nature*, 434/7033 (2005), 567.

26 Barbara M. Stafford, *Echo Objects: The Cognitive Work of Images* (Chicago: University of Chicago Press, 2007); Onians, *Neuroarthistory*; David Freedberg, 'From Absorption to Judgment: Empathy in Aesthetic Response', in Vanessa Lux and Sigrid Weigel (eds.) *Empathy: Epistemic Problems and Cultural-Historical Perspectives of a Cross-Disciplinary Concept* (London: Palgrave MacMillan, 2017), pp. 139–80. For a discussion of neuroaesthetics, see Semir Zeki, *Inner Vision: An Exploration of Art and the Brain* (Oxford: Oxford University Press, 2000).

27 Kinch, 'Re-visioning the Past', p. 262; Racine, Bar-Ilan and Illes, 'fMRI and the Public Eye', pp. 160–62.

28 Kate Mondloch, 'Wave of the Future? Reconsidering the Neuroscientific Turn in Art History', *Leonardo*, 49/1 (2016), 25–31; Bullot and Reber, 'The Artful Mind', 123–37.

[29] See Folgerø et al., 'Effects of Facial Symmetry', pp. 9–11, who state that 'experiments to test hypotheses about the intended or real effects of historical art on the audience of that time are of some merit and might provide us with insights about the plausibility of art-historical assumptions. However, the interpretation of such studies always has to take change in cultural knowledge of the audience into account'.

[30] Bullot and Reber, 'The Artful Mind', pp. 123–26.

[31] Johnson and Littlefield, 'Lost and Found in Translation', pp. 282–8.

[32] Roberto Casati and Alessandro Pignocchi, 'Mirror and Canonical Neurons are Not Constitutive of Aesthetic Response', *Trends in Cognitive Sciences*, 11/10 (2007), 411. Also see: Gregory Hickok, *The Myth of Mirror Neurons: The Real Neuroscience of Communication and Cognition* (New York: W. W. Norton & Co., 2014). See also Matthew Rampley in this volume.

[33] David Freedberg and Vittorio Gallese, 'Motion, Emotion, and Empathy in Esthetic Experience', *Trends in Cognitive Science*, 11/5 (2007), 197–203. For more discussion on the potential evidence of a human mirroring system, see: V. S. Ramachandran, 'Mirror Neurons and Imitation Learning as the Driving Force Behind "The Great Leap Forward" in Human Evolution', *Edge* (2000), *https://pdfs.semanticscholar.org/2bbd/122436b9446a34cab84cb283d717bfa90e58.pdf.*

[34] Freedberg and Gallese, 'Motion, Emotion, and Empathy', p. 197. The authors define an embodied response as 'embodied simulation [which is] a functional mechanism through which the actions, emotions, or sensations we see activate our own internal representations of the body states that are associated with these social stimuli, as if we were engaged in a similar action or experiencing a similar emotion or sensation'.

[35] Freedberg and Gallese, 'Motion, Emotion, and Empathy', p. 197; See also: Vittorio Gallese, 'The Manifold Nature of Interpersonal Relations: The Quest for a Common Mechanism', *Philosophical Transactions: Biological Sciences*, 358/1431 (2003), 517. Gallese writes, 'we empathize with others, we understand what others are feeling, be it a particular emotion or sensory state. Finally, when we witness the actions of others, we supposedly understand their meaning and the reasons that possibly promoted them'. Empathy is difficult to define, and neuroscientists have yet to formulate a concrete definition. Gallese's definition here most represents how I discuss the empathetic response of a medieval viewer to Figure 10.1.

[36] Freedberg, 'From Absorption to Judgment', pp. 146–8.

[37] Hickok, *The Myth*, pp. 3–7, 13–15. Hickok indicates that mirror neurons were initially discovered in the F5 region of the macaque brain, and that other scientists used this knowledge to hypothesise that humans have mirror neurons in Broca's area. The term 'mirror neurons' was first published in the following study: Vittorio Gallese, Luciano Fadiga, Leonardo Fogassi and Giacomo Rizzolatti, 'Action Recognition in the Premotor Cortex', *Brain*, 119 (1996), 593–609.

[38] Hickok, *The Myth*, pp. 27–8. Hickok notes that 'PET, fMRI, EEG, and TMS' scans are 'indirect' methods of observing brain activity when looking for mirror neurons.

[39] Hickok, *The Myth*, pp. 22–6.

[40] Freedberg and Gallese, 'Motion, Emotion, and Empathy', pp. 197, 203. On one hand, the authors state that embodied mechanisms 'are universal', yet ,on p. 203, they also assert that '[h]istorical and cultural or contextual factors do not contradict the importance of considering the neural processes that arise in the empathetic understanding of visual works of art'.

[41] Edward Nersessian, moderator, 'The Eye of the Beholder', Round-table discussion moderated with participants Suzanne Anker, Francis Baudry, David Freedberg, Vittorio Gallese, and Barbara Maria Stafford, The Philoctetes Center, 23 April 2007. (A video and transcript of this discussion are available at *http://Philoctetes.org/past_programs/eye_of_the_beholder.*) On p. 9, Gallese states that he does not want to 'reduce human nature, human experiences, and therefore art experiences, to cognitive enterprise solely mediated by our most highly sophisticated cognitive endowments'.

[42] Freedberg, 'From Absorption to Judgment', pp. 144–6.

[43] For a comprehensive review of studies that investigate mirror neurons and their role in universal artistic reception, see: Bartlomiej Piechowski-Jozwiak, François Boller and Julien Bogousslavsky, 'Universal Connection Through Art: Role of Mirror Neurons in Art Production and Reception', *Behavioral Sciences*, 7/29 (2017), 1–9.

44 Kraków, Biblioteka Jagiellónska, Ms. Berol. Germ. Oct. 109; fol. 28r.

45 Pamela Sheingorn, 'Making the Cognitive Turn in Art History: A Case Study', *Connexions* (11 June 2010), 22–3, *http://www.neurohistoriasztuki.umk.pl/pliki/sheingorn.pdf*.

46 Sheingorn, 'Making the Cognitive Turn', pp. 22–3.

47 Kinch, 'Re-Visioning the Past', pp. 262, 267. For another art historical study discussing the potential role of mirror neurons in aesthetic response, see: Elina Gertsman, 'Image and Performance: an Art Historian at the Crossroads', *Research on Medieval and Renaissance Drama*, 51, special issue: 'Opportunities in Medieval and Renaissance Drama', eds Mario Longtin and Jill Stevenson (2013), 5–13.

48 Also see: Mondloch, 'Wave of the Future?' pp. 26–7.

49 Mondloch, 'Wave of the Future?' pp. 26–7.

50 Racine, Bar-Ilan and Illes, 'fMRI and the Public Eye', p. 160. Reducing identity to its mere biological components is 'neuroessentialism', a process in which, Racine and colleagues suggest, 'the brain is used implicitly as a shortcut for more global concepts such as the person, the individual or the self'.

51 George Lakoff and Mark Johnson, *Philosophy in the Flesh: The Embodied Mind and its Challenges to Western Thought* (New York: Basic Books, 1999), pp. 37–8. For more information on anti-Cartesian interpretations of consciousness, see: Antonio Damasio, *Descartes' Error: Emotion, Reason, and the Human Brain* (New York: Grosset/Putnam, 1994); Antonio Damasio, *The Feeling of What Happens: Body and Emotion in the Making of Consciousness* (New York: Harcourt Brace, 1999). For more discussion on Cartesian and non-Cartesian views of cognition, see Victoria Blud's chapter in this volume.

52 Lakoff and Johnson, *Philosophy in the Flesh*, pp. 37–8.

53 Freedberg and Gallese, 'Motion, Emotion, and Empathy', p. 198.

54 Freedberg and Gallese, 'Motion, Emotion, and Empathy', pp. 197–8, 201–2.

55 Racine, Bar-Ilan and Illes, 'fMRI and the Public Eye', p. 160.

56 Emily Postan, 'Defining Ourselves: Personal Bioinformation as a Tool of Narrative Self-Conception', *Journal of Bioethical Inquiry*, 13 (2016), 133–51.

57 Mondloch, 'Wave of the Future?' p. 25.

58 V. S. Ramachandran, 'Consciousness and Body Image: Lessons from Phantom Limbs, Capgras Syndrome, and Pain Asymbolia', *Philosophical Transactions: Biological Sciences* 353/1377 (1998), 1854. Although Ramachandran states that our internal understanding of self is 'stable', he does not suggest this notion of self remains fixed throughout our lives. Instead, the word stable describes how we think of ourselves as whole beings despite the fact that we create these internal representations from 'evanescent and fragmentary evidence derived from multiple sensory systems'.

59 Ramachandran, 'Consciousness', p. 1851.

60 Ramachandran, 'Consciousness', p. 1854; Kinch, 'Re-Visioning the Past', p. 268.

61 Kinch, 'Re-Visioning the Past', p. 268.

62 Mondloch, 'Wave of the Future?' p. 25.

63 Metropolitan Museum of Art, 'Mirror Case, Acc. 41.100.160', *https://www.metmuseum.org/art/collection/search/467733* (accessed 17 December 2017). The museum lists the dimensions as 11.1 x 10.4 x 1.1 cm.

64 Peter Barnet, 'Gothic Sculpture in Ivory: An Introduction', in Barnet (ed.), *Images in Ivory: Precious Objects of the Gothic Age* (Princeton, NJ: Princeton University Press, 1997), p. 3. See also: Alexa Sand, 'The Fairest of Them All: Reflections on Some Fourteenth-Century Mirrors', in Sarah Blick and Laura D. Gelfand (eds), *Push Me, Pull You: Imaginative and Emotional Interaction in Late Renaissance and Medieval Art* (Leiden: Brill, 2011), pp. 531–4.

65 James A. Rushing, 'Adventures in the Service of Love: Yvain on a Fourteenth-Century Ivory Panel', *Zeitschrift für Kunstgeschichte*, 61/1 (1998), 64.

66 Sand, 'The Fairest', pp. 529–30; Susan L. Smith, 'The Gothic Mirror and the Female Gaze', in Jane L. Carroll and Alison G. Stewart (eds), *Saints, Sinners, and Sisters: Gender and Northern Art in Medieval and Early Modern Europe* (Aldershot: Ashgate, 2003), pp. 73–4. Also see: Alexa Sand, '*Materia Meditandi:* Haptic Perception and Some Parisian Ivories of the Virgin and Child,

ca. 1300', *Different Visions: A Journal of New Perspectives on Medieval Art*, 4 (2014), 2–4. Sand argues that mirrors invited interaction not just for their utilitarian value, but also for their smooth texture and smooth touch. These textural qualities, in Sand's opinion, would only further enhance the viewing experience.

67 Sand, 'The Fairest', pp. 529–30, 535–42. On p. 535, Sand comments that 'the act of looking at one's own reflection triggers a chain of mental events that heighten consciousness of relations between body, self, and other'. Sand cites Lacanian psychology, but her emphasis on the unity of vision and the human body suggests that a viewer would have an embodied response when looking at the mirror. Also see: Smith, 'The Gothic Mirror', pp. 73–5. Smith, unlike Sand, focuses most of her attention on the female gendered gaze. Sand and Smith's idea about the mirror's multivalent role does have precedence, as the mirror functions as an instrument for reflection in early fourteenth-century manuscripts such as the *De Lisle Psalter* (London, British Library, Arundel MS 83, *c.*1308–40) and the *Roman de Fauvel* (Gervais de Bus, Paris, Bibliothèque nationale de France, MS fr. 146, *c.*1316–20).

68 Richard H. Randall Jr, 'Popular Romances Carved in Ivory', in Peter Barnet (ed.), *Images in Ivory: Precious Objects of the Gothic Age* (Princeton, NJ: Princeton University Press, 1997), 64.

69 Richard H. Randall Jr, 'Medieval Ivories in the Romance Tradition', *Gesta* 28/1 (1989), 35–7.

70 Smith, 'The Gothic Mirror', pp. 75–6. Although Smith cites medieval inventories as evidence that both men and women owned such mirrors, she argues that women engaged in much of the use and viewing activities.

71 Harry Bober, 'French Gothic Ivory Mirror Case', *Fogg Art Museum Annual Report* (1952/1953), 5. Hunting appears in the *Lais of Marie de France*, *La Roman de la Rose*, and many Arthurian tales, among others. See: Marcelle Thiébaux, *The Stag of Love: The Chase in Medieval Literature* (Ithaca, NY: Cornell University Press, 1974). See also: William Calin, *The French Tradition and the Literature of Medieval England* (Toronto: University of Toronto Press, 1994).

72 Randall, 'Popular Romances', pp. 67–8.

73 Sand, 'The Fairest', 534, 547–8, 551–5. The author describes how hunting symbolises the conquest for love. On p. 555, she argues that carvers of these secular ivory mirror cases 'focused on themes of opposition and moments of tension rather than the fulfillment of love's promise'. See also: Thiébaux, *The Stag of Love*, p. 58.

74 Sand, 'The Fairest', pp. 534, 558.

75 Freedberg and Gallese, 'Motion, Emotion, and Empathy', p. 198.

76 Freedberg and Gallese, 'Motion, Emotion, and Empathy', p. 198.

77 Hickok, *The Myth*, pp. 128–9.

78 Hickok, *The Myth*, pp. 171–8. Hickok cites: S. Shultz, S. M. Lee, K. Pelphrey and G. McCarthy, 'The Posterior Superior Temporal Sulcus is Sensitive to the Outcome of Human and Non-Human Goal-Directed Actions', *Social Cognitive and Affective Neuroscience*, 6/5 (2011), 602–11.

79 Skyler S. Place, Peter M. Todd, Lars Penke and Jens B. Asendorpf, 'The Ability to Judge the Romantic Interest of Others', *Psychological Science*, 20/1 (2009), 22–6. For a cross-cultural assessment, please see: Skyler S. Place, Peter M. Todd, Jinying Zhuang, Lars Penke and Jens B. Asendorpf, 'Judging Romantic Interest of Others From Thin Slices is a Cross-Cultural Ability', *Evolution and Human Behavior*, 33 (2012), 547–50.

80 Nathalie George and Laurence Conty, 'Facing the Gaze of Others', *Clinical Neurophysiology*, 38 (2008), 198–200. Gazes also play an important role in social cognition, and the ability to decode social cues provides a valuable evolutionary advantage; anticipating the intentions of others increases one's chance of survival. See: Hickok, *The Myth*, p. 158.

81 Omri Gillath, Angela J. Bahns and Hayley A. Burghart, 'Eye Movements When Looking At Potential Friends and Romantic Partners', *Archives of Sexual Behavior*, 46/8 (2017), 2322–5. See also: Joan Kellerman, James Lewis and James D. Laird, 'Looking and Loving: The Effects of Mutual Gaze on Feelings of Romantic Love', *Journal of Research in Personality*, 23/2 (1989), 145–61.

82 Atsushi Senju and Mark H. Johnson, 'The Eye Contact Effect: Mechanisms and Development', *Trends in Cognitive Science*, 13/3 (2009), 127–30.

83 Folgerø et al., 'Effects of Facial Symmetry', pp. 1, 8–10. The scientists studied how contemporary subjects perceived Medieval and Renaissance Holy Faces of Christ. While the scientists 'observed that frontal faces with direct gaze were more highly associated with positive adjectives', they also concluded that 'many factors affect the impression of the face, and that eye contact in combination with face direction reinforce the general impression of a portrait, rather than determine it'.

84 Jari K. Hietanen, Terhi M. Helminen, Helena Kiilavuori, Anneli Kylliäinen, Heidi Lehtonen and Mikko J. Peltola, 'Your Attention Makes Me Smile: Direct Gaze Elicits Affiliative Facial Expressions', *Biological Psychology*, 132 (2018), 7.

85 Hietanen et al., 'Your Attention Makes Me Smile', pp. 6–7; Antonia F. de C. Hamilton, 'Gazing at Me: The Importance of Social Meaning in Understanding Direct-Gaze Cues', *Philosophical Transactions of the Royal Society B: Biological Sciences*, 371 (2015), 1–6; Áine Lorié, Diego A. Reinero, Margot Phillips, Linda Zhang and Helen Riess, 'Culture and Nonverbal Expressions of Empathy in Clinical Settings: A Systematic Review', *Patient Education and Counseling*, 100 (2017), 411–24.

86 Martha Easton, 'Was it Good for You Too? Medieval Erotic Art and Its Audiences', *Different Visions: A Journal of New Perspectives on Medieval Art* 1 (2008), *http://www.differentvisions.org/issue1PDFs/Easton.pdf.* Easton cites *The Art of Courtly Love* by Andreas Capellanus as evidence for her interpretation of the gendered gaze. The author states that 'there is something about seeing (as opposed to reading), which changes the nature of perception. The implications of the gaze, and specifically the gendered gaze, were addressed in the Middle Ages; in his famous treatise on the art of courtly love, Andreas Capellanus maintained that desire resided in sight, that it was created from the "inborn suffering" produced by looking at the opposite sex'. Andreas Cappellanus, *The Art of Courtly Love*, trans. John Jay Parry (1941; rpt New York: Columbia University Press, 1960), p. 28.

87 Charles T. Little, 'Mirror Case With Falconing Party', image description in Peter Barnet (ed.), *Images in Ivory: Precious Objects of the Gothic Age* (Princeton, NJ: Princeton University Press, 1997), pp. 235–6.

88 Smith, 'The Gothic Mirror', p. 76.

89 Jean Markale, *Courtly Love: The Path of Sexual Initiation* (Rochester, VT: Inner Traditions International, 2000), pp. 100–2.

90 Smith', The Gothic Mirror', pp. 75, 81–3.

91 Sarah Stanbury, 'The Virgin's Gaze: Spectacle and Transgression in Middle English Lyrics of the Passion', *PMLA*, 106/5 (1991), 1083–4. Stanbury supports her claim with a discussion of Beatrice from Dante's fourteenth-century *Inferno*. She argues that 'Beatrice's gaze, the object of Dante the spectator's intense desire, takes its power from the traditional iconography of Eros as well as from the imagery of divine rapture: love's arrows are transformed in the service of a visual apotheosis that suggests a beatific vision. Yet Beatrice's look, reciprocating Dante's impassioned stare, also takes its power from its violation of conventions condemning a woman's gaze.'

92 Smith, 'The Gothic Mirror', p. 76.

93 Stanbury, 'The Virgin's Gaze', p. 1084. Stanbury claims that a 'woman's gaze is most invitingly marked by its absence; in Chaucer's *Legend of Good Women* Lucrece meekly drops her eyes 'and mekely she let hyre eyen falle' (1734) – as a sign of wifely chastity'. Stanbury argues that Bernard of Clairvaux paints the sin of *curiositas* as an implication of 'a similar equation between a woman's gaze and her vulnerability in the world'. Regarding the rape of the biblical Dinah, Bernard states that 'you look inquisitively, yet you are looked at more inquisitively'. His assessment of Dinah's rape assigns blame to the woman rather than the sexual aggressor.

94 Molly Anne Martin, *Isn't The Gaze Male? Gender and the Visual Experience in the Romances of Chaucer and Mallory* (PhD dissertation, Purdue University, 2007), pp. 150–1. Martin cites Mallory's *Le Morte D'Arthur* (1469) as an example in which the woman maintains control by withholding her affections. Martin states that Uther is emasculated through the unrequited love of Igrayne.

95 Markale, *Courtly Love*, pp. 100–2; Smith, 'The Gothic Mirror', p. 76.

96 Marianne Schmid Mast, 'On the Importance of Nonverbal Communication in the Physician–Patient Interaction', *Patient Education and Counseling*, 67 (2007), 315–18.

97 Hietanen et al., 'Your Attention Makes Me Smile', pp. 6–7.

98 Elise Holland, Elizabeth Baily Wolf, Christine Looser and Amy Cuddy, 'Visual Attention to Powerful Postures: People Avert Their Gaze from Nonverbal Dominance Displays', *Journal of Experimental Social Psychology*, 68 (2017), 60–7.

99 Peter A. Andersen, 'Nonverbal Immediacy in Interpersonal Communication', in Aron W. Siegman and Stanley Feldstein (eds), *Multichannel Integrations of Nonverbal Behavior* (Hillsdale, NJ: Lawrence Erlbaum, 1985; New York, NY: Psychology Press, 2014), Kindle edition.

100 Sabrina Brugel, Marie Postma-Nilsenová and Kiek Tates, 'The Link Between Perception of Clinical Empathy and Non-Verbal Behavior: The Effect of a Doctor's Gaze and Body Orientation', *Patient Education and Counseling*, 98 (2015), 1260–5.

101 Andersen, 'Nonverbal Immediacy'. Also see: Kathryn M. Larsen and Charles Kent Smith, 'Assessment of Nonverbal Communication in the Patient-Physician Interview', *Journal of Family Practice*, 12 (1981), 486–8; Arne Nagels, Tilo Kircher, Miriam Steines and Benjamin Straube, 'Feeling Addressed! The Role of Body Orientation and Co-Speech Gesture in Social Communication', *Human Brain Mapping*, 36 (2015), 1925–36.

102 Andersen, 'Nonverbal Immediacy'. Andersen cites the following foundational works: Ernst G. Beier and Daniel P. Sternberg, 'Marital Communication: Subtle Cues Between Newly-Weds', *Journal of Communication*, 27 (1977), 92–7; Albert Mehrabian, *Silent Messages* (Belmont, CA: Wadsworth, 1971).

103 For a thorough discussion of mimicry and emotions, see: Eliska Prochazkova and Mariska E. Kret, 'Connecting Minds and Sharing Emotions Through Mimicry: A Neurocognitive Model of Emotional Contagion', *Neuroscience and Biobehavioral Reviews*, 80 (2017), 99–114.

104 Little, 'Mirror Case With Falconing Party', pp. 235–6.

105 Smith, 'The Gothic Mirror', pp. 78–9.

106 Sand, 'The Fairest', pp. 533, 551.

107 Smith, 'The Gothic Mirror', pp. 75, 81–3.

108 Sand, 'The Fairest', pp. 554–6; Randall, 'Popular Romances', p. 75.

109 Smith, 'The Gothic Mirror', pp. 81–2.

110 Smith, 'The Gothic Mirror', pp. 81–2.

111 Kinch, 'Re-Visioning the Past', pp. 266–7.

112 Sand, 'The Fairest', pp. 534, 558.

Select Bibliography

Barnet, Peter (ed.), *Images in Ivory: Precious Objects of the Gothic Age* (Princeton, NJ: Princeton University Press, 1997).

Bullot, Nicolas J. and Rolf Reber, 'The Artful Mind Meets Art History: Toward a Psycho-Historical Framework for the Science of Art Appreciation', *Behavior and Brain Sciences*, 36 (2013), 123–37.

Camille, Michael, 'The Image and the Self: Unwriting Late Medieval Bodies', in Sarah Kay and Miri Rubin (eds), *Framing Medieval Bodies* (Manchester: Manchester University Press, 1994), pp. 62–99.

Caviness, Madeline, 'Reception of Images by Medieval Viewers', in Conrad Rudolph (ed.), *A Companion to Medieval Art* (Oxford: Blackwell, 2000), pp. 65–85.

Damasio, Antonio, *The Feeling of What Happens: Body and Emotion in the Making of Consciousness* (New York: Harcourt Brace, 1999).

Doidge, Norman, *The Brain That Changes Itself: Stories of Personal Triumph from the Frontiers of Brain Science* (New York: Penguin Books, 2007).

Frith, Chris, *Making Up the Mind: How the Brain Creates Our Mental World* (Oxford: Blackwell, 2007).

Gallese, Vittorio, 'The Manifold Nature of Interpersonal Relations: The Quest for a Common Mechanism', *Philosophical Transactions: Biological Sciences*, 358/1431 (2003), 517–28.

Kandel, Eric R., *Reductionism in Art and Brain Science: Bridging the Two Cultures* (New York: Columbia University Press, 2016).

Kellerman, Joan, James Lewis and James D. Laird, 'Looking and Loving: The Effects of Mutual Gaze on Feelings of Romantic Love', *Journal of Research in Personality*, 23/2 (1989), 145–61.

Lakoff, George and Mark Johnson, *Philosophy in the Flesh: The Embodied Mind and its Challenges to Western Thought* (New York: Basic Books, 1999).

Mondloch, Kate, 'Wave of the Future? Reconsidering the Neuroscientific Turn in Art History', *Leonardo*, 49/1 (2016), 25–31.

Pickersgill, Martyn and Ira Van Keulen (eds), *Sociological Reflections on the Neurosciences: Vol. 13. Advances in Medical Sociology* (Bingley, UK: Emerald Group Publishing, 2011).

Ramachandran, V. S., 'Consciousness and Body Image: Lessons from Phantom Limbs, Capgras Syndrome, and Pain Asymbolia', *Philosophical Transactions: Biological Sciences*, 353/1377 (1998), 1851–9.

Randall, Richard H. Jr, 'Medieval Ivories in the Romance Tradition', *Gesta*, 28/1 (1989), 30–40.

Sand, Alexa, 'The Fairest of Them All: Reflections on Some Fourteenth-Century Mirrors', in Sarah Blick and Laura D. Gelfand (eds), *Push Me, Pull You: Imaginative and Emotional Interaction in Late Renaissance and Medieval Art* (Leiden: Brill, 2011), pp. 527–59.

Sheingorn, Pamela, 'Making the Cognitive Turn in Art History: A Case Study', *Connexions*, (2010), 1–46, *http://www.neurohistoriasztuki.umk.pl/pliki/sheingorn.pdf.*

Smith, Susan L., 'The Gothic Mirror and the Female Gaze', in Jane L. Carroll and Alison G. Stewart (eds), *Saints, Sinners, and Sisters: Gender and Northern Art in Medieval and Early Modern Europe* (Aldershot: Ashgate, 2003), pp. 73–93.

Stafford, Barbara M., *Echo Objects: The Cognitive Work of Images* (Chicago: University of Chicago Press, 2007).

Wells, Peter S., *Image and Response in Early Europe* (London: Duckworth, 2008).

Zeki, Semir, *Inner Vision: An Exploration of Art and the Brain* (Oxford: Oxford University Press, 2000).

11

Spoons, Whorls, and Caroles: How Medieval Artefacts Can Help Keep Your Brain on Its Toes

JEFF RIDER

Materially, for us today, the Middle Ages may be said to be the surviving artefacts that were created between roughly 500 CE and roughly 1500 CE within the geographical limits, roughly, of contemporary Europe and the Mediterranean coastal regions. Relatively few of these artefacts survive intact and many of them have been restored, changed or augmented since they were created. Few of them are immediately useful to us now for their original purposes and those that are, such as 'medieval' churches (which are never entirely medieval any more), have usually been substantially restored and modified.

When we refer to the Middle Ages, we are in fact not usually referring to this collection of artefacts but to the stories and imaginings we have woven around them and one of their principal values is, indeed, their ability to provoke such stories and imaginings. I have made a first attempt to define what one might call the psychological value of these objects elsewhere.[1] In this chapter, I would like to focus on a second value that is perhaps less well recognised than the first: the ways in which engagement with medieval artefacts can enlarge the '*vocabulary* of motor acts', 'mechanical knowledge' and repertoire of motor skills of someone who is unfamiliar with them because their affordances are different from those of modern ones insofar as they were made to facilitate actions that we no longer commonly practice.[2]

An object's affordances are 'those of its intrinsic properties that facilitate our interaction with it. [They] . . . incarnate the *practical opportunities* that the object *offers* to the organism which perceives it'.[3] They

> correspond to action possibilities resulting from animal-relative, biomechanical properties. For instance, a cup affords grasp-ability, throw-ability, or push-ability for a human adult, but support-ability for a fly . . . affordances exist independently of the act of perception. Said differently, the action possibilities offered by a cup do not need to be perceived by the human or the fly. They just correspond to what both of them could do with the cup, as a function of their biomechanical and morphological characteristics.[4]

All objects, even natural ones, have affordances. When humans make or modify objects, however, when they create artefacts, they provide them with artificial affordances to facilitate certain movements, certain 'action possibilities', in relation to them. They intend the artefacts to be used in certain ways and their intentions shape at least some of the objects' affordances. A soccer ball, for example, has clearly been made to roll smoothly along a flat surface; a brick has not. Because an artefact's affordances are 'extracted' from it by certain visuomotor neurons as part of perception, moreover, images of it, which I would term visual replicas of it, are sufficient to perceive its affordances – especially if the images are three-dimensional or show it from more than one point of view – and to form motor representations of how the object can be manipulated.[5]

All Souped Up

When I see a medieval spoon or an image of one, I recognise it as a spoon (that is, as an artefact with which I can eat soup, for example) because its affordances correspond by and large to those of a modern spoon (very grossly: a graspable handle attached to a recipient small enough for an adult human mouth to drink from conveniently or to be placed in a human mouth) and I can imagine how I would manipulate it to eat soup because I already have a motor neuronal representation of how to use an object with spoon-like affordances to eat soup. I do not, however, value the medieval spoon highly as a spoon. It does not offer me more action possibilities than a modern spoon and will probably, depending on its state of preservation, be more difficult to use. When I searched the British Museum's Portable Antiquities Scheme database for medieval spoons, for example, I discovered images of relatively few spoons that I could still use to eat soup and none that I would prefer, from a practical point of view, to those I have in my kitchen.[6] We do not collect and preserve medieval spoons and post descriptions and photos of them online because of their immediate instrumental value. We do so in part, as I mentioned above, because we enjoy and learn from imagining them in their original context and weaving stories about them – what it was like for a family to eat potage around their hearth on a windy October night in Autun in 1127, what it would be like for me to be eating potage next to a hearth in Autun on such a night – but also because their affordances are often different from those of modern spoons and thus enable us to develop our neural motor vocabularies.

When I look at the images of the relatively intact spoons in the Portable Antiquities Scheme database, they look odd to me in two ways.[7] First, as will, I hope, be clear from the following images, their handles appear to be round and rather thin in comparison to the flatter, broader handles of the soup spoons in my kitchen. It does not seem to me that I could hold and manipulate the medieval spoons in as many ways as I do those in my kitchen. Secondly, the bowls or heads of the medieval spoons seem broader and blunter at their end than that of my kitchen spoons. It seems to me that the makers of the medieval spoons intended their users to drink from the side of their bowls but not to place them entirely in their mouths. When I form a motor representation of using these medieval spoons based on their affordances, in sum, I imagine holding them and using them a little differently than I do my kitchen spoons because of the slight differences in their affordances.

It may well be that other people are used to modern soup spoons that resemble the medieval ones more than they do mine and that the affordances of my spoons are more

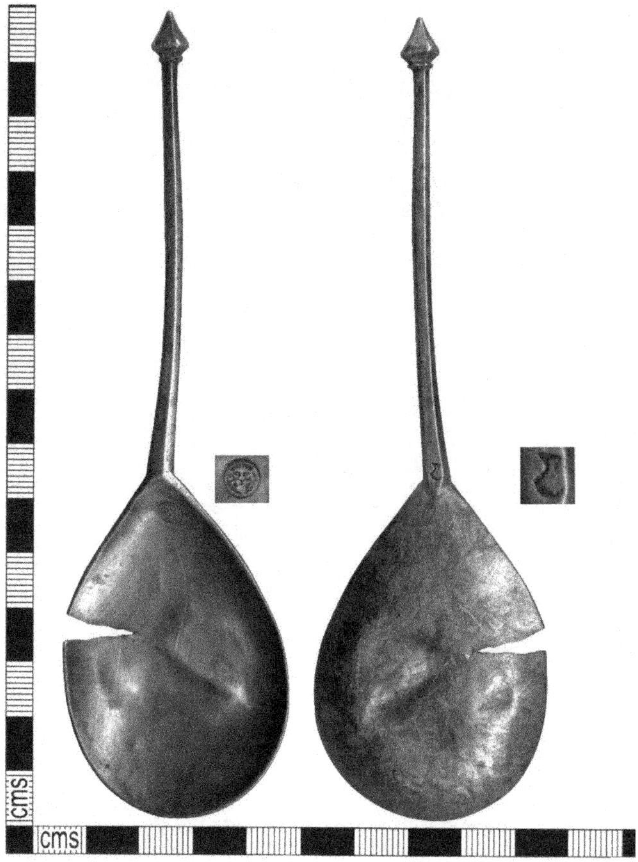

Figure 11.1: C. Hayward Trevarthen (2014) *DOR-235972: A medieval spoon.* Web page available at: *https://finds.org.uk/database/artefacts/record/id/631204* (accessed 10 September 2019)

novel to them than those of the medieval spoons. It may be, that is, that what I am imagining as a 'medieval' way of holding and using a spoon is also a contemporary way of doing so with which I am not familiar. From the point of view of my neurocognitive development, however, it does not matter whether the 'medieval' way of holding and using a spoon I imagine is authentically medieval or not. What matters is that thanks to the vision of these medieval spoons, I have enlarged my general motor representation or 'mental simulation' of using a spoon and, more generally, spoon-like objects.[8] Or, perhaps more precisely in this instance, I have become aware that my kitchen spoons can be used in more ways than a medieval spoon and more aware of those uses.

Now that I have seen these medieval spoons, moreover, I would like to try eating soup with one to see if I can manipulate it the way I imagine and if it truly is different from manipulating one from my kitchen. This desire seems to me a normal part of my efforts to use motor and visual feedback to test, refine and master the new aspects of the motor representation I have formed of eating soup with a medieval spoon. Medieval spoons are,

Figure 11.2: The spoons in my kitchen. *https://i.ebayimg.com/thumbs/images/g/49IAAOSwoudW6XIL/s-l225.jpg* (accessed 10 September 2019)

unfortunately, relatively rare and inaccessible and are not usually well-preserved. Only a couple of those catalogued in the Portable Antiquities Scheme database could still be used to eat soup and I doubt their owners would be willing to let me try. If I want to try to eat soup with a medieval spoon, my best bet is to create or buy a replica of one and in order to enhance my motor neuronal representation of eating soup with a medieval spoon as much as possible, my replica should reproduce insofar as possible the original's material composition as well as its shape. A useable replica will not be an exact copy of the original since it seeks to reproduce the original in its original rather than its current state and this effort will probably modernise the replica to some degree since the imagining of the medieval spoon in its original state will be done by a modern imagination. No two hand-produced spoons are likely to be identical, however, and as the degree of material variation between the replica of a particular late-twelfth-century Norman (let's say) spoon and the original approaches the degree of material variation between one late-twelfth-century Norman spoon and another, the replica becomes every bit as good as any late-twelfth-century Norman spoon for the evocation, refinement and enhancement of the motor representations that would have been evoked by the original in its original state. All that matters from the point of view of my neurocognitive development is the enlargement of my general motor neuronal representation of using spoon-like objects and in this regard a good replica is as valuable as the original, better ultimately because it can be used on a regular basis.

The Mind in a Whorl

When I see a medieval spoon, I recognise it as a spoon because its affordances are similar to those of a modern spoon and I have an idea of how I might use it to eat soup because I already have a motor neuronal representation of how to use a spoon to do so. But what happens when I encounter a medieval artefact I do not recognise? While browsing the Portable Antiquities Scheme database, I came across a picture of the object in Figure 11.3.

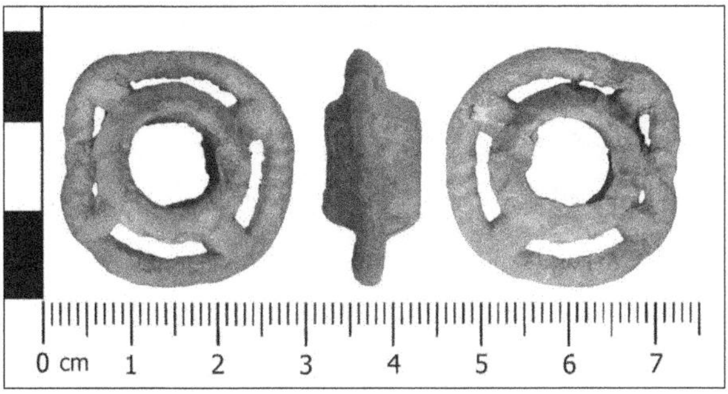

Figure 11.3: S. White (2016) *LVPL-2FFE5E: a medieval spindle whorl.* Web page available at: *https://finds.org.uk/database/artefacts/record/id/799769* (accessed 10 September 2019).

My perception of the object's affordances told me that it was made by a human being and thus for a purpose, but the purpose escaped me at first glance. I thought that I could probably pick it up, hold it in my hand and throw it (and that by placing my index finger on the outer rim and spinning it when I throw it, I would probably be able to throw it further and more accurately than otherwise). The object in my repertoire of objects whose affordances overlapped most with those of this unknown one was the handle of a water faucet (below) and I wondered if such handles existed already in the Middle Ages.

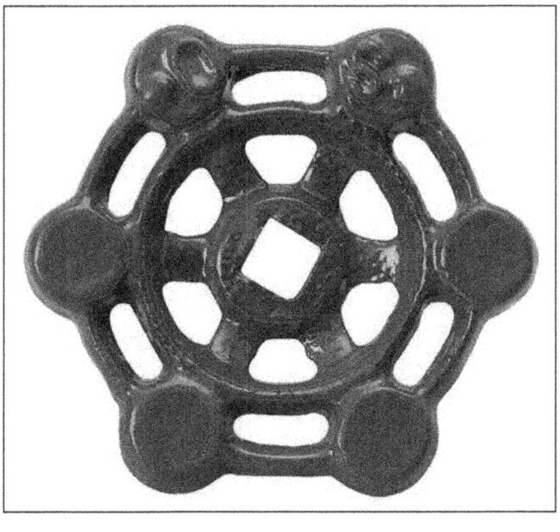

Figure 11.4: Wheel faucet handle. *https://www.doitbest.com/products/405272?gdffi=4685742 9cc1343fcae2c0324cc87e14a&gdfms=CB8C1D9E287245C1A23F89A86B8DBE6C&gclid= EAIaIQobChMInt_24-rp2AIV17rACh16ggMPEAQYAyABEgJUvfD_BwE* (accessed 10 September 2019).

The catalogue entry for the object informed me that it is a spindle whorl and while I had some idea of what a spindle is, I had no idea of what a spindle whorl is. A search on the internet brought up a series of videos that gave a good explanation of what a whorl is used for,[9] and when I then looked for medieval representations of spinning with a drop spindle, I of course found that they often include whorls.

Figure 11.5: London, British Library, Add MS 42130, f. 30v: drop spindle and whorl.

The video enactments of medieval spinning are also interesting because they demonstrate another way in which an engagement with medieval artefacts can contribute to the enhancement of neurocognition. The explanation of the whorls and their uses is enlightening and interesting, but I could learn a great deal from the videos even if I turned the sound off, thanks to my mirror motor neurons. Unlike visuomotor neurons, mirror motor neurons 'do not discharge at the sight of . . . three-dimensional objects . . . their activation depends on the observation of specific motor acts involving a body part . . . – object interaction'; 'the visual stimulus is not constituted by an object or its movements, but by object-related movements made by another individual with the goal of grasping, holding, or manipulating them'. These neurons, in sum, respond specifically to human object-related movement and 'are primarily involved in the *understanding of the meaning of "motor events", i.e. of the actions performed by others*'.[10]

If the observed action (or something reasonably like it) already exists in my repertoire of actions, the activation of these mirror neurons 'generate[s] an "internal motor representation" of the observed motor act, . . . a potential motor act is evoked in . . . [the] brain which is to all effects similar to that which was spontaneously activated during the organisation and effective execution of that action' in the brain of the individual who performed it and 'these movements take on meaning for the observer, thanks to the vocabulary of motor acts which regulates his own capacity to execute an action'.[11] If the observed action or something like it is not already present in its repertoire of actions, however, the brain learns it and adds this new action to its repertoire 'by the integration of two distinct processes: in the first, the observer segments the action to be imitated into its individual elements or, in other words, he converts the continuous flow of movements observed into a string of acts belonging to his motor repertoire; in the second he arranges these coded motor acts into a sequence that will compose an action replicating that of the demonstrator'.[12]

When I see someone spin thread with a drop spindle, I automatically, immediately and pre-reflectively generate a motor representation of spinning with a drop spindle, of which I may not even be conscious, that is presumably similar to the motor representation that was activated during the organisation and execution of that action in the brain of the spinner, whether or not I have ever spun with a drop spindle. If I have spun with one, I remember what it is like to do so; if I have never spun with one, my brain segments the action into a string of smaller motor acts that are in its motor repertoire and then combines them into a sequence that replicates as completely as possible spinning with a drop spindle. This is how we learn by watching. I can, of course, then attempt to perform the new action I have seen according to the motor representation my brain has generated, and the experience, in turn, provides motor and visual feedback that allows the brain to develop and refine the motor representation.[13]

My vision of the enactment of spinning with a drop spindle enlarged my repertoire of motor representations because I had never seen drop spindle spinning before. The more familiar with drop spindle spinning one is, however, the less these videos will enlarge one's repertoire of motor representations. The neurocognitive usefulness of seeing an enactment depends on one's familiarity with what is being enacted and this explains the value of accuracy in the enactment of old practices: the more accurate the enactment, the less familiar to us it is likely to be and the more seeing it (and eventually attempting to reproduce it) is likely to enlarge our repertoire of motor representations. Accuracy in the enactment of past practices is valuable because it decreases familiarity and thus increases neurocognitive learning.

It is important, however, to consider what accuracy means with respect to the enactment of an action that, like medieval spinning, cannot be observed. We cannot compare the enactment of an unobservable past practice to the original – at best we can compare the enactment to a static image like that in Figure 11.5 – and thus have to come up with other ways to make it as accurately unfamiliar as possible. If the past practice involved objects, a first step is to provide the enactor with replicas of them that reproduce their shape – their affordances – and material composition as closely as possible. One would presumably also study descriptions and visual representations of the past practice whose origins are as chronologically and spatially close to the past practice one would like to enact as possible. It would also be helpful to observe any modern practices that seem to be linked or analogous to the past practice. In the case of spinning with a drop spindle, it in fact appears that the practice is still used in a number of places and can be observed. On this page, for example, one finds a video of a Romanian woman born in 1931 for whom spinning with a drop spindle was the normal way of making thread for much of her life: *http://peasantartcraft.com/peasant-spinning-wool/* (although in the video she is not actually using the drop spindle as a drop spindle). Spinning with a drop spindle and whorl seems never to have disappeared as a practice, even if it is performed less now than it was during the Middle Ages, and the observation of this practice today can help us form a motor representation of how it may have been performed in the Middle Ages.

As the following video of a woman who did not grow up spinning on a drop spindle makes clear, moreover, doing so is a complicated motor action that requires practice or, in other words, the development and refinement of the initial motor representation one can form of the action through the above-mentioned means: *https://youtu.be/54RxwnRmmU4*. It may be, again, that, unlike me, many people are thoroughly familiar with drop spindles, whorls and their use. These people will learn little from forming a motor representation of medieval spinning with a drop spindle, no more than I learned from forming a motor representation of using a medieval spoon to eat soup. But, once again, what is important for me is that spinning with a drop spindle is a new kind of motor activity for me. I may not do much drop spindle spinning in the future, but my engagement with medieval whorls has enabled me to form motor representations of the small movements involved in it. They are now part of my neuronal vocabulary of motor acts, are available to me in my everyday life, and can be transferred to other activities I might want or need to perform. As a result of seeing that first whorl and then following up with searches on whorls and drop spinning, I have developed a series of motor representations and I have improved my ability to manipulate my environment, more than I did by seeing a medieval spoon. Forming, then developing and refining a motor representation of spinning with a drop spindle enlarge one's repertoire of motor representations and ultimately enhance one's ability to manipulate one's environment in a real, if not necessarily dramatic, way. This transferability of the motor representations formed by observing and attempting to imitate other people's actions to other activities is indeed the basis of new 'neurorehabilitation strategies' or 'mirror therapy', particularly in connection with stroke victims.[14] As Professor Alan Costall wrote in his pre-publication review of this essay: 'After all, we are not told to exercise by gripping rubber balls in order that we can leave hospital to deal better with rubber balls'.[15]

I will also note in passing that the presence of the cat in the second video (of a woman who did not grow up spinning on a drop spindle) is particularly interesting since medieval representations of spinning with a drop spindle show that medieval cats were equally intrigued by it (see Figure 11.6 below).

Keeping the Brain on Its Toes

There is a substantial body of evidence that shows that dancing develops the brain, and particularly the motor system, and that learning a new and thus unfamiliar dance leads to more neural development than dancing a dance one already knows.[16] It thus seems likely that learning an old, unfamiliar dance that was created according to aesthetic and social criteria we may no longer entirely share and may involve movements that are no longer common will lead to more neurocognitive development than learning a contemporary dance.

According to Robert Mullally, the *carole* was a French dance popular from the early twelfth century through about 1400.[17] The dance cannot be observed since it seems to have died out about 1400 and to have no direct, surviving descendants. The dance did

Figure 11.6: London, British Library, Stowe MS 17, f. 34r: spinning yarn with a cat.

not, moreover, involve any artefacts whose affordances might give us clues to its performance. As Mullally notes, a 'precise idea of the dance can only be gained from a comprehensive study of the different primary sources – literary (in the broadest sense), musical and iconographical. As no treatise or manual exists to instruct us on how the dance was performed, we must glean the requisite information from a variety of texts and iconographical items'.[18] Curiously, then, manuscripts are the medieval artefacts with which we have to engage to learn how to dance a *carole*, although some modern dances, as we will see in a moment, can perhaps help us to form a mental simulation of dancing a *carole*, and of course bodies, clothes and the ground, the only objects involved in the *carole*, have not changed much since the Middle Ages.

Based on his survey of the medieval sources, Mullally concludes that the *carole* was a circular dance involving roughly the same number of men and women (although single-sex *caroles* are also described) who, ideally, alternated woman-man-woman-man, etc. around the circle. The dancers joined hands and 'step[ped] to the left, and then join[ed] the right foot to the left. No other kind of step is mentioned in the sources'. 'The *carole* . . . was invariably accompanied by the singing of the dancers themselves' and 'several songs were usually sung in the performance of a *carole*'. The dance was not usually accompanied by instruments.[19]

It is difficult to imagine that the very simple dance Mullally describes remained one of the most popular in medieval France for three hundred years. It seems likely that much of what made the dance pleasurable is not transmitted by the manuscript sources available to us. The singing, first of all, must have been an important part of the experience. When the lover enters the garden created by Diversion in Guillaume de Lorris's part of the *Romance of the Rose*, he sees Lady Joy singing for a group of characters dancing a *carole*:

Figure 11.7: London, British Library, Ms Royal 20A XVII, f. 9: detail from *Le Roman de la Rose*, Love's dance ('La karole damours').

Bien sot chanter e plaisamment,
Ne nule plus avenamment
Ne plus bel ses refraiz n'assist.
A chanter merveilles li sist,
Qu'ele avoit la voiz clere e saine.
. . .
Ele estoit adès costumiere
De chanter en toz leus premiere,
Car chanters estoit li mestiers
Qu'ele faisoit plus volentiers.

(She knew how to sing well and pleasingly; no one arranged her refrains more beautifully or agreeably. Singing suited her wonderfully, for she had a clear, pure voice. . . . Everywhere she went, she was, customarily, always the first to sing, for singing was the activity that she performed most willingly).[20]

We have a few written fragments of songs and lyrics that may have accompanied *caroles*, but their performance, especially their performance in the context of the dance, escapes us. In order to form some idea of what it might have been like we can perhaps turn to the Faroese chain dance, one of the modern dances that may, it has been suggested, give us an idea of how the medieval *carole* was performed.[21] This dance, like the *carole*, is accompanied only by singing, but the songs themselves, it seems, are largely heroic ballads and thus unlike the amorous ditties to which medieval French carolers seem to have danced. It also seems that singing the ballads, which commemorate a common past,

Figure 11.8: Vienna, Österreichische Nationalbibliothek, Cod. 2568, f. 7r: miniature from *Le Roman de la Rose*.

is as important as the dancing (insofar as the two may be distinguished); perhaps the singing was as important as the dancing in a *carole* as well.

The simplicity of the dance described by Mullally would also have allowed the dancers great freedom in its performance and it is impossible to believe that some of them did not take advantage of it. There are indeed comments in the written sources suggesting there may have been a great deal of movement in the dancing and a sense of individual style. Dancers are sometimes said to move *cointement* (adroitly) or *affaitiement* (elegantly), or 'en passer cointement, en bras démener et hochier' ('to slip by adroitly, swinging their arms and moving them up and down').[22] When the lover in the *Romance of the Rose* comes across the *carole* in the garden of Diversion, the dancers invite him to join them. Most of the passage is given over to a description of the allegorical figures (Joy, Courtesy, Diversion, etc.) who participate in the dance, but the poet uses a few words at the beginning of the description that help us imagine the dancers' movements. He writes that Joy, for example, 'se savoit bien debrisier, / Ferir dou pié e envoisier' ('knew well how to break, stamp her foot and enjoy herself').[23] Other dancers likewise 'Bien se savoient debrisier' ('knew well how to break'), and are said to dance *mignotement* (adorably), *cointement* (adroitly) and *belement* (beautifully).[24] All this suggests that some people danced better, or at least more strikingly, than others and that the collective movements of the dancers were not homogeneous or monotonous. Mullally finds that 'whereas written sources generally give a coherent view of the *carole*, the iconography, while interesting, is varied and conflicting'. He suggests that this is because the iconography is 'mostly unreliable'

Figure 11.9: Oxford, Bodleian Library, MS. Douce 195 7r. Photo: Bodleian Libraries, University of Oxford: miniature from *Le Roman de la Rose*.

'as historical evidence',[25] but perhaps it in fact gives a better idea of the variety of movement and individual style involved in the dance. An occasional bent knee, raised foot or crooked elbow in the illustrations of the *carole* of the *Romance of the Rose* (Figures 11.7 to 11.11) do help us to form at least the beginnings of motor representations of some of the kinds of movements that might have enlivened the dance and distinguished one dancer from another. The lack of alignment between the upper and lower parts of some of the bodies in these illustrations may suggest a swaying of the torso and perhaps gives us a clue to what Guillaume de Lorris referred to as the dancers' *debrisement* or 'breaking'.

These images also help us sense the social, collaborative nature of the dance. Because the dance was circular, seeing and being seen were particularly important aspects of it. As the descriptions, and ecclesiastical condemnations, of the dance make clear, it also offered ample opportunities for flirtation and this emotional excitement should not be left out of our mental simulations of it.[26] The Faroese chain dance, which can last all night and seems in some cases to involve an entire community, can perhaps give us some sense of the social importance and effect of the *carole*, but the Romanian hora – performed at weddings, Unification Day celebrations and other festivities – can perhaps help us form a better representation of the dance's social quality.[27] Indeed, 'a se prinde in hora' ('to get caught up in the hora') can be a metaphor for, and a sign of, integration into the collective group. Perhaps the *carole* was a sort of elegant hora or a lively chain dance.

Figure 11.10: Paris, BnF, Fr 19137, 68r: miniature from *Le Roman de la Rose*.

It is interesting to imagine what would happen if one sought to form a group to *carole* every Friday evening, let's say. It would not take long to master the footwork. The singing would be a more difficult and anxious issue and take more time to work out since some people sing better than others and some more willingly than others and the question of being asked to sing, volunteering to sing, taking one's turn to sing, choosing what to sing, etc. would also be part of the experience of the dance (we know we always have to ask Joy to sing first and should never ask Generosity, although we have to let him sing if he volunteers, and oh my! what am *I* going to prepare for next week?). Once the moving and singing were running fairly smoothly, all the other aspects would come to the fore. What will I wear? Whom will I try to stand next to or across from (and the experience will vary greatly depending on the make-up of the group)? Will I dance as inconspicuously as possible or, on the contrary, kick up my heels? Will I squeeze his/her hand just a little? Bump 'clumsily' up against him/her? How will I welcome and evaluate a newcomer to the group? And so on. Forming a mental simulation of a medieval *carole*, in sum, involves forming not only motor representations of moving and singing but also visceromotor representations of dancing and singing with and in front of other people.[28] None of this, or almost none of it, is communicated in the medieval sources and yet all of it was surely part of dancing a *carole*. In this case, my interaction with the medieval artefacts – the manuscripts containing the texts and images – allows me to form only a rather incomplete mental simulation of dancing a *carole*. I then have to complete that simulation on the

Figure 11.11: Paris, BnF, Fr 19153, f. 7r: miniature from *Le Roman de la Rose*.

basis of observations of modern dances, but also on the basis of my experiences and memories, my existing repertoire of motor and visceromotor representations. This completion of the mental simulation also enlarges my repertoire of motor and visceromotor representations, however, insofar as it requires my brain to break apart the existing ones in my repertoire and rearrange bits and pieces of them in new ways to fit into the framework of the simulation formed on the basis of the medieval sources, a framework that I could never have anticipated or imagined on my own. When we form mental simulations of the dance we will, some of us more, some less, enlarge our motor and visceromotor repertoires through both the addition of new motor representations and the rearrangement of old ones, and if we enact the new representations thus formed, we will refine and enhance them. When we imagine old ways to move, we learn ways that are new to us and on which we can draw in our everyday movements. Thanks to this encounter with the *carole*, I am now able to break (*me debrisier*) or at least have an idea about how to do so.

Everything I have written about the ways an engagement with medieval artefacts can enhance one's neurocognitive abilities and one's ability to manipulate one's environment also holds true of an engagement with artefacts, let's say, from Nuragic Sardinia or eighteenth-century Denmark. Engaging with artefacts from any past milieu with which we no longer feel a direct connection enhances our neurocognitive abilities because it helps us form new motor and visceromotor representations of actions we could perform and feelings we could feel. This enhanced repertoire of potential actions and emotional possibilities helps us see new and more things in the world of our everyday experience, allows us to manipulate our environment more effectively, and enables us to sense more possibilities of being-in-the-world. It enriches our lives and, ultimately, makes us more competent, more resourceful and happier than we would be if we did not engage with them.[29]

What distinguishes an engagement with artefacts, let's say, from twelfth-century Flanders from an engagement with artefacts, let's say, from twelfth-century Denmark or third-century Flanders is not the nature of the engagement or the means by which we learn, but the nature of at least some of what we learn. The artefacts produced in twelfth-century Flanders are different from those produced in twelfth-century Denmark or third-century Flanders and each set enhances our neurocognitive abilities in different ways. We often speak of such differences in terms of style: a Romanesque style, a gothic style, a baroque style, an English style, a French style, and so on. This aesthetic concept of style, I would suggest, is a sign that our neurocognitive abilities are enhanced in different ways by an engagement with different sets of artefacts.

It would be possible presumably to analyse the way in which our neurocognitive abilities are enhanced differently through an engagement with third-century Flemish spoons, twelfth-century Flemish spoons and twelfth-century Danish spoons, but it is impossible to say if one of those engagements would be more useful to us than another because it is impossible for us to foresee the conditions of our future life in any detail. It may be that what we learn from an engagement with a twelfth-century Flemish spoon will be more useful to us in one set of circumstances and that what we learn from an engagement with a third-century Flemish spoon will be more useful to us in another. One could perhaps suggest that, in general, the less familiar the artefact the more one learns from it, but what one has learned from an unfamiliar one may be less useful in a particular set of circumstances than what one has learned from a more familiar one. In the end, some people will be drawn more to one set of artefacts and others to others, for largely undiscoverable reasons, because they prefer one style to another. In order to maintain as broad a set of human competencies as possible, it is important to maintain the engagement of living humans with the artefacts of as broad a set of milieus as possible, and especially with those of milieus with which they do not feel any direct connection. I cannot say that what one learns from an engagement with medieval artefacts is more or less useful than what one learns from an engagement with ancient Assyrian ones, for example (although I can say that, for reasons I do not understand, *I* feel that what *I* learn from an engagement with medieval ones is more useful to *me* than what *I* learn from an engagement with ancient Assyrian ones), but I can say that what one learns from an engagement with unfamiliar artefacts from a milieu with which one no longer feels a direct connection is likely to be more useful than what one learns from an engagement with familiar ones. It is likely to be more useful neurally to study a medieval church than a post-modern one and more useful to eat with a medieval spoon than a modern one . . . as long as one is able in the end to consume a roughly equal amount of soup.

Notes

1 Jeff Rider, 'L'Utilité du Moyen Âge', *Itinéraires LTC (Littérature, Textes, Cultures)*, 2010, no. 3, pp. 35–46 (*http://itineraires.revues.org/1800*). See also Jeff Rider, 'The Middle Ages Are within Your Grasp: Motor Neurons, Mirror Neurons, Simulacra, and Imagining the Past', in Karl Fugelso with Vincent Ferré and Alicia C. Montoya (eds), *Studies in Medievalism XXIV: Medievalism on the Margins* (Cambridge: D.S. Brewer, 2015), pp. 155–76.

2 For background, see Giacomo Rizzolatti and Corrado Sinigaglia, *Mirrors in the Brain – How Our Minds Share Actions and Emotions*, trans. Frances Anderson (Oxford: Oxford University Press, 2008), pp. 45–9; and François Osiurak, Yves Rossetti and Arnaud Badets, 'What is an Affordance? 40 Years Later', *Neuroscience and Biobehavioral Reviews*, 77 (2017), 403–17 (at pp. 409–14), *https://doi.org/10.1016/j.neubiorev.2017.04.014*.

3 Rizzolatti and Sinigaglia, p. 34.

4 Osiurak, Rossetti and Badets, pp. 409–10. The notion of *affordance* was introduced by J. J. Gibson, 'The Theory of Affordance', in R. E. Shaw and J. Bransford (eds), *Perceiving, Acting, and Knowing: Toward an Ecological Psychology* (New York: Lawrence Erlbaum Associates, 1977), pp. 67–82; and idem, *The Ecological Approach to Visual Perception* (Boston: Houghton-Mifflin, 1979).

5 Rizzolatti and Sinigaglia, pp. 21–52; Osiurak, Rossetti and Badets, pp. 406–7.

6 *https://finds.org.uk/database/search/results/objecttype/SPOON/broadperiod/MEDIEVAL/fromdate/500/todate/1500/thumbnail/1/show/100.*

7 *https://finds.org.uk/database/artefacts/record/id/744967; https://finds.org.uk/database/artefacts/record/id/631204; https://finds.org.uk/database/artefacts/record/id/616255; https://finds.org.uk/database/artefacts/record/id/570286; https://finds.org.uk/database/artefacts/record/id/247752; https://finds.org.uk/database/artefacts/record/id/183234; https://finds.org.uk/database/artefacts/record/id/138785; https://finds.org.uk/database/artefacts/record/id/130723; https://finds.org.uk/database/artefacts/record/id/86081; https://finds.org.uk/database/artefacts/record/id/64776; https://finds.org.uk/database/artefacts/record/id/54855.*

8 Rizzolatti and Sinigaglia, *Mirrors in the Brain*, pp. 139–53; Osiurak, Rossetti and Badets, 'What is an Affordance?', pp. 410–13.

9 *https://youtu.be/ocbRbd54Hiw, https://youtu.be/l9x-b0D9jHM, https://youtu.be/XPqWDYnrnNE, https://youtu.be/UUsDVFPYtGQ.*

10 Rizzolatti and Sinigaglia, *Mirrors in the Brain*, pp. 80, 98, 97.

11 Rizzolatti and Sinigaglia, *Mirrors in the Brain*, pp. 96–97, 98.

12 Rizzolatti and Sinigaglia, *Mirrors in the Brain*, pp. 145–146. For a more developed and nuanced discussion of mirror neurons, see Nadia Pawelchak in this volume. I am aware of the many reservations that have been expressed about the existence, role and functioning of mirror neurons over the last twenty years (see, for example, William Uttal, *The New Phrenology: The Limits of Localizing Cognitive Processes in the Brain* (Cambridge, MA: MIT Press, 2001); Eric Racine, Ofek Bar-Ilan and Judy Illes, 'fMRI in the public eye', *Nature Reviews Neuroscience*, 6/2 (2005), 159–64, *http://dx.doi.org/10.1038/nrn1609*; David P. McCabe and Alan D. Castel, 'Seeing is believing: The effect of brain images on judgments of scientific reasoning', *Cognition*, 107 (2008), 343–52, available online 4 September 2007, *https://doi.org/10.1016/j.cognition.2007.07.017*; Deena Skolnick Weisberg, Frank C. Keil, Joshua Goodstein, Elizabeth Rawson and Jeremy R. Gray, 'The Seductive Allure of Neuroscience Explanations', *Journal of Cognitive Neuroscience*, 20/3 (March 2008), 470–7, *https://doi.org/10.1162/jocn.2008.20040*; Victoria Southgate and Antonia F. de C. Hamilton, 'Unbroken mirrors: challenging a theory of Autism', *Trends in Cognitive Sciences*, 12/6 (2008), 225–9, available online 12 May 2008, *https://doi.org/10.1016/j.tics.2008.03.005*; Gregory Hickok, 'Eight Problems for the Mirror Neuron Theory of Action Understanding in Monkeys and Humans', *Journal of Cognitive Neuroscience*, 21/7 (2009), 1229–43, posted online 24 April 2009, *https://doi.org/10.1162/jocn.2009.21189*; Christina E. Erneling, 'The Limits of Mindreading', *Philosophy of the Social Sciences*, 40/1 (2010), 172–7, article first published online 15 December 2009, *https://doi.org/10.1177/0048393109352780*; Antony D. Passaro, 'A cautionary note from a neuroscientist's perspective: Interpreting from mirror neurons and neuroplasticity', *postmedieval: a journal of medieval cultural studies* 3 (2012), 355–60, *https://doi.org/10.1057/pmed.2012.23*; and Matthew Rampley's chapter in this volume), but it seems clear to me that something like mirror neurons exists in our brains and functions in the ways mirror neurons are said to function. Perhaps we should call them 'brain elves' in order to make clear our uncertainty about them.

13 For discussions of the ways in which motor representations or simulations are formed, see B. Calvo-Merino, D. E. Glaser, J. Grèzes, R. E. Passingham and P. Haggard, 'Action Observation

and Acquired Motor Skills: An fMRI Study with Expert Dancers', *Cerebral Cortex*, 15 (2005), 1243–9, *https://doi.org/10.1093/cercor/bhi007*; Emily S. Cross, Antonia F. de C. Hamilton and Scott T. Grafton, 'Building a Motor Simulation De Novo: Observation of Dance by Dancers', *NeuroImage*, 31 (2006), 1257–67, published online 10 March 2006, *https://doi.org/10.1016/j.neuroimage.2006.01.033*; and Diane Solway, 'How the Body (and Mind) Learns a Dance', *International Herald Tribune*, 28 May 2007, *http://www.nytimes.com/2007/05/28/arts/28iht-dance.html*.

14 See David de Léon, 'Building thought into things', in P. Graves Brown, R. Harrison and A. Picinic (eds), *The Oxford Handbook of the Archaeology of the Contemporary World* (Oxford: Oxford University Press, 2013), pp. 671–84; Giacomo Rizzolatti, Maddalena Fabbri-Destro and Luigi Cattaneo, 'Mirror neurons and their clinical relevance', *Nature Clinical Practice Neurology*, 5 (2009), 24–34, *http://www.nature.com/doifinder/10.1038/ncpneuro0990*; Frederik J. A. Deconinck, Ana R. P. Smorenburg, Alex Benham, Annick Ledebt, Max G. Feltham and Geert J. P. Savelsbergh, 'Reflections on Mirror Therapy: A Systematic Review of the Effect of Mirror Visual Feedback on the Brain', *Neurorehabilitation and Neural Repair*, 29/4 (2015), 349–61, article first published online 26 August 2014, *https://doi.org/10.1177/1545968314546134*; Wouter J. Harmsen, Johannes B. J. Bussmann, Ruud W. Selles, Henri L. P. Hurkmans and Gerard M. Ribbers, 'A Mirror Therapy-Based Action Observation Protocol to Improve Motor Learning After Stroke', *Neurorehabilitation and Neural Repair*, 29/6 (2015), 509–16, article first published online 21 November 2014, *https://doi.org/10.1177/1545968314558598*; and Feng Guo, Qun Xu, Hassan M. Abo Salem, Yihao Yao, Jicheng Lou and Xiaolin Huang, 'The neuronal correlates of mirror therapy: A functional magnetic resonance imaging study on mirror-induced visual illusions of ankle movements', *Brain Research*, 1639 (15 May 2016), 186–93, *https://doi.org/10.1016/j.brainres.2016.03.002*.

15 For an intriguing study of how an understanding of the related craft of knitting can help us understand the composition of a medieval text, see Godelinde Gertrude Perk in this volume.

16 For convenient introductions to the subject, see Steven Brown and Lawrence M. Parsons, 'The Neuroscience of Dance', *Scientific American*, 299 (July 2008), 78–83; Christopher Bergland, 'Why Is Dancing So Good for Your Brain?' *Psychology Today*, posted 1 October 2013, *https://www.psychologytoday.com/blog/the-athletes-way/201310/why-is-dancing-so-good-your-brain*; Scott Edwards, 'Dancing and the Brain', *On the Brain: The Harvard Mahoney Neuroscience Institute Letter*, posted December 2015, *http://neuro.hms.harvard.edu/harvard-mahoney-neuroscience-institute/brain-newsletter/and-brain-series/dancing-and-brain#*; and F. J. Karpati et al., 'Dance and the Brain: A Review', *Annals of the New York Academy of Sciences*, 1337 (2015), 140–6.

17 Robert Mullally, *The Carole: A Study of a Medieval Dance* (Farnham, Surrey: Ashgate, 2011), pp. 1, 19–29, 101. On the *carole*, see also Seeta Chaganti, *Strange Footing: Poetic Form and Dance in The Late Middle Ages* (Chicago: University of Chicago Press, 2018).

18 Mullally, *The Carole*, p. xvi.

19 Mullally, *The Carole*, pp. 49, 87, 85. For the description of the dance and music, see pp. 41–50, 63–91.

20 Guillaume de Lorris and Jean de Meun, *Le Roman de la Rose*, vv. 731–5, 739–42, ed. Ernest Langlois, 5 vols (Paris, Champion pour la Société des anciens textes français, 1914–1924), 2: 38; idem, *The Romance of the Rose*, trans. Charles Dahlberg, 3rd edn (Princeton, NJ: Princeton University Press, 1995), p. 40, trans. modified.

21 *https://youtu.be/LjrOFCM2Is8; https://youtu.be/3NMUn-92vo8*; *https://youtu.be/F5vhJXQqmKI*; and, for a longer explanation: *https://youtu.be/__iXQgJencw*.

22 Cited by Mullally in *The Carole*, p. 50. My translations.

23 *Debrisier*, which I have translated as *break*, is a curious word in this context. It generally means to break something, to break apart, or to torment, suggesting a rather violent motion. Perhaps the *carole* was a medieval forerunner of breakdancing.

24 *Roman de la Rose*, vv. 737–8, 771, 744, 765, 766, 2: 38–40. My translations.

25 Mullally, *The Carole*, p. 100.

26 For a sensitive description of the kind of romantic and erotic excitement such a dance might have created and our ability to understand it, see Pawelchak's analysis in the preceding chapter of possible medieval interpretations of a representation of a falconing party carved into the ivory case of a fourteenth-century mirror.

27 *https://youtu.be/rV_V4jPj_bc; https://youtu.be/mZpNzYcliSI; https://youtu.be/MSIaoEkMFpE; https:// youtu.be/0_U1__3l2Lw.*

28 The brain's network of visceromotor mirror neurons evokes the emotions that perceived motor-acts, even intransitive motor-acts like dancing, would evoke if we performed these motor acts. When I see someone laughing or kicking a vending machine, I know, approximately, what he or she is feeling because I form a visceromotor representation of what I would be feeling if I were performing those movements. 'Experiencing . . . [an emotion] and perceiving it in others appear therefore to have a common neural basis' (Rizzolatti and Sinigaglia, *Mirrors in the Brain*, p. 185). Just as the motor mirror neuron network seems to allow us to understand the object-related movements of others by imagining ourselves performing them, this visceromotor mirror neuron system seems to allow us to understand what other people are feeling by imagining what we would be feeling if we were performing the movements we see them performing.

29 My discussion of a modern person's interaction with medieval artefacts overlaps in a number of ways with Pawelchak's preceding discussion of the ways in which neuroscience and cognitive theory can perhaps help us understand to some degree a medieval person's interaction with medieval artefacts. What distinguishes our approaches, it seems to me, is Pawelchak's effort to understand how medieval people interacted with their artefacts ('how a long-dead audience perceived art'; 'how these [medieval] viewers likely arrived at their various interpretations' of an image). The object of her study, as I understand it, is the historical interaction between medieval people and their artefacts, whereas the object of mine is the present interaction between people like me and someone else's artefacts.

Select Bibliography

Brown, Steven and Lawrence M. Parsons, 'The Neuroscience of Dance', *Scientific American* 299 (July 2008), 78–83.

Calvo-Merino, B., D. E. Glaser, J. Grèzes, R. E. Passingham and P. Haggard, 'Action Observation and Acquired Motor Skills: An fMRI Study with Expert Dancers', *Cerebral Cortex*, 15 (2005), 1243–9, *https://doi.org/10.1093/cercor/bhi007.*

Chaganti, Seeta, *Strange Footing: Poetic Form and Dance in The Late Middle Ages* (Chicago: University of Chicago Press, 2018).

Cross, Emily S., Antonia F. de C. Hamilton and Scott T. Grafton, 'Building a Motor Simulation De Novo: Observation of Dance by Dancers', *NeuroImage*, 31 (2006), 1257–67, *https://doi.org/10.1016/j.neuroimage.2006.01.033.*

de Léon, David, 'Building thought into things', in P. Graves Brown, R. Harrison and A. Picinic (eds), *The Oxford Handbook of the Archaeology of the Contemporary World* (Oxford: Oxford University Press, 2013), pp. 671–84.

Deconinck, Frederik J. A., Ana R. P. Smorenburg, Alex Benham, Annick Ledebt, Max G. Feltham and Geert J. P. Savelsbergh, 'Reflections on Mirror Therapy: A Systematic Review of the Effect of Mirror Visual Feedback on the Brain', *Neurorehabilitation and Neural Repair*, 29/4 (2015), 349–61, *https://doi.org/10.1177/1545968314546134.*

Erneling, Christina E., 'The Limits of Mindreading', *Philosophy of the Social Sciences*, 40/1 (2010), 172–7, *https://doi.org/10.1177/0048393109352780.*

Gibson, J. J., 'The Theory of Affordance,' in R. E. Shaw and J. Bransford (eds), *Perceiving, Acting, and Knowing: Toward an Ecological Psychology* (New York: Lawrence Erlbaum Associates, 1977), pp. 67–82.

Gibson, J. J., *The Ecological Approach to Visual Perception* (Boston: Houghton-Mifflin, 1979).

Hickok, Gregory, 'Eight Problems for the Mirror Neuron Theory of Action Understanding in Monkeys and Humans', *Journal of Cognitive Neuroscience*, 21/7 (2009), 1229–43, *https://doi.org/10.1162/jocn.2009.21189.*

Karpati, F. J., et al., 'Dance and the Brain: A Review', *Annals of the New York Academy of Sciences*, 1337 (2015), 140–6, *https://doi.org/10.1111/nyas.12632.*

McCabe, David P. and Alan D. Castel, 'Seeing is believing: The effect of brain images on judgments of scientific reasoning', *Cognition*, 107 (2008), 343–52, *https://doi.org/10.1016/j.cognition.2007.07.017.*

Mullally, Robert, *The Carole: A Study of a Medieval Dance* (Farnham, Surrey: Ashgate, 2011).

Osiurak, François, Yves Rossetti and Arnaud Badets, 'What is an Affordance? 40 Years Later', *Neuroscience and Biobehavioral Reviews*, 77 (2017), 403–17, *https://doi.org/10.1016/j.neubiorev.2017.04.014.*

Racine, Eric, Ofek Bar-Ilan and Judy Illes, 'fMRI in the public eye', *Nature Reviews Neuroscience*, 6/2 (2005), 159–64, *http://dx.doi.org/10.1038/nrn1609.*

Rider, Jeff, 'L'Utilité du Moyen Âge', *Itinéraires LTC* (*Littérature, Textes, Cultures*), 2010, no. 3, pp. 35–46, *https://doi.org/10.4000/itineraires.1800.*

Rider, Jeff, 'The Middle Ages Are within Your Grasp: Motor Neurons, Mirror Neurons, Simulacra, and Imagining the Past', in Karl Fugelso with Vincent Ferré and Alicia C. Montoya (eds), *Studies in Medievalism XXIV: Medievalism on the Margins* (Cambridge: D.S. Brewer, 2015), pp. 155–76.

Rizzolatti, Giacomo and Corrado Sinigaglia, *Mirrors in the Brain – How Our Minds Share Actions and Emotions*, trans. Frances Anderson (Oxford: Oxford University Press, 2008).

Rizzolatti, Giacomo, Maddalena Fabbri-Destro and Luigi Cattaneo, 'Mirror neurons and their clinical relevance', *Nature Clinical Practice Neurology*, 5 (2009), 24–34, *http://www.nature.com/doifinder/10.1038/ncpneuro0990.*

Skolnick Weisberg, Deena, Frank C. Keil, Joshua Goodstein, Elizabeth Rawson and Jeremy R. Gray, 'The Seductive Allure of Neuroscience Explanations', *Journal of Cognitive Neuroscience*, 20/3 (2008), 470–7, *https://doi.org/10.1162/jocn.2008.20040.*

Solway, Diane, 'How the Body (and Mind) Learns a Dance', *International Herald Tribune*, 28 May 2007, *http://www.nytimes.com/2007/05/28/arts/28iht-dance.html.*

Uttal, William, *The New Phrenology: The Limits of Localizing Cognitive Processes in the Brain* (Cambridge, MA: MIT Press, 2001).

Afterword: The Medieval Brain and Modern Neuroscience

JOHN ONIANS

Long before I discovered this ambitious volume I was puzzling over the medieval brain and its relevance to medieval culture. It started when I set out to write a history of European art using the latest neuroscience, *European Art: A Neuroarthistory*.[1] The underlying challenge of this project was to explore how greater knowledge of the brain might add to our appreciation of the mind's role in the formation of culture. Previously, I, like others, had approached culture through an understanding of the roles of such manifestations as belief systems, mythologies, economic practices, political theories and interpretations of the natural world in the shaping of the conscious mind, a process in which words played a predominant part. But what is new about neuroscience is that it gives us access to the brain's mental processes of which the brain's owner is not and, in most cases, cannot be conscious. Hence those processes have left little or no explicit trace in the verbal record. How, then, are we to understand them?

Each person can develop their own framework to solve this problem, as the articles in this volume demonstrate. My own framework depends on reconstructing salient aspects of the neural formation of the people involved. This can now be achieved thanks to the new knowledge of such properties of the human nervous system as neural plasticity and neural mirroring, properties which govern the way our neural resources are shaped by our material and social environment. Once I had concluded that the principal influences on such neural formation were an individual's experiences and activities, it was possible to appreciate how that formation might affect that individual's behaviour, in my case particularly artistic behaviour. It was then a small step to recognise that to the extent to which those experiences and activities were shared in a community they would result in a sharing of neural resources, which over time would give rise to the sharing of behaviours, leading to the emergence of a common culture. This phenomenon can be observed both at the micro level of a small community at a moment in time, or at the macro level of a large population over a long period. This latter level is that at which we are operating when we talk of the culture of medieval Europe.

Neuroscience and the Hidden Roots of the Transition from Classical to Medieval Culture

There is an enormous literature on the broad differences between the culture which we call medieval and the most elaborate culture which preceded it, which we call classical, differences which have been too often structured around an assumed polarisation between a more 'enlightened' Age and one that is 'dark'. Most of this literature focuses on the role of texts as expressions of the conscious mind in articulating the shift in mentality. But, since I was interested in finding out whether neuroscience might illuminate new differences, I was looking for less explicit changes in people's neural formation, ones that might have emerged more directly out of changes in shared 'experiences and activities'. The first clue to a hidden neural change that was rooted in a change of experience, I found in a text by the Roman satirist Juvenal. Writing in the early first century CE, Juvenal was dismayed by the cultural changes of his time and sought to explain them. His conclusion was that a change in experiences had brought a change in mental activity. Having noted that a Roman of the past had concerned himself with: 'the distribution of military commands, magistracies, legions, everything' ('imperium, fasces, legiones, omnia'), the poet laments that 'a citizen of today restricts himself to an anxious desire for only two things: bread and circuses' ('nunc se / continet atque duas tantum res anxius optat, panem et circenses'; Juvenal, *Satire* 10:80–1). Juvenal thus makes a clear contrast between the higher level rational activity involved in the taking of informed decisions typical of earlier generations, and his contemporaries' lower level visceral and emotional relationship with material realities, food and entertainment, bread and blood-sports. A particularly telling feature of Juvenal's analysis is his description of people's relation to those goods in terms of 'anxious desire'. If there are neural correlates of such feelings they would be found not in the cortex where the rational processes involved in the decisions of earlier generations would have been located, but in the hypothalamus, seat of the autonomic nervous system, which, without us being aware of it, monitors critical aspects of our relation to the world. In this organ, buried beneath the cortex, neurochemicals, such as alcetylcholine, regulate our behaviour in vital 'feed and breed' situations, while others, such as noradrenaline, regulate that required when the issue is 'fight or flight'. Indeed, we can see how a desire for 'bread' relates to the former and a desire for 'circuses' to the latter. Juvenal, it appears, is drawing attention to the same stress-related neural processes as those discussed by Daniel Smail in this volume. Indeed, I suspect the satirist would have been sympathetic to Smail's larger enterprise of neurohistory and approved of his emphasis on the role of the arrival of a succession of psychotropic drugs in the shaping of 'deep history'.[2]

My own interest in Juvenal's text is as a clue to the identification of a potential driver behind the transition from classical to medieval culture which has been hitherto unnoticed. If there was frequent uncertainty about the supply of bread and blood-sports during the second and third centuries, with the economic collapse during the fourth and fifth this reached a critical level. In these circumstances, as the ruling elites realised that they were less and less able to guarantee the supply of bread and blood that the population craved, some of their members may well have sensed that Christianity might miraculously help to avert a social crisis by providing them. If the emperor had lost the ability to provide these 'anxiously desired resources' in quantity by traditional means, he could, by sponsoring this one religion, provide them reliably in small amounts: water at baptism, bread and blood at the eucharist, and the spectacle of violence in the commemoration of Christ's crucifixion and the deaths of the martyrs. There were many other reasons for the state to promote Christianity, but probably none was more neurally persuasive than the religion's unique ability to respond to a long-standing vital need in a way that was both economical and predictable.

Another hidden asset of Christianity to which neuroscience alerts us is the exploitation of the power of verbal metaphor. Texts played a greater role in Christianity than any other competing religion, including that of the Jews, from which it derived. And in those texts the part played by metaphors, which were already important in Judaism, was even greater, for reasons that are illuminated by neuroscience. One of its most revealing discoveries is that a word can have a real physical power that transcends the semantic, because it can activate the areas of the brain to which its reference relates. Thus a verb such as 'grasp' may activate the sensorimotor areas concerned with movements of the hand, while when we talk of an object, such as a cat, we are liable to activate the area of the temporal cortex where animals are categorised, so establishing links to all the knowledge with which they have become connected by our experiences. This means that when Christ said 'I am the bread of life' (John 6:35), the brains of his followers will have been liable to respond as they would have done to a real loaf, recalling its taste and its nutritional benefits. There were similar consequences in the case of other metaphors, as when Christ is said to be a 'shepherd', a 'light', a 'true vine', a 'lamb', a 'way', a 'door', or when he calls his followers his 'sheep'. People who felt themselves to be 'sheep' will have genuinely felt safer being cared for by Christ the 'shepherd'.

Equally reassuring were the architectural metaphors, in which Christianity is especially rich. These are likely to have been particularly comforting for individuals whose unstable social and material environment made them feel increasingly frail and vulnerable. So when people read or heard the words of St Paul: 'You are built upon the foundations of the apostles and the prophets, with Jesus Christ himself as the corner or key stone in whom the whole building is bonded together and grows into a temple of the Lord. In him you are being built with all the rest into a spiritual dwelling for god' (Ephesians 2:14–22), they will have felt that they joined Christ, the Apostles and Prophets in an empathy with the masonry of the churches in which they worshipped, and by doing so they will have acquired a greater confidence in the Church as an institution.

Similar benefits can be experienced in any context in which an intense and repeated experience of something lays down strong neural pathways. This is why Godelinde Perk rightly argues for the profound influence of knitting and needlework on the thought of Julian of Norwich. The more her readers shared the anchoress's experiences in such crafts, the more they will have shared her empathy with the certainties presented by regularly knotted fibres. Another verbal metaphor whose exploitation gave Christianity a special advantage over other religions because it engaged hidden neural processes was that of 'father'. Christians applied it to 'God the father', to teachers as 'Fathers of the Church', and to priests, especially the highest priest, the Papa or Pope, and the benefits of so doing are brought out by Danish research on the neural correlates of prayer.[3] What the experiment showed was that a prayer to God the father by a believing Christian is liable to activate the caudate nucleus in the dorsal striatum, an organ shown by other experiments to be associated with trust. Christianity's repeated use of the term 'father' for authority figures within the religion can only have contributed to the reinforcement of that feeling. We can also see that trust is one of the factors constantly in the background of Juliana Dresvina's article on attachment theory in this volume. Secure attachment certainly fosters trust, and when Margery Kempe says that God addressed her as 'daughter', we can feel that it is her trust in him that she is strengthening.

Such intense experience of metaphor by Christians is likely to have been reinforced by another omnipresent but obscure neural mechanism, that of priming. So essential for spiritual life were metaphors contained in scriptural texts that the faithful are likely to have become so habituated to responding to words as if they related to physical reality that they would have acquired neural networks not possessed by other people which accelerated and intensified this response. These networks were then available to be primed whenever a contextual cue suggested they were likely to be called on, as when one entered a church or just opened a religious book. Such priming is an omnipresent phenomenon, but everywhere its manifestation differs, depending on the concerns of that particular society. Thus, in ancient Greece, where athletics and military training were especially important, any male who attended a related event, such as the Olympic Games, was likely to have experienced a priming of the networks in his sensorimotor cortex that were responsible for neural mirroring, so making it more likely that he would be directly physically affected by looking at young men performing those activities, or even at representations of them in statues or reliefs. The more we know of people's interests in different places at different times, the more confident we can be of identifying the particular neural resources which would have been primed in different contexts.

For example, in both the poems discussed by Antonina Harbus, where the *Wife's Lament* imagines a figure under a cliff surrounded by water and the *Wanderer* 'sends his mind over the shackle of the waves', the mood of sadness is heightened by references to coasts and sea journeys. This reflects the special tensions associated with arrivals and departures by boat at a time when such travel was even more dangerous than it always had been. The sharing of an awareness of these dangers in what was an island community would have primed the neural resources of listeners to share the poet's distress, so intensifying the empathy through neural mirroring, that Harbus rightly emphasises.

In this way we are starting to think of what differentiates an Anglo-Saxon traveller's brain from someone else's, the type of difference that is a special concern of Nadia Pawelchak, as is demonstrated by her piece in this volume. Her discussion of 'cognitive style' takes its cue from Michael Baxandall's recognition of the phenomenon of the 'period eye' and the way it varies depending on what objects people have been looking at. She, though, takes it significantly further arguing that there will also be similar distinctions in 'cognitive style' shaped by other experiences, as in the case of the differences between those of lay and religious audiences.

Pawelchak's account of 'cognitive style' is one of many examples in this volume of how a cognitive or neural approach leads to a more or less familiar phenomenon being productively treated in a broader intellectual context. Another example is José Filipe Silva's discussion of the modularity of the mind, in which he first moves back from Jerry Fodor in the late twentieth century to Aristotle and then forward to the fourteenth-century Nicholas Oresme. And the same is true of Ralph Hood's treatment of mysticism, which builds on the ideas of the American philosopher and psychologist William James to ask whether mysticism is the core religious experience worldwide. A similar effect can be achieved with a narrower focus, as in Wendy Turner's review of medieval categorisations of mental illness, especially those preserved in court records, and Jeff Rider's study of the way contact with a particular object, such as a medieval spoon, can reveal unfamiliar 'affordances' and activate new sensorimotor processes. But perhaps the most striking example of a particular medieval cultural artefact being reinterpreted in the light of a very broad modern framework is Victoria Blud's bold presentation of Julian of Norwich's writings as illustrations of 4E cognition (i.e. cognition that is Embodied, Embedded, Enacted and Extended).[4]

Many conclusions can be drawn from these studies, but two struck me forcibly. One, in relation to the 'medieval brain', is that people in the Middle Ages had a view of mental activity which was often more flexible than in the preceding classical, or later Early Modern periods, and another is that such flexibility often depends on an acknowledgement of the importance of the body and of the emotions such as is only now being introduced to the life of the mind by modern cognitive and neural approaches. Such conclusions, however, do not please everyone, and, although the range of the themes of most of the pieces in this volume reflects the openness and innovation encouraged by new cognitive and neural approaches, such an open engagement with these new fields is not yet universal.

A Sceptical Point of View

Matthew Rampley, another contributor to this volume, is one of the few scholars using traditional humanities methods who has taken the trouble to learn about the new approaches, but persists in resisting their 'seduction', preferring to develop an extended critique.[5] The tone of his critique is evident from the statement in his review of *European Art: A Neuroarthistory* that many of its claims are 'vacuous, incorrect, bizarre and laughable'.[6] His assessment may seem extreme, but since it comes from a respected scholar who, in other contexts, is better informed than most on issues of theory, it needs to be taken seriously and its merits tested.

We can fairly take as our test object his illustration of the way 'research in the neurohumanities' wrongly assumes 'an unambiguous correlation between localisable brain activity and specific cognitive and other mental activities'. Rampley's prime example is my interpretation of a Michelangelo drawing (see Figure 3.1 on p. 63).[7] My argument is that Michelangelo's introduction of a Turkish face into the drawing of a column base for the Medici tombs in the New Sacristy of San Lorenzo, Florence, is so extraordinary as to require an explanation, and the one I offer is that it is a product of the way the contemporary Turkish threat to the Italian coast activated the fear centre in the sculptor's amygdala. This explanation Rampley describes as 'questionable', replacing it with his own suggestion that the face is only 'a playful visual pun'. Two things are remarkable about this response. The first is that, as Rampley ought to know, Michelangelo was not into such trivial creative acts as playful punning (which abound in the work of his contemporaries), a point illustrated by the contrast between his always serious and focused drawings and the much more varied oeuvre of his rival, Leonardo. The other is that he fails to mention that my interpretation is only one element in a much larger argument, in which I show that Michelangelo spent his life alternately frightened and being feared. Nowhere was this alternation clearer than in his relations with the Medici, his patrons in the Sacristy, who were themselves alternately frightening and fearful, especially in the 1520s, when they were ejected from Florence. Their involvement in such a cycle is even acknowledged in Michelangelo's note on the same page as the drawing where he tells how the occupant of one of the tombs in the Sacristy, Duke Giuliano, had closed the eyes of the statues of Day and Night to take 'vengeance' on them for having ended his life.

Threats were evidently very much on Michelangelo's conscious mind at the same time that they affected his unconscious imagery, and they didn't just impact the drawing for the column base. As I argue in the book, they also influenced the generation of an exceptional feature of the Sacristy as built, a moulding in which the eggs in a row of egg and dart are transformed into a sinister series of aggressive masks with threatening mouths very like that of the Turk, and we also see them influencing the forms of the bulwarks that Michelangelo designed at the same period to prevent the Medici re-entering Florence, which have long been seen as threatening in their jaw-like angularity. The power of all these works derives, I would argue, from Michelangelo's experience of fear and his interest in frightening other people, with the amygdala, seat of fear and aggression, fuelling his imagination by the distribution of noradrenaline. Given that Rampley himself is explicit that 'the amygdala is the seat of fear', old-fashioned logic alone justifies allowing it a role in the creative life of an artist, who was always seen as the embodiment of *terribilitá* – 'terrifyingness'. The only way Rampley can prevent his readers from following this logic is by concealing from them the core of the argument.

Elsewhere, in his treatment of mirror neurons, Rampley refers to the nineteenth-century theories of empathy advanced by Heinrich Wölfflin and the 'compelling arguments' of David Freedberg and Lisa Zunshine based on recent neuroscience, but draws attention to 'certain problems'. For a start, he is not persuaded by the idea of 'action understanding' unmediated by 'representation' advanced by David Freedberg and others. What he misses in the accounts of neurohumanists is any stage of 'inference' between observing and acting. As he says of Freedberg's claim that the sight of the gestural marks in a Franz Kline painting can provoke their spontaneous imitation: 'Observing and repeating an action ... consist of at least two separate actions: inferring and imitating'. This is a valid criticism in terms of the assumptions of traditional philosophy but it ignores the discoveries of neuroscience – because neural mirroring directly engages neural memories it is a single-stage phenomenon. Thus, we have 'action understanding' of others because seeing the traces of one of their actions engages neural memories of the traces left by similar actions that we have either performed ourselves or seen performed by others. Evidence for this is provided by experiments showing how in the brains of dancers the sensorimotor cortex is activated only by watching dances that the particular individual has already performed, those of ballet dancers by watching ballet, and those of capoeira dancers by watching capoeira.[8] So, in the case of the Franz Kline gesture paintings, anyone who had observed the visual consequences of applying paint with a brush would have been liable to instantly mirror, and empathise with, Kline's action. An 'inference' stage is redundant. Nor is this a new discovery. Already in 1860 Helmholtz argued that the brain's unconscious processes can make it unnecessary to invoke inferences and today theories of the mind's dependence on 'predictive coding' have greatly widened the field of such automatic responses.[9]

These illustrations of weaknesses in Rampley's argument should not be taken to invalidate all its elements. Many of the warnings he issues, as about the problems of interpreting fMRI images, are well founded and should be taken into consideration by anyone working in the neurohumanities. Yet, instead of undermining the whole project, they show how it can be refined and strengthened: researchers need to rise to Rampley's challenge. There is no activity of the mind which cannot be illuminated by study of the brain.

Conclusion

This ambitious volume fairly reflects the state of a field where innovation and experiment can be met with profound scepticism. At first sight the spectacle may seem depressing, but the fact that the two opposing points of view are presented together here is grounds for optimism. Indeed, if those in the neurohumanities take into consideration the well-founded criticisms of the sceptics, and the sceptics read with a more open mind the interpretations of the neurohumanists, a conversation will develop that should lead to a true meeting of minds, and a new understanding of old problems. An early, and isolated, demonstration of the fruits of such a process is provided by the 1973 volume *Illusion in Nature and Art*, edited by the neuroscientist Richard Gregory and the art historian Ernst Gombrich. A more recent example, and one of many today, is provided by the sequence of activities which made up the AHRC-funded Eye's Mind project, coordinated by the neuroscientist Adam Zeman and myself.[10] This volume thus now joins a growing number of publications competing to collaboratively penetrate ancient mysteries.[11]

Notes

1 John Onians, *European Art: A Neuroarthistory* (New Haven, CT and London: Yale University Press, 2016).

2 Daniel Lord Smail, 'Psychotropy and the patterns of power in human history', in Edmund Russell (ed.), *Environment, Culture, and the Brain: New Explorations in Neurohistory, RCC Perspectives*, 6 (2012), 43–8.

3 U. Schjødt, H. Stødkilde-Jørgensen, A. W. Geertz and A. Roepstorff, 'Rewarding prayers', *Neuroscience Letters*, 443 (2008), 165–8.

4 See Richard Menary, 'Introduction', in '4 E Cognition: Special Issue', *Phenomenology and the Cognitive Sciences*, 9 (2010), 459–63.

5 Matthew Rampley, *The Seductions of Darwin: Art, Evolution, Neuroscience* (University Park, PA: Pennsylvania State University Press, 2017).

6 Matthew Rampley, 'Fish, volcanoes and the art of brains', *Journal of Art Historiography*, 15, December 2016 (*online at https://arthistoriography.files.wordpress.com/2016/10/rampley-review-2.pdf*).

7 Onians, *European Art: A Neuroarthistory*, pp. 249–52.

8 Calvo-Merino, B. C. Glaser and P. Haggard, 'Towards a sensorimotor aesthetic of performing art', *Consciousness and Cognition*, 17/3 (2008), 911–22.

9 Hermann von Helmholz, *Treatise on Physiological Optics* (New York: Dover, 1860).

10 These include a special issue of *Cortex*, 105 (August 2018), 'The Eye's Mind –Visual Imagination, Neuroscience and the Humanities' and *Extreme Imagination, Inside the mind's eye* (2019), the catalogue of an exhibition curated by Susan Aldworth and Matthew MacKisack.

11 See also Suzanne Nalbantian and Paul M. Matthews (eds), *Secrets of Creativity. What Neuroscience, the Arts and Our Minds Reveal* (Oxford: Oxford University Press, 2019).

Index